AN INTRODUCTION TO CHILD AND ADOLESCENT MENTAL HEALTH

AN INTRODUCTION TO CHILD AND ADOLESCENT MENTAL HEALTH

Lester B. Ramirez

SOCIETY Publishing

www.societypublishing.com

An Introduction to Child and Adolescent Mental Health

Lester B. Ramirez

Society Publishing
4164 Lakeshore Road
Burlington, ON L7L 1A4
Canada
www.societypublishing.com
Email: orders@arclereducation.com

ISBN: 978-1-83441-050-0 (Hardcover)

ABOUT THE AUTHOR

Mr. Ramirez currently serves as a Senior High School Faculty member at Sta. Maria Integrated High School, and as a Part-Time Instructor at Balian Community College, Pangil, Laguna, where he teaches under the College of Public Administration, Entrepreneurship, Accounting Information System, and Midwifery programs. He also works as a Marketing and Promotion Consultant at Colegio De Sta. Isabel of Laguna, Siniloan, Laguna. Mr. Ramirez has earned 37 units toward a Doctor of Education major in Educational Management and Leadership at Arellano University-Manila. He holds 12 units in Master of Education, major in Teaching English, from the University of Perpetual Help System DALTA, and completed his Master's Degree in Educational Management, major in Administration and Supervision, at Dr. Carlos Lanting College in 2017. He earned his Bachelor of Secondary Education, major in English, from Laguna State Polytechnic University in 2007. With his extensive academic and professional experience, Mr. Ramirez has held key roles including Head of the Senior High School Department and Marketing Director at the College of St. Catherine, Quezon City (2016), Course Consultant at Informatics International College-Quezon City, and Part-Time Instructor at AMA University, Quezon City (2011). He is the author of four books published under Society Publishing and available on Amazon.

TABLE OF CONTENTS

LIST OF FIGURES

PREFACE

Children and adolescents go through developmental phases that are marked by profound shifts in thinking, feeling, and social cognition in addition to physical development. These are crucial years because they determine how young people develop their identities, interact with others, and respond to their environment. Early mental health can lay the groundwork for future responsibilities, healthy relationships, and stress resilience. Early emotional, behavioral, or cognitive dysregulation can have an impact on one's quality of life now and in the future. Integrating psychology, psychiatry, education, and community resources is necessary to understand the causes of these deficiencies.

Mental health for children and adolescents is distinct since it deals with individuals who are still growing and changing. In contrast to adults, children and adolescents are always changing—emotionally, socially, and neurologically. Treatment for anxiety, mood disorders, and behavioral issues must be tailored to the age at which they manifest. What would otherwise become chronic problems can be changed with early detection and care. At the same time, youth may lay the groundwork for a lifetime of well-being through prevention, education, and intervention at the family, school, and community levels. Therefore, it is essential that caregivers, educators, and professionals offer extra resources in the form of supportive environments and prompt responses

To provide a precise and methodical grasp of this topic, *An Introduction to Child and Adolescent Mental Health* was created. It combines clinical practice, theoretical ideas, and useful tactics to address mental health issues in kids and teenagers. The book is sufficiently detailed for practitioners who want to review or broaden their knowledge, but it is also written to be understandable to students who are new to psychology, social work, medicine, or education. In order to provide readers with both conceptual understanding and practical abilities, each chapter progresses from general ideas to more specialized illnesses and locales.

The fundamental ideas of the area are introduced in this chapter, including how mental health in younger age groups is assessed and comprehended. The chapter discusses the effects of peers, family, culture, and surroundings on psychological growth. The chapter also establishes the groundwork for understanding why children's and teenagers' mental health has to be given more consideration than that of adults, with a focus on early detection and intervention.

The development of the mind, emotions, and body during childhood and adolescence is emphasized. The brain's maturation, learning phases, and their connections to behavior and neurological development are discussed. In order to help readers comprehend how changes in the brain may affect learning potential, impulse control, and emotional regulation, psychological theories of development are explored alongside recent neuroscience research.

One of the most prevalent issues among youngsters is anxiety. This chapter covers phobias, social anxiety, generalized anxiety, and separation anxiety. Symptoms, diagnostic criteria, and risk factors are addressed, as well as evidence-based treatments such as cognitive-behavioral therapy, exposure techniques, and intervention at school. Attention is also given to how anxiety is expressed differently in children and adolescents.

This chapter discusses comorbid conditions, bipolar disorder, and depression. It outlines warning indicators of mood disorders, how frequently they occur, and how they affect day-to-day functioning. The role of familial processes, stress, and trauma is examined, along with therapeutic approaches and pharmacological therapy. Clinical management and the role that support systems play in healing are taught to readers.

This section discusses learning impairments, attention-deficit/hyperactivity disorder (ADHD), and autism spectrum disorder diagnosis. The chapter lists key characteristics, diagnostic issues, and therapeutic approaches. It draws attention to how these circumstances affect family ties, peer connections, and academic achievement. The need for long-term support networks and customized education strategies is given top importance.

The psychological effects of abuse, neglect, natural catastrophes, and other traumatic experiences are discussed in this chapter. It covers adjustment disorders, post-traumatic stress disorder (PTSD), and the long-term effects of negative early events on mental health. Effective practice examples are provided for intervention techniques such as community-based intervention and trauma-focused treatment.

The primary concern here is disruptive behavior, defiance, violence, and conduct issues. The chapter explains the causes and effects of conduct disorder and oppositional defiant disorder. Additionally, it reevaluates intervention techniques, such as family therapy and behavior control techniques. The focus is on supporting good behavioral change and improving detrimental behaviors.

Anorexia nervosa, bulimia nervosa, binge eating disorder, and more contemporary problems with teen body dissatisfaction are summarized in this chapter. It discusses the biological, cultural, and psychological factors that lead to these disorders as well as the grave health concerns they pose. Treatment approaches are discussed, including nutrition counseling, family-based therapy, and interventions to change body image.

Adolescence is usually the time when drug experimentation and risk-taking occur. The chapter discusses the hazards and trends of drug, alcohol, and nicotine use as well as behavioral addictions including internet and gaming addiction. It discusses risk factors, therapy and prevention, and dependent symptoms. The importance of preventative interventions at the school and community levels is emphasized throughout the chapter.

The last chapter discusses the role that community organizations and schools can play in fostering wellbeing. Outreach, peer support networks, school counseling, and mental health policy are among the subjects covered. In order to develop supportive systems that safeguard and advance adolescent mental health, the chapter highlights the necessity of interagency collaboration between educators, medical professionals, families, and legislators.

The intended audience for this book is anyone with an interest in children's and youth health. For students looking for an integrated introduction to the subject, it is especially appropriate for those studying psychology, psychiatry, social work, nursing, education, and public health. Teachers, counselors, doctors, and community workers who currently interact with young people will find it equally helpful as a guide to comprehending mental health issues and evidence-based interventions. Its straightforward explanation, which offers advice on identifying symptoms of difficulty and how to get expert assistance, may be appreciated by families and caregivers. This book aims to assist everyone committed to building healthier futures for kids and teenagers by bridging the gap between theory and practice.

Chapter 1

Foundations of Child and Adolescent Mental Health

Contents

INTRODUCTION

Facilitating youth overall wellness requires an understanding of child and adolescent mental health. Childhood mental health has an impact on family life, social skills, and academic achievement. Because mental health conditions including anxiety, sadness, and conduct disorders are so common in young people, effective techniques of assessment and intervention are even more crucial. Early detection of mental health problems can have a major impact on children's and teenagers' long-term trajectories as they negotiate challenging emotional and social environments. This emphasizes how important it is to incorporate mental health education into community activities and schools in order to provide prompt support and lessen the stigma attached to mental health issues.

By addressing these factors, the stakeholders may construct a future-focused plan that places mental health at the center of children's growth and wellbeing. When it comes to adolescent growth, accessing mental health assistance is quite difficult. Research has shown that systemic issues, such as healthcare quality and socioeconomic hurdles, actually make it more difficult for teenagers to get the mental health care they need. In particular, health systems research shows how managed care and health insurance can either facilitate or impede access to necessary services (Harriette et al., 2003). Planners, healthcare professionals, and legislators can implement creative programs intended to address the gaps and give underprivileged populations access to the mental health services they require by learning about such systemic problems. In addition, integration between various sectors, including social services and education, is vital to enable enhanced accessibility and efficacy of mental health care for adolescents, ultimately resulting in a healthier future generation. Disparities in mental health outcomes among adolescents are stark and need further investigation. Research indicated that race and ethnicity were significant determinants affecting the delivery and quality of mental health services among the minorities (Green et al., 2015).

These disparities can occur as a combination of socio-economic status, cultural stigmatization, and institutional biases affecting the availability of healthcare services for minority groups. In addressing these disparities, a developmental approach with an emphasis on barriers and protective factors to understanding mental health outcomes among such groups is needed. Initiating focused inquiry into these unique challenges provides rich information that can inform the development of inclusive mental health programs. By promoting equitable access to mental health resources, society can enhance the resilience and well-being of all children and adolescents and better promote a more inclusive mental health care response.

Definition of Mental Health in Children and Adolescents

A multifaceted approach that takes emotional, social, and psychological well-being into account is used to construct mental health in children and adolescents. The ability to maintain positive connections, overcome hardship, and discover oneself is regarded as mental health rather than the absence of mental illness. These are crucial since a child must navigate numerous developmental milestones in their early years. A child's mental health has a big impact on their general well-being, social connections, and academic achievement. As a result, a comprehensive definition of child mental health include the ability to do developmental tasks, engage in positive social roles, and preserve emotional stability. This broad notion must be understood by educators and mental health experts in order to develop interventions that promote inclusive developmental outcomes. During times of transition, like adolescence, when individuals are exposed to certain pressures that endanger their mental health, the foundations of mental health are especially important.

Figure 1.1. A child's academic achievement, social interactions, and general quality of life are all strongly impacted by their mental health.

Source: https://www.americanprogress.org/wp-content/uploads/sites/2/2023/06/GettyImages-1249924298.jpg.

Their mental health environment is complicated during this time because to social pressures, academic responsibilities, and identity construction. According to the literature, teenagers who feel disconnected or that they don't belong might bear a heavy burden of disconnectedness. These effects are lessened by protective factors including positive connections and access to mental health services, which foster resilience and normal growth. A increasing body of research indicates that in order to promote good coping processes among teenagers, both individual action and system support are essential (Fernandes-Alcantara et al., 2014). This highlights the need for effective models that assist these protective factors. In addition to strategies for defining and promoting mental health in children and adolescents, comprehensive policies and programs that cater to their particular needs must be implemented. These consist of improving primary care systems in order to integrate mental health service into other health promotions so that adolescents can be given holistic care. A study shows that addressing mental health as part of a unified approach to health can have better overall health outcomes. For instance, combined policy measures can rationalize access to resources, while specific programs may tackle the specific difficulties of vulnerable groups. It is therefore paramount that stakeholders promote mental health for children and adolescents by investing in effective programs that promote engagement, resilience, and overall well-being, and come to see ultimately mental health as a central aspect of youth development (Gootman et al., 2008) (Figure 1.1).

Importance of Mental Health in Early Development

It is impossible to overestimate the importance of mental health during early development since it establishes the foundation for long-term health. Children are acquiring social and emotional abilities during these formative years in addition to cognitive and physical abilities that will influence relationships and interactions for the rest of their lives. Early onset of problems like anxiety, depression, and behavioral disorders may cause these important developmental milestones to be neglected. Recent studies have shown that mental health is the primary determinant of an individual's well-being, influencing social interaction and family relationships. Preventive factors and care barriers must be closely examined because mental health disparities are more noticeable for minority kids (Green et al., 2015). By identifying these differences, we reinforce the importance of early identification and intervention, critical in creating healthy mental health trajectories and reducing long-term societal cost of untreated mental illness. In addition to overt emotional repercussions, early childhood mental health is fundamentally linked with academic performance and future employability. Children with mental health difficulties can perform poorly academically, leading to potential long-term difficulties in educational attainment. This can create a pattern of disadvantage, as poor mental health leads to underachievement at school, and underachievement at school reinforces poor mental health. The evidence suggests that robust mental health support systems at early stages of development will significantly improve outcomes at school. Mental health services integrated within school settings can assist in filling these gaps and providing children with the strengths needed to thrive. Innovative interventions that ensure access and address systemic barriers to care are essential. One such example is creating what supports or opposes access to mental health care, especially for marginalized populations, to guide service delivery and community outreach improvements (Harriette et al., 2003). Moreover, the general effects of early mental health care on society require crucial evaluation because they transcend individual well-being to encompass overall community well-being. Communities that invest in children's mental health programs will see a reduction in crime, drug use, and civic participation, making social conditions healthier. Not only do such programs serve the child's immediate needs but also build resilience in the child, allowing future generations of people to cope with life's challenges more effectively. Treating mental illness in early life not only reduces the risk of mental illness but also builds social cohesion and economic stability in communities. Early intervention thus emerges as not just a personal or family concern but an essential public health intervention. As emphasized in studies, inequalities in accessing these essential services highlight the need for an approach to mental health in early development at the system level (Green et al., 2015) (Figure 1.2).

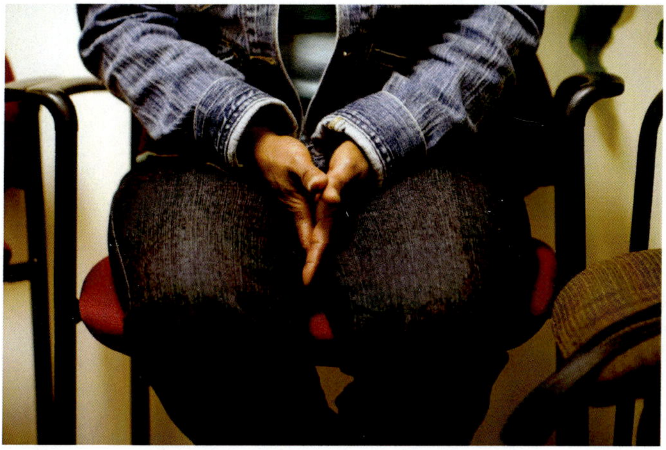

Figure 1.2. Minority youth experience particularly severe disparities in mental health outcomes, which calls for concentrated attention to protective variables and care-access barriers.

Source: https://www.americanprogress.org/wp-content/uploads/sites/2/2022/05/BehavorialHealthReport.jpg?w=1680.

Overview of Common Mental Health Issues

Designing successful preventative and intervention methods requires an understanding of the many mental diseases that affect children and young people. Anxiety disorders, which show up as excessive dread, concern, or avoidance behavior, are the most common of these conditions. They significantly impede social interactions and academic achievement, which affects long-term mental health. According to research, anxiety disorders can also co-occur with depression, which complicates diagnosis and treatment plans. Since untreated anxiety will persist throughout adulthood and cause chronic problems, early management and detection are essential. In order to provide specific interventions that address the individual experiences of teenagers, it is essential to address the underlying causes of such diseases, including biological inclinations and environmental influences (Fernandes-Alcantara et al., 2014). Depressive diseases also present a significant problem in teenage mental health, ranging from pervasive sadness to irritability and bad concentration. Depressive diseases among teenagers can be caused by numerous different reasons, including biological maturation, family dynamics, and peer pressures. Current research indicates a daunting rise in depressive symptoms among teens, particularly with regard to academic pressure and social media use. Further, depression will typically co-occur with other psychiatric disorders and complicate the clinical presentation (Amy, 2006).

Figure 1.3. Numerous factors, such as biological changes, familial dynamics, and social pressures, might contribute to the beginning of depression in adolescence.

Source: https://assets.betterhelp.com/advice/images/782844ee21880dcd67f6c8cdba420e00-x-ways-to-support-survivors-during-sexual-assault-awareness-month_2%20.jpg.

Such disorders require not only effective treatment but also building resilience and coping mechanisms in adolescents (Amy, 2006). Large-scale community initiatives aimed at reducing stigmatization of mental illness can further promote peer-to-peer, family, and teacher education and support. In addition to anxiety and depressive disorders, attention-deficit/hyperactivity disorder (ADHD) is another common mental disorder that affects adolescents and children. It is characterized by its symptoms of inattention, hyperactivity, and impulsivity and presents extremely unique challenges in school and relationship settings. When left unaddressed, these symptoms can lead to long-term problems like academic underachievement and the inability to establish a healthy interpersonal relationship. There are a number of treatments, including behavioral therapies and medication, which are intended to improve executive functioning as well as capacities for self-regulation. Moreover, involving family involvement in the treatment process can help promote improved outcomes via the creation of supportive home environments. Educators and healthcare providers must work together to tailor interventions toward enabling the management of ADHD and total development among impaired youth (Fernandes-Alcantara et al., 2014) (Figure 1.3).

1.1. THEORETICAL FRAMEWORKS

Because they identify the complex factors influencing psychological well-being, theoretical models serve as the foundation for information regarding the mental health of children and adolescents. Numerous theories in this subject explain how social, environmental, and biological elements interact to affect mental health outcomes. Researchers can address the complexity of mental health issues in children and adolescents by thinking child development within an ecological framework. For instance, secure attachment influences emotional resilience and regulation, which is explained by models that highlight responsive and stable partnerships. In order to explain the basis of social structure in the development of mental health in accordance with the established principles outlined in early childhood policies emphasizing supportive settings for healthy growth, models that emphasize relational considerations encourage interventions for strengthening family relationships and community support networks. Beyond relational factors, theoretical frameworks provide a context for evaluating the effectiveness of public health interventions aimed at supporting child welfare. A comprehensive economic worldview, as discussed in recent literature, integrates evidence from multiple disciplines to illustrate the importance of systematic intervention strategies in promoting child mental health. These models have a tendency to direct resources toward prevention aimed at addressing risk factors and promoting protective factors at the community level. The emphasis on early intervention and low-cost mental health care provides models that guide policymakers in evaluating current child well-being systems and making suggestions for gap filling that could undermine developmental potential. Strategies rooted in these frameworks guarantee service relevance to community needs, hence guaranteeing the optimal impact of interventions on child mental health, as highlighted by evidence compacting the effectiveness of such policies (Conti et al., 2012). Last but not least, ongoing advancements in theoretical frameworks in child and adolescent mental health indicate the necessity for ongoing research and responsiveness to future challenges. Because societal expectations and environmental pressures shift, the usefulness of dominant models must be critically reviewed and updated for efficacy in managing contemporary mental health concerns. Future research in this field should aim to redress existing knowledge gaps concerning how diverse cultural and socioeconomic contexts influence mental health trajectories. Theoretical models must be created to merge these factors so that interventions may become culturally responsive and fair. So, ongoing dialogue and fascinating are required to further advance these frameworks since common knowledge will result in the cultivation of innovative approaches that ultimately guarantee overall well-being for children and youths and reflect the existing state of child development scholarship and policy (Conti et al., 2012).

1.1.1. Developmental Psychology Perspectives

Understanding developmental psychology is essential for understanding the intricacies of child and adolescent mental health, emphasizing the importance of early life experiences and environmental interactions. Developmental psychology focuses on how a person's growth and development are shaped over time by biology, cognition, emotion, and social functioning. In order to detect potential risk factors and protective mechanisms, working professionals in the field of mental health must have a thorough understanding of these complex influences. For example, children who grow up in secure and supportive environments have stronger coping skills, which are critical for mental health. However, unfavorable situations like unstable families have the potential to halt emotional and psychological growth, highlighting the necessity of specific treatments that support young people's development in more positive ways. The significance of age-specificity in managing youth mental health disorders is also emphasized by developmental psychology. Adolescence is a particularly difficult stage of fast physical, cognitive, and social change that calls for measures tailored to these particular difficulties. The promotion of mental health and the reduction of harmful exposure to risks like drug use and social isolation must be the main goals of interventions and services for this age group. Researchers support full-range models that incorporate mental health promotion in primary care settings by analyzing adolescent health care and identifying primary needs. This has policy implications in that improved access to preventive care and mental health services can have an effect on developmental outcomes at this point in life (Gootman et al., 2008). In addition, central tenets of developmental psychology also imply advancing supportive environments that maximize the long-term mental health of children. Creating policies and programs that address the needs of children is of paramount importance to their overall development and psychological resilience. As emphasized by the appeal for stable families and safe environments, effective interventions need to incorporate not only healthy family environments but also community assets promoting healthy living. Food and physical health are also emphasized because these are strongly related to mental health outcomes throughout the life course. By the involvement of such fundamental building blocks at an early stage of childhood development, policymakers and mental health workers can join to introduce effective mechanisms and models of healthy life and disease prevention during an individual's lifespan (Figure 1.4).

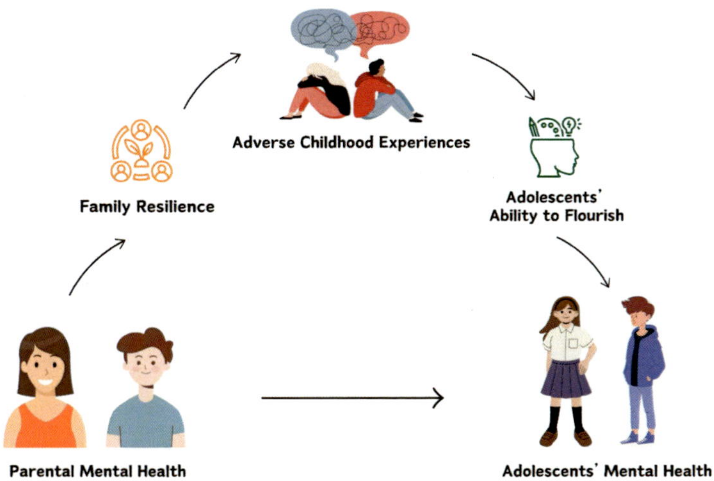

Figure 1.4. With an emphasis on the importance of early experiences and environmental interactions, developmental psychology perspectives offer crucial insights into the intricacies of child and adolescent mental health.

Source: https://pub.mdpi-res.com/children/children-11-01484/article_deploy/html/images/children-11-01484-ag.png?1733464714.

1.1.2. Biological Influences on Mental Health

Examining the mental health of children and adolescents requires an understanding of the biological processes that influence mental health. An individual's vulnerability to certain mental health problems, such as anxiety and depression, can be significantly influenced by genetic predispositions. Research has demonstrated that children from families with mental illnesses often have comparable vulnerabilities, underscoring the inherited nature of these disorders. Hormonal imbalance and neurotransmitter regulation are examples of biological factors. For example, imbalances in serotonin and dopamine have been implicated in mood disorders, suggesting that pathways of neurochemistry are essential to the study of mental health. This is the reason why, as a result, sensitivity to such biological roots can enhance improved early interventions and treatments that incorporate genetic and biological factors, ultimately affecting policies promoting healthy developmental outcomes for youth. In addition to genetic influences, environmental issues intersect with biological determinants to shape mental health consequences. The early childhood environment may assist or undermine healthy brain growth, which is key throughout the developing years. Protective and responsive relationships, as well as a supportive physical and chemical climate, are at the heart of a healthy childhood. Research emphasizes the importance of providing children with sound nourishment as a foundation for fostering long-term health and disease prevention. Also, the combination of adverse environmental experiences such as trauma or chronic stress could heighten biological vulnerabilities, thereby increasing the risk of developing mental illness.

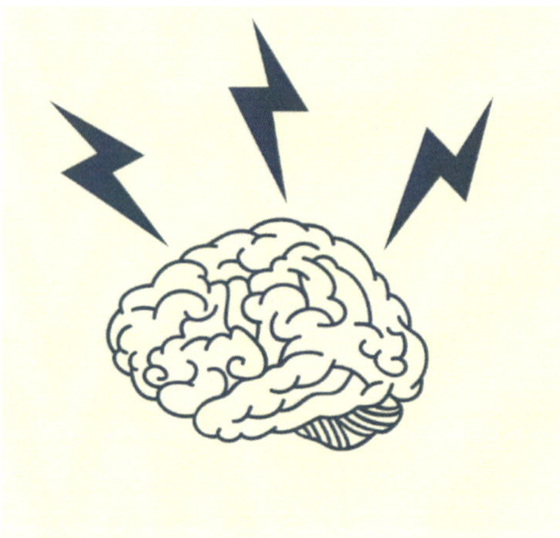

Figure 1.5. Hormonal imbalances and neurotransmitter modulation are examples of biological elements that are crucial.

Source: https://cdn.prod.website-files.com/615774abbceb093d7c7b77a5/6167145b81767e30917d9687_hormones%20mental%20health.png.

Through understanding these intricate relationships, stakeholders can develop interventions that address both environmental and biological determinants, leading to an encompassing approach to mental health care among adolescents and children. Furthermore, social determinants of health, in conjunction with biological determinants, create mental health inequities, particularly across racial and ethnic groups. Research conducted by Margarita Alegría and her colleagues suggests significant differences in mental health as well as in the receipt of care, pointing to the fact that minority youth have compounded risks resulting from systemic barriers (Green et al., 2015). Socioeconomic status, level of education, as well as available community resources, have significant influences on mental health outcomes, indicating the complicated nature of mental health issues. The acknowledgment of these differences is crucial to the development of targeted policies to reduce inequities and increase access to mental health services. By integrating biological information with sociocultural data, we might create more effective and equitable systems that meet the diverse needs of each child and adolescent and enable healthier mental well-being for all (Figure 1.5).

1.1.3. Environmental and Social Factors

The mental health of children and adolescents is directly impacted by the interaction of social and ecological factors. These influences usually include the immediate home environment, the community, and the larger social milieu. For example, a supportive family environment and easily available emotional support might help children develop resilience, whereas a busy home life may increase the likelihood of mental diseases. Furthermore, developmental outcomes are significantly influenced by easily accessible community resources like health care, education, and recreation. According to study on Bradford's Pakistani Muslim children, the psychosocial environment is particularly significant for some groups. In order to effectively treat their mental health, this demographic exhibits particular difficulties due to cultural and economic variables that need to be addressed with site-specific interventions (Bashford et al., 2002). In addition to family and community influences, environmental determinants like neighborhood safety, housing conditions, and access to social networks have an important role in influencing the psychological well-being of children and adolescents. Hazardous neighborhoods with high crime rates can create anxiety and conduct problems, while stable neighborhoods with resources can enhance mental health. The cumulative effect of these risk factors accounts for why understanding children's development requires an integrated perspective. Recent studies stress that the focus should be placed on how family support and social cohesion have the ability to neutralize negative consequences, thus resulting in healthier developmental patterns. The dynamic interplay among these environmental factors can either increase vulnerability or strengthen resilience in young people, confirming the need for integrated public health efforts to encourage mental health (Langher et al., 2015). The developing evidence concerning child and adolescent mental health emphasizes the importance of viewing environmental and social interaction as part of the integral elements in developmental trajectories. As a result, the trend towards bidirectional models of growth underlines the point that children do not just respond to their environment but also actively construct it, creating thus a two-way influence. As observed in many studies, the transactional approach provides a model for describing how individual factors, family milieus, and more universal societal conditions meet in such a way as to generate mental health outcomes. Consequently, child mental illness treatment is necessary in interventions that consider the complex and multi-faceted roles of such influences. Placing environmental and social supports in priority positions enables stakeholders to better focus interventions that build resilience, thus enabling healthier mental health status among children and youths in different settings (Bashford et al., 2002; Langher et al., 2015).

1.2. COMMON MENTAL HEALTH DISORDERS

Given the profound effects that mental diseases can have on children's and adolescents' development and health, the frequency of mental illness in this age group is a serious issue. The prevalence of conditions including anxiety, depression, and attention-deficit/hyperactivity disorder (ADHD) throughout this developmental stage attests to the necessity of early diagnosis and treatment. Overanxiety is a common symptom of anxiety disorders, which can affect social adjustment and academic performance. In a similar vein, untreated depression can have severe consequences, such as suicide thoughts and poor social functioning. This knowledge is thus crucial when providing mental health to young people in society to ensure healthier generations in the future. Differences in mental health outcomes are often observed among the different racial and ethnic groups, observing the differences that occur in mental health care systems. Research has shown that minority young people have usually faced barriers to accessing mental health care, including cultural stigma and a lack of appropriate resources. Alegría and colleagues' study highlight such differences in displaying the fact that systemic differences can increase mental health issues in such groups. With the examination of some protective factors and impediments to care, their findings promote a more balanced approach in the delivery of mental health services, with equal access to care for every child and youth regardless of background. Incorporating this in treatment practices is crucial to ensure inclusivity and improved outcomes in mental health. Access to mental health services continues to be very crucial in addressing common disorders among adolescents. Innovative programs, as identified in healthcare assessments in urban areas, provide evidence that treatment access is greatly influenced by conditions such as health insurance and managed care. Provider perceptions establish that whereas some systems easily allow youth to access necessary services, others unwittingly create a barrier that hinders youth access to timely treatment. Conclusions of these studies point towards the incorporation of holistic and culturally responsive healthcare models that address adolescents' unique needs. Through an understanding of the subtleties and diversity of mental health care, stakeholders can develop interventions to improve early diagnosis and treatment for common mental health disorders, which in turn can benefit adolescents across different populations and environments (Green et al., 2015; Harriette et al., 2003) (Figure 1.6).

Figure 1.6. Particularly common are anxiety disorders, which show themselves as excessive concern that can impair social interactions and academic performance.

Source: https://media.self.com/photos/6192d819e682190c49cddf5d/3:2/w_1875,h_1250,c_limit/GettyImages-1344713962.jpg.

1.2.1. Anxiety Disorders in Children and Adolescents

Anxiety disorders in children and adolescents are a major topic of study in the field of mental health, underscoring the significance of thoroughly comprehending their developmental characteristics. These include social anxiety disorder, generalized anxiety disorder, and specific phobias, which usually manifest in early infancy and have detrimental effects on interpersonal interactions, academic performance, and general well-being. In addition to personal psychological issues, a variety of external elements, such as social and familial pressures, contribute to the complexity of such circumstances. It is crucial to understand that early intervention can drastically change situations, highlighting the significance of awareness and education among parents, educators, and mental health experts. To properly address these disorders, there should be a multidimensional intervention that takes into account the unique experiences and needs of adolescents with anxiety, a hurdle aggravated by differences in mental health care services accessed by various demographic groups (Green et al., 2015).

Figure 1.7. A substantial portion of mental health research focuses on anxiety disorders in children and adolescents, underscoring the necessity of a thorough comprehension of their developmental implications.

Source: https://post.healthline.com/wp-content/uploads/2022/06/male-teenager-worried-in-school-1296-728-header.jpg.

Existing studies have determined the role of parental engagement in anxiety disorder onset and treatment among children. For example, parental anxiety and attachment styles may significantly contribute to a child's emotional regulation and coping mechanisms. Research that has been based on the Deakin Family Options study highlights the imperative of incorporating parental engagement in treatment models. The research from this study shows that when parents participate in therapy interventions, there is a significant reduction in the anxiety of parents, which consequently contributes to a better parent-child relationship and possibly relieves the symptoms of anxiety among children. Besides, where there is no parent involvement in therapy, maladaptive patterns such as avoidant attachment may continue or escalate in families. This brings to the fore the importance of collaborative treatment methods in mental health, highlighting the intricate association between family relationship and psychological child well-being (Bertino et al., 2013). To effectively address anxiety disorders in children and adolescents, continued focus on providing equal access to mental health treatment is vital. The nature and quality of mental health care continue to vary by race, ethnicity, and socioeconomic status, which also have a significant impact on treatment outcomes. Minority youth often face barriers to providing appropriate care, exacerbating their anxiety symptoms, and leading to other developmental problems. Research, for instance, by Alegría and colleagues, suggests the need to find protective factors in such populations to enhance resilience against anxiety disorders. Stakeholders who advocate individualized intervention based on cultural, social, as well as individual considerations can minimize the adverse effects of anxiety on adolescents and young adults and ensure improved outcomes, in addition to developing mental health-conducive environments among various groups (Green et al., 2015) (Figure 1.7).

1.2.2. Depression and Mood Disorders

A thorough description of the etiological mechanisms underlying the incidence of depression and mood disorders in children and adolescents is necessary. The development and maintenance of these illnesses are thought to be significantly influenced by cognitive biases. In particular, biased emotional processing has been identified as a causative mechanism that increases the risk of depression by combining attention biasing and memory distortion. These cognitive deficits can take many different forms, changing young people's perceptions of their emotional environments and, consequently, their mental health in general. Scientists draw attention to the complexity of depression by emphasizing the relationship between working memory, long-term memory bias, and attention. This encourages a shift away from reductionism and toward more integrated models of cognitive functioning that can offer more comprehensive guidance for interventions to reduce such risks (Bernstein et al., 2020). The complexity of depression and mood disorders is also shown by treating the effects of environmental stressors on children's mental health. For example, catastrophic events, such natural catastrophes, can trigger acute mental diseases, such as depression symptoms and posttraumatic stress disorder. The creation and use of reliable measurement tools, such the Hurricane Exposure, Adversity, and Recovery Tool (HEART), yield important information for identifying high-risk kids after traumatic exposures. These tools highlight the need for sensitive measurement of hurricane-specific and non-specific risk factors, such as prior trauma and ongoing adversities, which can synergistically compound the effect of exposure to catastrophes. As they accumulate, they highlight the need for sensitive interventions to assist involved adolescents to recover from natural traumas as well as their psychological aftermath (Dodd et al., 2019). Finally, knowing depression and mood disorders has implications far beyond patient care, extending to the necessity of community-based mental health services. Physicians, families, and schools must collaborate in creating supportive environments that enhance resilience in teenagers with emotional challenges. Early identification and intervention techniques should be emphasized, incorporating community stakeholder feedback to validate test measures and psychotherapy protocols. With increased consciousness regarding mental health, the importance of an integrated strategy that tackles cognitive, environmental, and social factors is clear. Taking an integrative approach not only has the potential to improve the mental health outcome for depressed adolescents but also lays the groundwork for more sustainable systems of care that acknowledge and respond to the specificity of child and adolescent mental health (Bernstein et al., 2020; Dodd et al., 2019).

1.2.3. Attention-Deficit/Hyperactivity Disorder (ADHD)

One of the most common neurodevelopmental disorders in children and adolescents is attention-deficit/hyperactivity disorder (ADHD). Persistent patterns of impulsivity, hyperactivity, and inattention that seriously hinder functioning in social, academic, and personal contexts are the hallmarks of definitional ADHD. Because it frequently co-exists with other diseases like learning difficulties and anxiety disorders, ADHD is a complex disorder that must be understood in light of the need for differential diagnosis. As demonstrated by earlier research showing the prevalence of ADHD in average and high IQ children with learning difficulties, the intercontextual relationships of the overlapping diseases complicate the management of ADHD symptoms. Therefore, a straightforward understanding of ADHD is not only to address symptomatology but must also consider the sophisticated cluster of related problems such children experience in their developmental trajectories (Spiliotopoulou et al., 2009). Successful treatments for ADHD require a multidisciplinary process that incorporates multiple therapeutic modalities. Current research indicates that pediatric occupational therapists may be crucial in managing the multi-domain needs of children with ADHD using individually developed strategies that promote developmental abilities. Treatments like sensory integration therapy and perceptual-motor training have demonstrated effectiveness in reducing some of the primary symptoms of ADHD by promoting self-regulation and organizational capabilities. The combination of different approaches results in a more tailored treatment plan that considers every child's unique difficulty. Multidisciplinary teams of professionals, including educators, psychologists, and occupational therapists, collaborate to create integral treatment plans that aim to help achieve better developmental outcomes and facilitate positive adaptation in educational and social environments (Spiliotopoulou et al., 2009). Importantly, the merger of psychotherapy with pharmacotherapy has also gained great popularity within ADHD treatment. This dual approach recognizes that medication might suppress symptoms, but psychotherapy can instruct coping strategies and behavior skills required to ensure long-term success.

Therapeutic interventions such as cognitive-behavioral therapy attempt to correct deficits in impulse regulation, organizational function, and interpersonal relationships. Both pharmacologic and psychotherapeutic interventions can be tailored to respond to unique treatment regimens, emphasizing the necessity of ongoing assessment and modification. This overall strategy ultimately reflects a developing appreciation for ADHD as not only a disorder of hyperactivity and inattention, but as a multifaceted construct that necessitates varied strategies for its productive management (Figure 1.8).

Figure 1.8. One of the most common neurodevelopmental disorders affecting children and adolescents is attention-deficit/hyperactivity disorder (ADHD).

Source: https://my.clevelandclinic.org/-/scassets/images/org/care-pages/pediatric/adhd-in-children-feature.jpg.

1.3. RISK FACTORS FOR MENTAL HEALTH ISSUES

Numerous risk factors that could have a detrimental effect on psychological health are linked to the foundation of mental health in children and adolescents. Socioeconomic circumstances are typically the main factors of this. Due to unstable surroundings, restricted access to nutritious food, and a lack of adequate educational facilities, children who live in substandard conditions may be more stressed. Because anxiety and hopelessness can be causally linked to the lack of supportive systems, the relationship between poverty and mental health is particularly troubling. Additionally, institutional barriers like shaky access to healthcare can make these issues worse, thereby depriving poor populations of assistance. Policymakers and healthcare professionals who are involved in putting into practice successful measures that can lessen the effects of these risk factors at an early age will find it useful to comprehend such socioeconomic variables. The adolescent's mental health profile is determined by familial ties in addition to socioeconomic issues. Adolescents' emotional development is greatly impacted by parenting practices, exposure to domestic violence, and substance misuse within the family. While dysfunctional or abusive situations increase the likelihood of mental health issues including depression and anxiety, supportive and warm surroundings typically promote resilience. Notably, children are protected from negative experiences by the presence of an involved caregiver. On the other hand, unpleasant family interactions can cause psychological damage that lasts a lifetime. According to research, family therapy and community support programs can help improve mental health outcomes by addressing family risk factors (Harriette et al., 2003; Gootman et al., 2008). Adolescent mental health is also significantly impacted by exposure to risk factors at the community level, such as bullying, violence, and isolation. Fear and stress are prevalent in urban settings, especially in high-crime cities with little recreational opportunities. Young people may experience increased anxiety and an overall sense of uneasiness as a result. In a similar vein, bullying of any kind—verbal, physical, or online—remains a major factor that can have a detrimental impact on mental health, resulting in low self-esteem and social isolation. Importantly, schools and local community groups can be crucial in implementing programs aimed at addressing and mitigating these contextual risk factors. Collective strategies aimed at creating secure spaces and creating social integration are essential in building resilience in children and adolescents, which ultimately results in healthier psychological outcomes (Harriette et al., 2003; Gootman et al., 2008).

1.3.1. Genetic Predispositions

Children's and adolescents' mental health trajectories are significantly influenced by genetic predispositions. Research has shown that certain genetic variables may affect susceptibilities to a number of mental health conditions, including attention-deficit/hyperactivity disorder (ADHD), anxiety disorders, and depression. It is challenging to comprehend mental health consequences since the predispositions interact with environmental factors rather than existing independently. The importance of the protective elements is further demonstrated by the fact that a child who is genetically predisposed to anxiety may never get sick if they are raised in a loving and secure environment. Therefore, studying hereditary components is essential to developing a comprehensive model for comprehending youth mental health symptoms. It is feasible to use customized interventions that could reduce risk and enhance wellbeing by finding such genetic markers.

Figure 1.9. Children's and teenagers' mental health trajectories are significantly influenced by genetic predispositions.

Source: https://www.verywellmind.com/thmb/KZMdZwjpwQSaxehvAA21uwbQHQ8=/3867x0/filters:no_upscale():max_bytes(150000):strip_icc()/528351183-56a795693df78cf772975e31.jpg.

The complex process of establishing mental health is exemplified by the interplay between genetic predispositions and environment. Environmental factors have a significant impact in determining the result, even while genetics may lay the groundwork for future mental health problems. The expression of genetic risks is mediated by family dynamics, socioeconomic position, and stress or trauma events. This emphasizes how important it is to provide supportive environments for kids and teenagers as a defense against the crippling consequences of unfavorable hereditary traits. Policies and interventions designed to foster building resilience—through the establishment of stable relations and safety of the environment—can make a considerable difference in the mental well-being of young people. These interventions underscore the necessity for an integrated perspective, accepting both genetic and experiential influences on mental health development. Against these background considerations, it is essential to set early childhood policies that consider genetic predisposition and its potential implications. Investing in policies that guarantee healthy environments has the potential to develop a proactive model that supports the enhancement of the mental health of children from the early stages. The strategy towards strategies that aim to produce caring relationships, quality nutrition, and safe physical environments is the most important factor in mitigating the effect of genetic susceptibility on mental health. As identified in current literature, an engagement with these underlying factors can encourage resilient behavior patterns and emotional health in young individuals. Initiatives that consider the interplay of genetics and environment can lead to meaningful child and adolescent mental health gains, ultimately yielding healthier adult populations (Trzcinski et al., 2025) (Figure 1.9).

1.3.2. Socioeconomic Status (SES) and its Impact

One of the main factors influencing the mental health outcomes of children and adolescents is their socioeconomic level (SES). Families with low socioeconomic status are more likely to experience a vicious circle of stressors, such as inadequate access to healthcare, subpar housing, and food insecurity. Children exhibit increased levels of anxiety and despair as a result of all of these. Research shows a direct correlation between changes in mental health and economic stability, and those from low-income families are more likely to experience psychiatric problems. Additionally, the strain of financial hardship may make parents less inclined to offer supportive interactions, which are crucial for emotional development. Understandings of these dynamics guide responses to children's and adolescents' mental health, highlighting the structural barriers that impact marginalized populations and the imperatives of policy interventions to diminish such disparities (Green et al., 2015). Furthermore, the environment of children's and teenagers' mental health is complicated by the convergence of race, ethnicity, and socioeconomic status. Young people of color, especially those from low-income families, frequently encounter discriminatory actions that contribute significantly to their psychopathology. Studies by Alegría and associates reveal differences in these young people's mental health and treatment utilization. The negative effects of low SES may be avoided by protective variables including involvement in the home and community support, but stigma and resource depletion continue to be major issues. In order to reduce these disparities and give all young people the opportunity to flourish in supportive environments, fair access to mental health therapies is crucial. Future research should focus on developing culturally responsive interventions that actively address these disparities (Green et al., 2015). In an effort to promote mental health in children and young people, policies and programs for early childhood must be designed with the fundamental elements of health in perspective. As highlighted in numerous research studies, developing strong and responsive relationships and encouraging safe physical environments are imperative to healthy development. For instance, offering children access to proper nutrition can prevent long-term health issues and can be a buffer in protecting against mental health challenges. As suggested by recent literature, holistic programs that include health promotion and disease prevention approaches can act as a buffer against the deleterious impact of low SES on mental health functioning. By placing resilient and supportive environments at the top of our agendas, we create the stage for healthier futures for every child, recognizing that socioeconomic factors are inextricably entwined with mental health and overall well-being.

1.3.3. Family Dynamics and Parenting Styles

Children's and teenagers' mental health is largely determined by the complex interplay between parenting and family relationships. The relational and emotional patterns that develop in family environments and impact each family member's conduct and viewpoints are referred to as parenting styles. Each of the four parenting philosophies—authoritative, authoritarian, permissive, and neglectful—has a distinct impact on a child's psychological and emotional growth. According to research, children who experience authoritative parenting—which combines love and structure—develop resilience and emotional control. This highlights the significance of supportive family contexts in contrast to authoritarian and negligent parenting, which tends to create increased anxiety and behavioral difficulties. It is crucial that these dynamics are appreciated by practitioners wishing to successfully use interventions that address the mental health issues of adolescents, emphasizing the need for interventionist treatments that address parenting behaviors and inter-familial relationships within the clinical setting. The value of parenting and family dynamics is further demonstrated by the success of family intervention in treating teenage mental health problems. According to recent research, structural-strategic family therapy and other systematic interventions can improve parental competence and family cohesion while reducing the incidence of behavioral issues in teenagers. These approaches create a more cohesive parenting unit by encouraging healthy communication habits within the family. Improved mental health has been associated with increased parental involvement and cooperation, highlighting the importance of a good parent-child relationship during adolescence. Effective parenting techniques combined with supportive family environments can help prevent the various mental health issues that teenagers face and encourage healthy coping strategies. Social relationships and subjective well-being which are declining in industrializing societies are closely related to evolving family roles and parenting strategies. As emphasized in contemporary appraisals, relational abilities that impact social relationships are predominantly established in infancy and are subject to being derailed by negative parenting practices. For instance, competition and consumerism among children could detract from the enjoyment of social relations, intensifying feelings of loneliness and impacting family relations. The trend emphasizes parents' need to create environments focusing on relational well-being and augmenting positive social relation. By enhancing family functioning through optimal parenting styles, families can ward off these negative social forces and assist in ensuring their children's and adolescents' general mental well-being, confirming the vitally important position of care-giving family support in promoting resilience and emotional health (Medina et al., 2019; Pugno, 2025) (Figure 1.10).

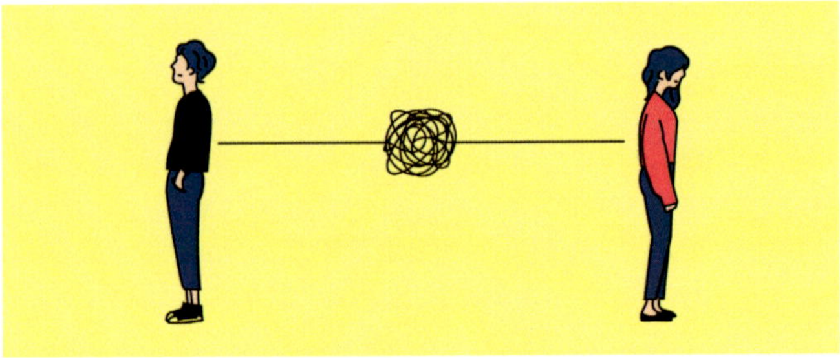

Figure 1.10. The emotional and relational patterns that develop in family environments and impact each member's behavior and perceptions are referred to as family dynamics.

Source: https://assets.psychologytools.com/uploads/509/reciprocal_cbt_cover_v3_1631x689.png.

1.4. SIGNS AND SYMPTOMS OF MENTAL HEALTH DISORDERS

Signs and symptoms of mental illness in children and teenagers can take many different forms and can change depending on the ailment and the person's developmental stage. Changes in mood, behavior, or academic performance, social disengagement, and elevated emotional discomfort are common indicators and symptoms. For instance, children with depressive symptoms may exhibit a loss of interest in once-enjoyed activities, and children with anxiety symptoms may frequently report preoccupations about school or peer interactions. Early detection may be challenging due to this small alteration. Parents, schools, and medical professionals must be aware of these indicators since early treatments can have a big impact on a young person's mental health outcomes. A healthy environment where teenagers can resolve mental health issues can be fostered by successfully identifying these symptoms, which can result in more educated strategies catered to particular requirements. Understanding the factors that contribute to the genesis of mental health issues is crucial for recognizing their symptoms. Numerous studies have identified parental participation and family interactions as important factors influencing children's psychological well-being. In one of the recent studies, families with adolescents aged between 12 and 25 years suffering from mental problems were investigated to observe the effects of treatment on parent-child relations. Parents and children who were part of a group treatment exhibited notable symptom reduction in anxiety among parents and children, which proves that family-based treatment strategies can eliminate distress and strengthen attachment among families (Bertino et al., 2013). These results highlight the relationship between mental health and family life, as well as the need for a comprehensive understanding of children's emotional environments in order to support early disorder diagnosis. Adolescents' symptoms will involve specific behavioral tendencies in addition to emotional discomfort. According to research, people with SSD frequently exhibit sensory anomalies in addition to motor and process skill impairments (Falk-Kessler et al., 2020). These disparities in perception have the potential to worsen psychiatric symptoms, making daily living and social integration more difficult. These complications show that mental illness can encompass a wide range of challenges, from processing sensory input issues to emotional irregularities. Practitioners must thus view assessment sessions with a holistic mindset, considering psychological as well as physiological aspects of mental health. By recognizing the diverse symptoms of mental health disorders, the stakeholders are then better placed to utilize appropriate interventions that address the unique needs of children and adolescents and nudge them towards healthier paths of development.

1.4.1. Behavioral Indicators

Behavioral markers, which represent the emotional and psychological well-being of children and adolescents, are important indicators of their mental health. They include a variety of observable behaviors that could indicate underlying mental illness, such as modifications in social interactions, academic achievement, or adherence to routines. For instance, declining grades may indicate stress or cognitive impairment, and increased hostility or avoidance of peers may indicate anxiety or depressive disorders. Additionally, a child's unique universe—which includes their family history and socioeconomic status—has a significant impact on how they behave. Teachers, parents, and mental health experts can then identify children and teens who need particular care by being aware of these symptoms. Monitoring such is required, particularly with the complexity of mental health issues in their initial stages, when treatment in these early stages is known to lead to better long-term outcomes (Amy, 2006). Bearing in mind the importance of behavioral indicators, significant research has emerged that describes the mental health picture of specific youth groups. For instance, the Lucile Packard Foundation for Children's Health-commissioned report highlights the preteen emotional, behavioral, physical, and academic health of Santa Clara and San Mateo counties. Such local data facilitates individual needs-based intervention and raises community knowledge of specific concerns and juvenile needs. Stakeholders can better grasp the unique issues faced by preteens in certain groups by combining economic, demographic, and behavioral data.

Figure 1.11. Behavioral indicators are essential measures for evaluating children's and teenagers' mental health because they provide information about their emotional and psychological wellbeing.

Source: https://heywellness.com/wp-content/uploads/2024/11/boy-with-phone-is-sitting-lifestyle-window-social-media-modern-children-article-about-developed-children.jpg.

As a result, there is increasing need to close current data gaps, and community-based interventions have the potential to strengthen the overall mental health infrastructure for children and adolescents (Amy, 2006). Furthermore, developing a comprehensive economic perspective to characterize behavioral variables offers a chance for well-informed child welfare policy. By using behavioral indicators in cross-national comparisons, one can gain a better understanding of the quality of child development. There is evidence to indicate that children's behavioral outcomes are influenced by both endogenous factors, such as temperament and genetics, and exogenous factors such as socio-economic status and maternal support. Such an understanding de-mystifies the complex interplay of factors that affect mental health and emphasizes policies that support integrative child well-being. Continued investigation and information gathering regarding behavioral markers are central to resolving current disparities and directing future action towards enhancing child and adolescent mental health (Figure 1.11).

1.4.2. Emotional and Psychological Symptoms

Understanding and promoting mental health in children and adolescents is severely hampered by emotional and psychological symptoms. These symptoms can manifest in a variety of ways, from anxiety and depression to behavioral problems and reactions to traumatic stress. Children and teenagers are particularly vulnerable to external stimuli that can create latent disorders since they are going through a tumultuous time of maturation. Their emotional sophistication is explained by the complex interactions between the environmental elements, such as family dynamics and school demands. For example, Alegría et al.'s study shows racial and ethnic disparities in mental health outcomes and observes that minority teenagers often encounter additional obstacles when trying to get mental health care. It is important to comprehend these variations in order to create inclusive interventions that address the unique needs of such groups and advance overall mental health (Green et al., 2015). The emergence of emotional and psychological symptoms is likely to be associated with certain demographic and contextual factors, suggesting the need for targeted assessment tools.

For example, after environmental disasters like hurricanes, adolescents can experience enhanced anxiety and depression symptomatology that are a result of trauma exposure. The Hurricane Exposure, Adversity, and Recovery Tool (HEART) are a self-report instrument used to quantify risk factors for the traumatic event. Its comprehensive approach measures hurricane-exposure-specific as well as underlying risk factors influencing post-disaster mental status. Evidence reveals that disaster exposure is highly correlated with post-traumatic stress responses in child victims, suggesting the importance of specific screenings and interventions following disasters. This information is crucial for practitioners in crafting effective support systems that address the multidimensionality of emotional distress (Dodd et al., 2019). The management of emotional and psychological symptoms in youth requires a multidimensional intervention incorporating prevention, intervention, and support. Schools, families, and mental health practitioners all need to collaborate to establish emotionally nurturing settings for emotional expression and resilience. Early intervention strategies have the capability of countering the development of more severe mental health problems by creating an emotionally nurturing framework for young people and adolescents. By using the resources of the community and creating open communication about mental health, stakeholders can enable young people to recognize and respond to their emotional difficulties.

Furthermore, a focus on developing protective factors, such as coping skills and social support networks, can foster resilience among adolescents suffering from emotional distress. Ultimately, addressing these symptoms holistically not only improves individual welfare but also contributes to the broader agenda of creating healthier, better adaptive future generations (Green et al., 2015) (Figure 1.12).

Figure 1.12. Youth are more vulnerable to outside pressures during this turbulent developmental stage, which might worsen pre-existing illnesses.

Source: https://dy7glz37jgl0b.cloudfront.net/advice/images/betterhelp/5568/c904365c1d728301ed04d66fb3e37bd3-teen-girl-holding-parents-hand-on-couch_l.jpg.

1.4.3. Academic and Social Performance Changes

Given that emotional well-being is directly related to cognitive functioning and learning success, there is ample evidence linking academic accomplishment and mental health in children and adolescents. Children with mental health issues frequently struggle with focus, memory, and organization, all of which have a negative impact on their academic performance. When these issues build up over time, children are more likely to experience chronic stress, which causes them to become disengaged from educational settings. Furthermore, social contexts including peer interactions and family life can exacerbate these illnesses since people with mental health problems may become socially reclusive or be the targets of bullying. Last but not least, the academic decrease of students with mental health issues highlights the necessity of integrating mental health services into educational systems and encouraging resilience and constructive coping strategies that can improve academic performance (Green et al., 2015). Since children's and teenagers' social interactions may be negatively impacted by their mood, social performance's influence on mental health is also crucial. The development of critical interpersonal skills will be hampered by conditions like depression and anxiety, which might show up as hostility or social disengagement.

Figure 1.13. Young people with mental health issues frequently struggle with focus, memory, and organization, which lowers their academic achievement.

Source: https://epe.brightspotcdn.com/fd/6f/8b70186f4260a182c8aa856d3a0c/1223-pisa-langreo-fs-1389037790.jpg.

Those with mental health problems are more likely to find it difficult to play cooperatively or make friends, which can result in feelings of loneliness and isolation. Furthermore, the school environment can be a mirror of broader society trends in which minority teenagers face inequalities in their access to support networks and mental health. Such disparities must be eliminated since collective intervention for mental health awareness and social integration can eventually result in more integrated schools with improved social interactions and a healthier learning environment (Farrow et al., 2014). In order to create successful interventions, it is also important to understand the long-term consequences of impaired social and academic functioning brought on by mental health problems. According to research, adolescents who perform poorly academically are more likely to face challenges in their future schooling and careers, resulting in a vicious cycle of disadvantage. Conversely, greater social support will moderate the negative effects of mental health, providing youth with resilience to manage academic stress and peer relationships. Mental health education and more available resources are policy interventions that help build resilience and facilitate help-seeking behavior in youth. When additional communities become aware of the place of mental health within educational settings, comprehensive strategies that integrate mental health interventions and educational curricula have the promise of providing joined-up support, enabling a generation of learners in a superior position to achieve academically and socially (Green et al., 2015) (Figure 1.13).

1.5. ASSESSMENT AND DIAGNOSIS

Effective intervention planning in child and adolescent mental health is mostly dependent on diagnosis and assessment. Due to the complexity of mental health conditions in these age groups, evaluation tools that take into account various developmental settings must be used. It is necessary to use multifaceted methods, such as behavioral observation, standardized rating, and family and kid interviews. Practitioners can discover prevalent problems including anxiety disorders, depression, and emerging personality disorders with the aid of such comprehensive exams. More recent studies on the validity of borderline personality disorder (BPD) in teenagers are particularly significant since they dispel theories on the treatability of personality problems throughout this stage of development (Fonagy et al., 2015). These developments underscore the central role evaluation plays not only in the establishment of a diagnosis but also in the development of personalized treatment plans that promote psychosocial functioning. The assessment of attention deficit hyperactivity disorder (ADHD) is a good example of the intricate dynamics of diagnosis. A thorough evaluation will often rely on collaborative working between pediatricians and child psychiatrists, especially due to the complexity of ADHD signs, such as impulsivity, hyperactivity, and inattention. It has been established that despite a high percentage of Child and Adolescent Mental Health Services (CAMHS) that provide specialist ADHD clinics, pediatrician involvement is very low. In fact, only 22% of pediatricians are engaged in medication management of ADHD, while 82% of child psychiatrists engage in such practice (Gavin et al., 2017). This disparity highlights the requirement for an interprofessional model that facilitates more effective and seamless communication and exchange of information between disciplines to deliver adequate and complete assessment and diagnosis. Moreover, achieving the engagement of families in the diagnostic process is pivotal towards successful mental health outcomes. Parents and caregivers provide valuable information about a child's behavior, emotional response, and developmental history that might otherwise remain latent in clinical settings. Incorporating family opinions allows clinicians to make more informed matchings of evaluations to accommodate a child's unique setting. Such a collaborative practice also serves to instill a sense of ownership on the families' part, encouraging them to be active participants and adhere to assigned treatment interventions. Education regarding the specificity and nuances of understanding mental health disorders—such as those illustrated in studies involving BPD and ADHD—can close knowledge gaps, which, in turn, results in improved diagnosis (Fonagy et al., 2015; Gavin et al., 2017). Assessment and diagnosis are, in overall terms, central elements in the child and adolescent mental health system, and they form the foundation for effective therapeutic intervention.

1.5.1. Standardized Assessment Tools

In order to identify and treat mental disease in children and adolescents early on, standardized tests are essential. The carefully crafted tests examine a range of psychological and developmental functioning, producing benchmarked results that allow comparisons across settings and groups. When identifying high-risk kids, standardized assessments are crucial because they allow practitioners to provide timely treatments targeted at particular needs. These tools aid in the more systematic delivery of mental health services by providing a uniform framework for evaluation, ensuring that children receive the proper care to improve their psychological and emotional development. The value of these standard instruments is even better emphasized by the imperative of national standards for preventive care that ultimately optimizes the impact of early childhood developmental services, including assessment, education, and care coordination (Stevens et al., 2005). Furthermore, the use of standardized assessment instruments is important in solving major public health problems, including those posed by adolescent substance abuse. The opioid epidemic is a quintessential example of the urgency for prevention and early intervention. Interventions to disrupt the cycle of addiction need to include not just those suffering currently but those who are still vulnerable. The use of standardized screening in children's Medicaid programs, the Early and Periodic Screening, Diagnostic and Treatment (EPSDT) benefit, places health professionals in a position to screen and serve vulnerable children effectively. These measures enable routine screening of mental health and alcohol and other drug problems within a clinical environment, enabling practitioners to pursue preventive approaches prior to harmful patterns developing (Cannon et al., 2019). Integrating standardized screens into mental health care for youth creates a basis in evidence-based practice while supporting health equity. Using these tools, mental health professionals can compare findings, leading to informed diagnoses and treatment plans that reverse new problems holistically. The method is also aligned with *Lifecourse Health Development* theory, underpinning preventive interventions for reversing risk factors at an early age. By prioritizing resources for initial assessment and intervention, healthcare systems can decrease the ultimate costs of under-treated mental illness. The integration of standard measures of assessment and developmental models eventually opens the door to avoiding future mental health crises, ensuring children receive care to thrive (Cannon et al., 2019; Stevens et al., 2005) (Figure 1.14).

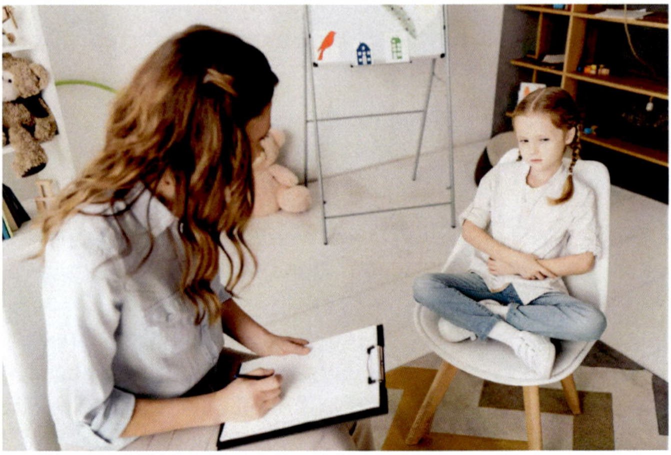

Figure 1.14. Standardized assessment tools play a crucial role in the early detection and intervention of mental health issues in children and adolescents.

Source: https://www.socialworkportal.com/wp-content/uploads/2023/02/child-mental-health-assessment-jpeg.webp.

1.5.2. Role of Mental Health Professionals

This not only benefits treatment in the short term but also lays the foundations for enduring mental health in the long term, reducing the likelihood of persistent issues taken into adulthood. Besides, mental health practitioners have a key role to play in advocating systemic changes that ensure children and adolescents receive better mental health service delivery. They understand the way things are now for mental health and steer policy direction towards ensuring more accessibility and better quality of care. According to Gootman et al. (2008), there is a critical need for enhanced primary care, integrated policy, and expanded coverage in response to the health disparities of youth populations. Mental health professionals also call for the incorporation of integrated services addressing diverse facets of a child's life, including schooling, family relationships, and social environments. By promoting a holistic approach, they aim to create supportive networks outside of clinical settings, hence creating a culture of mental well-being in communities. In specific contexts like in child welfare systems, mental health practitioners have a pivotal role to play in responding to the specific needs of vulnerable children. For instance, according to Farrow et al. (2014), African–American men and young men in these systems often encounter systemic barriers that have an impact on their mental health outcomes. Culturally responsive practices and policies can be implemented by mental health professionals to address the needs of these groups, rendering the services accessible and meaningful. By making their practice the focus of a balanced strategy to mental health care, these practitioners not only minimize the psychological impact of traumatic events but also drive systemic changes that maximize effects for vulnerable populations. Therefore, their practice transcends standard therapeutic practice, earning them the status of champions of social justice in mental health care (Figure 1.15).

Figure 1.15. When it comes to meeting the psychological needs of children and adolescents, especially during a developmental stage marked by fragility and change, mental health specialists are essential.

Source: https://cdn.who.int/media/images/default-source/hero-images/adolescent-mental-health-low-res.jpg?sfvrsn=d4b822cc_17.

1.5.3. Importance of Early Diagnosis

Effective treatment programs and better long-term outcomes depend on early detection of mental health problems in children and adolescents. Early detection of mental health problems enables early intervention, which can greatly reduce symptoms and improve developmental pathways. 10% of teenagers are thought to be experiencing mental health issues at any given moment, which is a startlingly high incidence. Healthcare systems must prioritize early diagnosis and intervention because these issues have long-term effects on emotional, social, and educational functioning. By addressing these issues in the early stages, practitioners and families stand a better chance to promote resilience and support coping mechanisms that are crucial during early stages of development. Furthermore, intervention is invariably associated with reducing social and economic costs that arise as a result of untreated mental illness. Delays in diagnosis will most often lead to more complex and entrenched issues that take so much time and resources attempting to unravel, hence clogging up healthcare systems and families. Research has emphasized the significance of easy access to CAMHS in achieving optimum treatment benefits and good family functioning, with qualitative summaries of the North Lincolnshire CAMHS Brief Intervention Service. Patients reported considerable improvement in symptom presentation and family adjustment and highlighted the central role of early intervention services in alleviating distress and improving quality of life. This serves to underpin the suggestion that investment in early diagnosis is not merely one of clinical imperative but a fundamental public health policy. In addition to the health benefits to the individual, action on early diagnosis also provides an opportunity to reframe community attitudes towards mental illness. Enabling conditions for early diagnosis and intervention can be created through successful school initiatives to increase awareness among parents, educators, and health professionals. By overcoming stigma and promoting open dialogue about mental illnesses, common responsibility can strengthen the support network for vulnerable populations. Programs that emphasize early diagnosis can provide more equitable routes to treatment for young people, while healthcare professionals encounter structural obstacles that may impede access to services. In addition to preventing immediate psychological stress, all of these actions are a component of broader public health initiatives to improve mental health and community resilience (Harriette et al., 2003; Gallagher et al., 2015).

1.6. TREATMENT AND INTERVENTION STRATEGIES

For children and adolescents with mental illnesses to develop and thrive, effective intervention and treatment are essential. Modern methods are based on an integrated strategy that includes person-centered community-based interventions, medication, and psychotherapy. For example, cognitive-behavioral therapy (CBT) has emerged as an evidence-based treatment for children and adolescents with anxiety and depression problems. CBT fosters emotional resilience and regulation in children by teaching them coping mechanisms, which are essential for adjusting to the ups and downs of growth. Additionally, treatment programs often include parents and caregivers as active agents due to the knowledge of the impact of family processes on mental health, creating an optimal setting that enhances therapeutic results. Through combining multiple modalities, clinicians are able to make available an all-encompassing treatment for the symptoms as well as etiology of children's mental health. Over the last few years, increased awareness of mental health disparities in the treatment of minority youth has led to the calls for focused interventions that address sociocultural factors. Studies have indicated that systemic inequalities influence access to mental health services and result in poorer outcomes for these groups (Green et al., 2015). In order to combat this, new models for treatment are being established that not only provide direct treatment but also engage communities and leaders from cultures in the process. Programs that incorporate traditional methods or community-based resources have been helpful in closing the gap in minority teenagers' access to mental health care. In addition to improving access, these community partnerships foster trust among groups that have previously faced obstacles to receiving equal care. These aspects must be given priority in order to provide an inclusive treatment environment that truly meets the requirements of every adolescent. In addition, teenage treatment and intervention decisions are strongly influenced by health care systems. Accessibility to mental health interventions is strongly influenced by managed care, health insurance, and resource availability, according to urban-based study (Harriette et al., 2003). To augment these measures, it is also important to advance policy reforms that recognize mental health care as a valuable component of the overall healthcare system. New initiatives that promote expanded service delivery models, such as school-based mental health programs, are effective ways of reaching teenagers where they are. These approaches de-stigmatize mental illness and offer an environment that encourages early intervention. Overall, an attempt to eliminate system barriers and design interventions that are youth-friendly will promote children's and adolescents' mental health and build a platform for healthier futures.

1.6.1. Psychotherapy and Counseling Approaches

The main elements of children's and teenagers' mental health are psychotherapy and counseling interventions, which use a range of approaches to address different psychological problems. Conventional therapies, like play therapy and cognitive behavioral therapy (CBT), rely on empirical foundations to direct interventions that let kids express their emotions and ideas. With a growing emphasis on the fusion of idiographic and nomothetic philosophies, the shift from static, protocol-based therapies to more process-based solutions has gained popularity in recent years. This change reflects a broader understanding that, in order to help practitioners better address the unique needs of adolescent clients as they traverse increasingly complex emotional terrain, psychological treatment must be tailored to individual biopsychosocial contexts (Carpenter et al., 2018). Increased emphasis on flexibility in treatment settings encourages adaptive processes that more deeply engage children and adolescents, setting the stage for increased therapeutic gain.

Figure 1.16. In the field of child and adolescent mental health, psychotherapy and counseling approaches are essential because they provide a variety of frameworks to address different psychological issues.

Source: https://upload.wikimedia.org/wikipedia/commons/3/3f/Psychosocial_sessions_for_children_in_kindergarten_Debaltseve_%2818728521230%29.jpg.

Therapeutic alliance between clinician and child or adolescent patient is a second critical ingredient to effective psychotherapy. Empirical evidence indicates that the quality of this alliance strongly influences outcomes and dropouts. Specifically, the frequency of ruptures—breakdowns in this alliance—can serve as indicators of unhappiness and can evolve into disengagement and incomplete therapy. Because unresolved conflicts can negatively impact the therapeutic process, research-based evidence is crucial when dealing with teenage populations to identify strategies to traverse these ruptures (Martin et al., 2020). Fostering resilience and maintaining long-term treatment commitment depend on enhancing communication and building trust in the therapeutic alliance. Mental health practitioners can reduce the chance of dropout and increase the overall effectiveness of their interventions by giving the healing of ruptures top attention as and when they happen. A key component of comprehensive child and adolescent mental health care is the integration of several therapeutic methods. As therapists adopt eclectic or integrative approaches, they are able to tailor interventions to suit the needs of unique clients while benefiting from the strengths of multiple methodologies. For example, younger individuals who are unable to articulate their feelings might express themselves when CBT is combined with art or play therapy. Additionally, therapists can effectively combine behavioral techniques with psychodynamic knowledge to help teenagers develop greater emotional awareness and self-regulation. In the context of psychotherapy and counseling, this flexibility guarantees results that are both dynamic and responsive to young people's developmental stages, ensuring a better understanding of mental health challenges as well as effective treatment strategies (Carpenter et al., 2018) (Figure 1.16).

1.6.2. Medication Management

Optimizing mental health outcomes for adolescents and young people requires effective drug management. It involves deliberate screening, monitoring, and adjusting pharmacologic therapies to meet the unique needs of younger people. Antidepressants and stimulants, for example, can greatly reduce the symptoms of mental health disorders, but their usage must be closely monitored to avoid unintended side effects and interactions, guaranteeing safety and efficacy. In mental health care settings, where therapeutic goals may need to be constantly adjusted based on factors like development and psychosocial maturation, medication management effectiveness is especially crucial. In order to create a treatment environment that is favorable for adherence and decision-making, multidisciplinary cooperation and patient and parent education are essential. The complexities that are required in the medication management of children and adolescents also point towards the importance of designing robust monitoring and evaluation procedures. Regular monitoring is necessary in order to identify the effectiveness of prescribed drugs and make changes accordingly. Evidence has shown that without regular monitoring, treatment can not only be ineffectual but even lead to the loss of trust in healthcare providers and a resulting fear of subsequent treatment. Secondly, the incorporation of de-escalation skills in medication management, especially in acute care settings, can enhance patient-clinician relationships. De-escalation aims to avoid crises from arising through the application of communication and assessment skills that focus on safety as well as empathy. Optimally applied, effective medication management, therefore, includes these practices as a strategy for establishing a therapeutic relationship sensitive to the emotional and psychological health of adolescent patients (Dickens et al., 2017). Systemic obstacles in the healthcare system may make it difficult to obtain the appropriate drug management services. It might be difficult for teenagers to obtain timely access to drugs due to health insurance constraints, managed care initiatives, and the accessibility of mental health services. According to clinician opinions, these systemic conditions may change significantly between cities, affecting the continuity and caliber of medication management treatments offered. Improving treatment delivery and outcomes for adolescents requires creative solutions to these access hurdles. Healthcare systems can create circumstances where medication management is a crucial component of all-encompassing mental health treatment by developing recommendations to address the aforementioned obstacles, hence promoting improved health trajectories among youth (Harriette et al., 2003) (Figure 1.17).

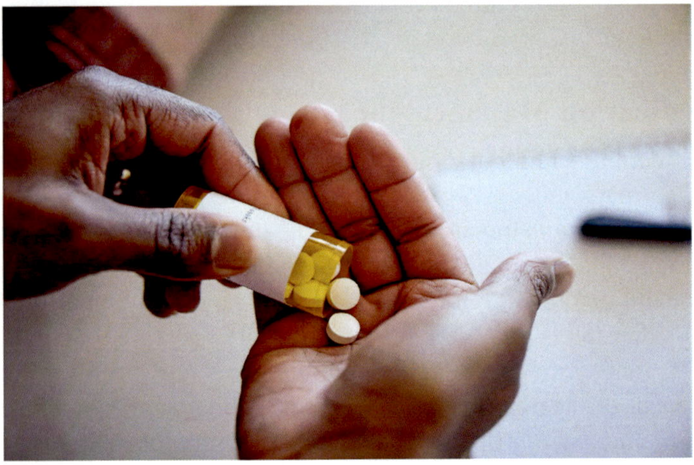

Figure 1.17. Medications such as antidepressants and stimulants can significantly alleviate symptoms of mental health disorders, yet their use necessitates thorough oversight to mitigate potential side effects and interactions, ensuring safety and efficacy.

Source: https://img.lb.wbmdstatic.com/vim/live/webmd/consumer_assets/site_images/articles/health_tools/ileocecal_resection_for_crohns_slideshow/1800ss_getty_rf_pills.jpg.

1.6.3. Role of Schools and Community Resources

Schools serve as both gatekeepers and coordinators of mental health services, and they are at the center of the youth and adolescent mental health system. Schools are typically the first places problematic adolescents go since they are socializing institutions. In addition to identifying adolescents in need of mental health interventions, teachers and counselors offer vital support. Children's sensitivity and resilience can be increased by incorporating mental health education into the curriculum, giving them coping mechanisms to deal with life's obstacles. Additionally, coordinated efforts between community health groups and schools can improve service delivery to guarantee that students receive timely and appropriate care. These initiatives can be improved by working together with the community and parents to foster an environment that values and supports mental health. Community resources are critical in providing additional support to the mental health needs of youth and children. Whereafter-school programs, youth organizations, and local health clinics can provide invaluable services outside the classroom.

These resources are typically designed to offer specialized interventions that address the particular needs of various demographic groups, particularly those who might have systemic barriers while trying to access conventional mental health care. For instance, such specifically targeted programs aimed at high-risk youth can give emotional space for expression and development and also connect participants with mental health professionals when necessary. When examining such systems, it is evident that access to community resources maximizes the support network of adolescents so that a more holistic approach to mental health treatment can be provided to address environmental and sociocultural factors (Harriette et al., 2003). Furthermore, some community programs identify the merit in intervening in focused programs to further maximize mental health outcomes. For instance, programs such as African–American boys and young men programming in child welfare systems aim to underscore the need for culturally responsive practice to meet their unique experiences and challenges (Farrow et al., 2014). Community-based responses not only increase access to fundamental services but also assist in fostering the sense of belongingness and support for marginalized groups. The efficacy of mental health interventions further depends on collaborative efforts involving schools, community organizations, and health care systems acting in unison. Prioritizing such interprofessional interventions enables stakeholders to establish comprehensive programs that tackle the multifaceted needs of children and adolescents appropriately, eventually creating a strong base for good mental health among extensive populations.

1.7. CONCLUSION

In synthesizing the conversation of child and adolescent mental health, it is necessary to recognize the complex interactions of contributory factors towards overall youth well-being. Mental health is increasingly recognized as an important determinant of not only individual well-being but also broader societal engagement. The importance of attending to mental health disparities cannot be overemphasized, particularly in minority youth, who have to contend with institutional obstacles impeding access to the required services and care. As highlighted in research on these disparities, it is essential to value the challenges facing marginal groups in finding relevant interventions that advance mental resilience and health equity in adolescents (Gootman et al., 2008). Therefore, integrative approaches are necessary, which include not only treatment but also prevention and early intervention actions that enable youth. Successful child and adolescent mental health care also requires an adequate support system in the form of families, schools, and healthcare providers. Multilateral strategies that engage these groups can enhance the impact of mental health promotion actions. Improving primary care settings, as emphasized in current research, will have to be combined with concerted policies aimed at expanding coverage and access for disadvantaged groups (Gootman et al., 2008). These system-level interventions hold the potential for making enormous improvements in the mental health climate of adolescents such that every teenager has an equal opportunity to thrive regardless of their economic or social status. Developing such frameworks requires continued research and a dedication to understanding the complexities of mental health issues encountered by young people in the contemporary era. Finally, the importance of a research agenda that places the priority on understanding and closing gaps in access to mental health care cannot be emphasized more. Subsequent research should seek to untangle the issues pertaining to mental health disparities across various youth populations, with an emphasis on main protective factors and barriers to care. Using a developmental perspective, researchers can access meaningful data about how various socio-economic, cultural, and family factors influence mental health outcomes (Green et al., 2015). In doing so, it is critical to inform policy and practice and ultimately create effective strategies that foster an environment of support for the mental health and well-being of all children and adolescents. As we proceed, applying these lessons to action will be vital in establishing a platform for healthier futures.

1.7.1. Summary of Key Points

The foundation of child and adolescent mental health rests in a multi-dimensional system comprising inter-related biological, psychological, and social aspects. Emerging evidence is reflective of the sophistication of children's development and signifies the imperative of intervention at an early point in order to foster mental wellness. Policies and initiatives aimed at child well-being must recognize these inter-relating aspects, which are vitally influential on outcomes of development. Of note, the debate identifies key markers of children's well-being, applied in cross-country comparisons, which allow for tracking progress in strengthening mental health across populations. This broad-based economic approach, as suggested by Conti et al. (2012), provides a framework for understanding how targeted investments in children's development can pay off for individuals and society in the long run. Beyond the basic factors, the significance of specially designed interventions and programs for teens has become increasing interest. With the brain continuing to develop during adolescence, susceptibility to mental health conditions is elevated. Models for Change are one such example of the potential for system change in both juvenile justice and mental health systems through integration with developmentally appropriateness. This emphasis on promoting effective, evidence-supported interventions is pivotal in addressing the special needs of adolescents with mental illness. Targeting adolescent needs in context, these interventions aim to reduce stigma and create supportive settings where there is open communication about mental health. As Ziedenberg (2006) notes, these collaborative efforts hold potential in reforming mental health care for this population. Ultimately, the mental health of children and adolescents looks to continued research and policy innovation in order to address the shifting landscape of mental health problems. Issues regarding the efficacy of existing programs suggest the need for strict testing and refinement of procedures for enhancing child well-being. Policies must be able to be modified in response to new evidence, considering the psychosocial determinants of mental health outcome. Through ongoing research and the promotion of inter-disciplinary working, stakeholders are able to learn more about the nuances of mental health development in early life and youth. A renewed emphasis on building a culture of well-being, as recommended in the literature, will most surely lead to more effective interventions and a brighter future for future generations.

1.7.2. Importance of Awareness and Education

Making the baseline level of awareness and education in adolescent and child mental health is important to construct a supportive environment that is healthy for growth. Awareness programs can de-stigmatize mental illness, such that youths and families have the ability to seek help without dreading social reactions. When communities are educated on the various mental health conditions that affect children and teenagers, they are better positioned to identify symptoms in time, thus enabling timely intervention. Integration of mental health education in schools and community programs can also help empower young people and their parents with essential information that improves resilience and coping skills. Without this systemic awareness, kids, particularly those from disenfranchised communities, may be left undiagnosed and have problems that get added upon later in life (Farrow et al., 2014). Education specifically tailored to the needs of vulnerable groups, including African–American boys and young men, is especially important in this system. By recognizing the unique issues these populations face in child welfare systems, stakeholders can implement unique policy and education practices that improve their experience and outcomes. Mental health education does not simply need to address symptoms and treatment but must also address more holistic socio-economic challenges that affect mental and emotional stressors among youth. Improved education of teachers and caregivers about the exact risks faced by these groups can help in designing support systems that can mitigate such risks and ensure better well-being. These gaps need to be bridged to provide equitable mental health care and support to all children so that none of them have to survive on their own (Farrow et al., 2014). Further, specific data on the emotional, behavioral, and academic health of preteens sheds light on the critical imperative for community education and public awareness campaigns. Reports, for example, compiled by the Lucile Packard Foundation for Children's Health, reveal entrenched knowledge gaps regarding the unique needs of preteens. These empirical conclusions illuminate the demographic, economic, and health-related characteristics of this age group, the significance of creating education programs that are responsive and knowledgeable to these challenges. These types of programs can have a direct impact on community resources, shaping the allocation of services aimed at preteens and their families. Reporting these findings back to communities encourages an anticipatory approach, a reaction to gaps that cause deleterious effects on adolescents' mental health and thus reinforcing the case for heightened awareness and anticipatory education efforts.

1.7.3. Future Directions in Child and Adolescent Mental Health Research

In recent years, child and adolescent mental health research has increasingly turned to combining several interdisciplinary approaches with a view to enhancing treatment interventions. This shift recognizes that quality approaches to mental health must take into account the intricate aspects of mental well-being, encompassing not only individual considerations but also family, social, and environmental considerations. Future studies will examine how domestic violence, and socio-economic disparities result in mental illness among youth. Targeting specific populations, such as troubled adolescents and young parents and fathers, allows interventions to be tailored to highlight preventive factors. Such development of targeted interventions, based on existing models, is a thrilling prospective for mental health research that aims to not only treat disorder but also to prevent likely risk factors and enhance resilience among high-risk groups (Rosewater, 2003). Policy planning during early childhood will also be a determining factor in shaping future trends in mental health research. Current evidence suggests that stable and supportive environments are central to enabling good mental health outcomes in children. Future studies must examine how developing secure foundations and sustaining physical and social conditions of support can become the bedrock for preventing mental health issues before they have a chance to occur. Early interventions require a forward-looking approach to conceptualizing these developments, prioritizing stable, responsive care and safe and supportive contexts for children and families. Prioritizing these core principles, mental health researchers can advance policy that not only invests in education in early childhood but also fosters overall health and well-being from early development. With the child and adolescent mental health research landscape ever evolving, the integration of technological advancements brings with it prevention and intervention opportunities. The use of technology platforms and software can potentially facilitate easy access to mental health care across large populations, particularly in underserved populations. Future research is indicated to assess the efficacy of such innovations in impacting mental health literacy and help-seeking barriers reduction. There is also a critical need for longitudinal studies exploring the long-term impact of interventions launched early in life through technology. The potential of real-time data collection and analysis through the use of mobile apps offers detailed information about behavior patterns and mental health. The interactive approach is capable of revolutionizing the provision of mental health services to make them flexible, accessible, and ultimately effective for children and youth in various settings.

REFERENCES

1. Arbreton, A. J. A. (2006). A portrait of preteens in Santa Clara and San Mateo Counties: What we know about 9- to 13-year-olds. https://core.ac.uk/download/71341361.pdf (accessed on 14th October 2025).
2. Baena Medina, M. S., Hidalgo García, M. V., Jiménez García, L., León, C., et al. (2019). Effectiveness of structural-strategic family therapy in the treatment of adolescents with mental health problems and their families. https://core.ac.uk/download/225123947.pdf (accessed on 14th October 2025).
3. Bashford, J., Kaur, J., Patel, K. K., Williams, G., et al. (2002). Healthy minds: A child and adolescent mental health research project: What are the mental health needs of Bradford's Pakistani Muslim children and young people and how can they be addressed? https://core.ac.uk/download/74206316.pdf (accessed on 14th October 2025).
4. Bernstein, A., Everaert, J., Joormann, J., Koster, E. H. W., et al. (2020). Mapping dynamic interactions among cognitive biases in depression. https://core.ac.uk/download/323232440.pdf (accessed on 14th October 2025).
5. Bertino, M. D., Knight, T., Lewis, A. J., Ricciardelli, L. A., et al. (2013). Reducing parental anxiety using a family-based intervention for youth mental health: A randomized controlled trial. https://core.ac.uk/download/77140438.pdf (accessed on 14th October 2025).
6. Cannon, Y. (2019). The kids are not alright: Leveraging existing health law to attack the opioid crisis upstream. https://core.ac.uk/download/225012727.pdf (accessed on 14th October 2025).
7. Carpenter, J. K., Ciarrochi, J., Curtiss, J. E., Hayes, S. C., et al. (2018). The role of the individual in the coming era of process-based therapy. https://core.ac.uk/download/360501487.pdf (accessed on 14th October 2025).
8. Conti, G., & Heckman, J. J. (2012). The economics of child well-being. https://core.ac.uk/download/pdf/30677962.pdf (accessed on 14th October 2025).
9. Dickens, G. L., & Hallett, N. (2017). De-escalation of aggressive behaviour in healthcare settings: Concept analysis. https://core.ac.uk/download/228178030.pdf (accessed on 14th October 2025).
10. Dodd, C. G., Hill, R. M., & Kaplow, J. B., et al. (2019). The Hurricane Exposure, Adversity, and Recovery Tool (HEART): Developing and validating a risk screening instrument for youth exposed to Hurricane Harvey. https://core.ac.uk/download/228022776.pdf (accessed on 14th October 2025).

11. Falk-Kessler, J., & Halperin, L. (2020). Schizophrenia spectrum disorders: Linking motor and process skills, sensory patterns, and psychiatric symptoms. https://core.ac.uk/download/286641346.pdf (accessed on 14th October 2025).
12. Farrow, F., Meltzer, J., Miller, O., & Notkin, S. (2014). Changing course: Improving outcomes for African-American males involved with child welfare systems. https://core.ac.uk/download/75780307.pdf (accessed on 14th October 2025).
13. Fernandes-Alcantara, A. L. (2014). Vulnerable youth: Background and policies. https://core.ac.uk/download/19523873.pdf (accessed on 14th October 2025).
14. Fonagy, P., & Sharp, C. (2015). Practitioner review: Borderline personality disorder in adolescence: Recent conceptualization, intervention, and implications for clinical practice. https://core.ac.uk/download/29416112.pdf (accessed on 14th October 2025).
15. Fox, H. B., Shejavali, K. I., & McManus, M. A. (2003). Is the health care system working for adolescents? Perspectives from providers in Boston, Denver, Houston, and San Francisco. https://core.ac.uk/download/71352449.pdf (accessed on 14th October 2025).
16. Gallagher, J., & Schlösser, A. (2015). Service users' experiences of a brief intervention service for children and adolescents: A service evaluation. https://core.ac.uk/download/151161466.pdf (accessed on 14th October 2025).
17. Gavin, B., Honorio Neto, F., McNicholas, F., Mulligan, C., et al. (2017). Attitudes and reported practice of pediatricians and child psychiatrists regarding the assessment and treatment of ADHD in Ireland. https://core.ac.uk/download/159108018.pdf (accessed on 14th October 2025).
18. Gootman, J. A., Sim, L. J., & Lawrence, R. S. (2008). Adolescent health services: Missing opportunities. https://core.ac.uk/download/71349202.pdf (accessed on 14th October 2025).
19. Green, J. G., McLaughlin, K. A., Alegría, M., & Loder, S. (2015). Disparities in child and adolescent mental health and mental health services in the U.S. https://core.ac.uk/download/75780891.pdf (accessed on 14th October 2025).
20. Langher, V., & Cataudella, S. (2015). Intervention strategies for children and adolescent with disorders: From intrapsychic to transactional perspective. https://core.ac.uk/download/54248559.pdf (accessed on 14th October 2025).
21. Mani, N., Pavuluri, S., & Kampani, S. (2005). Integrating pharmacotherapy

and psychotherapy for pediatric bipolar disorder: Translating science to service. https://core.ac.uk/download/pdf/86380.pdf (accessed on 14th October 2025).

22. Martin, P., Midgley, N., & O'Keeffe, S. (2020). When adolescents stop psychological therapy: Rupture-repair in the therapeutic alliance and association with therapy ending. https://core.ac.uk/download/266989997.pdf (accessed on 14th October 2025).
23. Pugno, M. (2025). The Easterlin paradox and the decline of social capital: An integrated explanation. https://core.ac.uk/download/pdf/6274676.pdf (accessed on 14th October 2025).
24. Rosewater, A. (2003). Promoting prevention, targeting teens: An emerging agenda to reduce domestic violence. https://core.ac.uk/download/71354063.pdf (accessed on 14th October 2025).
25. Spiliotopoulou, G. (2009). Management of children with ADHD and LD: A survey of pediatric occupational therapists in the UK. https://core.ac.uk/download/107200.pdf (accessed on 14th October 2025).
26. Stevens, G., Abrams, M. K., Inkelas, M., & Halfon, N. (2005). Quality of preventive health care for young children: Strategies for improvement. https://core.ac.uk/download/71354158.pdf (accessed on 14th October 2025).
27. Trzcinski, E., & Holst, E. (2025). Setting the set point: Initial predictors of life satisfaction in early adulthood. https://core.ac.uk/download/pdf/6492610.pdf (accessed on 14th October 2025).
28. Ziedenberg, J. (2006). Models for change: Building momentum for juvenile justice reform. https://core.ac.uk/download/71339533.pdf (accessed on 14th October 2025).

Chapter 2

Developmental Psychology and Brain Development

Contents

INTRODUCTION

The intricacies of human development and change throughout the life cycle are the focus of developmental psychology. The relationship between the stages of cognitive, emotional, and social development and the physical growth of the brain must be taken into account in order to understand these processes. There is evidence that early events have a major impact on neural development, especially in early childhood. Early aspects of a child's psychological portrait are organized by the responsiveness they receive from early interactions. The model of kinesthetic intersubjectivity, which describes embodied dialogues between caregivers and children in terms of the fine-grained connection realized through nonverbal communication and shared experience, reiterates this characteristic (Payne et al., 2012). This early relational context not only influences individual development but also grounds the child's later ability to engage in social relationships and emotional regulation. The interaction of environmental forces and brain growth is also complicated by the variety of viewpoints that inform early childhood policies and practices. For instance, a developmental view is focused on the consistencies in children's development, referring to their vulnerabilities at early periods. The economic and political view offers insight into how development principles become refracted into social interventions that foster child development in responding to economic models of human capital (Woodhead et al., 2006). Meanwhile, the social and cultural view illuminates differences in conceptions and practices of child development, indicating that norms and goals can be quite dissimilar across contexts. Conjoining these visions within developmental psychology is a three-dimensional understanding of a child's development and the environmental factors that support or inhibit brain growth. Along with this, the history of developmental psychology has also led to a human rights vision, which emphasizes the dignity and agency of young children. This shift makes professionals think of children as active participants in their own growth rather than as passive recipients of adult influence. By complimenting with this framework, practitioners and researchers resist mainstream approaches often relegating children's perceptions and contributions. Meanwhile, this human rights perspective reiterates the criticality of shared access to resources and services enabling maximum brain development and psychological health. As such models and conceptions persist in crossing over, one finds an integrated conception of developmental psychology emerging, which is critical to the formation of environments conducive to healthy psychological and neurological development throughout the life course (Woodhead et al., 2006).

Definition and Scope of Developmental Psychology

The study of psychological changes and development that take place during the course of a person's life, including cognitive, emotional, social, and physical development, is known as developmental psychology. Understanding human development from birth to old age with a focus on the interplay between biological and environmental factors is the focus of developmental psychology. Developmental psychology gives information on human development by analyzing several phases of life and finding milestones and patterns that define each stage. Additionally, the field acknowledges individual variances and contextual variations, providing a holistic picture of development that explains both culturally unique and universal experiences. This broad orientation is critical for the creation of effective interventions and policies to support development in diverse populations because precise descriptions of early childhood emphasize the necessity of attending to social, cultural, and economic factors on trajectories of development (Woodhead et al., 2006). Moreover, developmental psychology is also at the core of comprehending how brain development fosters psychological development. Understanding the mechanisms of neurodevelopment positions developmental psychology to ask questions regarding matters concerning the interaction between cognitive function and mind maturation.

Figure 2.1. Developmental psychology is a multifaceted field that examines the psychological growth and changes that occur throughout the human lifespan, encompassing cognitive, emotional, social, and physical development.

Source: https://cdn.prod.website-files.com/67ebf2aa4e72c068323f3dca/68021a9767e716b139cb7e93_6p1FwyfxFqnNi9Kruf6ig_43444dd732224fb4bb11c6a3d089180c.jpeg.

Research suggests that life during early childhood is dominated by high neural plasticity levels, whereby early childhood experience shapes brain structure and function. This neurobiological foundation impacts various domains such as language acquisition, social ability, and emotion regulation. Through integration of the neurobiological model, developmental psychology can greatly influence teaching and mental health treatment, emphasizing developmental timing and sensitivity to environmental signals. Within this framework, evidence favors an interrelation between cognitive and affective development facilitated through understanding of related neural mechanisms (Gelepithis et al., 2009). In broader contexts, developmental psychology has an extension of scope beyond individual development. It is critical of societal systems that constitute human development, such as political, economic, and cultural ones. By placing development within these contexts, researchers have been able to establish how inequalities at the system level affect the disadvantaged groups and the course of developmental trajectories. For instance, the application of a human rights framework puts special emphasis on the agency and dignity of children and demands policies that respect their rights and capacities. This not only reinterprets developmental goals but also brings psychological practice in line with social justice objectives, paving the way for inclusive and sustainable development. So developmental psychology sits in the space of individual and societal change, arguing the case for an integrated consideration of growth and development throughout the life stages (Woodhead et al., 2006) (Figure 2.1).

Importance of Studying Brain Development

Since the brain provides the foundation for a person's cognitive, emotional, and social development, understanding brain development is fundamental to developmental psychology. Early life and youth bring about significant changes to the brain, including myelination and synaptic pruning that affect the neuronal connections that govern behavior and learning. By comprehending these processes, educators and researchers can maximize developmental outcomes by gaining insight into critical windows of opportunity for intervention. For example, understanding how early childhood shapes the development of the brain highlights the importance of caring environments. Policies and initiatives that promote ideal developmental settings, particularly for populations at risk, can be informed by this information. Through an examination of how brain development is situated in context, psychologists can further our knowledge about the complexity of human behavior, ultimately yielding better intervention approaches to children's development and wellness. This interdependence of social interaction and brain development also underscores the importance of such research. Social actions, such as cooperation, are usually founded on underlying neurology, which reveals how both socially and biologically constructed development is. It is also proven that early cooperative experience strongly influences neural mechanisms that control social cognition and empathy. This suggests that cooperative play interventions can have lasting impacts on brain development, particularly in enabling children to cope with social complexities. Secondly, understanding the neural process of cooperation and interaction broadens the language about atypical development, like autism. As noted recently, ongoing research on embodied interactions reveals that even communicatively challenged children are able to engage in cooperative exchanges, challenging contemporary norms concerning social competence (Aldridge et al., 2014). Lastly, the investigation into the development of the brain has far-reaching consequences for educational processes and psychotherapy. Facts gathered from examining maturation in the brain can potentially inform the design of curricula as it maps onto cognitive preparedness to optimize learning outcomes. For example, understanding the sequence through which executive functions develop can inform age-compatible teaching methods conducive to self-regulation and critical thinking. In addition, involving a diversity of sources of explanation about brain development—e.g., culture and religious perspectives—enriches the discourse within developmental psychology. The collaborative effort of researchers from multiple backgrounds may provide new solutions that better address the complexity of learning and development, promoting psychological practice inclusivity (Behensky et al., 2006). Emphasizing research on brain development by scholars and teachers can empower them to create conditions that respect diversity among people while promoting collective human flourishing (Figure 2.2).

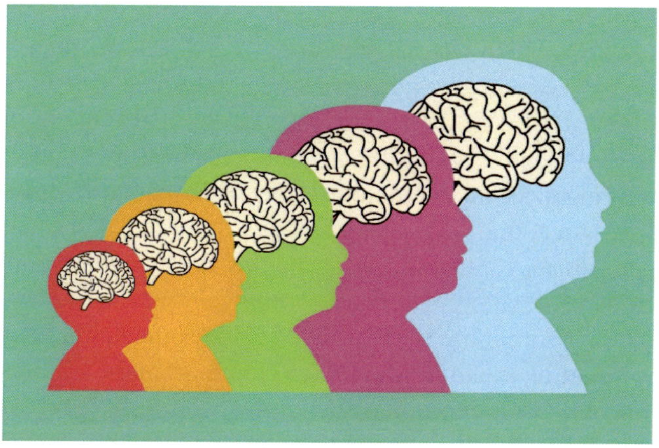

Figure 2.2. The brain undergoes significant transformation during infancy and childhood, with synaptic pruning and myelination processes shaping neural connections that influence learning and behavior.

Source: https://www.news-medical.net/images/Article_Images/ImageForArticle_24992_17201020278583427.jpg.

Overview of Key Theories in Developmental Psychology

Several well-known ideas that attempt to explain how people change emotionally, cognitively, and socially throughout the course of their lives make up developmental psychology. Jean Piaget's theory of cognitive development, which states that children go through four stages of cognitive development, is one of the most widely accepted theories. The phases of cognitive development known as sensorimotor, preoperational, concrete operational, and formal operational acknowledge how children's thinking evolves from simple reflex actions to sophisticated abstract thought. Piaget's focus on students actively creating their own knowledge serves as an example of the dynamic interplay between environmental interactions and cognitive development. The hypothesis provides a basis for understanding how brain growth naturally influences cognitive functions during the early years of life by assuming that cognitive development is intimately linked to biological maturation. An alternate viewpoint is offered by Vygotsky's sociocultural theory, which places a strong focus on the influence of culture and social interaction on the development of cognition. According to Vygotsky, language is an important tool for knowledge transfer and learning facilitation, and cognitive capacities are greatly influenced by the cultural tools that people currently employ.

He established ideas like scaffolding and the Zone of Proximal Development (ZPD), which characterize cognitive development as taking place when students are assisted by more seasoned individuals. It is a model that highlights the importance of collaboration with the learning environment and parental alliance, which are key to the promotion of healthy brain development. With growing sensitization of societies to the impact of early experience upon subsequent outcomes, Vygotsky's ideas result in a reconsideration of teaching procedures and intervention strategies designed to support children at critical periods of development. The ecological systems theory, which was formulated by Urie Bronfenbrenner, further broadens the field of developmental psychology by situating the individual's development in the frame of numerous interacting systems. Bronfenbrenner envisioned multiple levels of influence, from close environments such as home and school to more distant areas such as cultural and societal expectations. This broad framework accepts that a child's development is within a multi-faceted network of interaction and environmental pressures. These are particularly relevant when discussing the impacts of early childhood interventions on enhancing development. As highlighted in recent studies, public policy based on these ecological theories can significantly benefit when addressing the barriers to effective parent engagement in early childhood education. On this basis, ecological systems theory not only deepens the conversation concerning development but also offers essential frameworks for developing all-encompassing care systems for children and families (Aber et al., 2017; Huntington et al., 2017) (Figure 2.3).

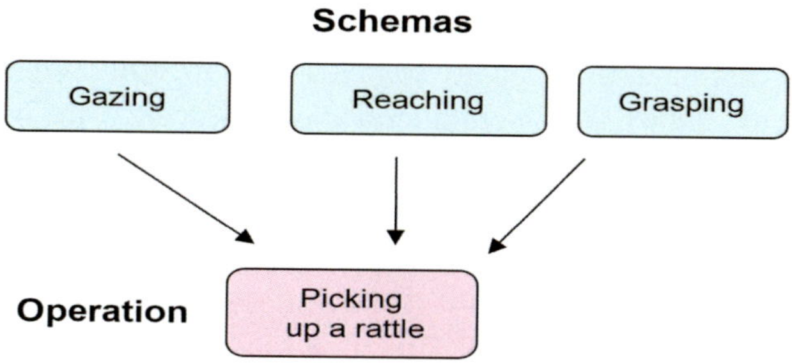

Figure 2.3. Piaget's emphasis on the active role of learners in constructing knowledge emphasizes the interplay between cognitive growth and environmental interactions.
Source: https://www.simplypsychology.org/wp-content/uploads/piaget-operations.jpg.

2.1. STAGES OF BRAIN DEVELOPMENT

The complexity of brain development occurs in distinct stages, each of which has unique neurobiological changes that serve as the foundation for both emotional and cognitive development. The neural tube has already established itself as the precursor to the central nervous system, and the foundation of the brain is formed during pregnancy. Many neurons are established at birth, but they are mainly disconnected. Synaptogenesis, the process by which neurons create synaptic connections, follows this phase of rapid growth and lasts throughout early childhood. The nature of these connections is shaped by experience with the environment, illustrating the interface between biological development and learning. Knowledge of these stages is how early experience has the capacity to organize brain architecture that can have a deep influence on later cognition and emotion, in accord with the developmental perspective that stresses regularities of development in this early period of life as has been pointed out by Woodhead et al. (2006). As kids move through early childhood, their brain undergoes a period of large brain plasticity defined by synaptic refinement and pruning. The brain undergoes use it or lose it mechanisms, where utilized neural paths become more powerful through repetition and the weaker ones are lost. This synaptic pruning is essential for optimal functioning to allow the brain to reserve its resources to the maximum extent possible based on the needs of learning and socialization. Besides, environmental influences, such as social interaction and language exposure, have the potential to significantly alter the trajectory of brain development during this time. Political and economic conceptualization of child development puts the role of fostering supportive environments that capitalize on these initial experiences at the center, thereby emphasizing the importance of policies encouraging educational practices and resources that have the capacity to nourish young children's development (Woodhead et al., 2006). In late childhood and adolescence, the brain continues to develop, with much alteration of regions responsible for higher-order thought, like the prefrontal cortex. This area is significant for decision making, control over impulses, and social conduct, and its maturation can influence the way adolescents think about danger and make choices. The steady growth across these stages emphasizes the necessity of a social and cultural perspective, underlining the manner in which society shapes the developmental milestones. In addition, a human rights perspective is necessary, as this necessitates respect for young people's dignity and their capacities to aid in their own development. Realization of brain stages of development interdependencies and complexity emphasizes integral solutions in development and education policy in fostering children's potential (Woodhead et al., 2006).

2.1.1. Prenatal Brain Development

The intricacy of fetal brain development is the main element affecting a child's intellectual and emotional development. For instance, the fetal brain undergoes substantial structural and functional changes during pregnancy as neural connections are developed and tuned. Notably, recent research indicates that listening to music while pregnant has a significant effect on brain development. This exposure not only fosters the creation of long-lasting brain images but also fortifies key areas associated with language processing and emotion. The literature review highlights the potential impact of prenatal musical exposure on a child's long-term cognitive and social development and finds a connection between it and increased brain plasticity. Furthermore, maternal music activities have also been found to be correlated with dramatic reductions in maternal anxiety, thus promoting a conducive atmosphere for maximum fetal brain development, wherein each song is not just an auditory experience but a design to be employed in the cultivation of mental capacities and emotional stability. No less significant is the role of the maternal environment during gestation, particularly as regards socioeconomic status (SES). Research indicates that maternal prenatal social disadvantage potentially has a detrimental effect on neonatal brain connectivity, particularly in areas of crucial importance in the amygdala and hippocampus. These brain regions are in charge of processing emotions and consolidating memories, respectively. Studies show that social disadvantage is linked to changes in functional connectivity in these brain regions, predicting behavioral consequences in newborns around the time of their first birthday. This illustrates the complex process of fetal brain development since socioeconomic status, which is a reflection of the mother's environment, plays a major role in neurological mechanisms that lead to behavioral effects. Understanding these correlations can therefore aid in customizing interventions to address brain development disparities brought on by socioeconomic circumstances, ultimately leading to healthier developmental trajectories for infants who are at risk (Max et al., 2024). Pregnant women's gestational care practices and the socioeconomic conditions of gestation will determine future understanding of fetal brain development. As science further elucidates the complexity of this developmental stage, it is increasingly apparent that the best opportunity for fetal brain development lies in optimizing conditions for such development. The inclusion of musical exposure as a form of therapy, in addition to recognition of socioeconomic stressors' effects, could have transformative outcomes not only in neural development but also in general developmental milestones. Hence, it is essential to draw evidence-based guidelines for prenatal care that incorporate these variables. These would encourage music as a regular practice within prenatal programs and, concurrently, address socio-economic determinants impacting maternal and fetal health. Through the process, one can have a uniform approach to prenatal brain development, resulting in a generation of people developing cognitively and emotionally robust (Max et al., 2024) (Figure 2.4).

Figure 2.4. Equally significant is the role of the maternal environment during pregnancy, particularly in the context of socioeconomic status (SES).

Source: https://www.americanprogress.org/wp-content/uploads/sites/2/2022/07/AStrongStartReport.jpg?w=1680.

2.1.2. Early Childhood Brain Growth

A child's brain grows and develops at its fastest rate during the first few years of life. The brain experiences a remarkable metamorphosis during this period, with the development of neuronal connections that set the stage for behavior and learning in later life. Since the brain is about 80% of its full size during the first three years of life, this is a crucial period for fostering both intellectual and emotional growth. In addition to being open to recognizing the underlying interdependencies and vulnerabilities that children exhibit during this stage of development, a developmental focus is eager to recognize the continuities in physical and psychosocial development seen throughout early childhood (Woodhead et al., 2006). This underlines the need to create supportive contexts that meet the special developmental needs of children, with particular focus on early intervention and good-quality care. Furthermore, the interplay between environmental conditions and neurological development sets the trajectory for a child's future health and learning potential. Research indicates that adverse conditions, such as poverty, can stifle not only cognitive development, but also emotional and social well-being. The neuroscientific evidence on child poverty explains how economic disparities long-term consequences on brain development might have, revealing a grim relationship between socioeconomic status and the neurological structure that plays a crucial role in emotional well-being and intellectual capability (Lipina et al., 2015). It is thus critical to address the challenges of children in poor environments to allow for optimal brain development. Developmental psychology provides a framework for comprehending these multifaceted influences, where it is emphasized that integrative strategies can enhance the brains resilience against adversity. Apart from environmental impacts on early brain development in children, cultural and societal circumstances also play a major role in shaping developmental trajectories. A. A social and cultural approach takes into account how early childhood status is constructed and interpreted within communities, as well as how this affects young children's lives and expectations. This viewpoint highlights the diversity of childrearing practices and educational intervention strategies used around the world, and it advocates for inclusive policies that honor and take into account diversity (Woodhead et al., 2006). This method promotes child empowerment initiatives and the recognition of children's rights by acknowledging them as agents in their own development. In order for academics and practitioners to support policies and practices that promote healthy development regardless of background, a comprehensive knowledge of early childhood brain development will ultimately need to take these varied perspectives into account.

2.1.3. Adolescence and Brain Maturation

The adolescent process is a crucial stage of neurodevelopment that involves significant alterations to the structure and function of the brain. During this stage, the brain undergoes a transformation that enhances emotional regulation and cognitive abilities. Since prefrontal cortex development is linked to higher-order functions including risk-taking, impulse control, and decision-making, it plays a crucial role in this process. In the meantime, heightened emotional reactions result from increased activity in the limbic system, which is responsible for processing emotions. Adolescents' propensity for risk-taking actions can be explained by this interaction between the limbic system and the developing prefrontal brain, since emotional cravings eventually take precedence over judgment. It is necessary to understand these neurological alterations in adolescence in order to comprehend the wider consequences for social interactions and behavior, thus making this developmental phase all the more significant in determining lifetime patterns of functioning. Teenagers' social behavior and emotional response are influenced by the activation of numerous brain circuits as they navigate connections with others. Adolescents go through several stages of social development, which are also greatly impacted by personal connections and social interactions, according to research. Subcortical systems manage affective motivation in social circumstances during transitions between the phases, which include intricate neurobiological processes. The executive components of the prefrontal cortex then control affective responses and connect them to cognitive techniques. Additionally, teenagers' perception and understanding of social cues are reinforced by processing of the visual and auditory systems in the occipital and temporal lobes. During development, these interactions between neurons contribute to the establishment of long-term brain functions and behavioral habits, underlining the significance of social experiences in the formation of neurological pathways and psychological developments during this stage of development (Guyer et al., 2016). Adolescent brain development can have profound long-term effects that affect behavior and cognitive functioning far into adulthood. Studies on the latent deficit hypothesis suggest that early brain trauma may have long-term repercussions on cognition. For example, people who experienced brain trauma prior to critical maturational phases may have long-term impairment of areas related to implicit cognition and executive function, which may show up later in life as more behavioral difficulties. When this kind of damage occurs, timing has a significant impact on the degree of cognitive impairment; individuals who are harmed at high-risk developmental stages struggle more with behavioral comprehension and cognitive flexibility than those who are injured later in life. This emphasizes the vulnerability of the adolescent brain to the environment and the necessity for supportive interventions during this period, which can induce resilience and promote healthier outcomes as one transition into adulthood (Andrade et al., 2010) (Figure 2.5).

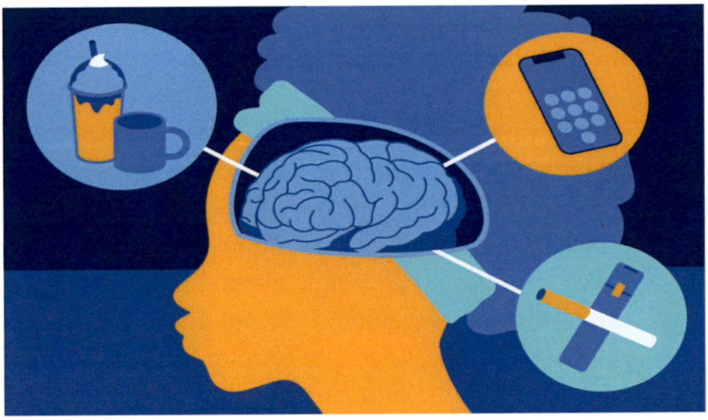

Figure 2.5. The process of adolescence marks a pivotal period in neurodevelopment, characterized by significant changes in brain structure and function.

Source: https://ktvz.b-cdn.net/2023/12/lead-image-teen-brain-stacker-1080.png.

2.2. THE ROLE OF GENETICS IN BRAIN DEVELOPMENT

Genetics is a powerful factor that controls many neurodevelopmental processes and serves as the master plan in the complex tapestry of brain development. From pregnancy to maturity, the structure, function, and overall development of the brain are determined by genetic factors. The relationship between genes and environment is especially important; while genetics determines the potential and blueprint for brain development, environmental factors, such as exposure to toxins during pregnancy or socioeconomic status after birth, can significantly impact the expression of the genetic inclination. According to Allen et al. (2020), a comparative integrative approach to developmental psychology is necessary in order to explain psychological phenomena such as emotional regulation, cognitive functioning, and vulnerability to psychopathologies. Further, the identification of specific genetic markers associated with neurodevelopmental disorders has presented new avenues for investigation and intervention programs. Development in molecular genetics has provided researchers with the means to extract genes that are associated with conditions like autism spectrum disorders (ASD) and attention-deficit/hyperactivity disorder (ADHD). Such knowledge of the genetic basis can help increase our understanding of the etiology of these disorders and, possibly, the development of more successful early interventions. For example, research has indicated that some of the genetic differences can lead to unusual patterns of brain connectivity that are frequently seen among ASD individuals. This genetic perspective allows clinicians and researchers to design targeted therapeutic interventions, such that the role of genetic studies in shaping our knowledge of developmental processes in psychology becomes evident (Rashid et al., 2020). Finally, the role of genetics in brain development is also observed within the neuroplasticity field, where genetic tendencies are blended with environmental factors to shape cognition and behavior across the lifespan. Neuroplasticity is the process by which the brain can reorganize itself by forming new neural connections due to learning and experience. Genetic dispositions can also influence a person's capacity for neuroplasticity, which can determine how much they can modify their response to change through their lifetime. For example, an individual with a high genetic disposition towards resilience can show greater neural adaptability in stress, hence mitigating the threat caused by environmental adversities. This genetic-neurodevelopmental-neuroplastic interaction identifies the complex and multidimensional nature of psychological development among individuals further bolstering the essential place of genetic research within the broader field of developmental psychology (Allen et al., 2020).

2.2.1. Genetic Influences on Brain Structure

Significant genetic influences on brain anatomy serve to shape the brain's functional capacities as well as its morphological characteristics. Numerous cortical metrics, including cortical thickness and surface area, have significant genetic contributions to their heritability, according to studies (Dale et al., 2014). These structural features contribute to cognitive functions and are differentially affected by age and environment during development. For example, the genetic basis of these elements can help us understand how people acquire abilities and skills like spatial reasoning, which has been linked to mathematical aptitude. Therefore, understanding the genetic basis of brain anatomy is essential to understanding the intricacies of developmental psychology and how it affects cognitive achievement. New research highlights the complex interplay between genetics and environment in the quest to understand how hereditary variables affect brain development. According to study, environmental factors also have a significant impact on cognitive performance, even while hereditary factors contribute a significant amount of diversity in the structure of the brain (Dale et al., 2014). In particular, it is predicted that hereditary factors account for 60% of the association between math performance and spatial aptitude, with shared and non-shared contextual settings playing a significant role. These results suggest that the identification of both genetic and environmental mediators may be beneficial for therapies aimed at improving cognitive functioning, especially in specific areas like mathematics. Thus, developmental psychology ought to consider both aspects in an attempt to ensure optimal brain and cognitive development. Moreover, the identification of specific genes responsible for brain structural variations further enhances our understanding of neurological and psychiatric diseases. Genome-wide association studies have identified genetic pathways responsible for brain development, such as the *Sonic Hedgehog* and *Wnt/β-catenin* pathways (Adams et al., 2019). These pathways not only shed light on typical mechanisms of brain development but also give insight into the ways in which deviations might lead to developmental disorders or intellectual deficits. By integrating genetic analysis with theory in developmental psychology, scientists can further understand how heterogeneity of genes affects variation in brain structure and function. It is imperative to this creation of targeted educational interventions and treatments matched to both the genetic predispositions and the individual's specific developmental needs (Figure 2.6).

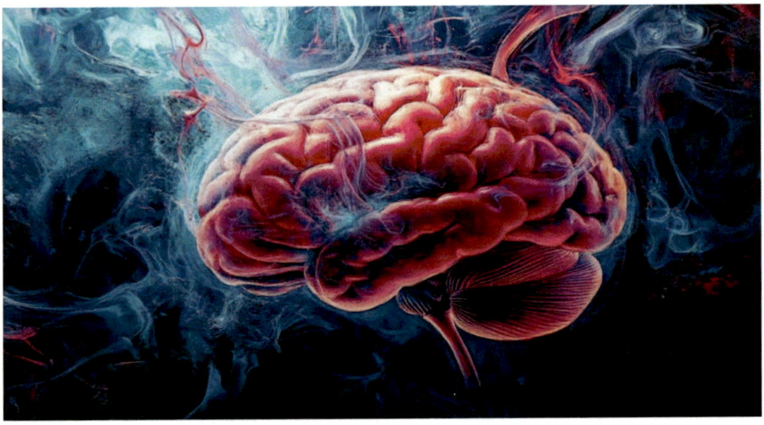

Figure 2.6. The genetic influences on brain structure are profound, shaping not only the anatomical features but also the functional capabilities of the brain.

Source: https://neurosciencenews.com/files/2025/05/memory-learning-hormones-neuroscience.jpg.

2.2.2. Heritability of Cognitive Abilities

Cognitive ability heritability has been at the forefront of developmental psychology research, illuminating the intricate relationship between environment and genes. Studies have shown that there are significant heritable components to cognitive ability, such as IQ and executive functioning. For instance, twin studies repeatedly demonstrate that twins raised apart will have remarkably similar cognitive capacities, indicating that genes are a major factor in cognitive development. Understanding cognitive heritability does offer insight into how genetic gifts may manifest across environmental settings, such as education and socioeconomic status, to have an impact on individual cognitive paths, even though it is true that heritability is not the same as determinism but rather the percentage of variance in cognitive ability that is explained by genetics for a given population. Furthermore, the environment also plays a significant role in shaping cognitive potential through a bidirectional impact of experiences and genetics. Factors including early childhood education and exposure to enriched environments have the ability to expand cognitive capacities and thus affect the expression of genetic potential. There is evidence to indicate that adverse environmental factors like trauma and instability may hinder cognitive development, the reality of which underscores the need for supporting environments. For instance, developmentally at-risk children, including those at risk for bipolar disorder, have varying cognitive outcomes based on their environments, which suggests that the expression of cognitive ability is not exclusively determined by hereditable factors but is also significantly contingent on their environments (Ghaleb et al., 2025). The understanding of cognitive abilities must thus have a balanced approach that appreciates both environmental and genetic determinants. Finally, cognitive heritability implications cut across academic writing, extending to educational practice and interventions. Parents and teachers should understand that the interaction between genetics and the environment can inform individualized interventions for cognitive development in children. Executive functions have been understood more clearly with the advent of neuroscience, with the complex processes by which cognitive abilities are built and expressed (Diamond, 2025). Through establishing an environment conducive to cognitive development—through social, emotional, and physical stimulation—stakeholders can optimize developmental outcomes. As research continues, it is essential to bear in mind the multidimensional nature of cognitive abilities and the way examining their heritability can influence developmental psychology and educational policy.

2.2.3. Interaction between Genes and Environment

Individual development, especially brain development and cognitive function, is fundamentally shaped by the interaction between genes and the environment. The relationship reflects both the dynamic nature of development and the tendency of genetic dispositions to require environmental activation in order to appear. Developmental psychologists, for example, support a concept in which genetic influences are not deterministic but rather interact with environmental circumstances to determine complicated behavioral consequences. In the context of the complex processes of neurodevelopment, where nature and nurture combine to produce cognitive capacities and emotion regulation, this is especially crucial. The previous genetic-environmental split is overshadowed by this recognition in favor of a more complete understanding of human development. Moreover, cognitive development can be shaped compellingly by various environments, which in turn can foster or inhibit genetic potential. Williams syndrome is just such a phenomenon; despite their unique cognitive profiles, people who are affected are not fixed by their biology. As researchers have pointed out, the uneven cognitive phenotype of adults with Williams syndrome demonstrates the way the environmental context may contribute to setting the expression of genetic tendencies.

Figure 2.7. Critical evaluations of genetic disorders further deepen our comprehension of the interaction between genes and environment in developmental psychology.

Source: https://www.verywellmind.com/thmb/O4GDMSiJqwBfKcs-7QPVesXeBPw=/1500x0/filters:no_upscale():max_bytes(150000):strip_icc()/168917706-56a7926b5f9b58b7d0ebcb35.jpg.

This development leads one to ask more questions about the manner cognitive modules are not necessarily pre-specified in the infant's brain, as the creation of cognitive abilities frequently arises from an interaction of combinations of complex mixes of genetic templates and environmental pressures. These findings illustrate that cognitive development is an emergent property of multifarious influences, rather than a straightforward product of genes. Philosophical criticisms of genetic disease also further clarify the connection between genes and environment in developmental psychology. The modularity thesis of some researchers stems from observation of selective cognitive deficits in individuals with genetic diseases. However, this perspective is false if it does not account for the ontogenetic mechanisms of brain development. Looking at behavioral research and neuroimaging evidence, cognitive modules are thus shaped by experience in development, rather than being innately programmed. Brain development and the social environments children are exposed to all contribute to how genetic elements are developed over the course of one's life. In this context, learning developmental psychology requires a sophisticated methodology that appreciates the intricate interdependence between genetic predispositions and environmental factors, informing future research and intervention models (Karmiloff-Smith et al., 2003; Machamer et al., 2002) (Figure 2.7).

2.3. ENVIRONMENTAL FACTORS AFFECTING BRAIN DEVELOPMENT

In developmental psychology, the relationship between the environment and brain development is a crucial area of study. For instance, cognitive functions and general brain health are greatly influenced by dietary status. Studies claim that diet quality, including macronutrient balance and micronutrient consumption, has a significant impact on executive functions and cognitive flexibility. According to Khodarahimi et al. (2018), a study conducted on adult Iranians revealed that individuals with a good eating habit had improved executive functions and cognitive flexibility, indicating that a balanced diet helps shape the brain. This highlights the need of early nutrition guidance and counseling as an anticipatory intervention in improving cognitive abilities and reducing cognitive impairments caused by improper eating. Parental drug use is another significant environmental factor in brain development that is a key risk factor for the cognitive and emotional growth of children. Exposure to drugs during pregnancy can lead to neurobehavioral deficits that surface throughout the life of a child. Children raised in families where drug abuse is prevalent have more adverse childhood experiences (ACEs), weakening their cognitive abilities as well as emotional regulation skills. Initial research points to young adults exposed to drugs early in their lives as typically showing deficits in attention and executive functioning, which are indicators of long-term effects that are likely to continue into adulthood. Acknowledging these risks is what makes the need for early intervention programs highly viable to help children from such backgrounds and reduce the psychological and cognitive challenges they may face (Afifi et al., 2016). Moreover, the role of socio-economic status as an environmental factor cannot be ruled out when the development of the brain is being discussed. Children from poorer socioeconomic backgrounds are more likely to experience a variety of cumulative developmental concerns, such as limited educational opportunities, ongoing stress, and unstable housing. These could lead to emotional issues and impaired cognitive performance. Economic insecurity and other general stressors can raise cortisol levels, which can harm brain regions like the hippocampus that are involved in learning and memory. A level playing field for children's cognitive and emotional development could result in better brain health if socioeconomic disparity is reduced through community assistance programs and public policy measures. Lastly, single holistic approach, considering nutrition, parental and socio-economic factors, is needed in order to enhance development outcomes among children (Afifi et al., 2016; Khodarahimi et al., 2018) (Figure 2.8).

Figure 2.8. Children from lower socio-economic backgrounds often face multiple and compounding challenges, including limited access to educational resources, chronic stress, and unstable living conditions.

Source: https://unitedwaynca.org/wp-content/uploads/2025/02/shutterstock_2332630597-scaled.jpg.

2.3.1. Impact of Nutrition on Brain Growth

It is indisputable that nutrition shapes brain development at times of sensitive growth. Given that certain nutrients are essential for neural development, it is more likely that a child in good health will experience the optimal developmental outcomes. Essential fatty acids like omega-3 and omega-6 are necessary for myelination, which makes it easier for impulses to travel between neurons. Furthermore, neurotransmitter function and neurogenesis are influenced by micronutrients such iron, zinc, and vitamins B, D, and E. Deficiency of such nutrients leads to cognitive retardation and impairment of learning and memory, which accentuate the importance of adequate levels of nutrition during developing years. Thus, detection of the intersection between developmental psychology and nutrition is essential to ensuring healthy brain development and decreasing disparities in cognitive outcomes among children. Therefore, healthy diets are not only beneficial; they are vital for long-term physical and mental health, particularly at early points in the life cycle. Equally effective, however, are the socio-economic factors that influence nutrition and brain development as a consequence. Disadvantaged children can experience food insecurity, with resulting chronic nutritional deficiencies that affect cognitions adversely. Evidence has increasingly highlighted the connection between child poverty and brain development, documenting significant alterations in brain organization and functioning due to inadequate nutrition (Lipina et al., 2015). Inadequate nutrition in early life might also harm school achievement and control of emotion, initiating a cycle of disadvantage.

Figure 2.9. Poor nutrition in early life can also impair academic achievement and emotional regulation, perpetuating a cycle of disadvantage.

Source: https://www.wfpusa.org/wp-content/uploads/2023/09/WF1774270_Barrera-01910-1024x683-1.jpg.

The long-term effects of these inequalities extend far into adult life, affecting educational qualifications, employment access, and health outcomes throughout the life course. To reverse these issues, strategic interventions are necessary, which address both the nutritional needs of children and the social determinants limiting access to healthy sources of food. Thus, an understanding of these complexities is essential for formulating policies that address the well-being and brain health of the child first. Moreover, the promotion of optimal nutrition is essential in crafting programs that lead to early childhood development. Educators and policymakers must collaborate for proper implementation of policies that give children proper nutrition. Children's brain development can be greatly impacted by policies that provide them with access to nutritious food in schools and their communities, as well as health education regarding eating habits. It also entails building settings that are responsive and stable. Children's cognitive and emotional development is aided by stable and safe environments since hunger does not interfere with their learning. Since early intervention is likely to result in long-term benefits, including improved cognitive function and general health, incorporating evidence-based practice into early childhood policy may ensure optimum developmental gains. As can be seen, combining these components with systemic measures will eventually strengthen the foundation for next generations (Figure 2.9).

2.3.2. Effects of Early Childhood Experiences

The early stages of a person's cognitive and emotional development are shaped by their early years. Children's brains undergo significant neurological changes between the ages of 0 and 8, with the majority of these changes being influenced either favorably or unfavorably by their experiences and surroundings. These early experiences influence many aspects of development, including social skills, language, and communication. For example, it has been demonstrated that intellectual stimulation through exposure to cognitively engaging learning materials and supportive relationships improves cognitive functioning; nevertheless, exposure to neglectful or unpleasant circumstances may result in long-term deficiencies in brain development. Hence, there is a need to learn of the significance of these early interactions to ensure healthy growth and to correct potential developmental delays or psychopathology later in life, facilitating interfacing between early experience and brain development. Moreover, the role of caregivers during early childhood experience cannot be overstated. Parents and teachers are immediate stakeholders in providing affective support and a learning-friendly environment. As required by existing research, interventions focused on parental education toward child development have been proven to enhance the quality of interaction and parent practices, which, in turn, have a beneficial effect on children's outcomes. For example, interventions in such areas as nutrition, sanitary habits, and affective caregiving have been shown to be effective in establishing bonds and healthy child development. This highlights the need for an integrated early childhood education approach that is able to empower parents and educators with information and skills necessary to create engaging environments that respond to the cognitive and social needs of young children (Suwahono et al., 2019). In addition to the effect of caregivers and learning environments, the socioeconomic status of a child's family is a significant determinant of early experience. Children in lower-income families often encounter more adversity, including fewer opportunities for quality instructional materials and experiences that promote cognitive development. These disparities can lead to the creation of alternate neural pathways, which impact cognition and social-emotional development in ways potentially of a lifetime duration. The interplay of these elements highlights the need for equitable access to resources and support systems that can possibly facilitate optimum growth across all segments. Correction of these disparities is essential to allow all children to learn skills for success in subsequent levels of life, thereby emphasizing the importance of early childhood experiences within the overall context of developmental psychology (Suwahono et al., 2019) (Figure 2.10).

Figure 2.10. Children from lower-income backgrounds often face greater challenges, including limited access to quality educational materials and experiences that stimulate cognitive growth.

Source: https://gem-report-2023.unesco.org/wp-content/uploads/2023/07/%C2%A9-Ismael-Martinez-Sanchez-ProFuturo-scaled.jpg.

2.3.3. Influence of Socio-Economic Status (SES)

A complex concept, socioeconomic status (SES) has significant effects on developmental processes, especially those related to brain development and psychological health. Numerous studies have repeatedly shown that children with low SES face a variety of challenges, such as reduced access to educational resources, poor nutrition, and greater stress exposure. All of these could potentially hinder the child's brain organization and cognitive development. For instance, being exposed to stimulating environments is quite critical during the best development of the brain during early childhood. Children brought up in poor settings have been shown to have language learning, attention, and executive functioning deficits, which can leave lasting impacts throughout their lifespan. The relationship between SES and brain development is complex, highlighting the necessity for more targeted interventions to eliminate these disparities and foster healthier developmental trajectories (Bryson et al., 2014). Moreover, the relative timing of environmental processes relative to genetic factors can shape developmental outcomes in powerful ways. The developmental period wherein a person is exposed to varying socio-economic conditions can lead to divergent trajectories depending on the interaction among genetic vulnerabilities and protective factors.

Figure 2.11. The developmental phase during which a child is exposed to various socio-economic factors can lead to divergent trajectories depending on the interplay of genetic vulnerabilities and protective factors.

Source: https://bidyapatibedstudy.wordpress.com/wp-content/uploads/2024/11/addressing-the-main-challenges-in-early-years-teaching.jpeg?w=1200.

Empirical data indicate that exposure to stress, typically more pronounced in lower SES environments, can lead to abnormal brain development patterns, increasing the risk for behavioral disorders and cognitive impairment. Such environmental stressors compounded by genetics underscore the need to understand how different individuals may possibly respond to interventions. It is central to designing tailored programs to provide support and access to resources for at-risk individuals, thereby improving equity in social and cognitive development (Bryson et al., 2014). The perceptions of early childhood development reveal even greater levels of complexity in understanding SES's role. Various discourses—development, political, social, and human rights—offer frames through which the impact of socio-economic status can be viewed. Developmentally, the vulnerability of children of low SES is obvious, and intervention must be informed by their unique needs. The political and economic frame emphasizes the importance of investments in early childhood education as a means for building human capital. In addition, the social and cultural approach highlights how childhood constructions differ in contexts and affect the availability of resources for children. Finally, a human rights orientation promotes the recognition of children's rights and dignity and urges us to prioritize their development needs irrespective of their socio-economic status (Figure 2.11).

2.4. NEUROPLASTICITY AND LEARNING

Neuroplasticity, or the ability of the brain to rearrange itself by generating new neural connections throughout life, is fundamental to learning and brain growth. This extraordinary suppleness helps individuals to absorb new knowledge, adapt to change, and mend brain damage. In developmental psychology, understanding the mechanisms of neuroplasticity is crucial because they explain how positive and unpleasant experiences influence brain structures and functioning. For instance, teenagers engaged in games that are building resilience and self-regulation may be boosting their brain connections in a favorable manner, which ultimately supports their transition into healthy adulthood. Such insight not only enhances our comprehension of normal developmental processes but also hints toward potential interventions that can foster adaptive behaviors in at-risk populations. Furthermore, application of neuroplasticity also holds in various domains of learning like physical exercise that results in significant neurobiological advantages. Engagement in movement-based activity, such as dance, has been associated with increased emotional well-being, cognition, and social interaction. Research indicates that dance fosters a unique combination of physical, emotional, and social engagement, enabling changes in brain structure and activity in neurotransmitters affecting the experience of well-being (Calmeiro et al., 2017). The cooperative and rhythmic locomotion of dancing provokes the formation of new neural pathways, which entrenches motor skills and cognitive abilities. Thus, creating spaces that integrate imagination-filled physical exercise can propel individuals' developmental processes significantly forward, particularly in educational and therapeutic environments. Ultimately, the relationship between learning and neuroplasticity emphasizes the significance of tailored learning practices that respond to the individualized needs of learners. By recognizing that the brain is not a static organ, but one that constantly develops and restructures itself, teachers can implement methods that take advantage of neuroplasticity to enhance the learning process. These findings provide the rationale for incorporating experiential education, emotional care, and creative expression into school curricula. Interventions that enhance resilience and self-regulation, particularly in adolescents, have the promise of leading to healthier developmental courses, such as that of foster youth who are most likely to struggle with the development of such essential skills. Knowledge of neuroplasticity, thus, not only is crucial to the understanding of brain development but also for the development of effective interventions that enhance lifelong learning and adaptive functioning.

2.4.1. Definition of Neuroplasticity

Neuroplasticity, which is often characterized as the brains incredible ability to reconstruct and restructure itself according to varied stimuli, is an important topic in developmental psychology. This process is done on various levels, ranging from the change of neuronal circuits to synapse formation, at the whim of learning, experience, and environment. It is needed for brain development, emotional regulation, and trauma recovery, highlighting how experience constructs the brain across an individual's life. As adolescents navigate complex social and emotional landscapes, neuroplasticity facilitates the development of self-regulation, coping skills, and resilience, particularly salient for foster care children who may lack secure support systems, ultimately determining their journey toward becoming healthy, connected adults. Knowledge of neuroplasticity also highlights the importance of engaging in activities that challenge brain development. Active engagement in physical and creative activities such as dance is capable of a direct influence on the improvement of neuroplastic change.

Research has begun exploring ways in which such activities can improve mental, as well as physical, health by exciting neural pathways as well as higher cognitive function. The dance itself, as an instance, has been associated with positive alterations in brain structure and function, which lead to improved mood and emotional control (Calmeiro et al., 2017). This indicates the interconnectedness of body movement, brain process, and overall psychological well-being, substantiating neuroplasticity's pivotal role in developing adaptive behaviors and improved quality of life. Moreover, neuroplasticity is not a single event but a continuum process that changes with the passage of time due to both genetic factors as well as environment. When individuals go through new experiences, the brain's structure can modify and develop, illustrating the life-long process of development and learning. In developmental psychology, understanding the definition and meaning of neuroplasticity provides a basis for discussing how early experience contributes to neural development and resilience. This recognition informs the idea that interventions during times of critical development have lasting consequences, prompting the need to create environments that build resilience capacities and healthy brain development across the life course (Figure 2.12).

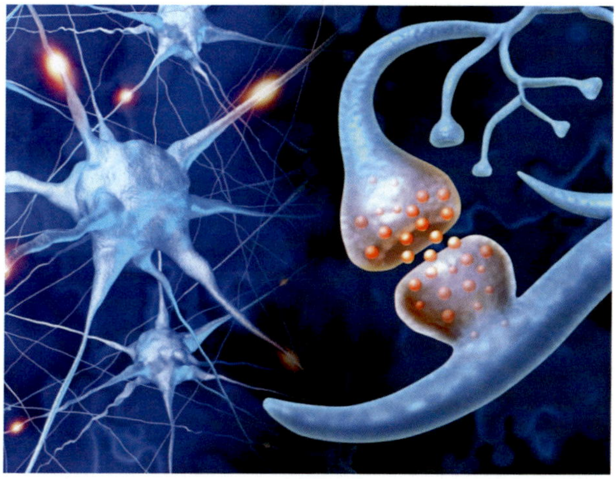

Figure 2.12. Neuroplasticity, often defined as the brains remarkable ability to reorganize and adapt itself in response to various stimuli, plays a critical role in developmental psychology.

Source: https://bayareacbtcenter.com/wp-content/uploads/2025/01/Untitled-design-631-1024x791.png.

2.4.2. Role of Neuroplasticity in Learning Processes

Neuroplasticity is the brains' extraordinary ability to recreate itself through the formation of unique neural connections during a person's lifespan. This quality is especially crucial in developmental psychology since the learning mechanisms of teenagers and children are driven by multiple experiences and interactions with the environment. As a person engages with the world, neural pathways become more or less effective, linking neuroplasticity to acquiring new skills and knowledge directly. This flexibility allows for the stimulation of cognitive functions, such as memory, attention, and problem-solving capacity, to result in a higher degree of understanding for abstract concepts. Additionally, research has discovered that supportive settings, such as those that foster social relationships and emotional health, further enhance optimal neuroplasticity, thereby allowing for healthy brain development throughout major growth periods. The uses of neuroplasticity extend beyond the traditional learning episodes in school; they impact emotional and social development significantly, too. To illustrate, adolescents experiencing processes of building up resilience and self-regulation can have changes in brain structures and functions, which are crucial for the control of emotions and social communication. With these processes supported, youth are likely to develop healthier, stronger adults who have coping strategies necessary for tackling life's challenges. Conversely, adverse experience or lack of appropriate support can prevent this process from occurring, and this points towards the intricate interdependence of neuroplasticity, learning, and overall psychological well-being. It is therefore essential that these processes be understood by teachers, parents, and mental health professionals who work with children. Neuroplasticity is not only involved in learning within the realm of cognition but also physical exercise and creativity. Engagement in activities like dance, for example, has been shown to enhance neuroplastic transformation that is of benefit to emotional and psychological well-being.

Dance not only drives the physical health but also mental stimulation and social connection, all of which are contributors to the brains potential to alter and evolve. The biochemical and cognitive-neuroscientific mechanisms underpinning such activities highlight the pedagogic and therapeutic benefit of adding motion and creative expression into learning and therapy contexts. Acceptance of these intertwined elements encourages a holistic education approach that is attuned to the plural causes of neuroplasticity, moving toward healthier pathways of development across childhood and adolescence (Figure 2.13).

Figure 2.13. Engaging in activities like dance, for example, has been shown to facilitate neuroplastic changes, positively influencing emotional and psychological well-being.

Source: https://www.n2y.com/wp-content/uploads/banner-neuroplasticity.png.

2.4.3. Implications for Educational Practices

The area of developmental psychology contributes greatly to educational practice in the sense that it describes the different development processes experienced by children and adolescents.

For instance, a developmental viewpoint underlines the need of identifying and caring for the particular physical and psychosocial development of early pupils at a developing age. This information leads teachers to design age-appropriate curricula and learning environments that recognize children's dependences and vulnerabilities, ultimately generating a supportive climate for learning. By incorporating principles from developmental psychology into educational plans, teachers can design pedagogies that foster resilience, self-regulation, and coping strategies, thus improving students' overall educational experiences and outcomes.

In addition, the political and economic framing of development highlights the imperative of coupling economic frameworks with educational policies. The recognition of the role played by educational interventions in the development of human capital highlights the imperative for systematic investment in early childhood education. These policies can pay rich dividends in the long term, as they aim to equip children with intellectual and social skills that are of paramount importance to ultimate success.

Implementing a curriculum that places an equal emphasis on developing skills and thinking will mean more balanced schooling opportunities, bridging gaps in performance that have the tendency to chain marginalized groups. This alignment with economic paradigms not only legitimates education practice but also compels policymakers to consider sustainable development and financing mechanisms in education. Finally, the complex social and cultural conceptualization of development emphasizes the various ways in which education is perceived and interpreted across contexts.

The understanding that education is a socially constructed place provokes teachers to examine their practices and the inclusivity of their pedagogic strategies. Therefore, it becomes vital to scrutinize the aims, models, and standards set in education systems to make sure that they address the heterogeneous cultural backgrounds of students. This strategy emphasizes developing a learning culture that respects the rights and dignity of all learners so that they become actively engaged in their own development. Moreover, it compels educators to consider how their practices are capable of empowering children, enabling them to contribute meaningfully to their learning processes as well as society at large, as claimed by Woodhead et al. (2006).

2.5. CRITICAL PERIODS IN BRAIN DEVELOPMENT

The crucial periods theory of brain development is significant in the explanation of how environmental experience impacts cognitive and behavioral result. Critical periods relate to various windows of a person's growth period within which the brain is improved sensitivity to specific sorts of stimuli or experiences. For instance, early childhood is often regarded as a sensitive period for language acquisition, such that exposure to linguistic input has a profound effect on the neural networks underlying language processing. Science indicates that not only is the brain predisposed to learn, but it is also plastic during these periods, in which it can make and break synaptic connections based on experience. This shaping of brain structure emphasizes the dynamic interplay between genetic predispositions and environmental influences, affirming the significance of supportive environments during these key developmental stages. The influence of socioeconomic determinants on brain development also emphasizes the significance of critical periods. Studies show that exposure to adverse conditions such as poverty and stress can leave a lasting effect on brain development, particularly during sensitive windows.

These adverse environmental stressors can lead to alterations in brain structures that are involved in executive function, emotional control, and social cognition. Consistent with new evidence, it is crucial that the exposure to these disadvantageous environments takes place at a particular point because this experience would modify gene expression involved in neurocognitive development. Of note, individuals may respond differentially to interventions based on genetic variation and development timing. This is a sign of the significance of employing supportive interventions at crucial points because such interventions have the potential to produce critical enhancements to cognitive capacity and resilience, eventually enabling the mitigation of the adverse effect of socioeconomic status on brain development (Bryson et al., 2014). Furthermore, the association of critical periods with neural correlates of psychological constructs shows a complex interaction between psychological and biological factors. While scientists will try to map neural mechanisms onto psychological processes, the correlation is not a straightforward reductionist system. The dynamic interactions of critical periods demonstrate that multiple neural pathways can account for the same psychological outcomes, suggesting many-to-many instead of one-to-one relationships. For example, while some mechanisms are perhaps essential for language acquisition during early development, there are alternative processes that can substitute if language exposure is delayed. This complex appreciation sheds light on how periods of criticality should be considered not just as strict timelines but as fluid stages in which adaptability can take place within the architecture of the brain, thus presenting new opportunities for intervention and enrichment (Khalidi et al., 2020) (Figure 2.14).

Figure 2.14. Critical periods refer to specific windows in an individual's developmental timeline during which the brain exhibits heightened sensitivity to certain types of stimuli or experiences.

Source: https://www.simplypsychology.org/wp-content/uploads/Sensorimotor-Stage.jpg.

2.5.1. Definition of Critical Periods

Critical periods are essential constructs within developmental psychology, indeed in brain development. The time-sensitive phases are windows of opportunity when the brain is more plastic, promoting maximum learning and adaption to external inputs. During such phases, some experiences have the most impact, organizing neural connections that continue to develop cognition, emotion, and social function. For instance, early life phases are correlated with revolutionary progress in the development of language, whereby exposure to linguistic stimuli must occur within a specific time frame to ensure mastery. Provision of an insufficient amount of such stimulation at a critical phase leads to irreparable deficits, underlining the importance of such defined temporal windows during human evolution. Theoretical models of critical periods reveal a variety of perspectives that inform early childhood practice and policy. Of the numerous perspectives, the developmental one focuses on consistencies of patterns of growth and the vulnerabilities that follow for children when these initial years are not fulfilled. These are crucial for understanding why early interventions mitigate risks of failed developmental milestones. Furthermore, a political and economic context further enriches this understanding with regards to how economic models translate developmental principles into effective social policies. This intersection also identifies the significance of fulfilling developmental needs within the broader socio-political structures, while understanding that the construction of early childhood as a status is founded upon cultural values and norms (Woodhead et al., 2006). Further, the effects of critical periods do not merely include developmental outcomes but also extend to include rights-based strategies in favor of children's rights. The human rights approach reframes developmental theory by emphasizing the agency and dignity of young children and establishing a context for them to take part in an active process of development. Through placing children's voice at the core, stakeholders can reframe education and social systems so that they enhance their provision in these critical years. This perspective not only promotes respect for the child as an agent but also prefers policies respecting and catering to their unique developmental phases. Separately and combined, these perspectives emphasize the intricate interplay between brain development and critical periods and provide a multidimensional perspective required to design effective interventions and foster overall childhood development (Ballhausen et al., 2016).

2.5.2. Examples of Critical Periods in Sensory Development

The crucial period notion of the senses has been a major aspect of understanding how the brain and sensory systems evolve with age. These essential phases are distinguished by heightened sensitivity toward specific environmental stimuli to assure correct sensory modality development. For instance, in visual development, research has demonstrated that infants show extreme sensitivity toward visual stimulation in the first few months of life. Unless adequate visual experience, such as vision of various shapes and colors, is given during this time period, long-term visual perception impairment can occur. This brings into perspective the hypothesis that the developing nervous system is plastic and vulnerable; without appropriate sensory stimulation, brain pathways responsible for sight may not form appropriate connections to provide optimal efficiency throughout life (Konczak et al., 2004). Hearing development is also a great case of critical periods, particularly language learning. Infants possess the biological aspect to be able to distinguish the sounds of their mother tongue. Studies indicate that there is a short period of time in childhood when children are most suited to learning a foreign language or grasping pronunciation nuances. Inability to captivate children with abundant sensory input during these formative years will lead to subsequent language challenges, pointing to the cooperation between sensory input and neural plasticity. Moreover, as the child ages, the capacity to acquire language diminishes, pointing to the intricate interaction among sensory experience and intellectual development (Guyer et al., 2016). This is an example of the broader implications of critical periods, demonstrating how exposure to certain stimuli at the proper time is crucial for laying the groundwork for higher-order cognitive functions. Social development also possesses critical periods that parallel sensory development, particularly in the domain of social and emotional relationships. As children encounter their first social environments, distinct stages are revealed corresponding to neurological changes in brain functioning. Early attachments to caregivers, play with friends, and finally romantic relations all activate different brain structures and emotional states. With these phases, the growing child accumulates a social repertoire that is inextricably bound up with their sensory experience, for instance, recognizing facial expressions or interpreting voice tones. The interplay between affective motivation and sensory experience highlights the pivotal role of critical periods in enabling both neural circuits and adaptive behaviors (Guyer et al., 2016). Such sensitive windows not only enhance short-term social competence but also underpin long-term trends of brain development and emotional well-being.

2.5.3. Consequences of Missed Critical Periods

The relevance of key times of brain development is deep, as these magical windows of time serve as the foundation for a variety of cognitive, emotional, and social competencies. The inability to fulfill developmental milestones within these windows leaves one with unwanted effects that might be disastrous and long-lasting. For instance, children who are not exposed to language adequately in early childhood may develop communication skills insufficiency at an older age, which can hinder education and integration. In this manner, brain plasticity declines, and issues are encountered that can even last through maturity. Studies also indicate that intervention for early development has to engage parents in an efficient way so that they understand the importance of such phases and set up environments that will support healthy growth. Resolving such issues through well-trained intervention strategies can reduce risks from lost critical periods, emphasizing recovery and optimal development paths in the future (Aber et al., 2017). The effects of missed critical periods are most obvious in social and affective development; wherein early bonding experiences play an important role. Disruptions at such early points, such as irregular maternal care, can profoundly disrupt the emotional regulation and attachment style of an individual. Empirical research shows that early maternal experience is to blame for establishing synaptic connections which underpin emotional response and regulation much later in life. For example, maternal separation has been shown to influence synaptic density in the key brain areas involved in emotional processing such as the basolateral amygdala and dorsomedial striatum, as indicated in maternal care variation studies (Chang et al., 2020). Therefore, individuals with poor or disorganized attachment during windows of opportunity will fare poorly on emotional regulation and social anxiety, which will be manifested into more diffuse psychological problems later in life as they reach adulthood. Furthermore, the missed opportunities in windows of opportunity do not only affect single paths but also create broader societal implications. When such children enter the school system without skill from the crucial early years, they are likely to face more problems in achieving academic success. Such disparity has long-term socio-economic consequences, as they might not be able to secure a stable career or contribute to society. Early childhood education and parent engagement programs can emerge as a primary tool against disadvantage that arises due to lost critical periods. By recognizing the importance of these programs and providing support through decisive means, society becomes capable of moving towards an even playing field for children, eventually evolving a system based on developmental equity and achievement (Aber et al., 2017) (Figure 2.15).

Figure 2.15. When developmental milestones are not met within these windows, the consequences can be severe and long-lasting.

Source: https://www.physio.co.uk/images/delayed-milestones/delayed-milestones1.jpg.

2.6. PSYCHOLOGICAL DISORDERS AND BRAIN DEVELOPMENT

The link between psychiatric problems and brain development is an attractive field of research in developmental psychology. Brain development is significantly influenced by psychological problems, and so it is likely that sequence and timing of the developmental milestones important. For instance, a number of neurodevelopmental disorders like autism spectrum disorder (ASD) impact not only cognitive processes but also social interaction and regulation of emotion. Because the brain goes through critical periods of development, disruptions during these phases—perhaps through genetic influence—can lead to atypical neural circuitry and consequent behavioral effects. This points to the significance of exploring how brain plasticity is modulated by both genetically programmed conditions and environmental interactions, particularly in developmental years, in which developmental trajectories may be particularly sensitive to extrinsic inputs and therapeutic interventions. Genetic disorders add more complexity to our understanding of psychological disorders and their effects on brain development. It is argued that conditions such as Williams syndrome can tell us something about cognitive modularity, with some cognitive processes potentially having neurobiological origins innately determined. The argument, however, remains contentious because due consideration must be given to the fact that cognitive modules would necessarily emerge through development rather than being pre-specified templates. As outlined in synthesizing accounts from various genetic disorders, through empirical behavioral assessment and neuroimaging, it can be observed that developmental restrictions exert influence on cognitive functioning in a non-linear fashion. This theoretical reshuffling delineates the significant viewpoint of genetic disorders not only as evidence of inborn modularity but as indicators of the individualized pathways due to ontogenetic development and the influence of environmental interactions. Considering the psychological disorder effects, particularly in the case of ASD, there is an implicit connection between social cognition and self-processing. Children with ASD, even though they have social functioning impairments, also exhibit a self-referential processing bias that strongly matches symptom severity. For instance, it can be observed that children with milder symptoms of ASD possess a stronger self-bias, speculating on a likely disconnection with social attention. On the contrary, more severe symptoms can be linked to lower self-bias, recognizing an "absent-self" effect. Having insight into such dynamics is significant because it reveals mechanisms whereby brain development interlinks with psychological notions of self and social integration. To estimate overlapping fields of psychological disorders and brain development, therefore, calls for an integrated approach that has room for both impairment and possible compensatory processes in cognitive and social contexts (Ballantyne et al., 2017).

2.6.1. Link between Brain Development and Mental Health

The delicate relationship between the development of the brain and mental well-being is an attractive subject area in developmental psychology. As the brain matures, particularly when under-going phases of important development such as childhood and adolescence, several neurobiological processes occur that contribute considerably towards the control of emotions, intellectual capabilities, and social function. Research indicates that during adolescence, the brain experiences a dramatic remodeling of areas concerning decision-making and impulse control. When teenagers experience interruptions in these stages of development, particularly under stressors from the environment, it can predispose them to mental illness. Moreover, this is the period when resilience and self-regulation are to be built, which are the tools necessary in facing the setbacks of life. Consequently, a holistic understanding of the methods by which brain development intersects with mental health outcomes is needed in detecting preventative variables and interventions designed to build psychological well-being through these initial years. Highlighting once more the brain-mental health interface, early interpersonal relationships are determined to be essential in both the creation of neural patterns as well as emotional responses.

Responsiveness of the caregiver in infancy and early childhood is what lays the foundation for secure attachment and positive self-concept. Developmental psychologists are certain that these initial interactions play a large part in one's sense of self and relatedness to others, which are crucial to social functioning later on. Unique to emotional regulation development is the fact that the brain's limbic system, which governs emotional response, is developed in significant part by the nature of early life attachment relationships. Without supportive interactions, children will struggle to learn self-regulation and coping skills and become increasingly at risk for later-life psychosocial issues. Thus, understanding early relational patterns is vital to inform mental health and intervention conversations (Payne et al., 2012). Lastly, emerging trends in developmental psychology emphasize the potential of embodied experiences to foster mental health. Therapies such as kinetic therapy and movement interventions highlight the value of physical activity in fostering emotional connection and self-knowledge. For example, kinesthetic intersubjectivity describes how shared movement brings a sense of connection to individuals, and this enhances understanding in both relation and emotional resonance. The understanding can be used in therapeutic treatment, particularly in individuals with developmental disorders, where normal communication may be challenging. By integrating these body-based interactions into therapy, practitioners are able to build deeper self-other relational processes that are required to maintain mental health. Hence, the recognition and harnessing of the energy of motion as an art therapy provide a new perspective towards cultivating mental well-being through combined insight from developmental psychology and brain science (Figure 2.16).

Figure 2.16. As the brain matures, particularly during critical developmental stages such as childhood and adolescence, various neurobiological processes occur that significantly influence emotional regulation, cognitive functioning, and social interactions.

Source: https://www.simplypsychology.org/wp-content/uploads/brain-critical-development.jpg.

2.6.2. COMMON PSYCHOLOGICAL DISORDERS IN CHILDHOOD

Childhood is a risk age of development where there is considerable cognitive, emotional, and social growth but also a time when some psychiatric illnesses can occur. Some of the frequent disorders that arise in youngsters are attention-deficit/hyperactivity disorder (ADHD), autism spectrum disorder (ASD), and anxiety disorders. These disorders frequently have a considerable impact on a child's capacity to succeed in daily activities, e.g., having friendships and academic accomplishment. For instance, ADHD children perceive inattention and hyperactivity as frequent concerns, as well as school settings particularly as a challenge. Such issues can lead to poor performance in school and rejection by their peers, consequently creating a cycle of poor mental health that could continue into adolescence and adulthood. In addition, interaction between psychological disorders and brain development in childhood cannot be underestimated. Research emphasizes that some of the conditions during early life, like preterm birth, lead to lifelong neurodevelopmental outcomes that enhance the susceptibility to psychiatric illness. For example, preterm children are at very high risk for emotional disorders, ADHD, and ASD, which emphasizes the relationship between psychological well-being and neurodevelopmental impairment. Studies reveal that approximately 25% of preterm adolescents suffer from psychiatric disorders, and this indicates the necessity of child psychiatry evaluations and intervention at an early age. Early intervention will contribute to improved psychosocial adaptation throughout the development of the child. Identification of the underlying developmental mechanisms of psychological disorders is imperative in preventing and intervening successfully. Current research contradicts the belief of innate cognitive modularity within the brain and suggests cognitive abilities such as language development are the result of complex interaction between environmental influence and the genetic basis. The model can be compatible with a more general explanation of disorders such as Williams syndrome, which involve selective cognitive impairment. Given the above conditions as an outcome of active ontogenetic development, there is a high need for personalized treatment regimens taking into account the specific neurodevelopmental trajectory of each child. Thus, holistic interventions addressing psychological as well as biological conditions are imperative in enhancing the well-being of children with psychological disorders and ushering in healthier generations ahead.

2.6.3. Early Intervention and its Effects on Brain Development

Early childhood intervention, particularly in children at risk of having developmental delay, has been of great importance in developmental psychology. Early intervention is meant to harness the fantastic neuroplasticity of the brain when it is young, an age characterized by rapid growth and learning. Early intervention can correct or even prevent long-term mental and emotional impairments that may be brought on by social or environmental disadvantage with special attention and stimulation. For example, early exposure to positive learning experiences can significantly improve young people's social, emotional, and intellectual capacities, enabling them to succeed academically and socially. Such a preventive intervention not only benefits the individual child but also has broader societal benefits in terms of reduced requirements of intensive developmental care later on in life and the development of a more competent and resilient generation. However, the impact of early intervention does not lie entirely in the area of short-term cognitive and behavioral impacts; it also has long-term impacts on brain maturation. Through research, it is established that there exist various interventions with the potential to evoke profound changes in neural structure, including the excitatory-inhibitory equilibrium that characterizes global brain function. The use of programmed intervention during developmentally critical phases can initiate the growth and development of synapses, thus enhancing cognitive capacities. Of particular interest are how such interventions influence the development of aperiodic activity in the brain, as in research employing electroencephalogram (EEG) measures. For example, the Bucharest Early Intervention Project investigated early adversity and age-appropriate intervention's impact on neural circuits, learning about mechanisms that characterize maturation of brain activity in such early years (Martín et al., 2024). Aside from the promise of early intervention, there still exist areas of research and issues requiring further investigation. For example, the complexity of the effect on neural development in early childhood from too much media exposure is not yet fully explored, particularly how it could interact with interventions that promote the building of cognitive and emotional resilience. As with increasing rates of children's media usage, particularly by those who have less parental monitoring, there is an urgent need for in-depth research (Donohue et al., 2025). Understanding the potential adverse consequences of this exposure will provide a better foundation for powerful intervention designs. Continuing studies on the subject not only will enlighten us to the importance of early adversities but also will maximize strategies that take advantage of the brain's flexibility, leading ultimately to more efficient intervention methods promoting healthy brain development during these initial years.

2.7. CONCLUSION

The complex relationship between biological development and the environment must be recognized while summarizing developmental psychology and brain development. Throughout life, the human brain experiences significant changes, especially between infancy and puberty. Major developmental milestones are made possible by changes that impact social, emotional, and cognitive development. Understanding how these brain processes interact with personal experience to influence a person's sense of self and connection to the outside world is essential to understanding human behavior. Because development never happens in a vacuum but rather is a process with dynamically conceivable outcomes in different persons, the interrelationship proposed by this approach is what makes adopting an integrated developmental psychology approach important. Additionally, when social development factors are taken into account, the reaffiliation motive theory (RAM) is also applicable. The influence of loneliness on psychological processes emphasizes how important social attachment is to human growth. People's innate need to reaffiliate after times of perceived social disengagement is explained by RAM. Comprehending this dynamic throughout the life span emphasizes how developmental interventions need to match support networks with promoting social engagement and avoiding long-term isolation. In order to promote mental health and well-being, it is essential to address these problems, which serve as a reminder that psychological development is not only a biological phenomenon but also a socially systemic one that necessitates interaction between families, communities, and schools (Bangee et al., 2015). Moreover, the discovery of moral development through observation work reveals subtle levels of children's interactions and decision-making. Research into sharing behavior among young children reveals moral character built up from complex negotiations rather than compliance with externally imposed values or rules. These results undermine classical accounts, bringing an increased understanding of children's subjective experience in dealing with moral issues. This approach highlights the importance of creating environments that facilitate ethical thought and empathic behavior, the very components of integrative development. As developmental psychology continues to evolve, including these multi-dimensional processes will improve our knowledge of brain and moral development, providing more effective education and psychological interventions (Arthur et al., 2012).

2.7.1. Summary of Key Points

A number of crucial concepts necessary for comprehending human development and behavior are highlighted by the convergence of developmental psychology and brain development. Neural plasticity, which takes place throughout crucial developmental periods, especially early life, is among the first. Experiences mold the structure and function of the brain during this crucial time for emotional and cognitive development. Research suggests that interventions based on developmental psychology can maximize brain development outcomes, resulting in improved social and educational outcomes. Additionally, this developmental process requires careful consideration of a number of elements, including family support and socioeconomic position. The influence of psychosocial factors in the process of brain development is also a significant factor that has been discussed in contemporary child development and behavioral economics literature. This discussion addresses how psychology can affect development practice and policy and alter the outcomes of children's lives. It is hoped by proponents that psychological approaches can promote well-being, but critics caution against prioritizing individual change over structural transformation. This tension unveils the complex relationships between psychological principles and broader socio-political contexts in shaping developmental pathways, suggesting a richer understanding of the conceptual framework of development across policy initiatives (Klein et al., 2017). Furthermore, emerging evidence from LGBTQ psychology indicates that affirming practices and positive environments are necessary for healthy brain and psychosocial development in LGBTQ individuals. This work prioritizes acceptance and representation within educational environments as a primary method by which the harmful effects of stigma and discrimination can be lessened. As social attitudes change, so also does the necessity for models that include various viewpoints on identity and development. By examining such concerns as same-sex parenting and the unique issues of LGBTQ youth, researchers point to the need for social support in maintaining resilience and healthy development. Overall, including the perspective of LGBTQ persons into developmental psychology not only broadens the field but also adds to our understanding of the complexity of human development.

2.7.2. Importance of Understanding Brain Development in Psychology

In psychology, knowing brain development is especially important because it provides the foundation for comprehending a wide range of behavioral and cognitive phenomena that occur throughout life. The brain constructs significant changes in times of critical development, such as during early childhood and adolescence, that not only influence individual cognitive ability, but also emotion regulation and social relationships. For instance, genetic mutations and the environment dynamically construct brain structure development pathways that influence behaviors, as found through research (Bryson et al., 2014). This interaction between biology and the environment testifies that psychological implications are often emergent rather than categorically predetermined, again with psychological theories seeing the value in such subtleties. Furthermore, an understanding of the full breadth of brain development allows psychologists to identify aberrant developmental patterns, and information regarding neurodevelopmental disorders is attained. For example, the neural mechanisms underlying disorders such as autism spectrum disorders demonstrate how different neural processes can lead to similar behavioral outcomes. The significance of genetic and environmental timing is made apparent by the observation that researchers investigate how intervention methods can vary in their efficacy for individuals as a function of their unique developmental contexts (Bryson et al., 2014). Understanding the processes that underlie brain development is therefore important not only for healthy psychological growth but also for formulating individualized treatment plans. In addition to illuminating clinical practice, the knowledge of brain development brings depth to more abstract psychological theory through relating cognitive and social development to evolutionary theory. The interconnections of psychology and neurobiology form the axis of comprehension of behaviors by recognizing that human cognition and emotional responses have evolved under specific environmental pressures. This intersection points to the significance of developmental processes, which impact not merely the psychological traits of an individual but also the behavior and versatility of groups of individuals. As learning explores further into these interlinks, it becomes increasingly clear that the necessity of integrating neuroscience findings into psychology is imperative, forming an integrated picture of human behavior throughout the life cycle.

2.7.3. Future Directions for Research in Developmental Psychology

Developmental psychology research stands on the threshold of sweeping developments in coming research, particularly with regard to the intersection of cognitive growth and sensory-motor exercises. Hypotheses introduced in recent years suggest mathematical reasoning as an advanced-level, abstract capability can be a product of subconscious integration with sensory-motor exercises, representing a fruitful area of study for coming research. While research continues studies the advantages of sensory-motor activities in learning contexts, it is vital to examine numerous moderators that influence learning, such as developmental stages and instructional aid. The equivocal character of earlier studies serves to underline the significance of a more precise line of investigation in exploring the conditions under which mathematics ability is improved by sensory-motor tasks. By defining these variables, researchers can more effectively recognize how integrated learning experiences may be structured to promote maximal developmental processes, thus enhancing pedagogical practice within schools (Durkee et al., 2018). A second valuable area for future research is in the field of embodied cognitive agents, such as humanoid robots. Scientific study of such agents provides a unique perspective on cognitive development, particularly in relation to sensorimotor, linguistic, and social skills of learning. Extending our understanding of how autonomous agents come to represent and manipulate objects can reflect important aspects of human cognitive processes. Revealing the richness of social interaction and learning processes in these systems can lead to enhanced developmental psychology and robotics frameworks. By developing a roadmap of key research challenges—e.g., compositional actions and lexica—researchers can facilitate the construction of robots that not only learn more effectively but that also engage in adaptive interaction with people and their worlds. Such grand tour is thrilling intersection of human development and technology that can revolutionize our understanding of cognition processes (Belpaeme et al., 2010). Together with valuing embodied cognition, future developmental psychology research must target interdisciplinary approaches involving neuroscience, psychology, and education. As next-generation developmental psychology discovers the nuances of brain development, results based on neuroimaging technologies should inform psychological theory regarding learning and behavior across different stages of development. Through bridging across disciplines, scholars will be better positioned to fashion an integrated theory of how biological, cognitive, and societal forces come together to impact developmental trajectories. Further, making inference from neuropsychological studies to transfer to applied interventions has the potential to shed light on designing resilience and adaptive behavior in varying contexts, particularly with vulnerable populations. As greater understanding of the interplay of neurobiological processes and developmental experience is achieved, researchers will be able to further explicate theory and create evidence-based practice that supports maximum growth throughout the life span (Durkee et al., 2018).

REFERENCES

1. Aber, J. L., Darling, M., & Gennetian, L. (2017). Behavioral economics and developmental science: A new framework to support early childhood interventions. https://core.ac.uk/download/80296482.pdf (accessed on 14th October 2025).
2. Adams, H., Ahmad, S., Ames, D., Amin, Z., et al. (2019). Genetic determinants of cortical structure (thickness, surface area and volumes) among disease-free adults in the CHARGE Consortium. https://core.ac.uk/download/231719760.pdf (accessed on 14th October 2025).
3. Afifi, M., Aharonovich, E., Alati, R., Alati, R., Anda, R. F., et al. (2016). Parental substance abuse as an early traumatic event: Preliminary findings on neuropsychological and personality functioning in young drug addicts exposed to drugs early. https://core.ac.uk/download/53527969.pdf (accessed on 14th October 2025).
4. Akmal, Y., Hikmah, H., & Hardono, I. H. (2019). Preparing for parenthood: Parenting training module on six child development aspect in East Jakarta. *JPUD–Jurnal Pendidikan Usia Dini.* https://www.semanticscholar.org/paper/74ff782ff7d47b7c9bbb1810dd0c719df4721426 (accessed on 14th October 2025).
5. Aldridge, J., Apperly, I., Baron-Cohen, S., Björne, M., Boucher, J., Boucher, J., Boucher, J., et al. (2014). We can work it out: An enactive look at cooperation. https://core.ac.uk/download/30609282.pdf (accessed on 14th October 2025).
6. Andrade, J., Barker, L., Bowles, D., Morton, N., et al. (2010). Investigating the 'latent' deficit hypothesis: Age at time of head injury, executive and implicit functions and behavioral insight. https://core.ac.uk/download/9426879.pdf (accessed on 14th October 2025).
7. Arthur, J., Aull Davies, C., Colby, A., Dunn, J., Gilligan, C., et al. (2012). Foundations of character: Methodological aspects of a study of character development in three- to six-year-old children with a focus on sharing behaviors. https://core.ac.uk/download/pdf/16279845.pdf (accessed on 14th October 2025).
8. Ballantyne, C., Branigan, H. P., Cunningham, S. J., Gillespie-Smith, K., et al. (2017). The I in autism: Severity and social functioning in autism is related to self-processing. https://core.ac.uk/download/162908423.pdf (accessed on 14th October 2025).
9. Ballhausen, N., Hering, A., Ihle, A., Kliegel, M., et al. (2016). Prospective memory in older adults: Where we are now and what is next. https://core.ac.uk/download/78911661.pdf (accessed on 14th October 2025).

10. Bangee, M., Harris, R., Lodder, G., Maes, M., et al. (2015). Loneliness across the life span. https://core.ac.uk/download/42136923.pdf (accessed on 14th October 2025).
11. Bashshur, R. L., Doarn, C. R., Frenk, J., Kvedar, J. C., & Woolliscroft, J. O. (2020). Telemedicine and the COVID-19 pandemic, lessons for the future. *Telemedicine Journal and e-Health, 26,* 571–573. https://doi.org/10.1089/tmj.2020.29040.rb (accessed on 14th October 2025).
12. Behensky, C., Flanagan, K. S., Gibson, N. J. S., Hicks, R. A., et al. (2006). Invitation to the table conversation: A few diverse perspectives on integration. https://core.ac.uk/download/84118523.pdf (accessed on 14th October 2025).
13. Belpaeme, T., Cangelosi, A., Dautenhahn, K., Fadiga, L., et al. (2010). Integration of action and language knowledge: A roadmap for developmental robotics. https://core.ac.uk/download/1640754.pdf (accessed on 14th October 2025).
14. Bryson, S. E., Clahsen, H., D'Souza, D., Gopnik, M., Guiraud, J. A., Karmiloff-Smith, A., Pinker, S., et al. (2014). Environmental and genetic influences on neurocognitive development: The importance of multiple methodologies and time-dependent intervention. https://core.ac.uk/download/20117923.pdf (accessed on 14th October 2025).
15. Calmeiro, L., & Jola, C. (2017). The dancing queen: Explanatory mechanisms of the 'feel-good effect' in dance. https://core.ac.uk/download/237029611.pdf (accessed on 14th October 2025).
16. Chang, I., Delevich, K., Thomas, A. W., Wilbrecht, L., et al. (2020). Variation in early life maternal care predicts later long-range frontal cortex synapse development in mice. https://core.ac.uk/download/323081762.pdf (accessed on 14th October 2025).
17. Dale, P. S., Davis, O. S. P., Hanscombe, K. B., Haworth, C. M. A., et al. (2014). Why do spatial abilities predict mathematical performance? https://core.ac.uk/download/19553507.pdf (accessed on 14th October 2025).
18. Diamond, A. (2025). Insights from a career at the border of developmental psychology and cognitive neuroscience. *Annual Review of Developmental Psychology.* https://www.semanticscholar.org/paper/2c850f52874126a28f0962c7ae056b2214e1eaf3 (accessed on 14th October 2025).
19. Donohue, M., Camacho, M., & Luby, J. (2025). Editorial: The pressing need to investigate the effects of media immersion in early childhood on brain and behavioral development. *Journal of Child Psychology and Psychiatry, and Allied Disciplines.* https://www.semanticscholar.org/pa

per/049c9147369179fda14a49d99d2c4911a3c2fee9 (accessed on 14th October 2025).

20. Durkee, C. (2018). Different methods of embodied cognition in pedagogy and its effectiveness in student learning. https://core.ac.uk/download/215422880.pdf (accessed on 14th October 2025).
21. Gelepithis, P. A. M. (2009). Outline of a new approach to the nature of mind. https://core.ac.uk/download/pdf/87224.pdf (accessed on 14th October 2025).
22. Ghaleb, C., Penney, D., Lavigne, K. M., & Raucher-Chéné, D. (2025). Exploring behavioral patterns in youth predisposed to bipolar disorder and the role of interpersonal trauma using the Adolescent Brain Cognitive Development (ABCD) dataset. *Early Intervention in Psychiatry, 19.* https://www.semanticscholar.org/paper/981139569b67ab1cc48b3b6a3b434a9a443d7b2d (accessed on 14th October 2025).
23. Guyer, A. E., Jarcho, J. M., & Nelson, E. E. (2016). Social re-orientation and brain development: An expanded and updated view. https://core.ac.uk/download/323070522.pdf (accessed on 14th October 2025).
24. Herzberg, M. P., Nielsen, A. N., Brady, R. G., Kaplan, S., Alexopoulos, D., Meyer, D., Arora, J., et al. (2024). Maternal prenatal social disadvantage and neonatal functional connectivity: Associations with psychopathology symptoms at age 12 months. *Developmental Psychology.* https://www.semanticscholar.org/paper/bf374bb2a567b2f3dc1ddb00871548d5ab16af46 (accessed on 14th October 2025).
25. Huntington, C. (2017). Early childhood development and the law. https://core.ac.uk/download/216957841.pdf (accessed on 14th October 2025).
26. Israel, A. C., Malatras, J. W., & Wicks-Nelson, R. (2020). *Abnormal Child and Adolescent Psychology.* Routledge eBooks. https://doi.org/10.4324/9780429286896 (accessed on 14th October 2025).
27. Johnson,S.J.,&Wolke,D.(2013).Behavioraloutcomesandpsychopathology during adolescence. https://core.ac.uk/download/9847191.pdf (accessed on 14th October 2025).
28. Karmiloff-Smith, A., & Thomas, M. S. C. (2003). What can developmental disorders tell us about the neurocomputational constraints that shape development? The case of Williams syndrome. https://core.ac.uk/download/5873.pdf (accessed on 14th October 2025).
29. Khalidi, M. A. (2020). Neural correlates without reduction: The case of the critical period. https://core.ac.uk/download/131179064.pdf (accessed on 14th October 2025).

30. Khodarahimi, S. (2018). Self-reported nutritional status, executive functions, and cognitive flexibility in adults. https://core.ac.uk/download/216809660.pdf (accessed on 14th October 2025).
31. Klein, E., & Mills, C. (2017). Psy-expertise, therapeutic culture and the politics of the personal in development. https://core.ac.uk/download/187115787.pdf (accessed on 14th October 2025).
32. Konczak, J. (2004). Neural development and sensorimotor control. https://core.ac.uk/download/pdf/86175.pdf (accessed on 14th October 2025).
33. Lipina, S. J., & Segretin, M. S. (2015). Strengths and weakness of neuroscientific investigations of childhood poverty: Future directions. https://core.ac.uk/download/159287533.pdf (accessed on 14th October 2025).
34. Machamer, P., Quartz, S., Scarantino, A., Sullivan, J., et al. (2002). Session 5: Development, neuroscience and evolutionary psychology. https://core.ac.uk/download/11920468.pdf (accessed on 14th October 2025).
35. Martín Antúnez, M., McSweeney, S., Zeytinoglu, S., Tan, E., Zeanah, C. H., Nelson, C. A., & Fox, N. A. (2024). Exploring background aperiodic electroencephalography (EEG) activity in the Bucharest Early Intervention Project. *Developmental Psychology.* https://www.semanticscholar.org/paper/4b72f30318b261bd8f87c55d4183562af1d46537 (accessed on 14th October 2025).
36. Payne, H., & Samaritter, R. (2012). Kinesthetic intersubjectivity: A dance-informed contribution to self-other relatedness and shared experience in nonverbal psychotherapy with an example from autism. https://core.ac.uk/download/9840405.pdf (accessed on 14th October 2025).
37. Suwahono, S., & Mawanti, D. (2019). Using environmentally friendly media (Happy Body) in early childhood science: Human body parts lesson. *JPUD–Jurnal Pendidikan Usia Dini.* https://www.semanticscholar.org/paper/bfd74ca258c94fcc10fab5b843693efc829a4ad2 (accessed on 14th October 2025).
38. Trevarthen, C. (2002). Can a robot hear music? Can a robot dance? Can a robot tell what it knows or intends to do? Can it feel pride or shame in company? –Questions of the nature of human vitality. https://core.ac.uk/download/pdf/85317.pdf (accessed on 14th October 2025).
39. Woodhead, M. (2006). Changing perspectives on early childhood: Theory, research and policy. https://core.ac.uk/download/799.pdf (accessed on 14th October 2025).

Chapter 3

Anxiety Disorders

Contents

INTRODUCTION

When it comes to the mental health of children and adolescents, anxiety disorders are a major and expanding concern. Anxiety disorders have a significant impact on families and schools in addition to having an impact on young people's developmental paths. Early identification and intervention are crucial since untreated anxiety has long-term ramifications that may express themselves in the forms of poor academic achievement, isolation, and risk for various later mental diseases. The complexity of anxiety disorders, which might include generalized anxiety disorder, panic disorder, and social anxiety disorder, necessitates informed knowledge of the numerous elements that prompt their onset and continuity in children and adolescents. Investigation highlights the necessity of considering both determinants within individuals and their environments while investigating anxiety disorders in adolescents and children. Parental mental health, for instance, plays a significant role in organizing a child's emotional climate. The parent-child relationship quality and parenting are some of the family dynamics that may significantly impact a child's susceptibility to anxiety. Moreover, studies have also established that challenging teen behavior is capable of enhancing parental distress and hindering parental mental health, even reinforcing the interdependent connection between parents' health and children's emotional adjustment. It is important to understand such inter-relations so that powerful intervention and treatment models for the whole family system, rather than for solitary individuals, can be developed. Apart from family considerations, socio-economic status and access to mental health care play an important role in influencing outcomes for anxiety. For instance, large surveys have found that nearly one in seven young Australians experience mental health issues, with impacts on their education and social lives in various ways. Such statistics based on working directly with families and young people not only provide the extent of mental health issues but also reveal the subtle emotional lives of young people and children that can be hidden from carers. These findings are essential to policymakers and service providers who desire to create supportive environments that augment mental health and mitigate stressors for young people. An understanding of anxiety disorders within this comprehensive framework is essential to addressing the pressing mental health problems facing children and adolescents in the present.

Definition of Anxiety Disorders

Anxiety disorders are a large range of mental illnesses that can interfere with functioning and well-being. They are typified by excessive concern or fear. Anxiety disorders can take many different forms in the field of child and adolescent mental health, including panic disorder, social anxiety disorder, generalized anxiety disorder, and particular phobias. Common symptoms include irritability, sleep difficulty, and somatic complaints including headaches and stomachaches. Teenagers experience a number of developmental challenges, and anxiety disorders can make it difficult to participate in daily activities, academic functioning, and routine activities. Above all, early identification and intervention are required to counteract long-term ill effects on emotional and psychological health, bringing forth the necessity for effective health and education services to address these disorders. The consequences of anxiety disorders extend beyond individual symptoms and impact families and communities too. The influence that anxiety disorders place on children has a knock-on effect in family patterns, usually generating added stress on caregivers who are often not well prepared to identify the internal conflict within their kids. Consistent with the results of recent studies with over 6300 Australian families, data that have been directly derived from young people reveal broad aspects of their emotional lives that are potentially concealed from parents and careers. The research underscores the importance of creating open communication between young people and their families and ingraining youth voices into mental health strategies. By so doing, one is able to create a recovery-friendly environment that promotes understanding, which is at the center of effective management of anxiety disorders and general mental health. Even though there has been growing awareness of the severity and prevalence of anxiety disorders among adolescents, a mismatch of monumental proportions in terms of resources for mental health care still persists.

Figure 3.1. Anxiety disorders represent a significant category of mental health conditions that are characterized by excessive fear or worry, which can impede daily functioning and overall well-being.

Source: https://unicorn-images.b-cdn.net/d23e1bca-5f6c-4de1-beee-d57fc3a-00ba6? optimizer=gif.

While the global community acknowledges the imperative of developing healthy mental growth among youths, various factors halt progress, including societal apathy toward children's worth and low levels of knowledge about developmental psychopathology. As the issue of the mental health of vulnerable populations, e.g., child soldiers and victimized children, illustrates, therapeutic interventions against anxiety disorders must be multi-faceted while considering the needs of both the individual and society. Here, positive mental health not only manifests itself as a personal imperative but also as an integral component of community cohesion and economic viability, thereby signifying that investments in mental health for the young are crucial in initiating robust communities as well as healthier future generations (Belfer et al., 2005) (Figure 3.1).

3.1. TYPES OF ANXIETY DISORDERS

The forms, manifestations, and symptoms of anxiety disorders in children and adolescents vary greatly. Among the most prevalent are social anxiety disorder, generalized anxiety disorder (GAD), and specific phobias. Excessive worrying that interferes with daily functioning and causes long-term distress is a hallmark of generalized anxiety disorder (GAD). Conversely, excessive dread of social engagement is known as social anxiety disorder, and it significantly impairs a young person's ability to interact with peers and grow socially. However, severe dread of certain things or circumstances, such as heights or spiders, are known as specific phobias. Identification of these categories is crucial for early diagnosis and successful intervention since each category requires tailored treatment protocols to meet the specific fears and coping mechanisms of each. In evaluating the implications of anxiety disorders, both prevalence and related risk factors need to be considered. Recent research indicates that children and adolescents experience high prevalence rates of anxiety disorders, which is due to varied genetic, environmental, and psychological factors. For instance, a child with a stressful early environment or a history of bad life events will be susceptible to suffering from an anxiety disorder. Furthermore, social media exposure and its connection to anxiety have been in the spotlight, particularly its interaction with adolescents' self-esteem and relationships. Interventions against such risk factors are essential in decreasing symptoms of anxiety throughout early life, thus optimizing mental health effects (Smith et al., 2008). Prevention and treatment of successful anxiety disorders are essential in fostering resilience and well-being among youths. Research has revealed that psychological treatments, such as cognitive-behavioral therapy (CBT), have good methods of tackling anxiety among this age group. In addition to helping children recognize and alter negative cognitions, these models of therapy also teach children skills for managing anxiety in general situations. School-based interventions that cover mental health promotion have been revealed to reduce levels of anxiety and enhance self-esteem. They can be installed for the broader context of the anxiety disorders as the encouragement of preventative interventions as integral components of children and adolescent mental health programs (Barlow et al., 2007). With these interventions made our priority, we can take an all-encompassing approach to the development of the mental well-being of children (Figure 3.2).

Figure 3.2. Effective prevention and treatment strategies for anxiety disorders are paramount in fostering resilience and well-being among youth.

*Source:*https://www.unicef.org/eca/sites/unicef.org.eca/files/styles/hero_extended/public/UN0775495.jpg.webp?itok=NjT6_zKi.

3.1.1. Generalized Anxiety Disorder (GAD)

Within the spectrum of anxiety disorders, generalized anxiety disorder (GAD) is a severe ailment that affects children and teenagers. Persistent anxiety about almost every facet of life, including health, social interactions, and academic performance, can significantly hinder a person's day-to-day functioning. Children with GAD have high levels of emotional distress, which can cause restlessness, irritability, and trouble focusing. Notably, GAD can develop at a young age, therefore early detection is essential for successful intervention. According to Woodie et al. (2009), the frequency of GAD in children and adolescents makes it more important to identify the disorder and raise awareness of how it affects mental health. As a result, schools and clinics must provide specialized therapy and strong support networks. The interconnectedness of GAD with other psychosocial variables makes its treatment in children even more challenging. Children with GAD are likely to be reinforced in the social environment in a negative way, and this is likely to intensify the symptoms further. Family, peer relationships, and school performance are all connected with the intensity of the anxiety experienced. Research has suggested that children with GAD are sensitized to social danger or negative feedback, resulting in heightened anxiety within school or social settings. Such knowledge is invaluable to mental health professionals to design in-depth treatment programs. Furthermore, the presence of comorbid conditions, such as depression or other anxiety disorders, necessitates careful evaluation and intervention strategies to ensure holistic treatment (Cooper et al., 2017). Cognitive Behavior Therapy (CBT) has been an evidence-supported therapy for youth and children suffering from GAD, contributing greatly to their healing and overall well-being. Meta-analyses indicate that approximately 60% of children overcome anxiety disorders following CBT interventions (Cooper et al., 2017). Recovery rates vary based on diagnostic criteria used in research. This highlights the necessity of standardized guidelines for reporting outcomes to detect the effectiveness of treatment. The adaptable nature of CBT allows therapists to tailor interventions based on an individual's needs, fighting against the cognitive distortions and behaviors toward anxiety. Further, the inclusion of parent training and treatment in school environments can enhance the efficacy of CBT even more, ultimately resulting in the development of resilience and coping behaviors in youth. As research evolves, an awareness of the complexities of GAD and successful treatment protocols remains the solution for enhancing child and adolescent mental health interventions (Woodie et al., 2009) (Figure 3.3).

Figure 3.3. Generalized anxiety disorder (GAD) represents a significant concern within the spectrum of anxiety disorders affecting children and adolescents.

Source: https://childmind.org/wp-content/uploads/2022/12/Generalized-Anxiety-scaled.jpg.

3.1.2. Social Anxiety Disorder (SAD)

Children and teenagers are greatly impacted by social anxiety disorder (SAD), a common mental illness that impairs socializing and academic achievement. Patients who have a persistent dread of social circumstances also experience extreme distress when confronted with social events, including speaking in class or at a party. This crippling illness may lead to avoidance habits, which hinder social development and foster loneliness and low self-esteem. Notably, in order to overcome SAD, early detection and intervention are crucial because untreated symptoms may persist into adulthood and exacerbate other psychological issues. Recent studies underscore the necessity to institute appropriate treatment modalities that can solve the special development needs of young populations and consequently encourage resilience against this disorder's long-term consequences on psychological well-being and health. The age of digitalization has come up with new opportunities in treating SAD, particularly through Digital Mental Health Interventions (DMHIs). These technologies provide an accessible source of intervention for youth with social anxiety, offering comparatively low-cost and often inconspicuous methods of treatment. It was discovered in a systematic review and meta-analysis that DMHIs were very effective in the treatment of symptoms of social anxiety in young people, yielding a sizable Hedges g effect size of 0.508. This highlights the strength of cognitive-behavioral constructs employed in these electronic media and the benefit of delivering interventions with human assistance. These findings not only highlight the necessity of introducing modernization to traditional forms of therapy but also suggest that interventions specially developed for specified populations, i.e., for SAD, are able to enhance uptake as well as improve outcomes. The identification of DMHIs is a milestone towards controlling the heightened rate of anxiety disorders among the youth. The COVID-19 crisis only contributed to elevating the cases of such mental illnesses as SAD in youth. Social distancing and disruption of routines have heightened the levels of distress and anxiety, magnifying problems for susceptible individuals with social anxiety. A systematic literature review endorses a significant increase in anxiety and depressive symptoms during the pandemic, especially among children who were inconvenienced by the emotional effects of sudden changes in their social environment. The shutdown of schools and limited interaction with peers served to worsen SAD symptoms, leading to behavioral and emotional disturbances. Against this backdrop, it is apparent that interventions aiming at special work, such as cognitive-behavioral therapy and internet mental well-being care, must be prioritized in order to curb the long-term psychological effect of the pandemic on children and teenagers. Emphasis on social support and continued research will become imperative in shaping effective measures to negate the adverse mental well-being consequences associated with these extraordinary times.

3.1.3. Separation Anxiety Disorder (SAD)

Separation anxiety disorder (SAD) is a significant but often under-treated component of anxiety disorders in children and adolescents. Pathological fear or worry of separating from attachment figures, SAD can significantly interfere with a child's everyday functioning and life quality. The disorder normally manifests as distressful behaviors such as inappropriate worry about losing a caregiver, nightmares about separation, and somatic complaints such as headaches or stomachaches, particularly when school hours or social hours are nearby. Parents and teachers must understand the meaning of such behaviors in order to build a more empathetic climate that addresses the emotional and psychological demands of the child. The incidence of Separation Anxiety Disorder has raised considerable interest in the last 10 years, given its implication for mental health in adolescents. A comprehensive survey of Australian families provided valuable data on the mental health status of children aged between 4 and 17 years, pointing towards a high rate of anxiety disorders among adolescents, including SAD. Thus, the report relies on children's own words in order to learn from these conditions, with a focus on aspects of their emotional lives and behaviors that are not necessarily obvious to parents and caregivers (Lawrence et al., 2015). These data highlight the importance of creating narratives about mental health, enabling improved interventions tailored to the specific needs of children with SAD. Treatment of Separation Anxiety Disorder is a multidisciplinary intervention with an eye to both assessment and treatment approaches that can be fashioned to address the unique needs of these children. Psychological treatments are shown to be highly effective in the treatment of SAD, employing cognitive-behavioral techniques that help the child cope and become resilient. Through emphasis on these therapeutic interventions, mental health clinicians are able to implement individualized programs that not only decrease anxiety but also empower children through skills acquisition (Smith et al., 2008). This anticipatory approach is required because untreated SAD can lead to exacerbated issues, including increased social isolation and problems within school, thereby again highlighting the necessity of early and effective mental health provision in child and adolescent care (Figure 3.4).

Figure 3.4. Separation anxiety disorder (SAD) represents a significant, yet often under-discussed, facet of anxiety disorders within child and adolescent mental health.

Source: https://www.simplypsychology.org/wp-content/uploads/attachment-anxiety.jpeg.

3.2. PREVALENCE OF ANXIETY DISORDERS

Mental health practitioners now frequently emphasize the prevalence of anxiety problems among young people. Numerous studies show that these conditions impact a sizable portion of kids and teenagers, frequently with far-reaching consequences. As an illustration of the worldwide trend, a recent survey revealed that 16% of teenagers in South Africa had anxiety disorders (Stansfeld et al., 2016). Vulnerable people are at higher risk since socioeconomic level and racial/ethnic status have been found to be important factors in determining the occurrence of these illnesses. In order to lessen the burden of anxiety during a crucial time of life, these statistics support the necessity for focused interventions that address the unique vulnerabilities experienced by these groups. In Australia, a national survey of over 6300 families revealed the prevalence of mental illness, including anxiety disorders, among youths aged 4 to 17 years. Involving adolescents and their parents provided a balanced representation of mental illness (Lawrence et al., 2015). Results of the survey validate that a large percentage of young Australians do experience anxiety, often in conjunction with other social and emotional issues. The results support the necessity to create not only an understanding of the quantitative prevalence but also the contextual determinants driving these disorders. By creating this understanding, more suitable early detection and intervention strategies can be created, which will ultimately result in a healthier generation. The social impact of anxiety disorders in teenagers is profound, influencing their academic productivity, social relationships, and overall quality of life. Early development of anxiety has the ability to lead to long-term problems, creating a cycle of mental adversity that may persist into adulthood. Literature illustrates the overlap of anxiety with other mental adversity such as depression and post-traumatic stress disorder, complexity to treatment models (Stansfeld et al., 2016). The requirement to treat anxiety disorders in children and youth is of vital necessity since early and effective treatment has the potential to alter the course of life. Hence, policymakers, educators, and mental health professionals must collaborate to ensure integrated support systems that address not just the symptoms of anxiety but also the underlying reasons for its widespread prevalence.

3.2.1. Statistics on Anxiety Disorders in Children and Adolescents

The prevalence of anxiety disorders among children and adolescents has grown exponentially in recent years, stressing the imperative for effective mental health care. Recent research estimates that around 7% of 3–17-year-olds have anxiety disorders, making it one of the most common mental illnesses among children and adolescents. These disorders present in a number of different ways, including generalized anxiety disorder, social anxiety disorder, and panic disorder, each with varying presentations and impact on daily function. Perturbing to the clinician is a high prevalence of anxiety-related diagnoses in this age group that suggests not just increased identification of the disease, but perhaps an increase in environmental stressors that are working on our children today. These trends call attention to the necessity of early detection and intervention strategies that can assist impacted children before their symptoms aggravate and severely disrupt their school and social life. Family life plays a significant role in the frequency and treatment response of anxiety disorders in adolescents. Family-based intervention studies show that incorporating parental involvement in treatment can improve outcomes among teenagers suffering from anxiety issues. Structural–strategic family therapy has been one of the methods that have been in increasing demand. This approach aims to enhance family interaction and communication patterns. In controlled studies, adolescents who were given the therapy demonstrated large reductions in both internalizing and externalizing behavior problems. Also, parents reported increased family cohesion and parental competence after treatment. The tension between family dynamics and adolescents' psychological well-being is complex, but one that is inevitable; familiarity with family dynamics has the potential to offer a climate of support that enhances affective strength and recovery from children experiencing anxiety disorders, as evidenced through the outcomes of various therapeutic approaches (Medina et al., 2019). Mindfulness-based treatments are also being found to be effective techniques to enhance affective well-being in adolescents suffering from anxiety. New research indicates school-based mindfulness training can have meaningful improvements in emotional control and resilience in early adolescence, especially. A study involving a cohort of sixth graders found that students who participated in a mindfulness program showed enhanced emotional functioning compared with a group in an active control condition. Interestingly, gender differences were observed, in that female participants registered greater gains in positive affect and self-compassion compared with male participants. This means that unique interventions may be called for to address the unique developmental needs and responses of the various genders. With growing popularity of mindfulness exercises among schools, they are one of the promising fields of intervention to not only suppress symptoms of anxiety but also build long-term emotional intelligence and resilience among teenagers (Britton et al., 2018).

3.2.2. Factors Contributing to Increased Prevalence

The growing prevalence of anxiety disorders among children and adolescents has become an issue of concern in contemporary mental health discourse.

The social environment in which youths live is one of the primary drivers of this increase. Empirical evidence from research indicates that poor social support and dysfunctional family environments can potentially exacerbate the symptoms of anxiety, as shown in a study indicating a substantial association between intimate partner violence and generalized anxiety disorders (GAD) in adolescent mothers (Tembo et al., 2024). This highlights the impact of external stressors on mental health. Secondly, the rapid changing social needs and scholastic pressure faced by youth may create a perfect storm for anxiety in those high expectations and paucity of coping skills blend to foster greater mental illness among them.

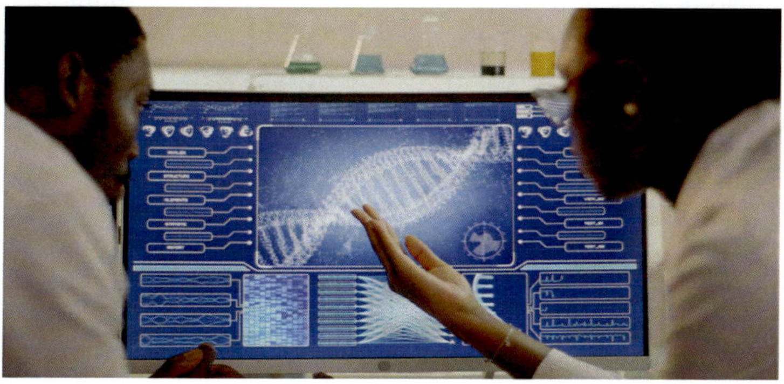

Figure 3.5. Genetic predispositions combined with stressors such as peer relationships and academic challenges can exacerbate vulnerabilities.

Source: https://www.verywellhealth.com/thmb/FW2aC0KwK-L4xzBI0QxbIn-Lm2bE =/1500x0/filters:no_upscale():max_bytes(150000):strip_icc()/VWH-GettyImages-1345098965-779be2ac96934cb998ab1ce83470318b.jpg.

A further important cause is the traumatic experiences faced by most children and youths, particularly in war zones. Recent research exemplifies that war and violence-exposed children have high degrees of anxiety disorders, in addition to comorbidities such as PTSD and depression (Skrypnyk et al., 2024). Witnessing or experiencing violence can lead to psychological trauma in the form of acute anxiety, having a profound impact on the mental well-being of a child. The prolonged length of such trauma incurs the likelihood of developing anxiety disorders a number of years following the initial experience of exposure. As evidence demonstrates, the prevalence of symptoms of anxiety can increase several times within 6 to 12 months following exposure to trauma, and it is hence essential to use specific interventions treating the immediate as well as long-term effects of such events. Finally, the interaction between environment and biology cannot be dismissed in comprehending the increased incidence of anxiety disorders among children. Genetic vulnerability coupled with stressors like social relationships and academic difficulties can create vulnerabilities that may expand. For example, kids with a history of anxiety disorders in their families are more vulnerable to these disorders, especially when confronted with other stressors in their lives. The research implications of teen mothers illustrate how cultural and social determinants can intensify these vulnerabilities to produce a higher incidence of GAD among populations where such determinants hold greatest influence (Tembo et al., 2024). Initiatives in reversing such complicated determinants with far-reaching preventative interventions and early intervention are imperative in curtailing the rising trend in anxiety disorders in child and adolescent mental health (Figure 3.5).

3.2.3. Comparison with Other Mental Health Disorders

When compared to other mental health illnesses, the prevalence of anxiety disorders in children and adolescents reveals significant differences. According to recent research, anxiety problems affect a large percentage of young people, often outnumbering diseases like depression and behavioral issues. For example, although depressive disorders are worrying, their prevalence is typically lower than that of anxiety disorders; hence, anxiety may typically appear first in children and, if untreated, may develop problems that include depression. Additionally, anxiety disorders can coexist with other conditions, exacerbating their symptoms. This fusion of anxiety with other mental health disorders necessitates an integrated assessment and treatment strategy among health providers because interventions aimed at the discrete disorder might not account for the underlying dynamics that prevail with multiple disorders. When viewing the risk factors of anxiety disorders compared to other mental health disorders, disparities become more conspicuous. Research has tracked that anxiety disorders typically have an intricate interaction of genetic, environmental, and developmental factors. For example, children suffering from anxiety disorders are usually over-sensitized to stress due to over-sensitivity in their neurological systems, a factor less stressed in other mental disorders such as conduct disorders. Additionally, Smith et al. (2008) indicates that factors of risk and protection identified are quite divergent, necessitating the need for tailored preventive interventions. While some like family history can influence the expression of various disorders, the distinct causes and maintenance factors of anxiety call for particular emphasis and intervention strategies, further solidifying its unique profile in child and adolescent mental health. Comparative study also indicates the course of treatment for anxiety disorders diverges considerably from others of psychological disorders. Findings demonstrate that effective psychological treatments for anxiety, particularly cognitive-behavioral therapy (CBT), are more effective than medication treatments commonly applied to other types of mental health disorders. In fact, Smith et al. (2008) reports the effectiveness of such interventions among primary school children, identifying an important age group to address. The effectiveness of psychological treatments in alleviating symptoms of anxiety emphasizes the need for early diagnosis and treatment, particularly in educational and health care environments. Accordingly, mental health professionals should be cognizant of these differences so treatment models may be optimized to best serve those with anxiety disorders by providing them with specialized care specific to their individual situation that can significantly differ from other mental health disorders.

3.3. SYMPTOMS AND DIAGNOSIS

Diagnosis of anxiety disorders in children and adolescents is difficult since their symptoms are multifaceted and take different forms based on developmental stages. The majority of young individuals are prone to generalized anxiety, where they are concerned with a number of things in life, including school life and social relationships. In addition, irritability, restlessness, and spontaneous physical reactions, including headaches or stomach pain, typically accompany anxiety disorders, which complicates diagnosis. Closely examining such symptoms indicates that generalized anxiety can coincide with symptoms of other mental disorders and thus requires accurate diagnosis. Providers are faced with the dilemma of differentiating anxiety symptoms from the normal developmental concerns, thus making the diagnosis more difficult, particularly if secondary illnesses like depression are also prevalent in the same cohort of adolescents (Susan et al., 2024). Anxiety disorder diagnosis is virtually solely reliant on standardized measures and rated interviews that review the severity and extent to which the symptoms interfere with functional life. Measures like the Screen for Child Anxiety-Related Disorders and the Kiddie Schedule for Affective Disorders and Schizophrenia are key in making this diagnosis since they provide quantifiable parameters on which to base conclusions about the degree of anxiety and related comorbidities. The retrospective analysis of children with medically unexplained symptoms underscores the need for stringent psychiatric evaluations in revealing concomitant, under-diagnosed anxiety-related disorders. In fact, in referred children with these symptoms, a high percentage were diagnosed with a psychiatric disorder, and this also reflects that anxiety tends to manifest in the form of physical symptoms. This further underlines the necessity for clinicians to employ an integrated assessment approach that showcases the relationship between psychological and physiological symptoms to reach the accurate diagnosis and suitable treatment protocol (Kodali et al., 2021). Finally, interactions between anxiety symptoms and other mental health trends, such as diet, are offered as additional consequences of untreated anxiety in adolescence. It has been established through research that adolescents with severe anxiety symptoms can also have low diet quality, leading to additional overall concerns for health and wellbeing. After controlling for comorbid depression, interactions between anxiety and lower diet quality are most prominently highlighted. This interrelation means that anxiety disorders not only manifest in psychological symptoms but also have implications on other aspects of physical wellbeing, hence necessitating a holistic approach in intervention in diagnosis and treatment methods. With greater awareness of these associations, further study is necessary to determine the optimal manner in which to treat both the mental and physical health conditions at the same time, in hopes of obtaining a more holistic approach to youth health (Susan et al., 2024).

3.3.1. Common Symptoms of Anxiety Disorders

Anxiety disorders in children and adolescents have a tendency to manifest in a range of common symptoms, which can easily impact everyday life and overall health. Among the symptoms, fear and worry are evident indicators of anxiety. Children will express frequent concerns about various aspects of their lives, such as school performance, social relationships, and family relationships. This increased preoccupation often leads to avoidance behaviors, where the child will steer clear of activities or situations that could lead to anxiety. Furthermore, this worry hyperactivity can lead to emotional distress, putting a strain on the child's relationship with friends and family members, thereby undermining their social growth and emotional health in early, developmental years. Physical symptoms of anxiety often arise in addition to the emotional symptoms as well. Young people and adolescents with anxiety disorders may complain of headaches, stomachaches, or other bodily complaints that are perplexing to parents and also healthcare providers. The somatic symptoms may arise as a reaction to heightened levels of anxiety and are not out of the ordinary in adolescents who are facing emotional challenges. As noted in anxiety prevalence and symptom studies, this dysfunction makes the condition of the child more difficult to break, as it becomes rigid and resilient. Recognition of these symptoms indicates that early treatment and intervention are necessary, as failure to treat anxiety disorders will hamper the academic achievement and social development of a child significantly, impacting their long-term direction of mental health (Lawrence et al., 2015). Finally, the emotional climate for anxious youth is generally marked by low self-esteem and hopelessness. They become disabled by negative self-perceptions, which are further aggravated by a growing sense of isolation and withdrawal from peers. These emotional symptoms are aggravated further by the performance anxieties in schools where children fear being evaluated by peers and teachers alike, further fueling their feelings of inadequacy. As seen from the research on risk factors and treatment for anxiety, access to these emotional challenges through appropriate psychological interventions can be vital in providing avenues for recovery. Ensuring extensive prevention programs and psychological treatments is essential, particularly for primary school children, who may go through various transitions and stressors within their development (Smith et al., 2008). Identification and validation of these symptoms are necessary to establish nurturing frameworks to facilitate resilient mental wellbeing in children and adolescents (Figure 3.6).

Figure 3.6. Children and adolescents experiencing anxiety disorders may report stomachaches, headaches, or other somatic complaints, which can be perplexing to both parents and healthcare providers.

Source: https://www.verywellmind.com/thmb/Pz-00WKShiPRUYwS4hhuw7ahw=/2128x0/filters:no_upscale():max_bytes(150000):strip_icc()/anxiety-579eacee5f9b589aa9d817c6.jpg.

3.3.2. Diagnostic Criteria

Diagnostic criteria for youth anxiety disorders rely on standardized classification, largely explained in the Diagnostic and Statistical Manual of Mental Disorders (DSM-5). The system categorizes various anxiety disorders, including Generalized Anxiety Disorder, Social Anxiety Disorder, and Specific Phobias, and highlights primary features such as excessive fear or worry that is out of proportion relative to the actual threat involved. For the conditions to be of clinical significance, as defined in the DSM-5, they must result in significant impairment in everyday functioning. Temporal considerations are emphasized by the criteria, in that symptoms must persist for a minimum time, usually six months, before acceptance as a diagnosis. This means that proper diagnosis arises through careful assessment, taking the developmental context of the child or adolescent into consideration, as symptoms manifest differently in children and adolescents than in adults. In practice, the process of assessment typically makes use of standardized instruments that assist in the estimation of anxiety symptoms and their severity.

Figure 3.7. It is essential to integrate the perspectives of parents and guardians, as they provide valuable context regarding the child's behavior and emotional state.

Source: https://cdn.cpdonline.co.uk/wp-content/uploads/2024/08/05113531/Recognising-Early-Signs-of-Mental-Health-Issues-in-Children-scaled.jpg.

Assessment tools such as the Anxiety Disorders Interview Schedule for Children (ADIS-C) and parent-reporting tools facilitate the gathering of ample information regarding the child's experience. Assessment tools are core to the distinction between normal development phobias and anxiety disorders, as most children exhibit transitory fears that do not need treatment. Furthermore, parents' and guardians' opinions need to be included because they provide informative background information regarding the mood and behavior of the child. Subjective reports from adolescents, especially older than 11 years, are informative and reflect customized details about their emotional experiences that may not be observed by caregivers, thus enhancing the validity of diagnostic assessments (Lawrence et al., 2015). Moreover, the interrelationship between physical health conditions and anxiety disorders cannot be downplayed. Studies have confirmed that conditions of preterm birth, for example, can confer an increased susceptibility to developing anxiety disorders, as well as other psychiatric disorders. This relationship is particularly important among adolescents, a stage of development where illness of the mind is more pronounced and prolonged in preterm individuals compared to those who are term-born. The increased prevalence of anxiety, as well as other conditions like ADHD and Autism, necessitates rigorous screening and early intervention practices towards early detection and management (Johnson et al., 2013). An interpretation of these diagnostic requirements in an integrated context, including general physical health, is necessary to ensure the right treatment of anxiety disorders in children and adolescents, eventually leading to better long-term mental health outcomes (Figure 3.7).

3.3.3. Challenges in Diagnosing Anxiety in Children and Adolescents

Because anxiety symptoms can manifest differently at different stages of development, diagnosing anxiety disorders in children and adolescents is extremely difficult. Children may not always exhibit anxiety in a consistent fashion as they become older, which makes assessment duties more difficult for medical professionals. It has been found that symptoms in two- or three-year-old toddlers are indicative of social phobia, separation anxiety, generalized anxiety, and obsessive-compulsive behavior. However, little study has been done to distinguish these symptoms into distinct diagnostic categories (Briggs-Gowan et al., 2012). The use of multifaceted assessment tools that are responsive to the developmental stage of the children being evaluated is necessary due to the intricacy of emotion in younger children. Therefore, early and accurate diagnosis requires an integration of care reports and observation-based strategies that consider the developmental condition of the child. Moreover, the comorbidity of symptoms of anxiety with other psychiatric disorders makes the diagnostic process more problematic. Children and adolescents tend to have co-occurring diseases such as learning disabilities or depression, which are like symptoms of anxiety in terms of their nature and, hence, can result in misdiagnosis. For example, individuals with learning disabilities often have psychosocial impairment in the form of higher anxiety and lower self-esteem, further clouding the clinical presentation (Short et al., 2013). Clinicians evaluating juvenile patients should be able to understand this association since symptoms manifest as behavioral issues, necessitating the employment of multi-dimensional assessment strategies. A systematic approach considering environmental, educational, and psychological variables will enable clinicians to distinguish the primary anxiety disorder from possible comorbidities. Stigma of mental illness as well as low awareness among educators and parents regarding anxiety disorders can further lead to underreporting of symptoms. They are usually under pressure to be liked, and thus their expression of self-anxiety is hindered. Consequently, a majority of adolescents do not receive any treatment for their anxiety, further aggravating their distress, as well as potentially resulting in adverse effects at school and in social settings. The condition of the prevailing diagnostic measures highlights the importance of raising awareness for caregivers and educators regarding the symptoms of anxiety disorders. More comprehensive educational courses in psychosocial matters, alongside more rigorous screening procedures for children in schools, could help condition adults to better recognize and treat symptoms of anxiety, resulting in better mental health among young people.

3.4. CAUSES AND RISK FACTORS

It is important to comprehend the causes and risk factors of anxiety disorders in young people because these factors have a big impact on how the illnesses develop and progress. Genetic risk factors are important to take into account; children who have a family history of anxiety disorders are often more vulnerable. A person's risk of developing these mental health issues may be increased by specific genetic markers or gene variations, according to research. Furthermore, in vulnerable youth, environmental variables such as exposure to stressful life events or chronic illness can trigger anxiety disorders. As an illustration of how genetic abnormalities might interact with psychological stressors to increase susceptibility to anxiety, research revealed that children with congenital adrenal hyperplasia (CAH) developed high rates of anxiety disorders (Ernst et al., 2010). Clearly, there is a transactional connection between environmental factors and genetic susceptibility that forms an important component of research on anxiety disorders in children. Moreover, parenting strategies and family functioning cannot be ruled out while researching anxiety disorders in adolescents and children. Children reared in households with excessive parental anxiety, overprotection, or critical parenting are likely to develop anxiety disorders. Conversely, supportive parenting can result in resilience and counteract symptoms of anxiety. Teens reared in either permissive or highly restrictive families can develop boundary confusion and emotional distress regarding what is expected of them. Furthermore, exposure to mental health issues in the family, including depression, further exacerbates a child's risk for developing anxiety disorders. As also illustrated in the evidence on psychoeducational interventions for adolescents at risk, supportive systems and effective family communication are also imperative in accessing and treating mental health issues and building resilience (Jones et al., 2017). This also affirms the need to consider familial factors in assessing anxiety risk among young people. Socioeconomic status in society, as well as cultural issues, also play a role in the development of anxiety disorders among young individuals. Lower socioeconomic status kids could be exposed to more stressors such as financial instability, poor health care access, and violence, which exacerbate anxiety symptoms. Cultural norms also make this more complex; in certain cultures, mental illness is a stigmatized condition, causing families to shy away from getting treatment, and hence longer onset of anxiety disorders. In addition, cultural expectations around achievements and behaviors might exert additional stress on adolescents, leading to greater anxiety. Understanding such broader societal influences is a first step towards creating effective prevention and intervention efforts that are culturally responsive and target the diverse experiences of different populations. By critically analyzing these multiple causes and risk factors, mental health practitioners can better tailor their interventions to help children and adolescents with anxiety disorders (Figure 3.8).

Figure 3.8. Adolescents raised in either excessively permissive or overly strict families might experience confusion about boundaries and expectations, leading to emotional distress.

Source: https://news.uga.edu/wp-content/uploads/2020/09/GettyImages-482548469.jpg.

3.4.1. Genetic Predisposition to Anxiety Disorders

An understanding of genetic predisposition is thus instrumental in advancing our strategies in addressing anxiety-linked problems in children. In addition to the genetic mechanisms, environmental factors also play an important role in triggering anxiety disorders. For instance, traumatic exposure in childhood, including loss of parent or emotional abuse, can enhance genetic risk. Children who experience these stressors may present increased symptoms of anxiety irrespective of their genetic risk. Epidemiological evidence has shown that somatic, anxiety, and depressive disorders are prevalent in children, and both risk and protective factors influence their mental health outcomes. Effective interventions must thus take into account both genetic and environmental contexts since the examination of the interaction between these contexts can help guide individualized treatment strategies. Increasing the focus of psychological treatments above the sole utilization of pharmacological interventions is a sound method of opposing anxious symptoms, especially in primary school children, as suggested by more recent studies in the field (Smith et al., 2008). Furthermore, the influence of media consumption on body esteem and mental well-being also emphasizes the interdependence of genetic predisposition and external pressures. As teenagers identify more and more with television characters, their effects perpetuate feelings of anxiety and body dissatisfaction. Another study that explored the relationship between media exposure and mental health among teenagers found that both immediate effects of media and comparison to peers significantly caused anxiety and depressive symptoms (Maria et al., 2017). These findings suggest that though inherited vulnerability offers a foundation for risk, contemporary environment can increase or decrease these natural tendencies. Therefore, the influence of media consumption, combined with genetic vulnerability, is essential in establishing practical strategies to support children's and adolescents' mental health. This multifaceted strategy is integral to enhancing resilience in adolescents with anxiety disorders.

3.4.2. Environmental Influences and Stressors

Environmental determinants are a key predictor of children's and adolescents' mental health, particularly in the context of anxiety disorders. These incorporate a range of factors that encompass family issues, socio-economic status, and community resources, all of which can heighten or mitigate symptoms of anxiety. For example, children who are brought up in chaotic home environments with severe conflict or parent mental illness are at risk of having anxiety disorders. Such stressors from such backgrounds interfere with emotional regulation and coping mechanisms, and it becomes difficult for adolescents to cope with social and academic challenges. Moreover, as highlighted by recent studies, interaction of specific environmental stressors and personal vulnerabilities can predispose the causation of anxiety disorders, particularly in vulnerable children who do not have adequate support systems to serve as cushions for such effects (Smith et al., 2008). Influence of peer relations and social settings cannot be overlooked while deliberating on anxiety disorders in children. Bullying, exclusion, and peer pressure are common stressors that have the potential to significantly raise anxiety levels in vulnerable adolescents. Relational stressors tend to create a feedback cycle of negative self-concept and avoidance behaviors, further amplifying anxiety. Additionally, teenagers' reliance on peer validation while at critical growth stages renders them particularly susceptible to social pressure influence. The result of such stressors generally manifests itself in numerous anxiety disorders, including social anxiety disorder, which restricts their ability to engage in regular social activities. The intense effect of social environments is such that interventions for enhancing peer relationships and interpersonal skills are central to the management of anxiety disorders in teenagers (Asarnow et al., 2017). Last but not least, the overall community context also plays a crucial role in establishing mental health outcomes. High rates of violence, financial hardship, and low access to mental health care in communities can be detrimental for children and adolescents with anxiety. Such adverse community conditions have been found to expose children to chronic stress, hence higher levels of anxiety and even the development of related disorders. Furthermore, following access, availability also varies significantly within communities, and variation in available services can hinder the intervention for those in need. Overlaid upon these environmental conditions is a collective effort by policymakers, teachers, and mental health professionals to assist in creating supportive, resource-rich environments. As has been underscored by recent research, protecting children from environmental stressors yet simultaneously providing robust supportive systems has a redemptive influence on the decline of anxiety disorders and general mental health (Smith et al., 2008) (Figure 3.9).

Figure 3.9. Children growing up in unstable home environments characterized by high levels of conflict or parent mental health issues are at an increased risk for developing anxiety disorders.

Source: https://s3.amazonaws.com/utep-uploads/wp-content/uploads/online-regis-college/2020/11/17034153/Parental-mental-health.jpg.

3.4.3. Role of Parenting Styles and Family Dynamics

Anxiety disorders in children and adolescents are primarily caused by parenting and family dynamics. Combining warmth and order, authoritative parenting promotes emotional well-being and resilience while acting as a buffer against anxiety. Conversely, children who experience authoritarian or inattentive parenting are more likely to experience worry and insecurity. When parents reject or are too critical of their child's emotional expression, the child is likely to internalize these messages and have increased anxiety symptoms. The problem is further complicated by family dynamics between parents or siblings. There is a high correlation between anxiety disorders and family functioning, according to empirical data, which calls for more research on family dynamics and their long-term effects on children's mental health. (Cerniglia et al., 2020). The relational patterns of family life exert a large influence on the trajectory of anxiety disorders in children. Research indicates that collaborative family lives are able to offset stress and offer a stage upon which to rehearse emotions. In contrast, conflict families with inconsistent parenting and poor communication are prone to increased vulnerability to mental illness. The developmental psychopathology model of conceptualizing anxiety disorders underscores the importance of attending to risk and protective factors within family relationships and how these might operate as precursors to anxiety disorders. In including these relational factors, practitioners are given rich targets for interventions that go beyond the child to the family system itself. This all-inclusive approach acknowledges the interconnectedness of family life and mental health results (Benelli et al., 2015). Given the strong impact of parenting and family processes on adolescents' anxiety, interventions that enhance family relationships must be prioritized. Techniques that enhance effective communication, empathy, and conflict resolution can significantly reduce symptoms of anxiety. Incorporating family therapy and psychoeducation into treatment plans offers an optimistic route for addressing the roots of anxiety in the home environment. Supplemental training in proficient parenting skills—such as positive reinforcement and active listening—can enable parents to create settings that nurture their children's emotional coping support. It is essential to recognize that anxiety disorders do not exist on their own but are embedded in a tangled network of family interactions when building effective and holistic mental health initiatives for children and youths (Cerniglia et al., 2020).

3.5. IMPACT ON DAILY LIFE

The impact of anxiety disorders on the daily life functioning of children and adolescents generally occurs in social relationships, school functioning, and overall functioning. With growing severity of symptoms, children may have severe limitations on their ability to engage with others and be productively involved in school. Social withdrawal not only has the potential to lead to isolation but also to result in the creation of secondary disorders such as depression. The importance of these issues being addressed early cannot be overstressed; child-specialized psychological therapy has been seen to build up resilience and improve coping strategies. Early intervention schemes can provide healthier social behavior, ultimately laying the ground for children to navigate through daily living with ease and confidence (Smith et al., 2008). By the identification of the special problems faced by children who are anxious, parents and educators are able to collaborate in creating supportive environments that emphasize psychological and emotional health. In addition to social impairment, anxiety disorders significantly disrupt academic performance and intellectual development at critical formative ages. Anxiety disorders have a propensity to cause concentration, memory, and task completion difficulties that adversely affect a child's academic performance at school. Fear of failure or poor assessment or anxiety hinders students from participating in class discussions or seeking help from teachers, which subsequently enhances feelings of inadequacy. Schools are becoming more conscious of the need to tackle mental illness and are creating supportive mechanisms unique to assist anxious students. By fostering a culture of understanding and anxiety disorder accommodations, schools are best placed to foster not just academic excellence but emotional resilience in young students (Johnson et al., 2013). The intersection of academic success and mental health care is thus still an important consideration when it comes to managing the long-term impact of anxiety. Moreover, anxiety disorder consequences extend to family and community function and impact daily functioning on multiple levels. Families will bear the responsibility of adjusting to the requirements of an anxious child, which may lead to changes in patterns and routines within the family. Parents will have heightened tension and concern regarding their child's health and wellbeing and future, and they may endure strained relationships and reduced overall family cohesion. Community intervention programs and existing resources are essential in curbing such pressures as they provide the correct support framework for both the children and their families. With community sensitization and awareness, society is also capable of reducing stigma related to mental illness issues, hence encouraging affected families to come forward and seek help. Lastly, all these collaborative efforts can construct a more facilitative environment in which children can grow and manage their anxiety and eventually have more fulfilling, richer everyday lives without being restricted by their disorders (Smith et al., 2008).

3.5.1. Effects on Academic Performance

Anxiety disorders affect school performance among children and adolescents significantly, with disorders presenting as difficulties in concentration, decreased motivation, and difficulty maintaining social relationships. Emotional distress arising from anxiety might lead to procrastination and school avoidance behavior, where the youth tend to steer away from school settings that cause them anxiety, to the detriment of their learning process. Avoidance can lead to missed learning opportunities and reinforce a pattern of underachievement at school. Research has shown that kids who have anxiety disorders tend to get lower marks and scores on tests compared to their peers, further highlighting the imperative necessity for early detection and treatment to stem such harm to their studies. Even academic involvement determined by peer interaction is likely to suffer adverse impacts as a result of anxiety disorders. School children with increased anxiety commonly complain of difficulty in establishing and sustaining peer relationships, which is critical to developing an effective learning climate.

Figure 3.10. Children experiencing heightened anxiety often report challenges in forming and maintaining friendships, which is integral to creating a supportive learning environment.

Source: https://www.nc2s.org/wp-content/uploads/2024/07/Trauma-Informed-Resilience-Oriented-Schools-Toolkit.png.

Social problems of this type can contribute to a sense of isolation, thus further complicating anxiety disorders and interfering with academic functioning. In the case of a comprehensive report about the mental health of young Australians, emotional distress among these people tends to translate into less participation in school activities, ultimately impacting on teacher and peer relationships. The issue is thus significant to tackle in a bid to provide a more supportive learning environment. Effective interventions against anxiety disorders have been cited as key to improving academic achievement in the youth. Psychologically based interventions rather than pharmacological treatment have been promising to reduce anxiety symptoms and enhance coping skills. Cognitive-behavioral therapy, for instance, has been referred to as successful in helping children manage their anxiety, therefore their ability to concentrate and perform academically. As demonstrated in the findings of previous research, timely and appropriate intervention can reverse the study trajectory of children and adolescents and, in the long term, guarantee both educational achievement and psychological well-being (Lawrence et al., 2015; Smith et al., 2008). The interlinkage between academic performance and psychological well-being necessitates holistic interventions that incorporate both psychological treatment and educational interventions to provide a wholistic strategy in child and adolescent development (Figure 3.10).

3.5.2. Influence on Social Interactions and Relationships

Its effect on peer relationships and social interaction among children and adolescents is a multifaceted issue with far-reaching consequences for their developmental trajectories. Anxiety can potentially severely hinder successful building and maintenance of social relationships, leading to withdrawal and avoidance behavior. Children who are under higher anxiety usually feel overwhelmed by peers in events, which equates to isolation and less access to healthful interaction with peers. Such avoidance is most prominently demonstrated during the formative years, when social abilities are imperative for building relationship ties promoting emotional support and coping resilience. The severity of such social impairments emphasizes the importance of early detection and intervention strategies in order to overcome anxiety's interfering effect on social functioning and relational development (Smith et al., 2008). The relationship between parental mental health and children's social experience is also an important consideration that needs to be taken into account. Anxiety disorders also affect the children themselves but echo throughout relationships in the family, ultimately affecting social interactions. Parents who are under a lot of stress or have mental illness may struggle to engage in effective communication and interaction, impacting the social learning experiences of their children. For instance, in children with autism spectrum disorder (ASD), parents' engagement and mental health are essential for optimal social skill acquisition. Challenges experienced by parents, including their mental state and stress levels, can lead to reduced social opportunities for children, creating a cycle of social skill deficiency and ongoing anxiety (Caiozzo et al., 2018). This implies that intervention on family factors is crucial in therapy for anxiety disorders. Symptom reduction interventions for anxiety are not only required to target the individual but also the social context. Effective psychologies, such as cognitive-behavioral therapy, have been very effective in enhancing coping mechanisms and interpersonal skills, thereby enhancing interpersonal relationships. Family-involvement programs can further enhance treatment by enhancing understanding and effectively eliminating stigma regarding anxiety disorders. By enhancing healthy family interaction, practitioners can establish an environment conducive to healthy social interaction, mitigating isolating proclivities present with anxiety. Ultimately, enhancing social competence and maintaining relationships through targeted intervention is more important to the long-term mental health and well-being of children and adolescents experiencing anxiety (Smith et al., 2008).

3.5.3. Long-Term Consequences if Left Untreated

The long-term consequences of left untreated anxiety disorders in children and adolescents are very adverse and affect numerous aspects of their development and well-being. The disorders, if left untreated, often lead to chronic impairment, whereby the distress infiltrates not only the life of the individual but also the life of the family. For instance, anxiety left untreated has the potential to significantly impact performance at school through issues with concentration and school engagement, and it can lead to low self-esteem and social withdrawal in a cycle. According to research studies on obsessive-compulsive disorder, the duration of untreated illness is linked with increased suffering and disability, an indication of the importance of early intervention to prevent these detrimental outcomes (Albert et al., 2019). This inability to successfully treat anxiety disorders early on robs youths of their full survival potential, predisposing them to other complications down the road in adulthood, like other mental illnesses. The effects of ineffective treatment stretch beyond the immediate psychological impact; they can also manifest as bodily illnesses. Studies indicate that chronic anxiety has the potential to lead to severe physiological symptoms, such as gastrointestinal symptoms and cardiovascular issues, thereby contributing to the overall health burden (Albert et al., 2019). In addition, anxiety disorders if left untreated have the potential to co-occur with other psychiatric conditions, including depression and substance abuse, making the clinical presentation complex and recovery more challenging. The interrelationship between physical and mental health reinforces the argument that there should be an integrated treatment to address these disorders early, which can prevent them from developing into full-blown mental illness in adult life. As adolescents and children continue to struggle with unresolved anxiety, their capacity to engage constructively with society is gradually destroyed, leading to a cycle of withdrawal and unhappiness. Treatment of the long-term consequences of untreated anxiety matters not only for individuals but also for society. Families are likely to report distress when experiencing their child's untreated anxiety, as suggested by parents reports of feeling overwhelmed and unsupported in mental health systems. Having adequate mental health treatment is still a significant problem, often exacerbated by narrow information and continuity of care that can interrupt effective treatment. In addition, the community burden of untreated anxiety disorders, including increased healthcare utilization and lost productivity, makes early, accessible intervention strategies essential. Fostering literacy in mental health, improving accessibility to services, and establishing collaborative practice between clinicians and families are necessary steps towards circumventing these long-term consequences, ultimately benefitting the individual as well as the broader community (Figure 3.11).

Figure 3.11. Untreated anxiety can severely impact academic performance due to difficulties with concentration and participation in school activities, which may perpetuate a cycle of low self-esteem and social withdrawal.

Source: https://eductive.ca/wp-content/uploads/2024/05/anxiety.jpg.

3.6. TREATMENT OPTIONS

Therapy for anxiety disorder in children and teenagers is immensely varied and can significantly influence mental health outcomes. Among the most conventional yet extensively effective therapies are Cognitive Behavioral Therapy (CBT), which consists of altering negative thoughts and behavior towards anxiety. In structured programs, as noted in the Deakin Family Options (DFO) study, teen-only interventions such as the BEST Plus are compared with interventions that involve parents, suggesting the necessity of engagement with parents. The pilot studies outcome indicates that families that have received group treatment experience greater decreases in youth and parent mental health symptoms, suggesting that involving family dynamics as well as individual therapy can enhance treatment effectiveness (Bertino et al., 2013). Through the engagement of parents in the healing process, treatments not only benefit the young individual but also relieve parental anxiety, thus toward a more supportive environment contributing to the recovery of the child. New models with an emphasis on the power of resilience, namely in young children aged 4–7, point toward a shift toward supporting emotional well-being through complete immersion in therapeutic practice. Programs like FUN FRIENDS, implemented within community mental health services, demonstrate the beneficial impacts of group interventions tailored for young individuals experiencing social phobia or generalized anxiety disorder. This approach encourages children to develop self-sufficiency and enhanced social skills over a structured 12-week period, showcasing significant improvements in anxiety scores as measured by validated assessment tools. These new treatments expand beyond the conventional modalities and highlight the significance of community-based interventions in the management of anxiety (Carlyle et al., 2014). Emphasis on emotional resilience offers a critical adjunct to more conventional treatments, enabling children to manage their anxieties effectively. Finally, treatment of anxiety disorders in children is becoming multidimensional, encompassing both individual and systemic approaches to address various causative factors. In addition to CBT, the use of family-based treatments suggests greater recognition of the psychosocial determinants of mental health. Additionally, new interventions for younger individuals show that age-specific treatment is needed that promotes emotional competence and resilience. As evident from studies, the inclusion of parental and family participation within treatment not only enhances its effectiveness for the child but also decreases large family anxiety dynamics. This integrated model is a whole-person approach to the treatment of anxiety disorders, ensuring treatment modalities directly targeted not only at the affected child but also at the environment surrounding him or her, creating healthier family interactions and emotional milieus that will foster healing (Bertino et al., 2013; Carlyle et al., 2014).

3.6.1. Psychotherapy Approaches (e.g., CBT)

Psychotherapy forms an integral part of the treatment of anxiety disorders, particularly in the developmental phases of childhood and adolescence. Cognitive Behavioral Therapy (CBT) is the most well-studied and documented intervention with efficacy established in the reduction of various anxiety disorders. CBT focuses on the detection and modification of erroneous thought patterns that are responsible for anxiety as well as the modification of behavior with the aim of gradually exposing patients to their feared situations. This two-part approach not only allows adolescents to challenge unproductive assumptions but also educates them in coping skills to manage anxiety in the day-to-day context. Meta-analyses have reported that 60% of adolescents recover following CBT treatment, underscoring its role as a first-line treatment in child and adolescent mental health (Cooper et al., 2017). The organized model of CBT is especially ideal for younger groups because it facilitates the easy explanation of therapeutic principles and promotes active engagement in the process. Even though it has been demonstrated to be effective, CBT and other treatment strategies must be carried out by suitably trained clinicians to guarantee adolescents receive proper and directed treatment.

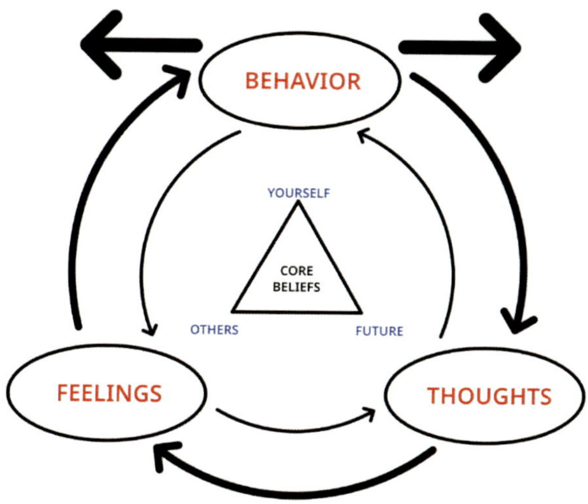

Figure 3.12. Cognitive behavioral therapy (CBT) stands out as one of the most extensively researched and validated approaches, demonstrating efficacy in alleviating various anxiety disorders.

*Source:*https://upload.wikimedia.org/wikipedia/commons/thumb/e/e2/Cognitive_behavioral_therapy_-_basic_tenets.svg/1200px-Cognitive_behavioral_therapy_-_basic_tenets.svg.png.

One study focusing on skills in Child and Adolescent Mental Health Services (CAMHS) found some concerning gaps in panic disorder training for clinicians, an illness that occurs in about 1% of adolescents. Surveys found fewer than half of the surveyed clinicians had the ability to identify panic disorder as a central concern, and this helped establish that there is a glaring gap in treating and diagnosing this illness. While the majority recognized CBT as their treatment of preference, few even utilized protocol-based therapies for adolescent panic disorder (Barlow et al., 2020). This discrepancy necessitates increased training for mental health professionals in recognizing the nuances of anxiety disorders to yield more solid and effective therapy. The effectiveness of psychotherapy for anxiety disorders among children is not only a function of the therapy procedure itself but also of regular surveillance and tailoring of treatment approaches. Heterogeneity of symptoms across anxiety disorders often overlap, and as such, accurate diagnosis is a challenging endeavor. This has necessitated agreement on outcome reporting in future clinical trials to optimize benefit from treatment and help guide clinical practice. Supported by findings indicating heterogenous rates of recovery in children undergoing CBT, it is important to address heterogeneity in response to treatment in an effort to enhance child mental health interventions (Cooper et al., 2017). Development of standardized methods for outcome assessment will enhance comparability of results across studies, which ultimately leads to a more robust evidence base on best practice in the treatment of anxiety disorders. By educating mental health practitioners with information and techniques, the path to more effective psychotherapeutic interventions can be laid, and hence better supporting the mental well-being of youth with anxiety disorders (Figure 3.12).

3.6.2. Medication Options for Anxiety Disorders

The treatment of anxiety disorders among children and adolescents is usually a multi-modal process, with medication being an important option. Selective serotonin reuptake inhibitors (SSRIs) have been widely used due to their efficacy and good side effect profiles. Fluoxetine and sertraline have been shown to exhibit significant efficacy in the treatment of various anxiety disorders such as generalized anxiety disorder, social anxiety disorder, and panic disorder. They operate by elevating the amount of serotonin in the brain, believed to stabilize mood and anxiety. The choice of drug must be modified to fit the individual's specific symptoms and needs based on potential side effects and the age of the child or adolescent, providing overall treatment style that complements other therapy. Besides SSRIs, some other medication options for the management of anxiety disorders include benzodiazepines and buspirone. Benzodiazepines, for instance, diazepam or lorazepam, are effective in treating short-term anxiety attacks due to their rapid action. However, their use is often limited in children and adolescents due to the risk of dependence and tolerance. Buspirone is another non-benzodiazepine anxiolytic available that may provide relief from anxiety without the addictive potential of the benzodiazepines. Its administration, although less common than the SSRIs, may be of value in some cases where immediate relief is required, although it takes a few weeks to achieve maximum effect. Thus, healthcare practitioners must closely consider the risk-to-benefit ratio in the determination of these drugs as part of a comprehensive treatment plan. Pharmacotherapy is a crucial aspect of the treatment for anxiety disorders among the young but should be combined with psychosocial interventions. Cognitive-behavioral therapy (CBT) has also been shown to be very effective in the treatment of anxiety, and this is usually employed as an adjuvant treatment in conjunction with drugs. Research increasingly highlights the importance of addressing cognitive dimensions of anxiety disorders, specifically through metacognitive processes. Understanding how thinking affects feeling can help children and adolescents develop more effective coping styles, crucial in managing symptoms of anxiety and improving overall mental health outcomes (Calderoni et al., 2017). Further, working with families incorporates them into the therapeutic environment where they receive support, and compliance and progress monitoring are facilitated, which is vital to long-term success in treating anxiety disorders (Emerson et al., 2009).

3.6.3. Importance of a Multidisciplinary Approach

The etiology of anxiety disorders in childhood and adolescent mental health demands multidisciplinary action, convening diverse disciplines to optimize the assessment and management process. Optimal management is an essential component of a multifaceted involvement of collaboration between child psychiatrists, psychologists, pediatricians, and allied health care professionals. Team-based approach is linked with enhanced diagnostic accuracy and treatment outcomes through the integration of diverse perspectives and expertise. For instance, while child psychiatrists can start medication, pediatricians are more likely to be accountable for essential physical health evaluations that guide general care. In Ireland, the evidence came from a study that showed widespread overlap and complementarity conducted by Child and Adolescent Mental Health Services (CAMHS) where a multidisciplinary model proved crucial to offering comprehensive care to children with anxiety disorders (Gavin et al., 2017). This dynamic interaction creates a supportive environment, addressing not only the psychological dimensions of anxiety but its physical and social effects as well. Further, this model suggests that one should take into consideration family dynamics and environmental factors in treatment. Families play a significant role in affecting children's mental health; thus, engaging caregivers can lead to successful interventions. By involving parents and family members in the process, clinicians are able to create customized plans that address the child's home life. Family-based interventions that educate family members regarding anxiety disorders engender knowledge and a sense of ownership of treatment. Additionally, interdisciplinary collaboration lays the groundwork for the integration of various therapeutic approaches, such as cognitive-behavioral therapy (CBT), occupational therapy, and sensory modulation techniques. A recently released review of sensory modulation approaches emphasized their effectiveness in diminishing symptoms of anxiety and promoting functional improvement in adolescents, demonstrating the clinical value of such multimodal interventions (Lloyd et al., 2017). Finally, implementation of a multidisciplinary model is critical to close the research-practice divide in addressing anxiety disorders in children. There is now an imperative for high-quality evidence to underpin interventions across professions, particularly in determining the long-term impact of multimodal interventions. By developing a culture of collaborative knowledge and inter-professional research, mental health professionals can enhance the quality of evidence-based practice. For example, research into pediatric settings reveals significant discrepancies in addressing ADHD, which attests to suboptimal application of holistic approaches by pediatricians compared to CAMHS (Gavin et al., 2017). Filling these discrepancies is part of informing subsequent training and practice guidelines so that all mental health professionals working with children and adolescents have the tools and knowledge necessary for holistic and effective treatment (Figure 3.13).

Figure 3.13. By bringing parents and family members into the therapeutic process, professionals can create tailored strategies that resonate with the child's home life.

Source: https://advice.cdn.betterhelp.com/md/family-smiles-at-computer.jpg.

3.7. CONCLUSION

Lastly, treatment of anxiety disorders in mental health in children and adolescents requires a proper and interconnected approach. The prevalence of these disorders in younger generations has not only individual psychological consequences, but also implications for the functioning of society as a whole. An optimal treatment plan, comprising Cognitive Behavioral Therapy (CBT) and psychoeducational interventions (PIs), hinges on the rationale that intervention at an early point is a significant contribution towards minimizing long-term effects. Promotion of awareness on such disorders is also of key significance since it helps in the provision of stigma-free environments where the victims can obtain help. Moreover, systematic application of evidence-based treatments ensures that children and adolescents receive the resources and therapy that best addresses their unique needs, thus ensuring better mental health outcomes. The growing body of literature concerning child and adolescent anxiety disorders requires ongoing examination and evaluation of treatment approaches. The findings are that, while treatments such as CBT have been incredibly effective at symptom reduction, with satisfactory rates of recovery, variability in outcomes complicates the evaluation of treatment effectiveness. Indeed, a meta-analysis illustrates that recovery rates vary considerably from one study to another, thus it is important to standardize parameters for diagnosis and reporting in later studies. This variability complicates the effective evaluation of the efficacy of various therapeutic approaches. Thus, the promotion of strict, standardized parameters for studies will enhance precision and applicability of results, which ultimately will benefit clinical intervention and treatment regimens. In addition, the significance of recognizing the pivotal position that psychoeducational interventions hold in the prevention and treatment of anxiety in adolescents cannot be overasserted. The evidence attests to the possibility that PIs hold the capability to significantly augment knowledge, symptom identification, and overall mental health outcomes among adolescents. Despite this, the persisting heterogeneity in program formats and definitions suggests that further refining their implementation and evaluation is required. Agreement on the salient features of effective PIs is central to the development of integrated models that can be generalized to diverse populations and environments. A collaborative effort to advance knowledge of the preventive as well as therapeutic factors of anxiety disorders will enhance the ability to implement customized interventions that are efficacious in reducing the needs of children and adolescents, ultimately leading to a healthier, mentally robust generation.

3.7.1. Summary of Key Points Discussed

In children and adolescents' mental health assessment of anxiety disorders, timely intervention importance is underscored in various research studies. A salient finding indicates that mental health self-care support intervention can have modest short-term to medium-effectiveness. This has been illustrated through systematic review of literature where a number of self-care interventions undertaken by children and young people (CYP) were analyzed. The review demonstrated how interventions in the areas of strengthening self-care knowledge and skills were significant in enhancing mental health results. Of importance, CYP and their families expressed a need for flexible and child-centered support services beyond traditional therapy sessions, calling for accessibility and the creation of supportive environments in fostering the mental health of vulnerable populations (Carlyle et al., 2014). Another significant subject discussed is the role of family dynamics in shaping children's and adolescents' mental health outcomes. Findings from the Deakin Family Options pilot study guide the relationship between parent anxiety and attachment styles, revealing that parental involvement with systematic treatments is useful to both youth and parent outcome. Especially, families engaging in intensive programs showed more pronounced reductions in symptoms of anxiety compared to families engaging in youth-only focused interventions. Additionally, the study indicated that parents' anxiety decreased remarkably with their engagement, which suggests an interactive relationship between child outcomes and parental mental health (Bertino et al., 2013). The results, therefore, bring into focus the critical role family-based interventions and treatment mechanisms play in alleviating anxiety disorders in this population. Furthermore, the discussions of anxiety disorders highlight the necessity of tailored mental health services encompassing both individual and systemic factors. Mapping exercise to locate self-care service providers revealed that there were poorly identified mental health support systems for CYP. The majority of the services do not have the structured support necessary for facilitating children to employ effective coping strategies. Integration of peer support systems alongside traditional therapy interventions played a key role as a major determinant of successful outcomes. This discovery affirms the requirement for stakeholders to revisit delivery frameworks for services to confirm they are effective in managing children and adolescents with anxiety's complicated needs. An enlightened strategy with merged multifaceted treatment modalities will most certainly achieve greater progress towards curing anxiety disorders and improving overall mental well-being in youth.

3.7.2. The Importance of Early Intervention and Support

Identification and intervention of anxiety disorders in children and adolescents at the early point is vital in encouraging effective mental health intervention. Early intervention not only minimizes the severity of symptoms but also postpones the onset of severe mental health disorders in children as they mature. The early years of a child's life are developmental and highly susceptible to the impact of various treatment modalities. Interventions for psychological therapies, as highlighted in literature, show a significant effect when provided at the primary school level. By focusing on early intervention, teachers and caregivers are able to create an enabling environment where there is open dialogue around mental health, enabling coping mechanisms and resilience among the youth (Smith et al., 2008). Early intervention thus becomes not merely a therapeutic need but a proactive measure for the overall wellness of children. Psychoeducational interventions (PIs) cannot be overemphasized in the case of anxiety disorders among adolescents. PIs are taught to provide accurate information regarding mental illness and facilitate self-management skills required of adolescents with anxiety. Through the integration of family engagement and community resources, PIs are well positioned to enhance symptom knowledge, improve communication, and promote mental health service utilization (Jones et al., 2017). It is indicated by research that through engaging in guided learning modules, young persons, especially at-risk individuals, are well positioned to recognize and express their emotions, which is central to responding to mental health issues. Early intervention in such measures not only helps in the management of symptomatology but also instills a sense of agency in adolescents to address the necessity of help in a proactive manner. Moreover, integration of early intervention and assistance at the systemic level can revolutionize the landscape of mental care for children and adolescents with anxiety disorders. Extensive support systems, including teachers, medical professionals, and families, play a key role in ensuring effective intervention is not only accessible but also tailored to the individual. A collaborative effort can enable a seamless transition from anxiety symptom identification to implementation of effective interventions. Effective implementation of early interventions creates a chain reaction, positively influencing the larger community and reducing the stigma related to mental health issues (Smith et al., 2008). Therefore, early intervention and sustained care are not only a treatment option; it is a social responsibility to safeguard the next generation's mental health against the prevalence of anxiety disorders.

3.7.3. Call to Action for Increased Awareness and Resources

In addressing growing numbers of anxiety disorders among children and adolescents, there must be a strong call to action to raise awareness and allocate resources. The mental health culture for these young people remains bleak, with huge numbers of youth enduring silently without adequate protective mechanisms. Increased awareness programs can be an important driver in de-stigmatizing mental illness and facilitating early identification of anxiety disorders. Schools, healthcare professionals, and communities must work together such that individuals are educated on the signs and symptoms of anxiety, and seeking help becomes the norm. This proactive approach is paramount in enabling interventions that are timely to have a significant impact on the mental health status of affected youths. For awareness campaigns to be effective, certain resources must be developed and provided. School-level interventions such as mindfulness interventions have been promising in improving the emotional resilience of adolescents, but their deployment across different education settings is anything but standardized. The evidence indicates that gender differences could be influential in shaping the impact of these types of interventions, calling for tailored interventions that account for developmental needs. For instance, mindfulness training has been found to be emotionally more beneficial for female students compared to male ones, thus illuminating the requirement for adaptive intervention that resonates with various groups of students (Britton et al., 2018). By equipping schools with the tools and frameworks that are required, it is possible to create comfortable environments that can manage better anxiety disorders. Besides, psychoeducational interventions (PIs) provide an exciting platform for enhancing understanding and anxiety management among adolescents. PIs are able to provide critical information on symptoms of anxiety, self-management, and communication skills, therefore inducing coping and resilience (Jones et al., 2017). Nevertheless, the current state of PIs requires enhancement and more integration into systematic adolescent mental health treatment processes. Few have described the existing imbalance in the effectiveness of such interventions, and we need more rigorous research to normalize PIs and analyze their components deliberately. In favor of greater investment and resources expended on developing and disseminating PIs, we can most effectively equip adolescents with the knowledge and competencies necessary to vanquish anxiety disorders, ultimately bolstering their overall mental health outcomes.

REFERENCES

1. Albert, U., Apergis-Schoute, A., Brakoulias, V., Carmi, L., et al. (2019). Early intervention for obsessive compulsive disorder: An expert consensus statement. https://core.ac.uk/download/287581694.pdf (accessed on 14th October 2025).
2. Angelo, M., Saliani, R., Baiocco, R., Barcaccia, B., Francesco, M., et al. (2017). Dysfunctional eating behaviors, anxiety and depression in Italian boys and girls: The role of mass media. https://core.ac.uk/download/127586647.pdf (accessed on 14th October 2025).
3. Asarnow, J. R., Hughes, J. L., Langer, D. A., Tompson, M. C., et al. (2017). Family-focused treatment for childhood depression: Model and case illustrations. https://open.bu.edu/bitstream/2144/24312/1/2015%20Accepted%20Tompson%20Langer%20Hughes%20Asarnow.pdf (accessed on 14th October 2025).
4. Baena Medina, M. S., Hidalgo García, M. V., Jiménez García, L., León, C., et al. (2019). Effectiveness of structural-strategic family therapy in the treatment of adolescents with mental health problems and their families. https://core.ac.uk/download/225123947.pdf (accessed on 14th October 2025).
5. Barlow, D., Barnes, D., Crenna-Jennings, W., Department of Health, Hargrave, D., James, A. C., Kendall, P. C., et al. (2020). The identification and psychological treatment of panic disorder in adolescents: A survey of CAMHS clinicians. https://core.ac.uk/download/287579423.pdf (accessed on 14th October 2025).
6. Barlow, J., Day, C., Goens, C., Stewart-Brown, S., et al. (2007). A systematic review of reviews of interventions to promote mental health and prevent mental health problems in children and young people. https://core.ac.uk/download/49361.pdf (accessed on 14th October 2025).
7. Belfer, M. L. (2005). Child and adolescent mental health around the world: Challenges for progress. https://core.ac.uk/download/pdf/86268.pdf (accessed on 14th October 2025).
8. Benelli, E., & Bianco, F. (2015). Models of collaboration between psychologist and family doctor: A systematic review of primary care psychology. https://core.ac.uk/download/80154468.pdf (accessed on 14th October 2025).
9. Bertino, M. D., Knight, T., Lewis, A. J., Ricciardelli, L. A., et al. (2013). Reducing parental anxiety using a family-based intervention for youth mental health: A randomized controlled trial. https://core.ac.uk/download/77140438.pdf (accessed on 14th October 2025).

10. Bevan Jones, R., Jones, I., Simpson, S., Smith, D. J., et al. (2017). Psychoeducational interventions in adolescent depression: A systematic review. https://core.ac.uk/download/132211505.pdf (accessed on 14th October 2025).

11. Briggs-Gowan, M. J., Carter, A. S., Godoy, L., Mian, N. D., et al. (2012). Patterns of anxiety symptoms in toddlers and preschool-age children: Evidence of early differentiation. https://core.ac.uk/download/215508112.pdf (accessed on 14th October 2025).

12. Britton, W. B., Eichel, K., Gold, J., Kang, Y., et al. (2018). Gender differences in response to a school-based mindfulness training intervention for early adolescents. https://core.ac.uk/download/186330305.pdf (accessed on 14th October 2025).

13. Brudniak, K., Czyczerska, M., Gadżała, K., Garbino, D., et al. (2025). Mental disorders in children and adolescents in crisis situations: The impact of the COVID-19 pandemic and armed conflicts - Types of disorders, effects, and intervention strategies. https://core.ac.uk/download/636385734.pdf (accessed on 14th October 2025).

14. Caiozzo, C., Carson, A. M., Dolan, B. K., Karst, J. S., et al. (2018). Examining the links between challenging behaviors in youth with ASD and parental stress, mental health, and involvement: Applying an adaptation of the family stress model to families of youth with ASD. https://core.ac.uk/download/213087175.pdf (accessed on 14th October 2025).

15. Calderoni, D., Cerutti, R., Faedda, N., Guidetti, V., et al. (2017). Metacognition and headache: Which is the role in childhood and adolescence? https://core.ac.uk/download/153366758.pdf (accessed on 14th October 2025).

16. Campisi, S. C., Savel, K. A., & Korczak, D. J. (2024). The relationship between anxiety and diet quality in adolescent populations: A cross-sectional analysis. *The British Journal of Nutrition.* https://www.semanticscholar.org/paper/18418706f063030665d74b186799edf049039fbd (accessed on 14th October 2025).

17. Carlyle, D. (2014). With a little help from FUN FRIENDS young children can overcome anxiety. https://core.ac.uk/download/286716166.pdf (accessed on 14th October 2025).

18. Cerniglia, L., Erriu, M., & Cimino, S. (2020). The role of family relationships in eating disorders in adolescents: A narrative review. https://core.ac.uk/download/296244843.pdf (accessed on 14th October 2025).

19. Cooper, P., Creswell, C., Murayama, K., Reardon, T., et al. (2017). Complete recovery from anxiety disorders following Cognitive Behavioral

Therapy in children and adolescents: A meta-analysis. https://core.ac.uk/download/74207012.pdf (accessed on 14th October 2025).

20. Coyne, I., Gower, C., Healy, M., McNamara, N., et al. (2015). Adolescents' and parents' views of Child and Adolescent Mental Health Services (CAMHS) in Ireland. https://core.ac.uk/download/30649897.pdf (accessed on 14th October 2025).
21. Emerson, C. P. (2009). *Exercise and its Effects on Depression in Young Adults.* https://core.ac.uk/download/5067419.pdf (accessed on 14th October 2025).
22. Ernst, M., Green-Golan, L., Leschek, E., Merke, D., et al. (2010). Psychiatric characterization of children with genetic causes of hyperandrogenism. https://core.ac.uk/download/55802070.pdf (accessed on 14th October 2025).
23. Gavin, B., Honorio Neto, F., McNicholas, F., Mulligan, A., et al. (2017). Attitudes and reported practice of pediatricians and child psychiatrists regarding the assessment and treatment of ADHD in Ireland. https://core.ac.uk/download/159108018.pdf (accessed on 14th October 2025).
24. Johnson, S. J., & Wolke, D. (2013). Behavioral outcomes and psychopathology during adolescence. https://core.ac.uk/download/9847191.pdf (accessed on 14th October 2025).
25. Kodali, M., Bodepudi, S., Benerji, T., Parvathaneni, K., & Manam, J. R. (2021). Psychiatric diagnosis of children presenting with medically unexplained symptoms. *Journal of Indian Association for Child and Adolescent Mental Health, 17*, 48–59. https://www.semanticscholar.org/paper/d48d8b16ecabcafb70952866513a4748ae2b1497 (accessed on 14th October 2025).
26. Lal, P., & Gupta, S. (2025). Psychological impact of COVID-19 on children and adolescents: A narrative review of mental health challenges, interventions, and long-term trajectories. *Cureus, 17.* https://www.semanticscholar.org/paper/81debd77aed1a896851371911 9eb9ddcd134cadf (accessed on 14th October 2025).
27. Lawrence, D., Hafekost, J., Ainley, J., Boterhoven de Haan, K., Sawyer, M., Johnson, S., & Zubrick, S. R. (2015). *The Mental Health of Children and Adolescents: Report on the Second Australian Child and Adolescent Survey of Mental Health and Wellbeing.* https://core.ac.uk/download/pdf/30671460.pdf (accessed on 14th October 2025).
28. Lloyd, C., Machingura, T., Molineux, M., Shum, K., et al. (2017). Effectiveness of sensory modulation in treating sensory modulation disorders in adults with schizophrenia: A systematic literature review.

https://core.ac.uk/download/196605658.pdf (accessed on 14th October 2025).

29. Short, J. D. (2013). *Psychosocial Implications for Students with Learning Disabilities.* https://core.ac.uk/download/60568983.pdf (accessed on 14th October 2025).
30. Skrypnyk, T., Martsenkovsky, I., & Martsenkovska, I. (2024). A longitudinal study of child and adolescent psychopathology in conditions of the war in Ukraine. *European Psychiatry, 67*, S74–S75. https://www.semanticscholar.org/paper/e3f8c9c39245f0ac5709149d512f8692074f56a7 (accessed on 14th October 2025).
31. Smith, M., & Storey, P. (2008). *Methods and Approaches to Improving the Emotional Health and Well-Being of Children: A Briefing Paper Concerning Interventions to Prevent Internalizing Disorders.* https://core.ac.uk/download/pdf/82102.pdf (accessed on 14th October 2025).
32. Stansfeld, S. A. (2016). Mental health inequalities in adolescents growing up in post-apartheid South Africa: Cross-sectional survey, SHaW Study. https://core.ac.uk/download/77040906.pdf (accessed on 14th October 2025).
33. Tembo, C., Portsmouth, L., & Burns, S. (2024). Cultural and social factors associated with generalized anxiety disorder among adolescent mothers during the postpartum period in Malawi: A cross-sectional survey. *BMC Global and Public Health, 2.* https://www.semanticscholar.org/paper/ad59c881b8af5ac893b0bd930ced4aa4e6e9a93c (accessed on 14th October 2025).
34. Walder, N., Frey, A., Berger, T., & Schmidt, S. J. (2025). Digital mental health interventions for the prevention and treatment of social anxiety disorder in children, adolescents, and young adults: Systematic review and meta-analysis of randomized controlled trials. *Journal of Medical Internet Research, 27.* https://www.semanticscholar.org/paper/4ff7a16dc6ca1491b85b9f7d04ba8202875a8ae6 (accessed on 14th October 2025).
35. Woodie, K. L. (2009). *Childhood Anxiety: How Schools Identify, Assess, Provide Resources to And Refer Students with Anxiety.* https://core.ac.uk/download/5067576.pdf (accessed on 14th October 2025).

Chapter 4

Mood Disorders

Contents

INTRODUCTION

The prevalence of mood disorders among children and adolescents is now a hot topic of conversation in current mental health discourse. Such disorders, with their persistent sadness, irritability, and emotional dysregulation, have the prognostic potential to curtail daily functioning and world quality of life. It is crucial that an individual take into account the developmental nuances in mood disorders since they manifest differently in youths than in adults and often co-occur with other psychiatric conditions. The impact of these disorders transmits beyond the individual to families, schools, and communities. There is thus a mounting need for a broad literature of research on the distinct environmental, biological, and psychological risk factors for mood disorders in early age groups. The successful battle against these issues demands sensitivity to the complexity of childhood experience, particularly as it sketches out emotional trajectories over the long term. Further, the complex interaction between mood disorders and comorbid conditions deserves close study. Literature is rich in evidence of high associations between literacy difficulties and psychiatric illness in youths, which implies the possibility that reading and comprehension difficulties can amplify mood-related problems. Current reports indicate that children with literacy difficulties often have elevated rates of emotional and behavioral problems, such as anxiety and depression. This two-way impact is due to literacy issues being able to not only introduce inadequacy and stress but also exacerbate mood disorders. This two-way impact demonstrates the need for interventions that address not only mood symptomatology but also the root literacy problems. As the study continues to unveil the interconnectedness, it becomes clear that comprehensive treatment approaches are needed in order to treat the mood disorders in addition to their comorbidities adequately (Angold et al., 2006). With these complexities in mind, it is imperative that early detection and intervention approaches be promoted that work to reduce the adverse impact of mood disorders on children and adolescents. Identification of symptoms at an early stage and their potential relation to more general developmental problems can lead to more effective treatment strategies. This needs the concerted efforts of parents, healthcare providers, and teachers in establishing the knowledge of mood disorders as tangible and treatable illnesses rather than as variations of normal child behaviors. Through open dialogues and awareness raising, the stakeholders can de-stigmatize these illnesses and empower their bared youth. With ongoing education about mood disorders in the context of developing youth, increasing research and real-world programs will be necessary in advancing a future generation that is emotionally stable and resilient (Emerson et al., 2009).

Definition of Mood Disorders

Mood disorders, which encompass widespread alterations in emotional states, are a wide range of mental illnesses that significantly affect the day-to-day life of children's and adolescents. Mood disorders can range from depressive disorders, such as major depression, to bipolar disorder, involving repeated cycles of mania and depression. Mood disorders can lead to interpersonal functioning impairment, problem in academic performance, and reduced quality of life. The onset is often in late childhood or adolescence, and thus early recognition and treatment are essential. Mood disorders, if not treated, will lead to long-term adverse effects, including susceptibility to self-injury and drug abuse. Practically, it is necessary to recognize the complexity of mood disorders, as they are influenced by genetic, environmental, and psychological factors that influence each other in a complex way. Symptoms of mood disorders in children and adolescents are very distinctive and thus make it hard to diagnose on time. In children, the depressive mood can be expressed in irritability or engaging in problem behavior rather than manifesting as usual expressions of sadness. For instance, a child with major depressive disorder may express loss of interest in activities previously enjoyable, appetite changes, and difficulty concentrating. Moreover, bipolar disorder presents with various challenges; manic phases normally come in the form of boundless energy, leading to impulsiveness and poor judgment.

Figure 4.1. Mood disorders can lead to challenges in interpersonal relationships, academic performance, and overall quality of life.
Source: https://atlanticbehavioralhealth.com/wp-content/uploads/2024/09/local-woman-suffering-from-mood-disorder.webp.

This variation in symptomology underscores the importance of the education of pediatric mental illness by parents, teachers, and health workers. If signs are detected early, stakeholders are able to ensure intervention strategies that can possibly decrease the long-term impacts of such diseases. Social attitudes and stigmas regarding mental health play a great role in the conditions of adolescents suffering from mood disorders. Stigma can make the children, and their families feel ashamed or stigmatized, deterring them from seeking necessary interventions. Moreover, pervasive media coverage by and social expectation has the potential to exacerbate feelings of hopelessness and inadequacy among adolescents. As implied by current research, mainstream cultural portrayals of mental health are superficial and unsophisticated and fail to convey the intricacies that are encountered by people with mood disorders. Shifting such cultural narratives and fostering more advanced ways of comprehending mental health is vital for the establishment of cultures that empower children and adolescents. Hence, mental health education is not just about symptoms and treatments but also the deconstruction of stigma and open communication regarding mood disorders (Schiller et al., 2008) (Figure 4.1).

Importance of Addressing Mood Disorders in Youth

Identification and intervention of adolescents' mood disorders are necessary to support healthy pathways of development. Research shows that depression is increasing among adolescents, with millions of adolescents experiencing major depressive episodes each year. This is a threat which requires collaborative interventions in school systems, particularly because adolescents from lower socioeconomics are more at risk for mental health problems. Around 80% of mental health treatment is accessed through schools, attesting to their pivotal position in providing services. Helpful measures, such as universal depression education and targeted screening programs, must be implemented within school environments in order to educate students about mental illness issues and create a helpful environment that encourages help-seeking (Hari et al., 2017). By addressing mood disorders early, we can prevent long-term mental health issues and improve academic and social relationships for those affected young individuals. The consequences of mood disorders among teens affect not just the individual but subsequently flow to the family and community as a whole. When teens and children struggle with these mental disorders, the family life becomes tense and interrupted. For instance, kids who have a parent stationed in combat zones are more likely to develop anxiety and emotional disturbance, as has been reported in a study conducted by the American Psychological Association. Such family disturbances may also exacerbate the mental illness of teens and create a cycle of distress that is perpetuating, undermining the quality of functioning in the family. Treating mood disorders among adolescents is more than a matter of mental health; it is a public health emergency that necessitates coordination among schools, families, and community resources. By providing an affirmative environment that promotes awareness and intervention, we can help families through the complexity of mental health and improve the well-being of all family members. Furthermore, neglecting mood disorders in young people comes with the result of experiencing long-term gains which endure into adulthood. Teenagers battling untreated mood disorders will likely encounter ongoing problems like poor grades, interpersonal relationship conflict, and increased drug and suicidal ideation risk. Evidence shows that earlier intervention is linked with improved outcomes, and thus proactive action is crucial in detecting and treating mental health issues while they arise (Hari et al., 2017). This necessity to society involves structural reorganization of the delivery of mental health care, particularly within schools where youth spend a significant portion of their time. By adopting comprehensive mental health measures encompassing screening, education, and intervention, we can profoundly alter the life course of adolescents with mood disorders, ultimately fostering healthier generations in the future (Figure 4.2).

Figure 4.2. As children and teens struggle with mental health issues, the dynamics within their families often become tense and fragmented.

Source: https://www.quickanddirtytips.com/wp-content/uploads/2023/01/shutter-stock_398804881.jpg.

4.1. TYPES OF MOOD DISORDERS

One of the most prevalent mood disorders among children and adolescents, Major Depressive Disorder (MDD) stands out due to its pervasive impact on daily functioning and general well-being. Characterized by prolonged sadness, loss of interest in activities previously enjoyed, and significant weight loss or gain or sleep patterns. Onset is typically in late adolescence, but symptom development can begin earlier. According to available research, MDD expression can lead to academic difficulties, conflicted family relationships, and increased susceptibility to self-harm. Notably, the psychological well-being impacts of depression also become evident outside of the childhood years, as studies have established that depression symptoms which arise during these developmental years may persist into the adult years, marking the importance of early intervention and support to at-risk adolescents (Emerson et al., 2009). Another severe mood disorder in teens and teenagers is bipolar disorder, which is typified by manic and depressive episodes. The manic episodes may include elevated mood, increased energy, and negligent behavior, while depressive episodes may be similar to what has been described in MDD. These pendulum swings back and forth between the two extremes would disrupt school performance and social relationships and thus result in significant impairment in daily functioning. The difficulty in diagnosing bipolar disorder in adolescents is because other mental disorders, such as ADHD, which they share similar behavioral manifestations, create overlapping. It is remarkable that it is important to identify and treat bipolar disorder in adolescents because inadequately treated episodes have severe consequences, such as increased substance abuse and suicidal ideation (Johnson et al., 2013). Additionally, Anxiety Disorders, although classified separately from mood disorders, are often found to co-occur with mood disorders in children, rendering clinical presentation more complicated. SAD and GAD in children can exacerbate depression symptoms in addition to augmenting depression symptoms, ultimately affecting emotional regulation and coping in children. These disorders usually present with inappropriate concern, fear of social performance, and somatic symptoms like restlessness and tiredness. Given that adolescents are susceptible to greater emotional fluctuation and social stress, the combination of anxiety and mood disorders means that they are in dire need of comprehensive evaluation and personalized treatment strategies. Unless it is intervened upon, kids and teens can go on being vulnerable to all manner of psychological issues that have the potential to impact their development and emotional health in the future (Emerson et al., 2009).

4.1.1. Major Depressive Disorder

Investigating the complexities of Major Depressive Disorder (MDD) in children and adolescents is central to gaining insight into the presentation of mood disorder within years of development. MDD consists of low mood, hopelessness, and considerable loss of interest in previously enjoyable activities. Presentation in children and adolescents is often misinterpreted or overlooked due to variations in emotional expression during development. Teachers and caregivers need to be observant as detection at an early stage can affect treatment considerably. Research affirms that teenagers are unlikely to seek help voluntarily and therefore emphasize the need for active detection and intervention strategies specifically tailored for this age group (Bertino et al., 2013). With treatment and care ongoing within this paradigm, understanding the unique presentation of MDD in adolescents also facilitates better communication between healthcare professionals, families, and individuals themselves. Interventions for MDD may involve, at times, not only individual therapeutic interventions but also family involvement to engage recovery processes. Most significantly, family therapies have gained much popularity since they target personal symptoms and context variables of the family that may be the cause of the disorder (Bertino et al., 2013). Family participation programs during treatment can de-mystify communication blocks and assist defiant adolescents who are not willing to accept conventional therapies.

Figure 4.3. Major depressive disorder (MDD) in children and adolescents is crucial for understanding how mood disorders manifest during formative years.

Source: https://mentalhealthcenterkids.com/cdn/shop/articles/depression_in_children_2048x.jpg?v=1749440158.

By employing a family system approach, practitioners can establish an open dialogue environment of understanding. Such holistic interventions also leverage family relationships to support and encourage positive behavior and coping mechanisms. This integrated methodology understands that adolescent mental health is not something that should be treated in a vacuum, with the family's active participation seen as essential to the therapeutic process. Furthermore, the impact of MDD goes beyond the patient and is expressed in family functioning, academic performance, and peer relationships. Chronic impact of depression on the adolescent can disrupt academic performance, leading to high-risk potential for future psychological distress. Research also established that early intervention does not just decrease symptoms but also works to increase family functioning and general well-being (Bertino et al., 2013). Thus, prevention of the occurrence of major depressive episodes to a level where they could become chronic is of utmost significance. Continued study of evidence-based interventions will specify best practices for family involvement and facilitating adolescents to handle their emotional landscape better. Early identification and treatment of MDD in the course of critical periods of development are essential in ensuring resilience and fostering mental stability over a lifetime (Figure 4.3).

4.1.2. Bipolar Disorder

Bipolar disorder, characterized by extreme mood, energy, and activity level changes, also has severe diagnostic issues in the child and adolescent population. Presentation of bipolar in the young can be quite different from the adult version and poses diagnostic challenges in making an accurate diagnosis and treatment. Because of the shifting perspectives regarding this disorder, consideration must also be given to the child's developmental status. Expression of symptoms is determined by variables such as normative behavior patterns, environmental influences, and hormonal fluctuations during adolescence. As clinicians sift through the subtleties, they must be capable of differentiating between bipolar symptoms and other psychiatric illnesses and understanding the prevalent comorbidities that complicate diagnosis. Thus, the fine-grained diagnosis of mood disorders in youth needs a robust framework that encompasses developmental considerations, so that adolescents and children are provided with appropriate and personalized treatment that addresses their unique presentations of bipolar disorder (Bossewitch et al., 2010). Studies on the topic in recent years have bridged tremendous leaps in the capacity to identify early-onset bipolar spectrum disorders (BPSDs); however, such increased rates of diagnosis carry with them serious ethical issues. As diagnosed BPSD prevalence has skyrocketed in clinical practice, there is concern that the diagnostic criteria are too sweeping or too poorly defined. Such broadening of diagnostic criteria would result in overlabeling, with a risk for harm through unwarranted treatment, specifically with the use of antipsychotic medications. Such concerns require critical attention to societal pressures upon adolescents and how these pressures might contribute to the clinician's interpretations of behavior. As the media has a deep impact on the public's attitude and information about mental health, it also helps in rising anxiety about child conduct and thereby affects clinical assessments and decision-making (Bossewitch et al., 2010). This interaction between social attitudes and clinical practice finds the significance of accurate diagnostic categories emphasizing the child's wellness. The changing environment of mental health assessment and treatment is further entangled by advancements in pediatric psychoactive pharmacotherapy for children with mood disorders. In growing awareness of pediatric bipolar disorder, the use of medication as the first line of treatment also increases. Whereas pharmacologic interventions have a place, they should be undertaken with care, bearing in mind the long-term effects on developing brains. The risks of psychotropic medication in children, particularly to psychosocial functioning and neurodevelopment, must be given careful consideration. Furthermore, the absence of complete guidelines for the evaluation and treatment of children with BPSDs increases the risk. Amidst all these complexities, there should be an effort from a multidisciplinary team to institute an atmosphere of teamwork between clinicians, researchers, and families. Lastly, determining effective treatments for adolescent bipolar disorder relies upon the intersection of clinical experience with developing research and public awareness (Arnold et al., 2009) (Figure 4.4).

Figure 4.4. Bipolar disorder, characterized by dramatic shifts in mood, energy, and activity levels, poses significant diagnostic challenges for children and adolescents.

Source: https://i.ytimg.com/vi/XQ2PbPr2AH4/maxresdefault.jpg.

4.1.3. Persistent Depressive Disorder (Dysthymia)

Persistent depressive disorder (dysthymia) is a severe mood disorder of children and adolescents, characterized by the long persistence of depression symptoms for one or more years in adolescents. Unlike major depression, dysthymia symptoms may be less severe but long-standing and significantly impair daily functioning and quality of life. This chronic condition of sadness can lead to difficulty in social relationships, school performance, and self-worth. Children and teens who have dysthymia are not necessarily openly showing symptoms of the disorder, making it difficult for parents and teachers to recognize the disorder. It is important to recognize the nuances of dysthymia in order to be able to intervene early and treat it, because overlooking these symptoms can have a lasting effect on the emotional and psychological development of an adolescent. There is evidence that an overwhelming number of mood disorders, such as chronic depressive disorder, exist in children and teenagers. Environmental stress and genetic predisposition can be reasons for the development of dysthymia in adolescents. Initial reports show that individuals with a family background of depression are at high risk of developing mood disorders like dysthymia.

Figure 4.5. Persistent depressive disorder (dysthymia) represents a significant mood disorder impacting children and adolescents, characterized by a prolonged duration of depressive symptoms lasting for at least one year in youths.

Source: https://www.verywellmind.com/thmb/D1Mm25h1LZHi-x4UK-k12AtLoK0=/2014x0/filters:no_upscale():max_bytes(150000):strip_icc()/dysthymia-5665f0875f9b583dc397ea35.jpg.

For example, studies have established that children of parents with recurring unipolar depression are at risk of developing a range of psychopathological conditions from mood and disruptive disorders which could occur in tandem with psychotic symptoms (Bevan-Jones et al., 2016). All these factors point to the importance of continuous observation of children's mental disorders in families with established evidence-based psychological problems, since intervention techniques would be able to minimize the long-term impact of dysthymia. Occupational therapy is essential to resolving challenges engendered by continuous depressive disorder among youths. A treatment guide to enable social engagement in adolescents with depressive disorders has increasingly been crucial (Marvel et al., 2015). Dysthymia symptoms can significantly hinder a teenager's social participation, and it has a negative influence on social as well as family relationships. Therefore, treatments focusing on the enhancement of social skills and enhancing healthy social interactions are essential treatment elements. By incorporating the Ecology of Human Performance model, occupational therapists are able to provide interventions that address depressive symptoms but also promote higher levels of participation in everyday social contexts. An integrated social focus is key to improving quality of life for those with persistent depressive disorder (Figure 4.5).

4.2. SYMPTOMS AND DIAGNOSIS

Diagnosis of mood disorders in children and adolescents is especially challenging since the symptoms are variable and may overlap with normal changes of development. Persistent sadness, irritability, fatigue, and change in sleep or appetite are the most common symptoms. The difficulty is that children's inability to communicate their feelings makes exact diagnosis impossible. Identification of these symptoms depends on astute observations by care providers and clinicians, in addition to standardized measurement tools that quantify the degree of emotional distress. Appreciation of the subjective symptomatology of mood disorders is important, given that children might report feelings of hopelessness or worthlessness in ways that differ from those of adults. Timely intervention depends on early identification of these symptoms, which can meaningfully impact long-term developmental pathways and resilience of impacted youths. The diagnostic assessment for mood disorders typically involves a comprehensive evaluation that consists of clinical interviews, observation of behavior, and collateral collection of information from family or caregivers. In children and adolescents, mental health professionals must take into consideration contextual factors like family history and psychosocial stressors. The multi-dimensional assessment is called for so that differential diagnosis can be made between normal mood fluctuations that occur during the adolescent phase and those that indicate a mood disorder. In addition, co-morbidity of disorders such as anxiety disorders or ADHD complicates diagnostic presentation. In one such sample of subjects with an At-Risk Mental State (ARMS), for instance, a high 70% of them had co-morbid mental health disorders, with mood disorders being particularly prevalent. Such findings further emphasize the importance of thorough assessment to determine individual challenges to a child's mental health (Preti et al., 2014). Accurate diagnosis is not only required for treatment planning but also for the development of supportive interventions in family and educational contexts. Observation of the child within their environment—e.g., viewing school or family interactions—can provide additional information about their mood state and functional capacity. Utilization of evidence-based rating scales and guidelines enables clinicians to assess the risks of mood disorders in a standardized fashion. For instance, longitudinal research indicates that even though many teens had alarming symptoms, low rates of long-term transition to psychosis persist, defying certain fears about the premature diagnosis of mood disorders (Preti et al., 2014). This underlines the importance of monitoring and treatment of children over a period of time, as most demonstrate a noteworthy symptom reduction with intervention. Therefore, precise diagnosis is critical in advancing better mental health outcomes among adolescents and children with mood disorders.

4.2.1. Common Symptoms in Children and Teens

When it comes to mood disorders among children and adolescents, one should also consider the vastness of common symptoms that may arise as separate emotional and behavioral problems. The symptoms would usually consist of ongoing sadness, irritability, or mood swings that have a profound effect on daily functioning. Children will exhibit a lack of interest in previously pleasurable activities, leading to withdrawal from social interactions. Furthermore, disturbances in appetite and sleep also usually follow such mood disturbances, producing weight shifts and fatigue that only serve to exacerbate their emotional state. They must be recognized because they often reflect typical developmental concerns, making identification and treatment of such states in younger individuals difficult. Another imperative aspect of mood disorders in children and adolescents is the impact on school performance and reading skills, especially the way they correlate with emotional difficulties. There is evidence to show that problems with reading skills tend to appear along with emotional and behavioral issues, which could suggest an interlinked connection between intellectual issues and mood disorders. For example, children with difficulties in reading might also feel greater anxiety and frustration, which further contribute to irritability or depressed mood. The repetitive aspect of such problems reveals that children with mood disorders are not only confronted with emotional issues but also with academic difficulties, making their development more complicated. Treatment of both literacy issues and mood symptomatology at the same time may be necessary if treatment is to succeed, as problems in one domain can compound difficulties in the other (Angold et al., 2006). Moreover, co-morbid anxiety and depressive symptoms may play a significant role in shaping child and adolescent behavioral tendencies, to present either as internalizing or externalizing behavior. Internalization of behaviors can be expressed as withdrawal or hypersensitivity to social settings, and externalization can be expressed as aggression or oppositional defiance. This co-morbid presentation complicates diagnosis of mood disorders, particularly since many of these children are capable of presenting symptoms that cross over ADHD or conduct disorders. The related nature of these symptoms requires an entire assessment that considers the child's emotional and behavioral world in its entirety. Effective management strategies should incorporate therapeutic treatment that is tailored to the individual needs of the child, with the understanding that co-occurring conditions require special treatments that focus on the co-morbidities of mood disorders (Emerson et al., 2009) (Figure 4.6).

Figure 4.6. Children may exhibit a decrease in interest in activities they once enjoyed, leading to social withdrawal and isolation.

Source: https://www.psychiatryadvisor.com/wp-content/uploads/sites/8/2019/10/Boy-Excluded_G_3523-000004.jpg.

4.2.2. Diagnostic Criteria According to DSM-5

The Diagnostic and Statistical Manual of Mental Disorders, Fifth Edition (DSM-5), presents a comprehensive system of diagnosis for mood disorders in young people, a significant evolution in the diagnosis. It is especially detailed in specifying criteria for major depressive disorder (MDD) and persistent depressive disorder (dysthymia), with emphasis placed on duration of symptoms and impairment in functioning. For instance, MDD is to be diagnosed in a child who exhibits five or more listed symptoms for two weeks, including changes in mood, energy, and interest. Of note, the DSM-5 places particular stress on variability of presentation among younger individuals, and that clinicians are careful to stay vigilant for departures from adult expression that may involve irritability or somatic complaints. This personalized method was a new acknowledgment of development factors in mental health. In addition, the DSM-5 also categorizes other mood disorders, such as bipolar disorder, which prove to be difficult to diagnose in adolescents. Teenagers may be impulsive and experience mood swings that could bewilder clinicians, particularly in terms of distinguishing between mood symptoms and normal developments. Transparent diagnostic criteria involve a requirement to observe discrete episodes of mania or hypomania, with criteria specifying the intensity and duration of the symptom. These are crucial nuances in diagnosis because misinterpretation can lead to inappropriate treatments, which can permanently impact a child's psychological development. With mounting prevalence of mood disorders among teens, correct diagnostic processes as defined by the DSM-5 become essential in delivering timely and suitable interventions. In the case of mood disorders in youth, research evidence illustrates alarming tendencies in accordance with DSM-5 criteria. For example, in line with studies, the majority of secondary school students display symptoms of various mood disorders with a very high rate of prevalence for anxiety disorders (Direkvand-Moghadam et al., 2017). Moreover, those studies investigating risk mental states among young people indicate huge functional impairment with the majority fulfilling the criteria for comorbid disorders, most significantly affective disorders, as shown in studies where 70% of the participants had such disturbances (Preti et al., 2014). Therefore, the application of DSM-5 criteria is not only used to enable diagnosis but to act as a foundation for measuring the prevalence and risk of mood disorders in children and adolescents. These are considerations to be aware of by teachers and mental health professionals who must develop and implement effective support mechanisms within schools.

4.2.3. Challenges in Diagnosing Mood Disorders in Youth

The challenges of mood disorder diagnosis among youth are multi-faceted and are based on developmental problems as well as societal culture. Kids and adolescents all exhibit wide ranges of behavior in attempting to balance emotional and psychological development through their formative years. Such developmentally based variability often complicates the assessment process since normative behaviors in one phase can represent mood disorders elsewhere. For instance, mood swings or irritability might be explained by normal adolescence and hence not be seen as an indicator of serious conditions.

Second, clinicians are faced with the issue of how to make a discrimination between situational stressors that cause short-term emotional responses and extended mood disorders that require treatment. These nuances emphasize the need for greater vigilance and improved training of health practitioners to deliver accurate diagnoses in such a vulnerable population. Adding to the diagnostic difficulties of pediatric mood disorder is the changing world of mental health criteria and the possibility of over-diagnosis. Over the last decade, the growing trend of diagnosing pediatric bipolar disorder has sparked great concern among mental health professionals.

Figure 4.7. Children and adolescents exhibit a wide range of behaviors as they navigate emotional and psychological changes during their formative years.

Source: https://www.verywellmind.com/thmb/yceFMrVdR0isaJ_ApIFaLanxq2Y=/3867x0/filters:no_upscale():max_bytes(150000):strip_icc()/522302201-56a795723df78cf772975eb0.jpg.

The critics believe that expanding the criteria might lead to pathologizing normal childhood behaviors, as seen in the growing practice of administering youth's anti-psychotic medications. This practice falls under ethical scrutiny of treatment techniques and long-term effects of treating youths who are likely experiencing normal development issues and not pathological disorders. For instance, the mood variation typical of children needs to be distinguished from the damaging effects caused by misdiagnosis and further research has to be conducted on the socio-cultural reasons for these emerging diagnoses (Bossewitch et al., 2010). Besides, the presence of social expectations and media portrayals of mental illness makes diagnosis more complicated. The pervasive influence of media has a tendency to shape parents' and teachers' definitions of normal behavior and normal emotional reaction. Increased anxiety over mood disorders has coincided with hypersensationalized portrayals of teen activity, which have fostered ignorance and fear surrounding mental illness. Cultural myths have a tendency to pressure practitioners into following current trends in diagnosing and treating adolescents at the danger of misdiagnosis or over-medication. For example, behaviors characterized as irrational or defiant are also viewed in a clinical context, and the multitudinous context of the stimuli for these behaviors is dismissed. Understanding such dynamics is needed to guide more accurate diagnostic criteria based on children's and adolescents lived experiences and psychological nuances so that in the end, mental health care can be more efficient (Emerson et al., 2009) (Figure 4.7).

4.3. CAUSES AND RISK FACTORS

Identifying the etiology and risk factors of mood disorders in children and adolescents requires a multifaceted process since these disorders are typically the result of a mixture of genetic, environmental, and psychologic factors. Genetic susceptibility is the most important factor, with investigations indicating that children who have a family history of mood disorders tend to develop the same disorders. Environmental factors, such as exposure to trauma, stress, and conflict in the family, may further elevate this risk. Additionally, the role of adverse childhood experiences, such as abuse or neglect, is also critical, as these experiences can lead to the learning of dysfunctional emotional regulation and coping mechanisms, thereby leaving an individual at risk for mood disorders. The interconnection of the factors demonstrates why early identification and intervention are needed to counteract these risks. The contribution of psychological problems to mood disorder etiology cannot be overstated. Cognition patterns, particularly poor emotional regulation and dysfunctional thinking, can serve as a window into understanding the onset of depressive and anxiety disorders in children. Dysfunctional thinking in a child, based on external pressures such as performance demands or peer dynamics, can put them at higher risk for mood disturbance. In addition, peer relationships are essential; bullying or exclusion can lead to worthlessness and helplessness, classic symptoms of mood disorders. Comorbidities such as attention deficit hyperactivity disorder and learning disabilities add additional layers of complexity to the dynamic by presenting additional barriers to the development of healthy emotionality. It is therefore critical that these psychological underpinnings are fully understood to facilitate effective prevention and treatment. Current studies have highlighted the interactions between reading problems and mood disorders and indicated that academically struggling children are more likely to develop emotional and conduct problems. Reading problems are often present alongside anxiety and depression, in which stress and frustration over reading difficulties can fuel feelings of inadequacy and low self-esteem (Emerson et al., 2009). The relationship is bidirectional; not only do literacy problems result in mood disorders, but the emotional pain of having these problems can interfere with academic achievement, creating a vicious cycle. Furthermore, children with neurodevelopmental disorders, such as autism, may have specific trouble with reading comprehension, complicating their emotional lives further. Therefore, literacy issues are essential in any combined mental health intervention strategy, since they may diminish some of the resulting mood disorder risks (Emerson et al., 2009).

4.3.1. Genetic Predisposition

The concept of genetic predisposition offers meaningful information regarding the progress of mood disorders in children and adolescents. Experiments indicate that genetic influences can have a significant influence on one's likelihood of acquiring such conditions. For instance, familial aggregation studies have proven that children whose parents suffer from mood disorders have greater possibilities of developing the same and indicating a significant genetic influence. In addition, specific genes that are involved in neurotransmitter regulation, such as the genes controlling serotonin transport, have been implicated in susceptibility to depression and anxiety disorders. Such genetic predisposition can manifest in children not as a mere transmission of traits but as a function of the interaction of multiple environmental and genetic factors, as the instance strongly supports the need for an integrated strategy in the understanding of mood disorders as end products of both biological make-up and environmental factors. The interactive dynamic between genetic vulnerability and environmental stress is essential in the explanation of mood disorders among adolescents. Even if an adolescent has a history of mood disorders in their family, the presence of protective factors—like a solid home environment and positive relationships with peers—can weaken their risk. Conversely, aversive experiences such as trauma, bullying, or adverse family environments can trigger the onset of mood disorders, often accentuating prior genetic risk. This dynamic means that while genetic disposition establishes a foundation risk, environmental conditions under which a child develops may augment or diminish such risk. Thus, understanding mood disorders must incorporate both behavioral health and ecological factors as children sort through their specific processes of development on the backdrop of their genetic origins. Interventions in children's and adolescents' mood disorders need to be balanced between the influence of genetic propensity and employing evidence-based psychological therapy. Due to potential hereditary associations in mood disorders, screening at an early stage and interventions are particularly beneficial in vulnerable children. Psychological therapy, i.e.,

Cognitive Behavioral Therapy (CBT), proved to decrease symptoms and foster resilience, while preventive interventions reinforce protection against genetic risks. At the same time, realizing that genetic predisposition is not determinism is crucial; children can be taught coping strategies and support systems that allow them to function well in spite of potential genetic vulnerabilities. This transdisciplinary approach acknowledges that, while genetics play a significant role in mood disorders, environmental and therapeutic factors remain powerful agents of beneficial change, as indicated by outcomes within recent literature for the treatment of children's mental health issues (Cham et al., 2015; Smith et al., 2008).

4.3.2. Environmental Influences

Environmental influences are of decisive importance in the etiology of mood disorders in children and adolescents. Family life, socio-economic status, and social interaction in the community are the salient factors that play a profound role in emotional well-being. To illustrate this, children living in unstable family systems where there is frequent conflict or neglect are at increased risk of having mood disorders. Inconsistent parenting may also add to emotional regulation being even more complicated, even leading to stressors like depression and anxiety. Socio-economic status has been observed to increase stressors over access to educational resources and healthcare that can intervene in mental health outcomes. Such environmental factors underscore the complicated interaction between environmental contexts and psychological inner worlds influencing how young people cope with stress and emotional struggles. Education is a key contributor to the development of mood disorders in youngsters, where literacy and academic performance contribute to mental well-being. Children having problems with literacy may develop increased anxiety and depressive symptoms due to the stress of poor academic achievement. Current literature finds a high correlation between literacy issues and a variety of emotional and behavioral disturbances, meaning reading trouble has a genetic component which may be common to disorders such as attention deficit hyperactivity disorder (ADHD) (Angold et al., 2006). In addition, the reversible nature of the correlation indicates that reading failure may intensify behavioral struggle, trapping the child in a cycle reinforcing the educational and emotional anguish. This intricate relationship between learning problems and emotional well-being demonstrates the important influence environmental factors have on development. Examining further the influence of environmental factors, social relationships and peer relationships become important factors in influencing mood disorders in youth. Adolescents are particularly vulnerable to peer influence and social relationships that may affect their self-esteem and emotional well-being. Negative social interactions such as bullying or social exclusion can provoke or aggravate mood disorders, leading to increased feelings of loneliness and hopelessness. Positive friendships are also protective against mental disorder, hence the importance of a friendly social environment. Empowering communities that promote positive social interactions play a crucial role in mood disorder prevention. Hence, it is also important to understand the internal and external determinants of social and environmental impacts on mental well-being while developing effective interventions for mood disorders, with multifaceted approaches taking into consideration the internal and external determinants of mental health (Emerson et al., 2009) (Figure 4.8).

Figure 4.8. Inconsistent parenting styles can further complicate emotional regulation, potentially leading to issues such as anxiety and depression.

Source: https://thriveworks.com/wp-content/uploads/2024/11/AdobeStock_284000839.jpg.

4.3.3. Psychological Factors

It is important to know the psychological factors that contribute to mood disorders in children and adolescents so that effective interventions can be developed. One of the key factors is anxiety, which tends to advance symptoms of depression and accompanies mood disorders in most cases. Such children are likely to exhibit irritability, sadness, or emotional lability, rendering diagnosis complex. The interconnection among depressive and anxious symptoms indicates that holistic treatment and assessment approaches are needed, as a child's internal world can be characterized by emotional responses to stressors. Understanding these psychological processes through observation can enable caregivers and mental health professionals to tailor interventions to suit the specific needs of young people, thus facilitating resilience and emotional well-being. The effectiveness of targeted psychological treatments is exemplified by findings that show how diligent intervention can lead to successful outcomes among children with such complex emotional states. Aside from anxiety, the impact of extraneous stressors also needs to be addressed in the evaluation of mood disorders in children and adolescents. What happens at home, what pressures are faced at school, and how the individual relates socially can have a significant impact on the mental health of a child. For instance, kids exposed to domestic conflict or parental abuse are more prone to developing mood disorders. Such psychological stresses influence not just immediate emotional responses but also have long-term effects on a child's development and adaptation. It is crucial to comprehend how these outside psychological pressures combine with temperament and resilience in the individual. By looking at both the individual and their immediate surroundings, prevention strategies and treatment interventions can more effectively be modified to address the underlying issues that are causing mood disturbances and, in turn, foster more constructive emotional development (Emerson et al., 2009). The fact that children and adolescents are able to survive psychological adversity would mean that there should be protection factors addressed as well when referring to mood disorders. Positive relationships, coping skills, and healthy self-esteem have been suggested as protective factors to prevent the onset of mood disorders. Having one or more such supportive adults may temper the effects of stressors and promote emotional control among adolescents. In addition, psychosocial interventions involving skill development, such as cognitive-behavioral approaches, may help children develop useful tools to manage their emotions and challenging circumstances. They recognize and strengthen these protective factors, not merely precluding the development of mood disorders, but equipping youth with the coping skills necessary to navigate the risk of adolescence, that they might remain psychologically healthy in the face of life's challenges (Emerson et al., 2009).

4.4. IMPACT ON DAILY LIFE

The influence of mood disorders on the day-to-day life of children and adolescents is profound, reaching into a number of aspects of their growth and health. One important one is their influence on school; students who are depressed or anxious have difficulty with attention, motivation, and engagement. This can lead to worse grades and more absenteeism since the emotional distress hinders them from participating intensively in their school life. Additionally, the disgrace of mental illnesses can further increase feelings of loneliness, which subsequently can help cultivate more disengagement from school and social peers. A supportive climate must be established, as studies demonstrate that early awareness and intervention on the part of teachers can potentially curb the negative effects of these disorders, resulting in better academic performance and a greater positive school experience (Emerson et al., 2009). Social relationships are also distorted by mood disorders, and friendships and peer relationships for these adolescents become complicated. Mood-disordered teenagers and kids will retreat from individuals or struggle with maintaining relationships due to the emotional uncertainty that pervades their lives. The social retreat alone can then perpetuate loneliness and strengthen the symptoms of mood disorders in a vicious cycle difficult to break. Others around them further will not have an idea of what to do with their behavior, and they are likely to be bullied as a result. It is essential to raise awareness and provide supportive environments that encourage comprehension and support from peers, something that can significantly improve the quality of life for such individuals. It is suggested by studies that positive social relationships are key to emotional resilience and can enable children and adolescents to deal with their issues more effectively (Smith et al., 2008). Additionally, the effects of mood disorders on family relationships are significant, tending to put significant stress on family relations. The parents and siblings of the affected teenager or child tend to be confused about the changed emotional and behavioral patterns presented by the child or teenager, creating arguments and heightened tensions among family members. The response of the family towards mood disorders can be a significant determinant of the treatment and recovery path; families who engage in supportive behaviors tend to create a more conducive environment for the child's or teens recovery process. Conversely, such environments with a backdrop of frustration and misunderstanding are more likely to worsen the child's mental health, hence making communication and expressed empathy key elements in the way families interact. It can be achieved through recognition of the interconnectedness of individual circumstances to facilitate families in dealing with the challenges of mood disorders and establishing a support environment that facilitates healing and comprehension (Emerson et al., 2009).

4.4.1. Effects on Academic Performance

Children and adolescents' mood disorders significantly impact their schoolwork, typically manifesting themselves in terms of lower concentration, low motivation, and persistent tiredness. Children with such conditions as depression or anxiety typically struggle to cope with the class work, achieving lower grades and lower academic achievement. The mood disorders can interfere with critical thinking processes, including memory and problem-solving, which are required in learning as well as understanding complex subject matter. Also, emotional distress leads to absenteeism, as the children avoid those surroundings that evoke their symptoms. If mood disorders are not treated, their overall effect on a student's educational journey can be devastating, ultimately influencing their educational and vocational career opportunities. Moreover, the effect of external influences such as physical activity also plays an important role in academic achievement in teenagers with mood disorders. For instance, physical activity interventions have been proven to alleviate depression and anxiety symptoms, which in turn will enhance academic functioning.

Figure 4.9. Children experiencing conditions such as depression or anxiety frequently find it challenging to engage in classroom activities, resulting in lower grades and diminished academic achievement.

Source: https://childmind.org/wp-content/uploads/2023/12/iStock-1517454 070-640x427.jpg.

It has been shown by evidence that programs of organized exercise, particularly those that are integrated into school learning programs, can significantly enhance students' physical fitness levels and mental well-being. The students participating in such programs have reported lower perceived stress levels, increased self-efficacy, and more satisfaction with physical activity, all of which improve the overall learning experience. Developing such an environment, therefore, not only improves mental health but also facilitates better academic performance and therefore yields a comprehensive approach to supporting students with mood disorders (Brown et al., 2015). Along with this, the increasing use of media devices among teenagers poses other challenges to academic achievement. With smartphones and tablets increasingly available among teenagers, excessive screen time can detract from schooling and social interaction. Studies reveal that overindulgence in social media leads to distraction and reduces students' ability to focus during key learning phases. It is such overuse of the media that could lead to sleep disorders, to add to the issues of mood disorders and further lose academic engagement. When adolescents are unable to juggle their virtual world with academic requirements, the negative effect on performance has to come first, and families and clinicians must have strategic intervention to counteract such effects under a technology era (Agostiniani et al., 2019) (Figure 4.9).

4.4.2. Influence on Social Relationships

Child and adolescent mood disorders dramatically affect the capacity to build and maintain social relationships, leading to isolation and miscommunication with one's peers. Anxiety, depression, or other symptoms of mood disturbance in adolescents are typically manifested as withdrawal from social life. That withdrawal is typically misinterpreted by peers as aloofness or unapproachability, thereby increasing feelings of isolation and loneliness experienced by the child. Therefore, the safety nets available in childhood become stretched, denying youngsters and adolescents the social support to enhance resilience and mental well-being. Moreover, stigma associated with mood disorders can lead to bullying or exclusion, extending the negative effects on interpersonal relationships and even generating a cycle of worsening symptoms of mental illness. In addition to withdrawal, mood disorders affect social behavior and communication patterns, thus making it challenging for adolescents to relate well with others. For instance, adolescents and kids become overly sensitive or irritable, responding negatively to social cues and inadvertently pushing their friends away. Such alterations may disrupt learning of essential social skills, including empathy and negotiation skills, which enable good relationship constructions. Additionally, when mood disorders are left untreated, the compounding effect may result in the overall perception of inadequacy and low self-worth within social situations. This battle not only has an impact on existing friendships but also has a lasting effect on subsequent social interactions because one tends to internalize the negative experiences and shy away from new avenues of bonding and support. Therefore, the destructive effect of mood disorders on interpersonal relationships reinforces the need for systemic intervention and supportive environments. The mental health education in schools and communities must be set higher than other interests, and to open dialogue to restrict the stigma and to promote acceptance. Educational programs for empathy, peer support, and active listening have the ability to create a more empathetic climate, where children feel safe to speak and access assistance. Moreover, encouraging coordination with mental health professionals will allow teachers and families to identify signs and intervene, bridge the gap between at-risk children and their peer groups. Addressing such problems holistically will not merely enhance social ties, but overall adolescent mental well-being, eventually contributing to society at large (Emerson et al., 2009) (Figure 4.10).

Figure 4.10. When young individuals experience anxiety, depression, or other mood-related issues, their emotional dysregulation often manifests in withdrawal from social interactions.

Source: https://nexusteenacademy.com/wp-content/uploads/2025/02/Long-Term-Consequences-of-Ignoring-Emotional-Dysregulation%E2%80%8B.jpg.

4.4.3. Consequences for Family Dynamics

The impact of mood disorders on family cannot be overstated as these tend to create a ripple effect of relationship and emotional issues in the household. Families who have children or adolescents with mood disorders are likely to experience a complex array of challenges, including heightened stress levels and communication breakdown. Parents may find they are unable to understand their child's symptoms and behavior, and frustration and feelings of helplessness result from this. Such a state of uncertainty has a detrimental effect on family relations; wherein previously intimate relationships are strained or even adversarial. Families may develop unhealthy coping mechanisms, which could enhance the mood disorder of the concerned adolescent and complicate the family relationship further. With such challenges raised, families can engage evidence-based therapies to enhance empathy, establish communication, and ultimately restore order in the household. Besides, presence of mood disorder can cause significant variation in parenting styles, impacting adolescent emotional well-being. For instance, studies indicate that parental psychological control and warmth as family variables form the core of adolescent emotional well-being with an emphasis on mood disorders and eating pathology. The psychological dynamics within the family tend to affect how adolescents regulate their emotions, and highly controlling families may promote emotional dysregulation among their adolescents, thereby worsening mood disorder symptoms. As such, the relationship between adolescent emotional control and family practices is of such ultimate significance in terms of consideration of family life and mood disorders that it is such failures as these that are likely to lead to unwanted outcomes in terms of emotional and psychological health. The identification of such patterns has potential as a foundation for effective intervention aimed at facilitating better family life and mitigation of the impact of mood disorders on youth. Moreover, the implications of mood disorders are felt among siblings as well, who may also develop emotional and psychological disturbances themselves. Siblings of mood-disordered individuals also feel neglected or resentful as parental affection is inappropriately divided among the child with mood disorders. This dynamic can lead to sibling competition, feelings of loneliness, or even the development of mood-congruent pathology in the siblings themselves that further makes family dynamics difficult. Furthermore, parental weight-based teasing (WBT) has the ability to exacerbate these issues, as supported by research that links family WBT to mood-congruent psychopathology in adolescents. The pervasive sense of tension can generate an environment in which negative emotional outcomes are more likely. Identifying these brother/sister relationships and encouraging good communication in the family can repair and strengthen relationships such that all family members receive attention and support from each other in order to cope in the midst of mood disorder problems.

4.5. TREATMENT OPTIONS

Effective treatment strategies for mood disorders in children and adolescents are multimodal, often consisting of a mix of therapeutic interventions geared to individual needs. One of the first-line treatments is psychotherapy, more specifically cognitive-behavioral therapy (CBT), which helps the young patients acquire coping skills and change negative thought processes. Therapeutic interventions have been shown to yield remarkable gains in mood management and social adjustment. Furthermore, family therapy is useful as it engages members of the family in the therapeutic process, thus providing a supportive environment that facilitates emotional learning. The involvement of parents is crucial in maintaining reinforcing strategies learned in therapy, thereby ensuring continuity and stability in the child's recovery process (Emerson et al., 2009). Pharmacological therapies are also essential parts of treatment for mood disorders in this group. Selective serotonin reuptake inhibitors (SSRIs) are commonly employed and could be beneficial in the alleviation of depression and anxiety symptoms in youths. Careful monitoring must be undertaken due to side effects and the risk of increased suicidal ideation with certain of these medications. Clinicians should weigh medication advantage against such risks. Collaborating with the child patient and family through a shared decision-making process can facilitate a more individualized approach. Ensuring that families are educated and involved in the management of medication helps in adherence and overall treatment success (Schiller et al., 2008). Apart from psychotherapy and medication, lifestyle changes are also significant in the overall treatment of mood disorders among children and adolescents. Encouraging exercise on a regular basis, healthy eating, and sleeping well can all have a considerable influence on mood. Exercise, for instance, has been shown to discharge endorphins, help to alleviate anxiety, and increase self-esteem, all of which are key factors in lessening depressive symptoms. Mindfulness training and stress management techniques such as meditation and yoga can also contribute to emotional resilience. By integrating these modifications in lifestyle into an overall treatment plan, professionals and caregivers can empower adolescents to become active partners in controlling their mental health, producing both short-term relief and lasting coping (Emerson et al., 2009).

4.5.1. Psychotherapy Approaches

The treatment of mood disorders in children and adolescents typically relies primarily on various psychotherapeutic techniques, and of them, cognitive-behavioral therapy (CBT) has gained attention to a significant level. CBT focuses on identifying and modifying negative thought patterns contributing to emotional distress. Its structured nature empowers the youth by equipping them with mechanisms for coping with anxiety and depressive symptoms effectively. Research has indicated that early interventions with CBT can achieve substantial improvements in the psychological health of adolescents and thus serves as an indispensable foundation for therapeutic intervention. By its focus on the dynamic interaction among thought, feeling, and behavior, CBT offers a means for young people and adolescents to understand and control their emotional lives more effectively, as the basis for long-term emotional well-being and thus as an effective therapy for mood disorders. A second highly valuable method in child and adolescent psychotherapy is interpersonal therapy (IPT) that addresses the interpersonal setting of a teenager's mood disorders. IPT aims to enhance interpersonal relationships and social support structures, recognizing the impact relationship patterns play on emotional health. Examining how relationships produce depression or anxiety symptoms allows therapists to help youths better communicate, be more assertive, and resolve conflict. This focus on interpersonal relationships is particularly relevant to teenagers, who are often negotiating peer and social status hierarchies. The evidence for the effectiveness of IPT for treating adolescent mood disorders is robust, suggesting that addressing social and relational concerns can lead to significant and enduring improvement in mental status, as well as develop resilience to subsequent adversity. Lastly, adding family therapy to the treatment package for mood disorders in adolescents has been encouraging. Family therapy recognizes that the family has a significant role in the psychological and emotional development of adolescents and children. By involving the members of the family during the therapy sessions, the practice aims to improve emotional support and communication within the family so that it becomes convenient for the youth to resolve their psychological issues. Families are taught ways to more fully understand mood disorders and communicate within family interactions in a way that allows healing. This collaborative treatment not only acknowledges the young person's perceptions and emotions but also promotes parental consciousness and engagement in the healing process, which is crucial for lasting healing. The success of family-based interventions confirms the necessity for a comprehensive response to the treatment of mental illness, as developed in studies of effective psychotherapeutic approaches to various disorders, e.g., mood disorders (Smith et al., 2008).

4.5.2. Medication Management

Effective medication management is also critically essential in the treatment of mood disorders among children and adolescents, particularly with regard to the complexity involved with psychiatric drugs. With the rising incidence of mood disorders such as depression and anxiety among young people, medical practitioners are increasingly exploring pharmacological management in addition to therapeutic interventions. The intention of medication management is to benefit as much therapeutically as possible while causing minimal negative effects; this entails careful monitoring of drug dosages, drug interaction, and individual responses among adolescents. Families must also be involved in making decisions to help ensure that medication is appropriate for individual children's needs as well as treatment plans in general. Evidence-based practice incorporation is required, as utilization of validated measures is capable of providing critical information concerning differential medication efficacy prescribed with an ultimate goal of enhancing the quality of care provided to youth and adolescents with mood disorders. However, medication management complexity for mood disorder in youth does not have a simple picking-and-giving approach to medication treatments. Follow-up visits at periodic intervals are important to assess the overall development and progress of the patient. Regular check-ups can diagnose the emergence of side effects, which are particularly threatening in children whose neurodevelopmental patterns are rather diverse from those of adults. Proper dosages also have to be regulated because growth and metabolic alterations in children and adolescents can affect their responses to drugs over a period of time.

Figure 4.11. The objective of medication management is to ensure optimal therapeutic outcomes while minimizing adverse effects; this requires careful monitoring of dosages, drug interactions, and the individual responses of young patients.

Source: https://viveinfuse.com/wp-content/uploads/2024/02/what-is-medication-management.jpg.

Parents, guardians, and clinicians must have regular meetings to facilitate a mutually managed management of medicines so that any problems or changes in symptomatology are addressed promptly. Such planning can lead to better compliance with drug treatment and overall better results for adolescent patients with mood disorders. Moreover, it is notable that medication management is optimally effective in combination with other forms of therapy like psychotherapy and changes in lifestyle. For instance, group-oriented social skills training has been found to be effective in the treatment of mood disorders, particularly in HFASD children as explained in recent studies. A randomized controlled trial that evaluated the effectiveness of such interventions showed that improvements in social responsiveness, along with a reduction in depression and anxiety symptoms, are achievable when combined with medication management. This points to the necessity of employing a multidisciplinary approach involving both pharmacological as well as non-pharmacological methods of treating mood disorders. Therefore, optimization of medication management involves not only judicious prescribing habits but also a commitment to coordinated care with family engagement and treatment modality coordination (Bender et al., 2013; Schiller et al., 2008) (Figure 4.11).

4.5.3. Alternative and Complementary Therapies

Increasing prevalence of mood disorders in children and teens has generated greater interest in complementary and alternative treatments as adjuncts to traditional care. These treatments encompass a variety of methods ranging from meditation, yoga, and mindfulness practices that have been shown to augment emotional regulation and overall mental well-being. For instance, meditation is now an effective intervention in lessening scholastic stress, a common precipitant of mood disturbance in this population. In a study focusing on adolescents, meditation was found to significantly reduce scholastic stress, enhancing emotional resilience and concentration in the participants (Andriyani et al., 2012). These findings emphasize the importance of incorporating mindfulness strategies into the treatment arsenal for youth with mood disorders, offering them pharmacologic-free avenues to improving their mental health. Yoga and other alternative strategies also represent suitable add-on therapies for mood disorders in youth. By the integration of body movement, breathing, and meditation, yoga brings about a sense of grounding and relaxation that can reduce symptoms of depression and anxiety. A study at the 3rd Java International Nursing Conference touches on the suitability of complementary therapies, such as aromatherapy and yoga, to enhance the outcomes of patients in various settings of health (Nurmalia et al., 2015). In their promotion of physical health and mindfulness, these therapies not only alleviate the acute symptoms of mood disorders but also provide children and adolescents with tools with which to handle daily stress and anxiety. For this reason, health care providers need to consider whether or not to recommend such treatments as part of a comprehensive treatment plan. The combination of alternative therapies with standard therapeutic models calls for close scrutiny and regulation. While some of these alternative therapies hold much promise, they are highly variable in their success and may be affected by others, necessitating individualized treatment modalities. Mental health professionals will need to inform themselves about these treatments so that they can guide young clients into appropriate and proper treatments. There also needs to be ongoing research to confirm the efficacy of these therapies and to standardize procedures for their use in clinical settings. Lastly, inclusion of complementary therapies not only complements existing interventions but also fosters a more holistic understanding of mental health treatment in children and adolescents to recognize the multifaceted nature of mood disorders.

4.6. PREVENTION AND EARLY INTERVENTION

While treating mood disorders in children and adolescents, prevention and early intervention can be the crucial aspects that can best manage the impact of such disorders. Evidence indicates that there needs to be an understanding about the frequency of mood-related disorders, and the risk and protective factors, for the planning and execution of effective preventive interventions. Through placing greater emphasis on psychological therapies in relation to the application of pharmacology, practitioners can introduce evidence-based programs specially tailored for children, particularly primary school age. This early strategic intervention serves not only to identify at-risk individuals but also to foster resilience and emotional stability so that children may develop coping mechanisms prior to the occurrence of mood disorders (Smith et al., 2008). This preventive approach is important, as earlier intervention can result in better long-term outcomes and less overall burden of psychiatric disorders among child populations. Importantly, the link between literacy issues and psychiatric disease further supports targeted interventions at an early stage. Recent evidence indicates a strong association between literacy difficulties and numerous emotional and behavioral issues among children. The link between literacy issues and attention deficit hyperactivity disorder and anxiety disorders indicates that unless literacy problems are treated, they may exacerbate mood disorders and lead to a cycle of deteriorating symptoms (Angold et al., 2006). Therefore, intervention programs that operate in the intersection of literacy and mental health have the capability of providing a comprehensive support system for at-risk children. By integrating educational intervention with mental health programs, practitioners not only enhance children's academic performance, but emotional strength as well and therefore work on many dimensions of their well-being. Secondly, the impact of comorbid conditions is widespread and goes beyond academic performance; they have significant bearings on emotional growth and self-worth. Children struggling with both literacy difficulties and mood disorders tend to become increasingly susceptible to low mood and anxiety as a result of classroom experiences. This twofold experience requires treatment to reflect the interaction of different disorders. Intervention needs to interrupt the risk cycle by offering specialized assistance suited to the unique needs of each child (Angold et al., 2006). By creating an environment in which both academic and emotional needs are responded to concurrently, we can lay the foundation for healthier patterns of development. As such, coordinated early intervention strategies working toward both academic success and emotional well-being are integral in preventing the escalation of mood disorders among teenagers to ultimately enhance life outcomes.

4.6.1. Importance of Early Detection

Early detection of mood disorders in adolescents and children is necessary in order to avert the potential serious consequences of the disorders. With early detection, appropriate interventions can be performed to treat the symptoms and prevent worsening of the disorders. Adolescents are at highest risk for mood disorders because of the intense development process of the brain in their stage, which may affect emotional regulation and decision-making. Research that highlights variations in development while making decisions has shown that teens may hold a varying sense of risk perception that can hinder them to recognize and respond to their mental health issues (Bonnie et al., 2017). Early recognition thus not only offers the possibility of treatment but also equips individuals with the competencies necessary for coping with their emotional difficulties, ultimately establishing resilience and pushing them towards better outcomes in life. In addition, the importance of early diagnosis is highlighted by the age-at-onset/long-term outcome association. Research suggests that the sooner a mood disorder is diagnosed, the more positive the cognitive, mood, and behavioral outcomes are likely to be (Bourlas et al., 2013). This relationship highlights the importance of active screening programs and mental health education, particularly through school networks whereby early signs are more apt to be detected by teachers and peers. A promoting condition with active discussion of mental health can reduce the stigma of seeking assistance so children and youth can more openly describe their feelings and situations. Implementation of such programs not only leads to early detection but also promotes support and compassion culture among adolescents. Early detection is also important in minimizing the overall family and community burden of mood disorders. Early identification allows families to receive adequate treatment and counseling, avoiding massive suffering from mental illnesses. This proactive approach can lead to decreases in emergency treatments as well as lower rates of co-occurring disorders, such as anxiety or substance abuse disorders, which can arise when mood disorders are not treated. Moreover, early treatment in adequate numbers can improve scholastic performance as well as social functioning, which can subsequently favor communities by building healthier, more engaged citizens (Bonnie et al., 2017). Thus, developing a model for early detection and intervention is not only beneficial for the individual; it serves the collective good by creating a balanced, mentally healthy society (Figure 4.12).

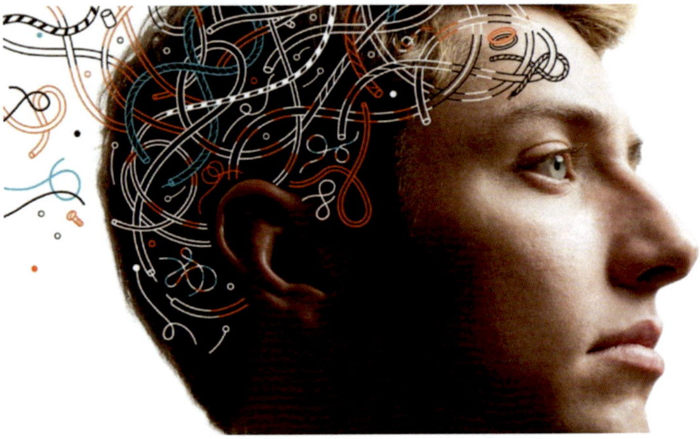

Figure 4.12. Adolescents are particularly vulnerable to mood disorders, given the rapid brain development occurring during these years, which may affect emotional regulation and decision-making.

Source: https://static.scientificamerican.com/sciam/cache/file/E9D 2DE3E-798F-4A22-A7C653D41DC12EB5_source.jpg?crop=16%3A9%2Csmart&w=1920.

4.6.2. Strategies for Prevention in Schools

Prevention of mood disorders in children and adolescents in school environments involves a multi-modal approach that integrates psychological support, education, and community involvement. Schools are in the best position to implement early identification programs, which identify at-risk students who may be displaying anxiety or depression symptoms. Effective prevention approaches involve educating teachers to better recognize such signs and offering an environment that places value on mental health. By incorporating workshops and training sessions on identifying mood disorders, schools can prepare teachers to hold discussions, guide students, and refer them to the services they require. Effective interventions have been found to incorporate elements of psychological treatments, and therefore, schools must create effective support systems to provide emotional well-being (Smith et al., 2008). Along with academic programs, the encouragement of exercise in school curriculum is also a significant method of preventing mood disorders. Physical activity has been associated with improved mental health status, such as enhanced mood, reduced stress, and social connection with peers. Schools should recognize the worth of pioneering initiatives such as sports, dancing, or marathon challenges that, in addition to enhancing physical health, encourage social interaction and coping against emotional duress. Examples of interventions on student preparation for marathon running have shown good effects on their aerobic fitness, as well as self-reported indicators of stress, thereby indicating an overall relationship between physical exercise and mental health (Brown et al., 2015). Such structured activities have the capacity to offer a community support environment, critical in helping students through the emotional turmoil of adolescence. Schools also need to actively involve families and communities in order to realize the best benefits from promoting mental health. Creating alliances with parents and community organizations can assist with providing access to resources and support networks beyond the school environment. Schools can also organize workshops for parents educating them on how to identify mood disorder symptoms and how to better support their children. Community involvement can also include creating safe spaces for teenagers to talk with other teenagers and positive role models so they can openly discuss mental health. Having these programs integrated into the school system can work to eliminate stigmas surrounding mood disorders and create a culture in which mental health is encouraged and discussed openly. Overall, a cooperative strategy with the community, families, and teachers can have a significant boost in the effectiveness of prevention for reducing mood disorders in children and adolescents.

4.6.3. Role of Parents and Caregivers in Support

Parent and caregiver engagement is critical in helping children and adolescents with mood disorders because they are typically the first to react in identifying and coping with emotional challenges. Parents play an important role in monitoring the behavior of their children, creating a secure place in which they can discuss their feelings, and establishing an environment for uninhibited flow of information concerning mental health. By being sensitive to mood and behavioral changes, caregivers are able to apply early intervention, and this is central in managing mood disorders effectively. Such anticipation not only works to improve the immediate needs but also helps avoid long-term consequences of these disorders since research shows delayed intervention leads to more pronounced effects later in life (Benelli et al., 2015). An active parental role can have the potential to result in enhanced coping ability, resilience strength, and adaptive capability among affected youth. Secondly, cooperation of parents with mental health professionals significantly enhances the system of support available to youth. Parents are also most likely to be involved in instigating help, promoting counseling options, and adhering to treatment regimens, thus advocating the need for professional help in the case of mood disorders. By participating in family therapy sessions and educational interventions, caregivers get a chance to learn communication skills and behavior management techniques specific to their children's needs. This partnership not only informs parents but also generates an integrated treatment plan, where caregivers act as advocates of their children's mental health in the family setting and the healthcare system (Cooper et al., 2016). This collaborative practice is essential in decelerating the stigma of mental health issues since it offers a healthy platform for adolescents. Furthermore, parents and guardians are influential in offering emotional and practical support, which can be extended to positive lifestyle choices having a great influence on mood stabilization. Engaging children in physical activity, fostering healthy nutrition patterns, and establishing routines not only improves global well-being but also serves as a protective agent against the exacerbation of mood disorders. Regular exercise, for instance, has been found to decrease symptoms of anxiety and depression, further reinforcing the importance of an active lifestyle. When these behaviors are modeled and supported by caregivers, they contribute to an overall treatment plan that complements therapeutic interventions. Therefore, establishing an environment conducive to emotional and mental health enables a platform for prolonged recovery and resilience in children and adolescents facing the brunt of mood disorders. Through these complex roles, parents and caregivers yield positive outcomes on mental well-being and emotional health (Figure 4.13).

Figure 4.13. Parents play a pivotal role in monitoring their children's behavior, offering a safe space for expression, and fostering an environment conducive to open dialogue about mental health.

Source: https://manochikitsa.com/wp-content/uploads/2024/05/asian-beautiful-young-woman-teacher-teaching-a-les-2023-11-27-05-22-08-utc-1200x900.jpg.

4.7. CONCLUSION

In concluding an investigation into mood disorders in children and adolescents, it is important to recognize the multifaceted nature of such illnesses. The emotional and behavioral problems manifesting among young individuals are much more than symptomatic in scope, generally infecting their social development, academic performance, and general well-being. With such disorders becoming increasingly prevalent, their causality continues to be a point of serious inquiry for developing effective intervention strategies. Genetic vulnerability, environmental pressure, and interpersonal relationships are causative factors in the development of such mood disorders, referring to the importance of an integrative perspective that considers interaction between several causative factors. Education and awareness regarding mental health can empower educators and caregivers with the ability to recognize early signs, thus facilitating timely support and intervention. Furthermore, the integration of physical exercise into the lives of adolescents and youth has also been promising in reversing the effects of mood disorders. Regular physical exercise programs not only enhance body health but have also been linked with increased psychological benefits. A recent study of a marathon training program, for instance, demonstrated significant improvements in adolescents' aerobic fitness, perceived stress levels, and exercise self-efficacy. These outcomes favor the inclusion of physical activity in educational curricula since it can be very effective in helping young people develop resilience and enhance mental health (Brown et al., 2015). Since mental health services are usually not available in most communities, these approaches provide an alternative way of treating mood disorders through enjoyable and low-cost access. Finally, understanding the cognitive styles specific to anxiety and mood disorders, particularly in special populations, is essential to evidence-based treatment planning. Children with spectrum disorders with high functioning have cognitive evaluations that are significant in emotional responding, which means there is a need for tailor-made therapies that work against these particular biases (Hunter et al., 2013). This recognition provides the basis for the development of therapeutic interventions with a focus on cognitive restructuring and emotional regulation strategies. Schools, as well as mental health professionals, must cooperate to create supportive environments that promote mental health, ultimately resulting in healthier outcomes for youths with mood disorders. With the integration of physical health interventions and cognitive-behavioral strategies, society can have an overall strategy to help young individuals overcome the challenges.

4.7.1. Summary of Key Points

The research on mood disorders in children and adolescents reveals most important details regarding the prevalence and impact of the conditions. The research, as it stands currently, indicates the excessive prevalence of anxiety and depressive disorders among them, which further indicates the necessity of early intervention and diagnosis. Understanding somatic symptoms that define these mood disorders is critical as such symptoms prove to be challenging for the diagnosis and treatment process. In addition, the identification of risk and protective factors of the disorder is essential while developing suitable preventive interventions.

For instance, environmental factors, family functioning, as well as genetic vulnerabilities are some among several factors that lead to provocation or protection against the effects of mood disorders among young people (Smith et al., 2008). Addressing these regions can enhance the overall treatment modalities that are aimed at enhancing the mental health of children and adolescents. Psychological therapy has come forward as central interventions for the treatment of mood disorders among children and adolescents. It is seen that treatments such as cognitive-behavioral therapy (CBT) have been very effective in reducing symptoms in depression and anxiety. Such treatments not only relieve symptoms but also empower the young by giving them coping mechanisms and resilience to face future attacks. Unlike pharmacological treatment, which has the disadvantage of side effects, particularly among younger people, psychological treatment has been effective without such additional complexities. Moreover, the focus on the psychological approaches guarantees that the treatment is tailored to the unique needs and growth stages of children, thereby resulting in more efficient treatments (Smith et al., 2008). The customized therapy is the centerpiece in guaranteeing a more holistic knowledge and treatment of mood disorders among young individuals.

Yet, challenges remain in addressing the intricacies of mood disorders in young people. There is a pressing demand for more research to clarify the intricate relationships among medication side effects and changes in mood in this population. New evidence supports a possible link between the use of certain medications, such as statins, and the onset of mood dysregulation, including depression and anxiety. Because adolescents frequently are prescribed medications for comorbid medical illness, it is essential to mental health practitioners to identify these adverse drug reactions. This complexity is what highlights the need for thorough assessments taking into account both the psychological and the physiological aspects in making treatment decisions. The most effective approach, therefore, may be a multidisciplinary one that brings together psychological therapies and vigilant pharmacological treatment monitoring to ensure both safety and efficacy in the mental health process of children and adolescents.

4.7.2. The Importance of Awareness and Education

Awareness and education are essential in the fight against mood disorders among children and adolescents. As it stands, studies indicate a record rise in depression among teenagers, with a staggering 2 million cases annually. Significantly, depressive symptoms appear as early warning signs of other severe mental health challenges in adulthood, highlighting the urgency of intervention at a young age.

Identification of mood disorders can help minimize stigma, often a barrier to treatment. Schools are particularly valuable in this case since they offer the first place for education. Universal depression education programs that teach students about symptoms and enhance help-seeking behavior may potentially foster an environment of high regard for mental health, ultimately the betterment of individuals with mood disorders, most notably in at-risk groups such as socioeconomically disadvantaged adolescents (Hari et al., 2017). Schools need to introduce vast educational measures for effective intervention and prevention of mood disorders.

Evidence suggests the importance of incorporating mental health literacy in the curriculum, including knowledge of the mental health issues, building strengths for resilience, and aiding access to assistance. For low-income youth, up to 80% of mental health services are offered through school systems, which makes schools central to assist. By enriching the instructional framework with explicit guidelines on mood disorders, schools become more likely to prepare students to recognize symptoms in themselves as well as among their peers. Being proactive can reap much on early intervention and treatment because knowledge-empowered students are more likely to advocate for their mental health and seek the proper intervention when needed (Hari et al., 2017). Teacher and school staff mental health awareness preparation is also essential in order to establish an understanding climate for students who live with mood disorders.

Teachers are often the first to respond to indicators of distress before the professionals in mental health respond. With the preparation of teachers to identify changes in behavior and moods, schools can create a climate where mental health conversations become a part of the daily routine. Schools' teacher training programs should include resources on the appropriate response and referrals for pupils evidencing depression or anxiety. Furthermore, integrating elements with open mental health discussions can assist in de-stigmatizing mental health issues and empowering pupils. It is by these multiple pronged education and sensitization programs that schools can most effectively tackle the adolescent mental health epidemic and make access available to those most in need.

4.7.3. Call to Action for Further Research and Support

The prevalence of mood disorders in children and adolescents demands an urgent need for more research and support to remedy the looming public health crisis. With the astronomical rates of young people experiencing depression, anxiety, and other mood disorders, the psychological and emotional impact is astronomical and far-reaching. The American Psychological Association has recognized the need for research efforts aimed at distinct groups, especially those who are underserved and exposed to outside stressors, such as military deployment. The Task Force on Military Deployment Services for Youth has specifically recognized the potential risks of children of deployed parents, and the knowledge gaps and services deficiencies. This highlights the need for extensive research that examines the interaction between environmental stressors and mood disorders in adolescents, leading to the eventual development of individually targeted interventions to alleviate these issues. Further, developing our understanding of mood disorders in adolescents necessitates interdisciplinary collaboration to create effective support systems. Educational services, health service providers, and community organizations must work together to establish a multi-level program that not only identifies vulnerable children but also provides ongoing emotional and psychological support. For instance, the use of evidence-based practices, such as screenings and interventions proven effective within similar settings, will be important in ensuring mental well-being among adolescents. It is also important to include families in treatment programs, particularly those with families residing under special stressors. By encouraging collaborative research efforts and developing resources tailored to various family configurations, we can optimize the support delivered to children with mood disorders to create more resilient and better-equipped future generations.

Finally, by leveraging data from other disciplines like psychology and solid research, what works effectively to help children with mood disorders may be explained better. As researchers investigate the physical and emotional impact of sound, discoveries based on these experiments can be accessed to design better emotional climates for teenagers. New interventions, including soundscapes or music therapy, could be tried to establish effectiveness in improving outcomes for mental health. The call for action also extends to policymakers, who handle the provision of funding for mental health initiatives that are aimed at children and youth separately. The resultant effects of failure to address this condition will leave the person with lifelong struggles with mood disorders, as evidenced in cases justifying early interventions. It is thus a collective responsibility to drive research and support systems to avert the unhappiness of children today so that they possess what it takes to survive in an ever-more-complex world.

REFERENCES

1. Agostiniani, R., Banderali, G., Bozzola, E., Bozzola, M., Caruso, C., Chiara, A., Corsello, G., et al. (2019). Media use during adolescence: The recommendations of the Italian Pediatric Society. https://core.ac.uk/download/286528669.pdf (accessed on 14th October 2025).
2. Andriyani, R. T. (Riska), & Suhartini, S. (Suhartini). (2012). Meditation in school adolescents who sit in Olympic and Acceleration Class. https://media.neliti.com/media/publications/89754-EN-meditation-in-school-adolescents-who-sit.pdf (accessed on 14th October 2025).
3. Angold, A., Banaschewski, B., Maughan, B., Byrne, D., Carroll, J., Craig, T., et al. (2006). Literacy and mental disorders. https://core.ac.uk/download/49099.pdf (accessed on 14th October 2025).
4. Arnold, L. E., Birmaher, B., Danner, S., Demeter, C., et al. (2009). Early-onset bipolar spectrum disorders: Diagnostic issues. https://core.ac.uk/download/159572415.pdf (accessed on 14th October 2025).
5. Bender, S., Cholemkery, H., Elsuni, L., Freitag, C., et al. (2013). The group-based social skills training SOSTA-FRA in children and adolescents with high functioning autism spectrum disorder–Study protocol of the randomized, multi-center controlled SOSTA-net trial. https://core.ac.uk/download/14528049.pdf (accessed on 14th October 2025).
6. Benelli, E., & Bianco, F. (2015). Models of collaboration between psychologist and family doctor: A systematic review of primary care psychology. https://core.ac.uk/download/80154468.pdf (accessed on 14th October 2025).
7. Bertino, M. D., Borojevic, N., Knight, T., Lewis, A., et al. (2013). Adolescent depressive disorders and family-based interventions in the Family Options multicenter evaluation: Study protocol for a randomized controlled trial. https://core.ac.uk/download/77140386.pdf (accessed on 14th October 2025).
8. Bevan-Jones, R., Collishaw, S., Craddock, N. J., Mars, B., et al. (2016). Prevalence and correlates of psychotic experiences amongst children of depressed parents. https://core.ac.uk/download/74223679.pdf (accessed on 14th October 2025).
9. Bonnie, R. J., Breiner, K., Casey, B. J., Chein, J., et al. (2017). At risk of being risky: The relationship between “brain age” under emotional states and risk preference. https://core.ac.uk/download/323078009.pdf (accessed on 14th October 2025).
10. Bossewitch, J. S. (2010). Pediatric bipolar and the media of madness.

https://core.ac.uk/download/161435957.pdf (accessed on 14th October 2025).

11. Bourlas, A. P. (2013). The effects of level and duration of play on cognition, mood and behavior among former football players. https://open.bu.edu/bitstream/2144/12058/6/Bourlas_Alexandra_2013_nosig_nocv.pdf (accessed on 14th October 2025).
12. Brown, K. P. (2015). Marathon training improves perceived stress, self-efficacy, and aerobic fitness in adolescents. https://core.ac.uk/download/211348918.pdf (accessed on 14th October 2025).
13. Cham, S., Golomb, B. A., & Koslik, H. J. (2015). Mood, personality, and behavior changes during treatment with statins: A case series. https://core.ac.uk/download/323064248.pdf (accessed on 14th October 2025).
14. Cooper, S. A., Philo, C., & Young-Southward, G. (2016). What effect does transition have on health and well-being in young people with intellectual disabilities? A systematic review. https://core.ac.uk/download/42373210.pdf (accessed on 14th October 2025).
15. Direkvand-Moghadam, A., Hashemian, A., Mehrdadi, A., Sadeghian, F., et al. (2017). The prevalence and risk factors of mental disorders among students in Ilam: A cross-sectional study. https://core.ac.uk/download/143840379.pdf (accessed on 14th October 2025).
16. Emerson, C. P. (2009). *Exercise and Its Effects on Depression in Young Adults.* https://core.ac.uk/download/5067419.pdf (accessed on 14th October 2025).
17. Ewigman, B., Hickner, J., Smith, S., Van Voorhees, B., et al. (2008). Treat depressed teens with medication and psychotherapy. https://core.ac.uk/download/62762449.pdf (accessed on 14th October 2025).
18. Flouri, E., & McEwen, C. (2008). Fathers' parenting, adverse life events, and adolescents' emotional and eating disorder symptoms: The role of emotion regulation. https://core.ac.uk/download/pdf/82499.pdf (accessed on 14th October 2025).
19. Hanks, E. (2019). The physio-emotional effects of audio in the global Christian church. https://core.ac.uk/download/213463595.pdf (accessed on 14th October 2025).
20. Hari, G. (2017). Depression in low-income adolescents: Guidelines for school-based depression intervention programs. https://core.ac.uk/download/130354083.pdf (accessed on 14th October 2025).
21. Hunter, S. C., Sharma, S., & Woolfson, L. (2013). Maladaptive cognitive appraisals in children with high-functioning autism: Associations with

fear, anxiety and theory of mind. https://core.ac.uk/download/9559312.pdf (accessed on 14th October 2025).

22. Johnson,S.J.,&Wolke,D.(2013).Behavioraloutcomesandpsychopathology during adolescence. https://core.ac.uk/download/9847191.pdf (accessed on 14th October 2025).

23. Marvel, A. L. (2015). *Social Participation: An Occupational Therapy Guide to Intervention for Youth with Depressive Disorders.* https://core.ac.uk/download/235073473.pdf (accessed on 14th October 2025).

24. Nurmalia, D., Padmasari, S., Rokhana, N., Utami, N., et al. (2015). *Proceeding: 3rd Java International Nursing Conference 2015 "Harmony of Caring and Healing Inquiry for Holistic Nursing Practice; Enhancing Quality of Care," Semarang, 20–21 August 2015.* https://core.ac.uk/download/76930906.pdf (accessed on 14th October 2025).

25. Preti, A., Simon, A. E., Morrison, A. P., Yung, A. R., Yung, A. R., Yung, A. R., Yung, A. R., et al. (2014). The 'at-risk mental state' for psychosis in adolescents: Clinical presentation, transition and remission. https://core.ac.uk/download/16293271.pdf (accessed on 14th October 2025).

26. Schiller, K. A. (2008). Cutting: What school counselors should know about students who self-injure. https://core.ac.uk/download/5067317.pdf (accessed on 14th October 2025).

27. Smith, M., & Storey, P. (2008). *Methods and Approaches to Improving the Emotional Health and Well-Being of Children: A Briefing Paper Concerning Interventions to Prevent Internalizing Disorders.* https://core.ac.uk/download/pdf/82102.pdf (accessed on 14th October 2025).

Chapter 5

Neurodevelopmental Disorders

Contents

INTRODUCTION

The field of child and adolescent mental health has become increasingly interested in neurodevelopmental disorders due to their profound effect on developmental trajectories and overall health later in life. The disorders, which are conditions such as attention deficit hyperactivity disorder (ADHD), autism spectrum disorders (ASDs), and tic disorders, affect a variety of cognitive, emotional, and social processes in children. Understanding the nature of these conditions is important, not just for effective diagnosis and treatment, but also to overcome the problems related to such persons and their families. These conditions usually develop at early stages in the development process, with consequent and serious effects on school performance and social integration of such children and youth, and hence, research and intervention in this area become highly relevant. Research has indicated a stark relationship between neurodevelopmental disorders and adverse outcomes, including increased risks for co-morbid mental illnesses and potential involvement in criminality. Specifically, studies depict that individuals with ADHD are at greater risk for violent criminality than their counterparts without the condition (Forsman et al., 2013). Furthermore, under-diagnosis of ADHD in both children and adults renders it impossible to recognize and assist the vulnerable individuals, resulting in unattended symptoms that further lead to risks such as substance use and educational failure. The research into these dynamics is essential because it points to the need for the timely intervention and appropriate management that can avert these risks and improve the overall life outcomes of individuals with neurodevelopmental disorders. Preventive and treatment strategies to neurodevelopmental disorders do not only have to be strongly guided by empirical evidence but also sensitive to changing knowledge regarding the disorder. Methylphenidate is a medication that has proved to be an effective first-line drug therapy to ADHD, with a significant proportion (80%) of patients responding to such therapy positively (Camilleri et al., 2013). This highlights the imperative requirement for thorough training of mental health professionals in recognition and management of such disorders in an effective way. Along with drug interventions, an interdisciplinary approach of psychoeducation, behavioral therapies, and environmental adaptation is required in treating children and adolescents with neurodevelopmental disabilities. Finally, a solid and advanced knowledge of these disorders will enable practitioners to facilitate more healthy outcomes and enhance the quality of life for individuals and families involved.

Definition of Neurodevelopmental Disorders (NDDs)

Neurodevelopmental disorders (NDDs) are a broad range of conditions that arise on the way to childhood developmental stages, influencing cognitive, behavioral, and emotional functioning. Examples of NDDs include ADHD, autism spectrum disorders (ASD), dyslexia, and intellectual disabilities, among others. In most cases, most of these disorders arise before the age of 18 years and influence the manner in which a child participates in activities of daily living, school, and social interactions. The complexity of NDDs is that they are multifactorial, where genetic susceptibility interplays with the environment to create diverse symptoms and complications, which can largely vary from individual to individual. Heterogeneity thus necessitates a sophisticated understanding and treatment regimen of diagnosis because early treatment can significantly improve the prognosis of affected children. The neurodevelopmental disorders diagnosis requires good understanding of the changes that occur in a child's developmental trajectory. For instance, research has shown that language regression is an important predictor of ASD, whereby children lose previously acquired skills, affecting social interactions and communication abilities. In population-based research, regression of language was found to occur in 30% of narrowly diagnosed autistic children, thereby further indicating the central function of monitoring developmental milestones (LeCouteur et al., 2008).

Figure 5.1. Neurodevelopmental disorders (NDDs) encompass a broad range of conditions that originate during the developmental phase of childhood, impacting cognitive, behavioral, and emotional functioning.

Source: https://www.verywellmind.com/thmb/JBTL8biEBPOJGZJbrvrJFwc7UVY=/1500x0/filters:no_upscale():max_bytes(150000):strip_icc()/GettyImages-1315878411-c95fb285737e46c3916fc148581c7ce6.jpg.

Regression suggests the importance of regular follow-up while the child grows up so that effective interventions may be introduced in good time to allow no further developmental delays. Hence, the early identification and diagnosis of NDDs are important since they may have enduring educational and social issues that last throughout adolescence and even adulthood. Research on the epidemiology of neurodevelopmental disorders is revealed to possess high prevalence rates, which emphasizes the importance of increased awareness among health professionals. ADHD, for example, is one of the most commonly diagnosed NDDs, with a 5.29% incidence among children and 2.5% among adults (Camilleri et al., 2013). The disorder, characterized by symptoms of inattention, impulsivity, and hyperactivity, highlights the ways in which such disorders are likely to outlast early childhood, necessitating lifelong intervention and care. Unaddressed ADHD will also create co-morbidities such as anxiety and depression, which exacerbate the problems for individuals and families. Effective intervention and evaluation strategies, such as behavioral treatments and medication, show the potential for encouraging outcomes when NDDs are properly treated. An understanding of the meaning and nature of neurodevelopmental disorders is essential to enhance child and adolescent mental health programs (Figure 5.1).

Importance of Studying these Disorders in Mental Health

Neurodevelopmental disorders such as autism spectrum disorder, attention-deficit/hyperactivity disorder (ADHD), and learning disabilities come with serious consequences for affected children and adolescents. Understanding the prevalence and symptomatology of these disorders is key to the development of effective interventions and support mechanisms. For instance, the COVID-19 pandemic has exacerbated symptoms of depression and anxiety in these populations, with studies indicating that 1.8–49.5% and 2.2–63.8% of infected individuals exhibited significant distress under lockdown (Panchal et al., 2021). By recognizing the psychological and emotional toll of these conditions, mental health providers can employ prevention strategies and foster resilience in children to improve their well-being. Additionally, such an understanding facilitates early detection and targeted therapeutic interventions that can dramatically restructure development trajectories, further highlighting the imperative for ongoing research on these disorders. Consideration within mental health discourse also relies on understanding of neurodevelopmental disorders complex interplay with other areas of life. Family dynamics, social stresses, and environmental influences can precipitate or modulate the manifestation of such disorders. The gut-brain axis, a relatively emergent area of investigation, highlights the interconnectedness of physiological and psychological well-being. Microbiota composition, which can be influenced by diet and stress, has been linked to a variety of mental diseases, including anxiety and autism (John et al., 2019). This way, their investigation not only adds to the discovery of individual-risk markers but also system concerns, enabling an integrated mental health care model. Understand the intricate nature of neurodevelopmental disorders ultimately leads to an integrated model for mental health treatment, one that addresses the interaction between biological, environmental, and psychological factors. The mental health impact of neurodevelopmental disorders continues into adulthood, affecting not only the well-being of individuals but also the functioning of society. Individuals with untreated mental health issues regarding neurodevelopmental disorders may find themselves confronting immense difficulties in educational, vocational, and social spheres. By investing in research and intervention approaches focusing on this group, we can improve their life outcomes and save long-term societal expenditures. Systematic analyses that account for these correlations are most in need; results can immediately inform public health policy and resource allocation, so that allocations for individuals with neurodevelopmental disorders are prioritized. As highlighted by the literature at present, intervention for these issues earlier on can enhance resilience, enhance quality of life, and lower the healthcare system cost burden. The importance of research on these disorders, thus, goes beyond individual health to include societal implications for which adequate attention and response are needed (Figure 5.2).

Figure 5.2. Inclusivity in mental health discourse also hinges on understanding neurodevelopmental disorders nuanced interactions with other life factors.

Source: https://cdn.prod.website-files.com/63b83bdb00cc281dd370dcf0/652e21a7753971053028779d_pexels-yan-krukau-8612932%20(1).jpg.

5.1. TYPES OF NEURODEVELOPMENTAL DISORDERS

Neurodevelopmental disorders are a broad array of conditions that make nervous system development complicated, affecting cognitive, emotional, and social competence in children and adolescents. Foregrounded among them are autism spectrum disorder (ASD), attention-deficit/hyperactivity disorder (ADHD), and learning disability. ASD is characterized by social communication deficit and the presence of stereotyped behavior, which can seriously impair daily functioning. ADHD is exhibited with symptoms of hyperactivity, impulsivity, and inattention that can disrupt learning settings and interpersonal relationships. Furthermore, learning disabilities such as dyslexia and dyscalculia can also interfere with academic achievement despite normal intelligence. Diagnosis and understanding of these disorders are critical since early identification and intervention can greatly enhance long-term prognosis for the patients. One of the striking characteristics of neurodevelopmental disorders is the way they correlate with environmental factors, particularly prenatal and early life exposure. For instance, studies indicate that preterm birth increases the vulnerability to cognitive impairment and other long-term mental illnesses, particularly anxiety and attention disorders. Studies indicate that preterm adolescents are at a greater risk for psychiatric and emotional disorders, with approximately 25% of them being affected. These observations underscore the need for monitoring neurodevelopmental issues within this population and early intervention to avert adverse outcomes. As the prevalence of such disorders increases, understanding their multifaceted etiology and manifestations becomes increasingly crucial to healthcare providers and educators alike. In addition to the direct effect on cognitive and emotional functioning, neurodevelopmental disorders also influence social and occupational level later in life. The English and Romanian Adoptees (ERA) study illustrates the manner in which early institution deprivation with extreme stress leads to long-term neurodevelopmental issues, ultimately translating to disorders of emotion in adolescence and adulthood. Individuals with early neurodevelopmental challenges are often unable to gain employment and still experience challenging interpersonal relationships as they age towards adulthood. This cascade of development highlights the necessity to intervene on the initial neurodevelopmental problems in children since these can exert strong effects on later social adaptation and mental health. By employing certain interventions, clinicians are able to develop resilience and promote healthier developmental trajectories for individuals with neurodevelopmental disorders.

5.1.1. Autism Spectrum Disorder (ASD)

The prevalence of autism spectrum disorder (ASD) has attracted significant concern over the last few years, with specific significance given to its impact on child and adolescent mental health. The findings indicate that ASD is predominantly found during early childhood but is likely to show significant difficulties that carry forward to adolescence and adulthood. Indications such as social communication impairment, restricted behaviors, and sensory processing difficulty need a broader grasp of the disorder. In addition, the intricacy of ASD is aggravated by comorbidities like anxiety and attention-deficit/hyperactivity disorder (ADHD), which render diagnosis and treatment challenging. It is therefore critical to realize the multidimensional nature of ASD in formulating effective therapy interventions and support networks for individuals afflicted by the condition. Literature suggests neurodevelopmental factors as central to the etiology of ASD, backed up by evidence that preterm birth and adversity in child are risk factors for developmental disorder. Indeed, Johnson et al. (2013) indicates preterm birth and higher risk of psychiatric disorder, with a higher rate of emotional disorder and communication impairment being reported in such individuals.

Figure 5.3. Understanding the multifaceted nature of ASD is essential in developing effective therapeutic approaches and support systems for individuals affected by this disorder.

Source: https://cdn-hkbbb.nitrocdn.com/QTCJbUazKnWUNTVqagKZShXFbBtZ-ByZg/assets/images/optimized/rev-2937d83/www.cadabamshospitals.com/wp-content/uploads/2022/06/preschool-development-of-children-with-autism-spec-2022-03-31-06-38-51-utc-scaled.jpg.

The findings bring into focus the need for preterm infants to be identified and treated early, as these individuals can suffer from long-lasting developmental issues. By the detection of the same risk factors and their effects on mental well-being, healthcare professionals can render broad-spectrum care tactics aimed at focusing on the individual needs of children afflicted with ASD to enhance overall well-being. Longitudinal research is beginning to explain how early neurodevelopmental problems appear as emotional difficulties later in life, particularly in teenagers. Studies within the English and Romanian Adoptees (ERA) study have demonstrated a proven link between earlier neurodevelopmental disorders and later emotional difficulties such as anxiety and depression (Barker et al., 2020). This cascade of development illustrates how early delays and disorders may impact social functioning and access to employment, and through this, increase vulnerability in the transition to adulthood. Healthcare professionals can mitigate this risk of later emotional problems by addressing these early issues, and in the process promote resilience in adolescents with ASD, ultimately improving their quality of life as they face the challenges of adulthood (Figure 5.3).

5.1.2. Attention-Deficit/Hyperactivity Disorder (ADHD)

The multifaceted nature of Attention-Deficit/Hyperactivity Disorder (ADHD) renders it one of the most common neurodevelopmental disorders among children and teenagers. The condition is characterized by symptoms of inattention, impulsivity, and hyperactivity and impacts academic performance as well as interpersonal relationships. Epidemiological studies estimate that the prevalence rate stands at 5.29% among children, reflecting a wide recognition of the condition across child mental health services. Further, ADHD is very hereditary, with research indicating that parents and siblings of individuals with the disorder are four or five times more probable of being diagnosed with the disorder too. The genetic factor, coupled with several environmental factors, emphasizes the multiple-determined etiology of ADHD and the need for broad diagnostic approaches that consider both genetic and situational determinants of the disorder (Johnson et al., 2013). The implications of untreated ADHD extend, however, far into the future and well beyond childhood to adolescence, where it can result in a number of comorbidities, such as anxiety, depression, and learning disability. For instance, research highlights how preterm birth is associated with increased risks for the development of ADHD and psychiatric illness and how this implies an intersectional turning point between developmental history and mental health outcome. Research has indicated that anxiety and communication problems, which are common among preterm adolescents, are accompanied by increased rates of ADHD symptoms. During adolescence into adulthood, the stability and continuity of these problems underscore the need for early identification and treatment (Johnson et al., 2013). Prevention is critical in minimizing the long-term effects of ADHD on mental health and general satisfaction with life. Successful ADHD treatment is a multi-component approach, where pharmacological treatment such as methylphenidate is largely practiced. Methylphenidate has documented successful outcomes in approximately 80% of individuals diagnosed with ADHD. Methylphenidate is the first-line drug that emphasizes the need for clinicians like child and adult psychiatrists to have confidence diagnosing and treating ADHD in adults and children (Camilleri et al., 2013). Also, intervention methods have to incorporate behavioral treatments and educational support, which significantly enhance rates of treatment and provide coping mechanisms for affected persons. As ADHD is continuously raising its profile in the field of child and adolescent mental health, knowledge of its complexity, risks involved, and treatments is essential in the creation of better clinical interventions and outcomes of treatment among affected subjects (Figure 5.4).

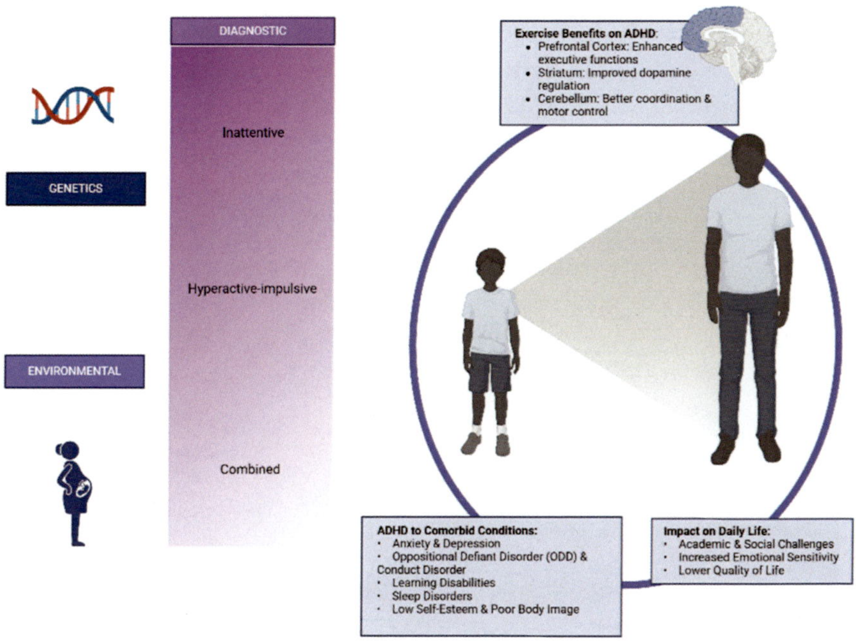

Figure 5.4. Effective management of ADHD employs a multi-faceted approach, predominantly utilizing pharmacological treatments such as methylphenidate, which has shown favorable responses in approximately 80% of diagnosed cases.

Source: https://pub.mdpi-res.com/children/children-12-00338/article_deploy/html/images/children-12-00338-g001.png?1741349880.

5.1.3. Learning Disabilities

In the context of neurodevelopmental disorders, learning disability is a significant problem of child and adolescent mental health. Reading, writing, and mathematics impairments in the presence of normal intelligence and appropriate educational arrangements are typical of such disorders. Increased awareness of learning disability has prompted extensive investigation of the etiologies of learning disabilities involving multiple genetic, environmental, and neurologic factors. Early intervention and diagnosis are critical, since delays can exacerbate academic challenges and lead to more severe psychosocial issues like low self-concept and worry. Additionally, the social significance of learning disabilities highlights the necessity of caring educational systems providing assistance with varied learning capabilities, fostering an integrated education culture positive to the attainment of all students. Learning disabilities may also interact with other neurodevelopmental disorders to make educational life more complex. For instance, research indicates a large comorbid connection between learning disability and mental illness, particularly in teenagers. This is usually a variable that leaves people at higher risk of acquiring secondary emotional disorders, including depression and anxiety.

Figure 5.5. The increasing recognition of learning disabilities has prompted an expansive investigation into their root causes, which encompass a range of genetic, environmental, and neurological factors.

Source: https://cdn.prod.website-files.com/65cb6a13e28e17a9782545c2/664336fad4a520f23ffaf856_Causes%20of%20Learning%20Disabilities.jpg.

Active mental health intervention cannot be overemphasized, particularly for people who have been diagnosed with disorders like ADHD or autism spectrum disorder, which tend to occur together with learning disabilities. By analyzing such intersections, interventions must be multi-faceted so that they address both academic as well as emotional needs in order to accomplish overall development. The schools therefore play a significant role in recognizing such complexities, modifying educational interventions to navigate the impacted students through their respective concerns. The effects of learning disability extend beyond the education domain, influencing long-term trajectories of mental health throughout the life course. Teenagers with learning disabilities are especially at risk for developing emotional disorders since high levels of psychiatric illness have been found among such individuals. Findings indicate that almost 25% of preterm teenagers, who themselves are already at risk of neurodevelopmental issues, have learning disabilities alongside other mental health issues. This dual burden can potentially create a cycle of vulnerability, as the identification of learning disabilities adds to stressors that exacerbate emotional and psychological concerns. Keeping this in mind, comprehensive screening and sustained intervention plans are essential. Through reinforcing and fostering resilience, caregivers and teachers may provide teenagers with learning disabilities the resilience to navigate their lives, ultimately enhancing their mental health and life trajectory through informed, guided interventions (Johnson et al., 2013) (Figure 5.5).

5.2. CAUSES AND RISK FACTORS

Identifying the etiology and risk factors for neurodevelopmental disorders within child and adolescent mental health is key to the development of efficacious intervention and prevention strategies. Complications in pregnancy and birth are an important factor, such as maternal infection, use of drugs, and complications in giving birth. These conditions may affect brain development during gestation periods that are critical in importance, having long-term consequences upon cognitive and affective function. For instance, preterm birth has been discovered to be associated with increased risk of residual neurodevelopmental disability. The evidence leads towards preterm persons displaying higher prevalence rates for emotional disorders, ADHD, and Autism, pointing towards early trauma and brain development mechanisms being utmost crucial in establishing later-life mental health outcomes (Johnson et al., 2013). Discovery of these biological mechanisms is crucial to enabling timely screening and the application of targeted intervention processes among risk-taking populations. Environmental factors make a major impact on the etiology of neurodevelopmental disorders through interference with brain development and functioning. Education access, socioeconomic status, and exposure to environmental pollutants such as lead have a massive impact on the mental health development trajectory of a child. Children with low socioeconomic status are exposed to more stressors in their life, including housing instability, safety concerns, and lower exposure to quality healthcare, which all get in the way of optimal brain development. Moreover, intensive traumatic childhood experiences like abuse and neglect have been indicated to exert long-term effects on neurodevelopment as well as psychiatric disorder development. Through the study of such risk factors, researchers are better able to understand the intricate nature of neurodevelopmental disorders and how gene and environment interact to influence a child's state of mental health. The nuances of brain development in adolescents also play a vital role in the explanation of mental illnesses at this age. As adolescents deal with complicated social worlds, their brains, particularly areas in charge of decision-making and impulse control, are still exposed to unique vulnerabilities. Research suggests that adolescents are prone to voluntary challenges in making decisions, which affect their susceptibility to developing mental illness disorders (Pustilnik et al., 2015). Regulatory legislative frameworks for managing adolescent behavior tend to be disconnected from the scientific evidence of developmental neuroscience and, as such, end up treating adolescent crimes in an unequal manner. This necessitates revisiting policies impacting adolescents grounded on an understanding of their stage of development. By marrying conclusions drawn from developmental neuroscience with legal concerns, we can better bolster support systems for teens and create environments that are supportive in terms of cultivating healthier mental health developments (Figure 5.6).

Figure 5.6. As adolescents navigate complex social environments, their developing brains—particularly areas responsible for decision-making and impulse control—remain susceptible to unique vulnerabilities.

Source: https://www.softmindindia.com/userfiles/Blog/a9e2596a753a4675abd0eb-89ca2fba1d.png.

5.2.1. Genetic Influences

It is necessary to consider genetic influences while examining neurodevelopmental disorders among children and adolescents because these disorders show a familial pattern. It has been studied that genetic influences play a strong role in the variance of the symptoms of attention-deficit/hyperactivity disorder (ADHD), and the estimates are that genetic influences can account for 54% to 73% of variance in attention and 31% to 73% of variance in activity levels in adolescence. This validates the argument that neurodevelopmental disorders are not only environmental in nature; rather, they are deeply rooted in genetic susceptibility. Familial contributions, including both inherited genes and new familial contributions, play a vital role in shaping these neurodevelopmental features over time, which is essential in developing targeted interventions individualized for each case. As studies investigate deeper into these genetic underpinnings, it seems increasingly that a full understanding of such influences is essential to effective treatment. The pursuit of effective interventions in neurodevelopmental disorders also requires the study of interaction between genetic predispositions, environmental factors, and developmental outcomes. For instance, while genetic components can dominate the manifestation of disorders like fragile X syndrome (FXS), environmental interventions can improve outcomes along development. In a randomized controlled trial, researchers demonstrated that the combination of parent-implemented language interventions and lovastatin treatment was capable of enhancing language skills in teenagers with FXS. Notably, both groups experienced similar improvement, proving the synergistic interaction between genetic and environmental intervention. This approach shows the importance of pediatric mental health professionals considering not just the genetic background of their patients but also the importance of particular, evidence-supported treatment based on family involvement and environmental engagement.

As a result, a combined focus on genetic and environmental factors may lead to more successful treatment. Moreover, the recognition of the significant role of genetic factors not only exceeds treatment measures but also gives data for preventive measures in neurodevelopmental disorders. Genetics has the possibility to provide cues for risk and resilience processes that can develop in initial phases of development. It can recognize children and adolescents who possess genetic markers associated with neurodevelopmental challenges and begin early screening and prevention programs in high-risk individuals. This preemptive approach is pivotal in warding off the late-life consequences of disorders such as ADHD and FXS. Consequently, genetic research not only informs us on the pathogenesis of these disorders but also enhances our capacity to act proactively, leading to improved mental health outcomes in child and adolescent life. In achieving this, the merging of genetic information in mental health paradigms will be key to driving the enhancement of treatment and prevention strategies within the sector (Figure 5.7).

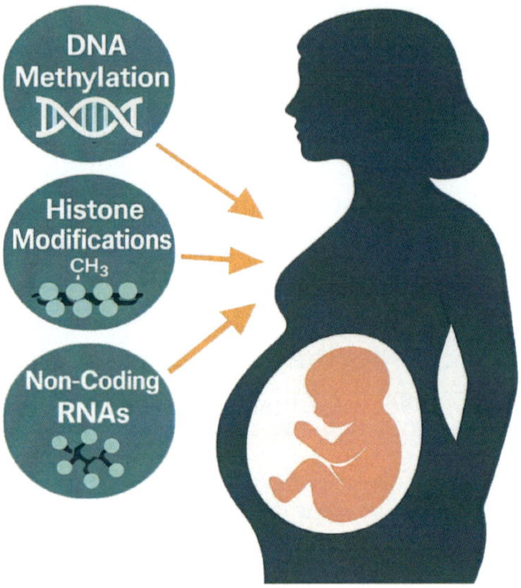

Figure 5.7. By identifying children and adolescents who possess genetic markers associated with neurodevelopmental challenges, clinicians can implement early screening and preventative programs tailored to high-risk populations.

Source: https://www.mdpi.com/ijms/ijms-26-06096/article_deploy/html/images/ijms-26-06096-g001.png.

5.2.2. Environmental Factors

The role of environmental factors and neurodevelopmental disorders in children and adolescents is a highly important area of study in the field of mental health. Multiple variables such as exposure to prenatal toxicity, socio-economic status, and family dynamics contribute significantly to neurodevelopmental outcomes. For instance, gestational exposure to environmental pollutants, including endocrine-disrupting chemicals and heavy metals, in mothers has been associated with increased risks of diseases like attention-deficit hyperactivity disorder and autism spectrum disorders. Further, traumatic experiences in childhood, as well as neglect, have been reported to have adverse effects on neural development with long-term psychiatric consequences. Understanding these environmental determinants can guide prevention through strong focus on the creation of a healthy prenatal environment and favorable socio-economic status in order to serve as a buffer against risk for neurodevelopmental disorders among vulnerable populations. Additionally, lifestyle factors, including diet and physical activity, play significant roles in shaping the neurodevelopmental trajectory of children and adolescents. For example, a diet rich in essential nutrients such as omega-3 fatty acids and antioxidants has been found to relate to improved cognitive functioning as well as behavioral results. A diet rich in processed foods and sugar can deteriorate behavior disorders and influence mental health negatively, though. The advantages of physical activity have also been the focal point of scientific attention, which improves neurogenesis and cognitive resilience. Therefore, addressing nutrient deficiency and promoting physical exercise are essential components of public health policy in a bid to reduce the prevalence of neurodevelopmental disorders. By focusing on eating habits and exercise, communities can promote healthy environments that maximize children's overall health and can short-circuit the onset of mental illness. Finally, the role played by early intervention in mitigating the effects of environmental factors cannot be overemphasized. Early recognition and management of neurodevelopmental disorders such as obsessive-compulsive disorder (OCD) significantly improve clinical outcomes and global quality of life. Delays in treatment have been shown to cause chronic disability and added misery for sufferers and families and thus provide justification for earlier access to mental health care. Differences in access to such resources, particularly in low- and middle-income nations, identify some of the most important gaps in health equity and unmet demand for early intervention services. With the establishment of inclusive support systems, integration of mental health care into primary care, and prioritization of education regarding environmental risks, public health interventions can positively address the issues of neurodevelopmental disorders, in the end assuring a healthier adolescence future (Albert et al., 2019; Dueñas et al., 2014).

5.2.3. Prenatal and Perinatal Complications

The prenatal growth phase is also the period when fundamental cognitive and emotional capabilities are established, and any disruption during this phase may have long-term effects on mental health. Maternal infections, teratogenic exposure, and nutritional insufficiency in pregnancy have all been linked with an increased risk of neurodevelopmental disorders later in life. Other factors like gestational diabetes and hypertension can also disrupt fetal growth and development, causing negative outcomes at birth. Such early disturbances may increase susceptibility to emotional disorders and developmental delay that may be prolonged to adolescence and beyond. Studies indicate that children with a history of prenatal complications are at higher risk of developing anxiety, attention deficits, and social adjustment problems, which highlight the importance of interventions at an early stage to arrest such risks and promote mental health resilience in the long run. The perinatal period too is equally important as it covers a chain of complications that directly impact neurological development. It is interesting to note that preterm birth is associated with a highly increased risk of neurodevelopmental impairment, such as cognitive disability and psychiatric disease.

Figure 5.8. Prenatal complications, such as maternal infections, exposure to teratogens, and nutritional deficiencies, have been linked to an increased risk of neurodevelopmental disorders later in life.

Source: https://www.thetransmitter.org/wp-content/uploads/2022/12/1200-maternal-inflamation.webp.

A large proportion of preterm infants experience long-term morbidity in the form of attention-deficit/hyperactivity disorder (ADHD) and autism spectrum disorders (ASD) (Johnson et al., 2013). Morbidity typically manifests at the transition phase of adolescence when already prevailing vulnerabilities are escalated. Regular monitoring and management in preterm infants can contribute to the early alleviation of these complications and their remission over time. Consequently, healthcare systems must address screening and treatment for these infants during development, supplying them with the right mental health interventions based on their unique developmental trajectories. Additionally, paternal age has been found to be a causative factor contributing to neurodevelopmental complications and impacting mental health status in the child. Increased paternal age has also been shown to be associated with greater risks for ASD and schizophrenia, suggesting that environmental and genetic factors coincide with the older age of fathers (Ek et al., 2015). This dimension of parental health invokes a broader conceptualization of the etiology of neurodevelopmental disorders as connecting maternal as well as paternal contributions to being key determinants. With mental illness in youth increasingly being better understood as a multifaceted construct, this association calls for increased investigation into how parental age and accompanying characteristics can impact child development and mental health. Public health and clinical considerations of knowledge regarding these factors are paramount to reducing risks associated with advanced parental age (Figure 5.8).

5.3. SYMPTOMS AND DIAGNOSIS

Symptoms of neurodevelopmental disorders may present in various forms, often compounded with emotional, cognitive, and behavioral challenges. Children will most likely have difficulties with attention, communication, and social interactions. For instance, attention-deficit/hyperactivity disorder (ADHD) is characterized by signs of impulsivity, inattention, and hyperactivity, while autism spectrum disorders (ASD) can involve social communication impairment and repetitive behaviors. These symptoms not only hinder learning but also interfere with social relationships and interpersonal relationships within the family. Identification of these symptoms then becomes essential as they are often comorbid with other mental illnesses, requiring careful evaluation by qualified personnel trained in child and adolescent mental health. Early detection and intervention are of essence in preventing the long-term sequelae that come with these disorders, allowing children to get the needed intervention and strategies designed specifically for them. Diagnosis of neurodevelopmental disorders is multifaceted and takes into account developmental history and current functioning. Clinicians utilize standardized assessment and observational techniques to determine behavioral and affective reactions. Categorizations in manuals of diagnosis, such as the DSM-5, form the foundation to determine specific disorders based on predetermined criteria. Diagnostic complexities of conditions like ASD or ADHD are augmented with the prevalence of co-occurring disorders, making symptom profiling more complex. For example, it has been identified that preterm birth greatly predisposes an individual to mental disorders, as evident from symptoms that are normally found with anxiety, social disorder, and communication disorder. This commingling of symptomatology with diagnostic criteria underscores the significance of ongoing assessment in clinical practice, particularly when symptoms change in salient developmental periods. The presence of regression in developmental milestones poses even more challenges to diagnosis and treatment of symptoms in neurodevelopmental disorders. There is evidence to suggest that narrowly defined children with autism are at risk of language regression, which stands at 30%, far above in the case of broad categories of ASD where it is 8%. Regression defined by a divergence of paths of development not only suggests a loss of learned skills but also accompanied by an increase in autistic symptoms. It is essential that clinicians understand these regression patterns in order to navigate the complex landscape of child development and mental health. Moreover, the impact of such findings extends beyond close clinical observation; it requires ongoing monitoring and intervention strategies to mitigate the added risk factors of various neurodevelopmental disorders, including the prevalence of emotional disorders among preterm adolescents, as highlighted by the ongoing need for long-term screening and treatment (Johnson et al., 2013; LeCouteur et al., 2008).

5.3.1. Behavioral Symptoms

Behavioral manifestations of neurodevelopmental disorders are significant indicators of underlying cognitive and emotional challenges typically encountered in children and adolescents. Disturbances in behavior can include hyperactivity, impulsiveness, withdrawal, and anxiety typically encountered with disorders such as attention-deficit/hyperactivity disorder (ADHD) and autism spectrum disorder (ASD). Not only do these complications disrupt a child's social life but also impact school performance and self-esteem. Involvement of environmental influences, such as prenatal influences and early-life stressors, can contribute to these behavioral manifestations. It has also been demonstrated that preterm-born children, for instance, are at higher risk for behavioral issues, such as anxiety and communication issues, and that these have been identified to extend into adolescence and adulthood and thus be in need of long-term intervention and support measures (Johnson et al., 2013). In neurodevelopmental disorders, the conflict between early behavioral difficulties and subsequent emotional pathology stands at the forefront of what determines the trajectory of mental health. England and Romanian Adoptees (ERA) project research describes the cascade from early neurodevelopmental issues caused by severe institutional deprivation. Kids who are exposed to such extreme environments usually present with central behavioral issues, which stabilize into adolescent emotional issues like depression and anxiety. By early adulthood, such individuals usually have difficulty with stress reactivity and relationship issues that reinforce early behaviors. This chain of development emphasizes the relevance of careful assessments that include the long-term consequences of early behavior disruption (Barker et al., 2020). Treatment of the behavioral symptoms of neurodevelopmental disorders requires particular intervention methods attuned to the individualized requirements of the affected individuals.

Early identification and intervention can play a pivotal role, particularly in children with symptoms similar to those associated with preterm birth or institutional deprivation. Individualized treatment methods, including cognitive-behavioral therapy, social skills training, and family intervention, can decrease symptom severity and improve functioning. Moreover, ongoing monitoring of high-risk populations is crucial in order to implement early interventions that ensure resilience and mental wellness. Because manifestations of behavior are generally reflective of underlying neurodevelopmental pathology, treatment in early stages not only benefits the patient but also aids in enabling healthier developmental pathways across all child and adolescent mental health (Barker et al., 2020; Johnson et al., 2013).

5.3.2. Cognitive Symptoms

Cognitive symptoms are an essential part of considering neurodevelopmental disorders and hold a significant role in impacting learning as well as social interaction among kids and adolescents. These symptoms, such as difficulty with attention, memory, and problem-solving skills, can often set off a chain of problems affecting the overall mental health of a child. Kids diagnosed with disorders such as attention deficit hyperactivity disorder (ADHD) often experience deficits in executive functions, which govern organizational as well as planning capabilities. These impairments not only hinder academic achievement but also impact social skill, risking social rejection and contributing to feelings of isolation and anxiety in these children. In teens, these cognitive challenges complicate the evolution of other mental health disorders too, leading to early recognition and targeted interventions in an effort to minimize risks for long-term outcomes. Research has shown the association of premature birth with subsequent cognitive expressions, disclosing that preterm children are at a higher risk of experiencing various neurodevelopmental disabilities that are manifested in the form of learning disabilities and conduct issues. The cognitive deficits are usually multifaceted, nonisolated events; instead, they become highly enmeshed with psychiatric disorders. For instance, studies indicate that individuals born preterm are vulnerable to a higher incidence of emotional disorders, ADHD, and Autism, and underlining the specific risk factor for the cognitive dysfunctions resulting from neurodevelopmental disorders. Longitudinal nature of the problems must be determined as the cognitive deficits that develop in early childhood tend to carry over into adolescence, which means that persistent monitoring and treatment are required. The prevalence of such issues highlights the necessity for strong supportive mechanisms for people so affected, as a way of ensuring resilience and more positive developmental outcomes over the life course (Johnson et al., 2013).

Studies of the cognitive impact of early severe deprivation further highlight the long-term effects of neurodevelopmental impairments. One engaging study of Romanian adoptees revealed that institution-based early deprivation is highly consonant with cognitive deficit and the development of emotional problems later in life. Cognitive deficits observed in the early years typically provide the basis for later problems with social function and vocational achievement in adolescence and beyond. This stressful section is compounded by the long-term continuity of cognitive symptoms, making for increased vulnerability to stress and emotional disturbance during adulthood. The result of such studies points to the need for long-term care and interventions aimed at not just the cognition impairment among children and adolescents but also the associated psychosocial issues that arise as they develop into adults (Barker et al., 2020) (Figure 5.9).

Figure 5.9. The cognitive issues presented in early childhood often lay the groundwork for difficulties in social functioning and vocational achievement during adolescence and beyond.

Source: https://childdevelopmentinfo.com/wp-content/uploads/2022/03/cognitive-development-min-scaled.jpg.

5.3.3. Diagnostic Criteria and Assessment Tools

Diagnostic procedures and criteria employed in the diagnosis of neurodevelopmental disorders in children and adolescents are crucial for guiding effective intervention and support. Standardized classification systems, including the Diagnostic and Statistical Manual of Mental Disorders (DSM-5) and the International Classification of Diseases (ICD-10), form a basis for the specification of the symptoms and behaviors which are typical of conditions like autism spectrum disorder (ASD) and attention-deficit/hyperactivity disorder (ADHD). These standards not only inform clinicians in arriving at accurate diagnoses but also ensure consistency in different health care settings. Furthermore, the utilization of valid assessment instruments, including structured interviews and behavior checklists, enhances reliability of diagnosis, thereby informing relevant treatment plans. These systematic methods are vital in decreasing the stigma routinely ascribed to these disorders, increasing education among educators and families.

Assessment tools serve to establish the complicated nature of neurodevelopmental disorders. While clinicians typically rely on clinical interviews and rating observations, standardized questionnaires may yield data about the severity and frequency of symptoms reported by the parents, teachers, and the children. Measures like the Conners Comprehensive Behavior Rating Scales and the Autism Diagnostic Observation Schedule have been found to be effective in evaluating various aspects of functioning, including social skills and cognitive abilities. Moreover, these measures can identify comorbid conditions, which are frequent among neurodevelopmentally disordered adolescents, and hence enable comprehensive treatment planning. As neurodevelopmental trajectories are influenced by several environmental and genetic factors, accurate measurement is key to the prediction of long-term outcomes and the provision of early interventions that can lead to improved mental health and well-being. Early identification and intervention cannot be overstated, particularly in light of the complex interrelationship between neurodevelopmental disorders and long-term outcomes in mental health. Research has established that neurodevelopmental disorders-associated conditions, such as those due to preterm birth, increase the risk of adolescence's many psychiatric issues, such as ADHD and emotional disorders, which need to be closely followed (Johnson et al., 2013). Furthermore, Transition from Child and Adolescent Mental Health Services (CAMHS) to Adult Mental Health Services (AMHS) pathways once more underscore the necessary need for effective assessment and diagnostic procedures. Studies have shown that a poor transition process has the potential to exacerbate existing mental health issues, while the potential for discontinuity of care results in impaired emotional status (Adamson et al., 2015). With this in mind, ongoing efforts at simplifying diagnostic criteria as well as creating secure assessment methods are essential in managing the long-term mental health care of children and adolescents with neurodevelopmental disorders.

5.4. IMPACT ON CHILD AND ADOLESCENT DEVELOPMENT

The impact of neurodevelopmental disorders on child and adolescent development is substantial and multifaceted. Preterm-born individuals have been found to be extremely susceptible to neurodevelopmental disabilities persisting in the long term, and they are usually cognitive impairments and affective disorders. The susceptibility is not randomly distributed but has some relationships with mental disorders, namely anxiety and attention disorders. In fact, preterm-born teenagers are far more likely to develop emotional disorders, ADHD, and autism compared to those born at term. Therefore, the course of development in such individuals must be monitored closely since continuity of symptomology from childhood through adolescence means there is an established pattern of neurodevelopmental impairments whose management may require ongoing intervention to avert adverse outcomes in emotional and social adjustment (Johnson et al., 2013). Substantial evidence demonstrates that early adverse experience, such as severe institutional deprivation, has significant impacts on child and adolescent development. The English and Romanian Adoptees (ERA) study recognizes a distinct pathway whereby early neurodevelopmental challenges can predispose to later emotional challenges. Children who are deprived have increased risks of neurodevelopmental challenges that can hinder their social performance when they become adolescents and adults. These initial problems are likely to be the forerunners for a cascade of consequences as neurodevelopmental impairment results in social and occupational challenges. The evidence suggests a significant relationship between experience of early deprivation, subsequent neurodevelopmental challenge, and the onset of anxiety and depression during adolescence and early adult life, emphasizing the need for early intervention in those at risk (Barker et al., 2020). The implications of the research are wide-ranging, in the sense that they indicate a requirement for individualized interventions and continuous support to children and adolescents with neurodevelopmental disorders. Early identification and intervention practices can avert unfavorable developmental outcomes through the reduction of long-term effects. By establishing conditions that foster emotional, social, and cognitive development, educators and caregivers can play an influential role in the outcomes of vulnerable youth. Besides, a focus on resilience and coping aspects in promoting resilience in those affected by neurodevelopmental disorders can be a welcome development. Extended research and screenings, particularly with regards to groups identified as vulnerable such as preterm birth or institution, will be critical in fostering effective ways of improving overall mental health outcomes and offering an improved quality of life for such populations (Barker et al., 2020; Johnson et al., 2013) (Figure 5.10).

Figure 5.10. Adolescents born preterm demonstrate a markedly higher prevalence of emotional disorders, ADHD, and autism when compared to their term-born peers.

Source: https://cdn.prod.website-files.com/64271cf7f88ba128857fe9b7/643857e0921205343f589cd5_IMG_1087.PNG.

5.4.1. Academic Challenges

The cognitive impairments of children and teenagers with neurodevelopmental disorders are multifaceted, with a wide-ranging impact on education and social interaction. The sufferers have impaired processing of cognitive function that affects their ability to acquire and store knowledge under normal learning conditions. The difficulties also manifest themselves in other forms, for example, difficulties with attention, memory, and executive function. Therefore, the students with neurodevelopmental disorders are likely to perceive themselves as being inadequate and frustrated compared to their peers, and a negative self-image will further hinder academic achievement. Educators and mental health professionals must identify such challenges since they must adapt their teaching methods to accommodate these children's ways of learning and enable an enabling learning environment. Moreover, children in out-of-home care or protective custody, a group frequently impaired through neurodevelopmental disorder, need also to deal with compounded academic difficulties. According to studies, youth in these placements have poorer health status overall, including mental health, which can interfere with their educational participation and performance. For instance, studies show that 41.6% of youth in protective custody have a mental health diagnosis, with most having ongoing medical conditions and acting-out behaviors. These issues crosscut one another and merge to form a nexus of problems that not only affect educational performance but also erode potential for social integration and skill attainment. Breaking these learning barriers requires targeted interventions and collaboration between mental health services and schools to create individualized networks of support for such vulnerable children (Beal et al., 2019). Additionally, the presence of fetal alcohol spectrum disorders (FASD) among children within different care systems disproportionately exacerbates their educational struggles. The intellectual and physical disabilities due to prenatal exposure to alcohol can lead to impairments in major areas of language development, memory processing, and executive functioning. This can often lead to more problems in schools in the form of relationship difficulties among peers and learning environments that are disturbed. FASD's lack of public recognition in school and healthcare systems renders it even harder to develop effective intervention systems. To ensure that such children are properly supported, instructional experts must be trained to recognize the signs of FASD and adjust their pedagogical approaches for this reason. Multidisciplinary coordinated interventions have to be implemented in order to minimize the learning difficulties associated with FASD and ensure that these children receive equal learning opportunities (McLean et al., 2025).

5.4.2. Social Interactions and Relationships

Social relationships and interactions have a significant bearing on the mental well-being and general development of children and youth, especially those who have neurodevelopmental disorders. Neurodevelopmental disorders can interfere with social competence, such that affected individuals have difficulties participating in normal peer relations. Consequently, kids with such disorders as autism spectrum disorder (ASD) or attention-deficit/hyperactivity disorder (ADHD) may become rejected or isolated by other children, which will perpetuate a vicious cycle of self-concept and emotional disturbance. The complicated interaction between neurodevelopmental disorders and social processes is significant in understanding to create successful interventions. Additional social skills training and supportive environments can facilitate positive interaction, consequently, improve the well-being of such children and encouraging them to establish healthy relationships essential to their emotional well-being. Family greatly affects social interaction and relationships and cannot be overlooked, especially for neurodevelopmental disordered children. Families are primarily supportive and influence children's self-esteem and social skills. Parents and caregivers typically have the role of identifying and treating the special needs of disorders such as fetal alcohol spectrum disorders (FASD), which involve a range of cognitive and physical abnormalities that further complicate social interaction. Misunderstandings about these disorders can lead to labeling, which in turn can disrupt peer relationships and hinder overall growth. Efforts directed at educating families about FASD can equip them with the knowledge and ability to facilitate healthier interactions and guide children towards more successful social experiences and preventing the risk of emotional and behavioral issues due to isolation (McLean et al., 2025). Moreover, the overall societal environment also plays a vital role in shaping the social experiences of children with neurodevelopmental disorders. Schools and community environments must foster inclusive approaches acknowledging and addressing the diverse needs of affected individuals. Such environments can facilitate friendships and peer relationships through formal social programs that allow children with various abilities to interact with each other. Awareness and sensitivity training among caregivers and peers also can decrease stigmas generally associated with neurodevelopmental disorders, which in turn will enhance positive social interactions. By creating inclusive settings, the scope of effective relationship-building becomes greater, thereby enhancing the emotional and psychological adjustment of such children. Multidisciplinary actions combining family, educational settings, and community resources are needed to facilitate social development in neurodevelopmental disorder children, finally resulting in resilience and safeguarding mental health (Browne et al., 2019) (Figure 5.11).

Figure 5.11. Social interactions and relationships significantly impact the mental health and overall development of children and adolescents, particularly those diagnosed with neurodevelopmental disorders.

Source: https://www.verywellmind.com/thmb/JBTL8biEBPOJGZJbrvrJFwc7UVY=/1500x0/filters:no_upscale():max_bytes(150000):strip_icc()/GettyImages-1315878411-c95fb285737e46c3916fc148581c7ce6.jpg.

5.4.3. Emotional Well-Being

Emotional well-being is one of the key aspects of mental health in children and adolescents, particularly for individuals with neurodevelopmental disorders. Neurodevelopmental disorders can pose a critical influence on the development of emotional regulation and social interactions, thereby influencing long-term psychological functioning. For example, children with neurodevelopmental issues might display impaired identification and response to emotion cues, which might lead to isolation and other emotional problems later in life. It is necessary to understand how neurodevelopmental disorders relate to emotional well-being, as interventions that address developing the skills required to be emotionally healthy early on can avoid the long-term detrimental effect these disorders have on mental health. The research is centered on how neurodevelopmental struggles intertwine with emotional well-being, particularly in cases of early deprivation. The English and Romanian Adoptees (ERA) study illustrates the manner in which children subjected to severe institutional deprivation will present with early neurodevelopmental problems that progress to subsequent emotional difficulties such as depression and anxiety in adolescence. These subsequent emotional disturbances are in turn exacerbated by social and vocational functioning in the transition from adolescence to adulthood, emphasizing the strong need for targeted therapeutic interventions. The resolution of these issues holistically through continued mental health treatment can ride the complex terrain of emotional health in affected individuals, fostering resilience and adaptive coping strategies. Furthermore, the preterm adolescent age group is the critical juncture of neurodevelopmental diseases and emotional health. Evidence would indicate preterm birth to be defined by increased rates of psychiatric disease, most prominently symptoms of anxiety, attention deficits, as well as difficulties with social communication. As a result, preterm adolescents are at higher risk of encountering mental health issues that can be expressed as emotional disorders, ADHD, as well as even autism. This background also underscores the necessity to implement long-term monitoring and intervention measures to help ensure emotional and psychological development in such susceptible individuals. By focusing on emotional health, mental health professionals can assist in ensuring that teenagers overcome these struggles well, leading to better emotional and overall mental health.

5.5. TREATMENT AND INTERVENTION STRATEGIES

Effective intervention and treatment of neurodevelopmental disorders involve a multidisciplinary approach involving pharmacological and behavioral treatments. Research suggests the therapeutic value of pharmacological medication, such as lovastatin, with positive outcomes in children affected by fragile X syndrome (FXS). In the controlled trial, the lovastatin patients demonstrated significant improvement in social and language skills, determining the efficacy of medication combined with very structured interventions like parent-implemented language intervention (PILI) that is offered through distance video teleconferencing. This comprehensive approach highlights the importance of collaboration between healthcare professionals, including psychologists, speech and language specialists, and behavioral analysts, in designing harmonized treatment plans to address an individual child's needs in the context of their developmental problems (Abbeduto et al., 2020). Behavioral treatments form a core component of the treatment of neurodevelopmental disorders with an emphasis on engaging caregivers during therapy protocols. Focused interventions that target the growth of parental involvement, such as the PILI used in the lovastatin experiment, bring to light the feasibility of training parents in effective communication practices while they converse with the child. This not only improves the child's learning environment but also parent-child relationship, which has the potential to be outcome linked to long-term developmental change. Greater parental competence in applied communication strategies not only improves the language development of the child but also fosters a support system that promotes emotional and social development, thus highlighting the interconnected nature of such therapy interventions (Abbeduto et al., 2020). Also, the treatment model for neurodevelopmental disorders is continuously evolving, and there are high degrees of emphasis on prevention, particularly on fetal alcohol spectrum disorders (FASD). Within the realm of evidence accumulated from a variety of studies, varying from those which have proved the effectiveness of targeted interventions for both Indigenous and broader Australian populations, it is increasingly clear that prevention programs can be utilized effectively to reduce the incidence and severity of such disorders. Current measures are directed towards educating pregnant women on the risk involved with alcohol consumption during pregnancy, with the general intent to reduce the prevalence of FASD. By adopting culturally appropriate interventions applicable to targeted populations, such programs make it clear how important individualized care is in addressing neurodevelopmental difficulties.

5.5.1. Behavioral Therapies

Behavioral therapies are a cornerstone in the treatment of neurodevelopmental disorders in children and adolescents for the management of a variety of conditions such as autism spectrum disorder, attention-deficit/hyperactivity disorder (ADHD), and fragile X syndrome. The behavioral therapy is intended to modify overt behaviors through varied approaches like reinforcement, modeling, and behavioral modification interventions. By applying these principles consistently, clinicians aim to reduce maladaptive behavior while augmenting positive behavior, eventually progressing toward skill acquisition and social interaction. These interventions are particularly crucial in the treatment of the unique challenges neurodevelopmental disorders embody because they provide children with tangible strategies with which to interpret their worlds. Notably, these therapies can be adjusted according to individual needs, thus offering one flexible instrument in maximizing developmental courses and enhancing overall mental health outcomes for affected youth. Evidence highlights the effectiveness of such behavioral interventions, especially where they are introduced early in a child's life. For instance, a study examining the interplay between pharmacologic treatment and parent-implemented language intervention in adolescents with fragile X syndrome noted significant gains in language and social communication abilities in both treatment conditions. Participants exhibited effective implementation of behavioral strategies advised by expert clinicians using video teleconferencing, demonstrating parental participation is critical in transferring skills to naturalistic settings (Abbeduto et al., 2020). Second, the supportive structure of behavioral treatments can allow for the consistent reinforcement of desired behaviors, again implying why early intervention not only yields better short-term outcomes but can also decrease developmental impacts of neurodevelopmental disorders. Third, the cascading effects of early behavioral interventions transfer to long-term emotional and cognitive processes. As indicated in the English and Romanian Adoptees study, early neurodevelopmental impairment has adverse effects on subsequent emotional health, and in suggesting a developmental pathway in which early intervention can prevent long-term adverse outcomes. Specifically, the impact of early behavioral treatment on vocational and social adjustment in adolescence as a protective factor in preventing the development of anxiety and depression in adulthood (Barker et al., 2020). This highlights the need to blend behavioral treatments with more holistic interventions that consider the scope of mental health, ultimately forming resilience in children and adolescents confronted with neurodevelopmental challenges.

5.5.2. Medication Management

Proper medication management is an integral component in managing neurodevelopmental disorders in child and adolescent mental health. With the prevalence of diseases such as attention-deficit/hyperactivity disorder (ADHD), autism spectrum disorder (ASD), and learning disabilities, medical professionals often resort to pharmacological interventions as part of a comprehensive treatment plan. Medication can significantly enhance symptoms, enhance functionality, and play a role in the overall well-being of patients who are affected. But the challenge is to correctly diagnose such disorders because they have overlapping symptoms. Regular monitoring and adjustment of treatment are required in order to optimize effectiveness while preventing untoward side effects. Where these considerations become particularly significant is in the selective taking into account of the individual developmental trajectories of children and adolescents because their neurobiological systems differ quite markedly from adults' and may respond differently to pharmacotherapy. The transition from Child and Adolescent Mental Health Services (CAMHS) to Adult Mental Health Services (AMHS) is even more difficult in the area of medication management.

This is a crucial period of transition because adolescents can go through fluctuating mental health needs, which call for different therapeutic approaches or a modification in their drug schedule. Studies like the ITRACK study demonstrate the importance of clear communication among providers at this stage, pointing out the adverse consequences that might be induced by breakdown in information transfer. Where clinical information pertinent to them is not shared, adolescents may find it difficult to obtain appropriate drugs or will not benefit from timely interventions aimed at managing their conditions adequately. Therefore, uninterrupted transition facilitated by thorough medication histories and ongoing monitoring can be particularly impactful on continuity and stability of treatment in this high-risk population, ultimately leading to improved long-term outcomes. Given the very high prevalence of neurodevelopmental disorders in preterm adolescents, uniquely tailored approaches to medication management become ever more critical. Preterm birth has been found by studies to be highly associated with an increased risk of various mental disorders such as anxiety, inattention, and emotional disorders such as ADHD and autism. The conditions manifest in early life and persist into adolescence, which implies that there is a need for high-level long-term screening and intervention strategies. Effective medication management among this population must address both the pharmacologic and psychosocial components of care and incorporate mechanisms to adapt treatment plans to meet the changing individual needs over time. As psychiatric disorders affect an estimated 25% of preterm children, it is critically important to embrace evidence-based approaches that couple medication management with therapeutic care to promote healthy holistic developmental trajectories that align with their individualized neurodevelopmental profiles and mental health needs (Johnson et al., 2013).

5.5.3. Educational Support and Accommodations

The requirement for teaching assistance and adjustment in children and youth with neurodevelopmental disorders cannot be overstated. These children and youth often come with issues the typical education systems are ill-equipped to address, presenting significant barriers to learning and social adaptation. In a bid to create effective learning settings, teachers must implement individualized strategies that satisfy specific needs in terms of disorders such as attention deficit hyperactivity disorder (ADHD), autism spectrum disorder (ASD), and Fetal Alcohol Spectrum Disorders (FASD). Empirical evidence underscores the fact that effective interventions not only yield better outcomes in learning but also instill a sense of belonging and worth among affected students, which is highly crucial to the overall well-being of affected students. As implied by existing studies, early identification and special interventions make it possible to have enhanced academic performance, which means such children get to attain their full potential while minimizing the negative effects of their conditions (McLean et al., 2025). Moreover, school accommodations normally include modified methods of teaching, differential curricula, and customized assessments created to address varying learning styles. For example, students with Tourette's syndrome would welcome less stigma and greater awareness by teachers and peers.

Positive communication and self-advocacy can be empowering for such students since they will be able to communicate their needs, therefore a welcoming classroom. Moreover, through assistive technologies, learning gaps can be filled, particularly in reading comprehension and math, which may be challenging for neurodiverse students. Education facilities must accord proper priority to teacher professional development so that they become competent enough with the required knowledge and tools to offer an effective support system. Finally, identification of and response to the special education needs of such children are important for nurturing an inclusive culture and an egalitarian environment to learn (Forrester-Jones et al., 2015). Finally, communication and collaboration between schools, families, and mental health professionals are required for the successful implementation of educational supports and accommodations. Being multidisciplinary, this endeavor guarantees intervention methods being multifaceted and taking into account several facets within a child's life, such as social skills and mental health. Fluid channels of communication between parents and teachers allow for a united front in addressing issues and embracing success. Second, community outreach programs can foster awareness and reduce the stigma often associated with neurodevelopmental disorders, making the school and community more accepting. When stakeholders work together, they can create extensive support systems that not only promote educational success but also help children and adolescents with neurodevelopmental disorders become intellectually and socially successful. All these collective endeavors are crucial for developing a path towards a more integrated society (McLean et al., 2025) (Figure 5.12).

Figure 5.12. To create effective learning environments, it is essential for educators to implement tailored strategies that accommodate specific needs related to disorders such as attention deficit hyperactivity disorder (ADHD), autism spectrum disorder (ASD), and fetal alcohol spectrum disorders (FASD).

Source: https://cdn.prod.website-files.com/5b69a01ba2e409501de055d1/6798b0f22873361d21fcd7cf_6685219e279173ac0b4a2549_Learning%2520disability.webp.

5.6. ROLE OF FAMILY AND COMMUNITY SUPPORT

Family and social support are central in the development and management of neurodevelopmental disorders among children and adolescents. Families form the majority setting for early interventions, shaping the emotional and psychological well-being of those affected. On a regular basis, evidence emphasizes that an appropriate environment not only enhances intellectual development but also social competence and resilience against potential mental issues. An active family life can assist in minimizing some of the adverse effects that are associated with neurodevelopmental disorder by providing stability and unconditional love. This approach is also observed in studies that identify familial participation as an imperative factor towards long-term accomplishment in children with

ADHD and Autism. Through evoking a sense of belonging and understanding in the family, families come up with an adaptive system through which children are better able to negotiate their experiences of neurodevelopmental disorders. Support from the community also enhances the success of efforts at the family level by providing resources and networks essential for the well-being of children facing neurodevelopmental disorders. Community programs that offer specialized services, such as education and therapy, have been shown to have highly positive outcomes for youth and children. By uniting to form inclusive communities, communities decrease stigma and raise awareness of such conditions as those caused by prenatal alcohol exposure, as outlined in existing FASD research. Such programs are often in need of intersector collaboration, such as health, education, and social services. Successful policies for prevention and management of the disorders can be rooted on this cohesiveness within the community. The interplay between family support and community sources encapsulates an integrated response to stemming the multifaceted challenge of neurodevelopmental disorders. Moreover, efforts towards improved mental health outcomes among the children reinforce the importance of an integrated effort among the community and families. Long-term monitoring and intervention are imperative, especially among vulnerable groups, including preterm individuals, who are under increased risks of emotional disorders and ADHD, which continue through adolescence, as supported by recent studies (Johnson et al., 2013). The community's contribution transcends the provision of mere support; it involves making access to information and services facilitating the empowerment of families to gain further knowledge and control over these disorders. Through encouraging multidisciplinary collaboration, communities have the ability to offer education and support to families for guiding their children toward healthy productive lives. In effect, the synergistic benefit of family and community intervention not only reduces immediate concerns but also contributes toward a more integrated solution to the long-term issues of neurodevelopmental disorder.

5.6.1. Family Dynamics and Involvement

Family functioning is a key predictor of the mental health condition of neurodevelopmental disorder children. Family functioning encompasses the interaction and relationship among family members, which ultimately influence children's behavior and emotional development. Open communication and caring from the home environment play a significant role in the growth of resilience and coping mechanisms in children who are faced with neurological challenges. Conversely, negative family relationships such as conflict or neglect can serve as precipitants to symptom increase in a variety of disorders, hindering the child's social adjustment and emotional well-being. Parental involvement, particularly in education and therapy, is discovered to be crucial to enhancing treatment outcomes. Family involvement actively in the care of their child's can confer a secure supportive environment, promoting adjustment and better mental health status for children with neurodevelopmental disorders.

Figure 5.13. A supportive familial environment, characterized by open communication and nurturing, is essential for fostering resilience and coping strategies in children facing neurological challenges.

Source: https://renewneurotherapy.com/wp-content/uploads/2024/02/5-Ways-Family-Support-Can-Positively-Impact-a-Child_s-Learning-Disorder.webp.

The transition to adolescence is a critical phase for individuals with neurodevelopmental disorders, often highlighting the importance of family involvement in navigating this transition. Since children develop neurodevelopmentally within a social environment, family life takes on a predominantly influential role. The interplay between family support and individual development may facilitate successful transitions or advance the heightened vulnerabilities. Effective communication in the family is a cornerstone at this stage of development, which allows teenagers to openly express their needs and concerns. Families that emphasize understanding and empathy can ensure healthy coping strategies, which are needed when addressing the issues of adolescence. Moreover, healthy family functioning reduces the risk factors of peer influence and drug consumption because it enables active communication about these actions, thus enhancing resilience against the adolescent socio-environmental context (Arroyo et al., 2018). Besides, family quality impacts the general well-being and health of adolescents while growing up to adulthood with neurodevelopmental disorders. Research indicates that as such subjects move to adulthood, they will likely suffer from an unusual set of issues, including health complications and social integration challenges (Cooper et al., 2016). Ongoing emotional and practical support from families can be a very effective means of countering the stresses of such transition, leading to better health. For instance, the management of physical health problems, such as obesity and sexual health concerns, requires active engagement from families to facilitate needed lifestyle change and care. By remaining involved and vigilant, families can ensure that adolescents navigate through these complex changes while making sure that the latter receives what they need to achieve their full potential. Ultimately, building healthy family relationships not only enhances the well-being of the individual but also a healthier family system that can weather adversity around neurodevelopmental disorders (Figure 5.13).

5.6.2. Community Resources and Programs

Community resources and programs are also key in addressing neurodevelopmental disorders affecting child and adolescent mental health. These resources, typically coordinated by schools, healthcare systems, and community organizations, provide specialized services that cater to the particular needs of the affected. A case in point is early intervention programs, which play a pivotal role in providing interventions to children with conditions such as fetal alcohol spectrum disorders (FASD). By the implementation of personalized educational treatments and therapies, the programs aim to minimize the adverse impacts on emerging cognition and sociality. Moreover, education and information shared with parents as well as teachers can assist in developing a facilitative environment for the growth of children with neurodevelopmental disorders and therefore display the necessity of an approach that is community-oriented in striving for successful mental health programs. Intersectoral collaboration is necessary in creating a wide system of care for neurodevelopmental children with disorders. Specifically designed programs targeting the expansion of screening and preventive interventions are becoming more prominent, presenting an opportune intervention to high-risk populations. Research highlights the need for diversified strategies that engage families, teachers, and health professionals in the process of handling disorders like FASD. Adhering to community-based solutions does not only enhance the distribution of resources but also reduces the stigma surrounding such disorders. By integrating information across various disciplines and introducing participation from the community, programs are better suited to address the particular issues of children, generating improved results in mental health as well as overall well-being. Secondly, the need for ongoing assessment of community resources underscores the importance of evidence-based practice in program design and implementation. Assessing the efficacy of ongoing initiatives allows for improvement and adaptation that is more relevant to the needs of children and families. For instance, evidence has attested to the positive impact of family-centered interventions in raising awareness and knowledge about FASD among caregivers. Such programs can support open communication and more informed decision-making, which are key to cultivating supportive environments. Further improving community awareness can be achieved through targeted campaigns that educate the public about the effects of prenatal alcohol exposure. All these measures, in turn, will contribute to a decrease in the prevalence of neurodevelopmental disorders. The coordination among robust community resources and knowledge-guided policies is pivotal to the advancement of children's mental health initiatives within the neurodevelopmental disorders spectrum (McLean et al., 2025).

5.6.3. Advocacy and Awareness Initiatives

Awareness and advocacy campaigns are essential to expanding the understanding and awareness of neurodevelopmental disorders in children and adolescents. The purpose of such campaigns is to bridge the information gap surrounding disorders such as fetal alcohol spectrum disorders (FASD) and autism spectrum disorder (ASD), raising awareness among parents, teachers, and medical professionals. For instance, pregnancy educational campaigns can reduce prenatal alcohol exposure by half, one of the primary causes of FASD and its associated cognitive impairments. Public education about developmental consequences of prenatal alcohol exposure supports advocacy groups to advocate for a better-informed approach towards maternal health and social responsibility. Comprehensive strategies with an emphasis on community engagement are essential to resist the stigmas and complexities of these disorders. Of central importance to advocacy success is synchronizing policy guidelines with family need. Early intervention and multi-disciplinary programs supporting it are essential in preventing neurodevelopmental disorder long-term consequences in children. Research indicates that the majority of those with FASD remain undiagnosed, particularly in high-risk groups such as children who are in out-of-home care. For this issue to be successfully tackled, advocacy must target legislative backing of compulsory screening and professional training within the appropriate sectors. Promoting policy change towards prioritizing early diagnosis and targeted intervention is one method by which advocacy can lead to improved outcomes for children who are dealing with problems related to FASD and other associated disorders. These collective efforts develop a more responsive, empathetic, and skilled healthcare atmosphere. Moreover, ASD awareness programs focus on postsecondary education and the difficulty that adults with autism face in accessing higher education. Outcomes show that students with ASD have equal academic capability to their neurotypical peers but experience greater psychological stress and reduced social confidence. It highlights the necessity for advocacy that promotes inclusive learning environments and specialist support services in colleges and universities. Through advocating for institutional change that enhances social contacts and resources intended for students with neurodevelopmental disorders, advocacy groups can facilitate the integration of these students into adulthood. Lastly, the effectiveness of all these initiatives depends on fostering a culture of acceptance and tolerance that not only advocates for the rights of persons with neurodevelopmental disorders but also enhances their general well-being (Baczewski et al., 2020; McLean et al., 2025) (Figure 5.14).

Figure 5.14. Advocacy and awareness initiatives play a crucial role in enhancing the understanding and support for children and adolescents with neurodevelopmental disorders.

Source: https://www.mentalhealth.com/wp-content/uploads/2025/05/Development-Disabilities-Lifespan.jpeg.

5.7. CONCLUSION

In outlining the review of child and adolescent neurodevelopmental disorders of mental health, it is imperative to recognize the complicated nature of the illnesses and the extensive impact on individuals and families. Fragile X syndrome and fetal alcohol spectrum disorders are neurodevelopmental disorders that pose significant challenges to the affected youth, often yielding a chain reaction of social, emotional, and academic issues. Studies have shown that intensive interventions, both pharmacologic and individually tailored behavioral interventions, are able to achieve significant gains in developmental outcomes in participating children. One such example is research on using lovastatin in adolescents with fragile X syndrome that identified the potential merits of simultaneous treatment plans in enhancing significant gains in language and social abilities, proving the potential of multimodal interventions (Abbeduto et al., 2020). These findings serve to emphasize the necessity of ongoing investigation and refinement of treatment strategies in order to more fully meet the needs of these at-risk populations. Furthermore, familiarity with the incidence and characteristics of various neurodevelopmental disorders is essential for public health policy development and for educational treatments. The growing body of evidence regarding fetal alcohol spectrum disorders is a reflection of the urgent need for prevention and targeted intervention, particularly in high-risk groups such as Australia's Indigenous population. By addressing the social determinants and risk factors for the development of neurodevelopmental disorder, practitioners and policymakers can more effectively target resources to promote early diagnosis and supportive intervention. Reducing the gap between practice and research will enable a more integrated model of mental health care, eventually enhancing the quality of life for children and adolescents affected by these multifaceted disorders. Lastly, the neurodevelopmental disorders landscape of child and adolescent mental health is promising but challenging. As the evidence base increases, it is equally important that findings be made operational at the level of clinical practice so that children receive timely and appropriate interventions. Healthcare professionals, teachers, and families, through cooperative intervention, have a key role to play in establishing resilience and development in affected youth. Besides, with investments in research, public health programs, and community-based interventions, stakeholders can create a supportive platform that not only addresses the needs of such individuals but also encourages prevention strategies. This multi-dimensional approach is critical in decreasing the long-term impacts of neurodevelopmental disorders, eventually reflecting into better health status and quality of life for the next generation.

5.7.1. Summary of Key Points

Neurodevelopmental disorders such as attention deficit hyperactivity disorder (ADHD) and fragile X syndrome (FXS) are core in child and adolescent mental health. ADHD is especially prevalent, with an estimated 5.29% prevalence in children and 2.5% in adults and often leading to significant referrals to mental health care. Heritability of ADHD is high with afflicted family members having a higher likelihood of successive identical diagnoses. Major environmental influences, as well as genetic vulnerabilities, play a role in the multifactorial nature of ADHD. Notably, left untreated, ADHD can result in a wide range of comorbidities as well as long-term morbidity, further emphasizing the importance of early intervention. Pharmacological interventions, with a focus on methylphenidate, exhibit a favorable response rate of around 80%, highlighting the treatability of the disorders and the significance of practitioners being knowledgeable about ADHD management (Camilleri et al., 2013). In yet another and similar context, Fragile X Syndrome presents unique challenges for a multidisciplinary approach. One recent controlled trial examining lovastatin's effect in adolescents 10 through 17 years old with FXS included a parent-implemented language intervention along with medication. While there was significant improvement in both treatment and placebo groups for communication skills, the study underscored the efficacy of the parental position in therapeutic treatments. The research design was founded on behavioral as well as pharmacological interventions and showed how making use of techniques of scholarly communication can benefit cognitive results. This dual approach clearly identifies the potential of tailored interventions in meeting the multimodal needs of children with neurodevelopmental disorders to enhance their overall development and academic achievement (Abbeduto et al., 2020). The intersection of genetic, environmental, and therapeutic factors emphasizes the polygenic basis of neurodevelopmental disorders and their impact on child and adolescent mental health. The greater understanding by clinicians of the disorders increases the necessity for early diagnosis and intervention. ADHD, due to its high heritability and impact on daily living, necessitates an active approach in school and clinical settings. Similarly, treatment of FXS through coordinated treatment that stimulates parental engagement is emphasizing the necessity for overall care tailored to developmental nuances. The greater the study continues to illuminate the processes of such disorders, the more effective a holistic approach can be used as a foundation for intervention and support in vulnerable groups (Abbeduto et al., 2020; Camilleri et al., 2013).

5.7.2. Importance of Early Intervention

Early treatment is indispensable when it comes to treating neurodevelopmental disorders in children and adolescents and plays an important role in long-term outcomes. The earlier the signs are identified, and intervention strategies are implemented, the more likely the chances of reducing the adverse impacts of these disorders on a child's growth. In the realm of mental health, intervention at an early stage has positive implications for the quality of life in youth as well as on decreasing the burden for families and health care systems. By providing support early on, such as cognitive-behavioral therapies or specifically tailored educational services, professionals can lower the intensity of symptoms and facilitate healthier development patterns. It is important, since unless addressed, mental illnesses have the potential of becoming long-term in their nature and extending to adulthood, thereby increasing the suffering of the victims and their relatives. In addition, the importance of early intervention is compounded by the findings from current research that highlight the consequences of waiting until it is too late to intervene. For instance, conditions like obsessive-compulsive disorder (OCD) generally manifest in childhood, with studies documenting a staggering duration of untreated illness (DUI) that may last up to 10 years among adults. Such an extended period is associated with enormous misery and is characterized by increased familial and societal costs. By recognizing the worth of early clinical intervention, stakeholders can treat not only OCD but other neurodevelopmental disorders for which prompt treatment ensures positive outcomes. The literature shows that early intervention can have a major impact in lessening the size of suffering and enhancing significant health care outcomes, emphasizing the critical role of early help within child and adolescent mental health care. In addition to improved individual outcomes, early intervention can also assist in ensuring smoother continuity between child and adolescent mental health services (CAMHS) and adult mental health services (AMHS). A study that examined these transitions revealed that possible discontinuities in continuity of care may jeopardize effective treatment pathways. Thus, effective communication and coordination of services, from the pediatric phase, are critical in avoiding that adolescents fall through the cracks as they grow up. Clinicians must be adept at identifying transitional cases so that the appropriate information is passed to CAMHS and AMHS so that the patients have a smooth transition. By prioritizing early intervention and intensified coordination between service levels of health, mental health professionals can enhance service delivery and outcomes for adolescents with neurodevelopmental disorders, ultimately identifying the necessity of strategic early interventions that strengthen care transitions (Adamson et al., 2015; Albert et al., 2019).

5.7.3. Future Directions in Research and Policy

As researchers press on to unravel the complexity of neurodevelopmental disorders, agendas for research and policy in the future will need to grapple with the intersection of aging and autism spectrum disorder (ASD). Current debates show that the field is at a fork in the road when it comes to understanding aging within the context of autism science. Notably, establishment of special interest groups, such as those formed during the International Society for Autism Research conferences, has led to critical debate regarding cognitive and physical autistic issues among autistic adults above the age of 50. The outcome of these conferences reveals an impending necessity for correct diagnostic workups tailor-made for the elderly. This shift will develop research agendas and policy paradigms to encompass the heterogeneity of older adults with ASD that, consequently, can enhance quality of life in this group (Roestorf et al., 2019). In the context of adolescent decision-making under the banner of neurodevelopmental disorders, progress in neuroscience is reshaping legal and ethical responsibilities. Legal systems governing adolescent autonomy normally reflects an incoherent devotion to their capacity to make wise decisions. Consistent with the growing knowledge forwarded by developmental neuroscientists regarding how brain development influences judgment, this empirical information must be addressed in policymaker reform. Policymakers are tasked with evaluating existing legal systems in a manner that distinguishes between those behaviors adolescents can master and those behaviors that will exacerbate their volitional impairments. By adopting a matrix-based approach to evaluation, the new law will be more in line with psychological research in fostering a supportive atmosphere for adolescents with neurodevelopmental disorders as they face the complexity of their autonomy (Pustilnik et al., 2015). Lastly, the inclusion of a multidisciplinary framework will be essential for future research and policy exploring neurodevelopmental disorders in child and adolescent mental health. Collaboration among clinicians, researchers, educators, and policymakers will facilitate increased insight into the multifaceted issues posed by these groups. Prioritizing collaboration will allow stakeholders to ensure that research findings guide public health interventions and education programs. Furthermore, inclusion of voices from the affected communities, namely individuals with autism, will make interventions more accessible and effective. The convergence of scientific understanding and good policy can give rise to the development of integrated programs that address the varied needs of children and youth with neurodevelopmental disorders, opening the way for improved outcomes throughout their lifespan.

REFERENCES

1. Abbeduto, L., Banasik, A., Bullard, L., Hagerman, R., et al. (2020). Controlled trial of lovastatin combined with an open-label treatment of a parent-implemented language intervention in youth with fragile X syndrome. https://core.ac.uk/download/323068901.pdf (accessed on 14th October 2025).
2. Adamson, M., Barry, S., Coyne, I., Cullen, W., et al. (2015). Who is in the transition gap? Transition from CAMHS to AMHS in the Republic of Ireland. https://core.ac.uk/download/30650016.pdf (accessed on 14th October 2025).
3. Albert, U., Apergis-Schoute, A., Brakoulias, V., Carmi, L., et al. (2019). Early intervention for obsessive compulsive disorder: An expert consensus statement. https://core.ac.uk/download/287581694.pdf (accessed on 14th October 2025).
4. Anokhin, A. P., Grant, J. D., Heath, A. C., Mulligan, R. C., et al. (2015). Familial influences on the full range of variability in attention and activity levels during adolescence: A longitudinal twin study. https://core.ac.uk/download/70385321.pdf (accessed on 14th October 2025).
5. Arroyo, J., Feldstein Ewing, S. W., Fuligni, A., Gonzalez, M. R., et al. (2018). Assessment of culture and environment in the Adolescent Brain and Cognitive Development Study: Rationale, description of measures, and early data. https://core.ac.uk/download/323079766.pdf (accessed on 14th October 2025).
6. Baczewski, L. M. (2020). Self-reported experiences of students with autism spectrum disorder in higher education: A population-based sample. https://core.ac.uk/download/323063011.pdf (accessed on 14th October 2025).
7. Barker, E. D., Golm, D., Hill, J., Kennedy, M., et al. (2020). Why does early childhood deprivation increase the risk for depression and anxiety in adulthood? A developmental cascade model. https://core.ac.uk/download/287579405.pdf (accessed on 14th October 2025).
8. Beal, S. J., Crosby, I., Greiner, M. V., Nause, K., et al. (2019). Understanding health risks for adolescents in protective custody. https://core.ac.uk/download/212897226.pdf (accessed on 14th October 2025).
9. Browne, J., Cohen, S. S., de Camargo, O. K., Delaney, K., et al. (2019). Pediatric feeding disorder: Consensus definition and conceptual framework. https://core.ac.uk/download/286544045.pdf (accessed on 14th October 2025).

10. Camilleri, N., & Makhoul, S. (2013). ADHD: From childhood into adulthood. https://core.ac.uk/download/46602345.pdf (accessed on 14th October 2025).
11. Cooper, S. A., Philo, C., & Young-Southward, G. (2016). What effect does transition have on health and well-being in young people with intellectual disabilities? A systematic review. https://core.ac.uk/download/42373210.pdf (accessed on 14th October 2025).
12. Cryan, J. F., O'Riordan, K. J., Cowan, C. S. M., Sandhu, K. V., Bastiaanssen, T. F. S., Boehme, M., Codagnone, M. G., et al. (2019). The microbiota-gut-brain axis. *Physiological Reviews, 99*, 1877–2013. https://doi.org/10.1152/physrev.00018.2018 (accessed on 14th October 2025).
13. Dueñas, N., Giulivi, C., & Napoli, E. (2014). Potential therapeutic use of the ketogenic diet in autism spectrum disorders. https://core.ac.uk/download/323068211.pdf (accessed on 14th October 2025).
14. Ek, M. (2015). Paternal age as a risk factor for schizophrenia in offspring. https://core.ac.uk/download/70341284.pdf (accessed on 14th October 2025).
15. Forrester-Jones, R., Malli, M., & Murphy, G. H. (2015). Stigma in youth with Tourette's syndrome: A systematic review and synthesis. https://core.ac.uk/download/30708470.pdf (accessed on 14th October 2025).
16. Forsman, M., Kerekes, N., Larsson, H., Lichtenstein, P., et al. (2013). Childhood neurodevelopmental disorders and violent criminality: A sibling control study. https://core.ac.uk/download/70340707.pdf (accessed on 14th October 2025).
17. Johnson, S. J., & Wolke, D. (2013). Behavioral outcomes and psychopathology during adolescence. https://core.ac.uk/download/9847191.pdf (accessed on 14th October 2025).
18. LeCouteur, A., Pickles, A., Prizant, B. M., Taylor, B., Molloy, C. A., Lord, C., et al. (2008). Regression, developmental trajectory and associated problems in disorders in the autism spectrum: The SNAP study. https://core.ac.uk/download/pdf/82619.pdf (accessed on 14th October 2025).
19. McLean, S., & McDougall, S. (2025). Fetal alcohol spectrum disorders: Current issues in awareness, prevention and intervention. https://core.ac.uk/download/pdf/30673146.pdf (accessed on 14th October 2025).
20. Panchal, U., Salazar de Pablo, G., Franco, M., Moreno, C., Parellada, M., Arango, C., & Fusar-Poli, P. (2021). The impact of COVID-19 lockdown on child and adolescent mental health: Systematic review. *European Child & Adolescent Psychiatry, 32*, 1151–1177. https://doi.org/10.1007/s00787-021-01856-w (accessed on 14th October 2025).

21. Pustilnik, A. C., & Tennison, M. N. (2015). And if your friends jumped off a bridge, would you do it too? How developmental neuroscience can inform legal regimes governing adolescents. https://core.ac.uk/download/56360509.pdf (accessed on 14th October 2025).

22. Roestorf, A., Anderson, J., Ayres, K., Van Heijst, B. F. C., et al. (2019). "Older adults with ASD: The consequences of aging." Insights from a series of special interest group meetings held at the International Society for Autism Research 2016–2017. https://core.ac.uk/download/288395613.pdf (accessed on 14th October 2025).

Chapter 6

Trauma and Stressor-Related Disorders

Contents

INTRODUCTION

The topic of trauma and its long-term impact on child and adolescent mental health is an important topic that needs to be thoroughly researched. Trauma exposure during childhood, ranging from maltreatment to violence witnessing, can potentially impact the trajectory of mental health development. Existing research indicates that disruptions in the development of stress response systems are the cause of the emergence of various psychopathologies among such youth. For instance, Alves et al. (2014) hypothesizes that maltreatment underlies dysregulation of physiological reactivity, leading to patterns of response that make it harder for emotional regulation. These profound effects can only be understood by constructing effective interventions that can minimize the psychological effects experienced by individuals exposed to traumatic conditions. Additionally, diagnosis and identification of trauma disorders among children and adolescents are marked by unique challenges. There is growing evidence that the traditional diagnostic criteria may not fully capture the symptoms and experiences of youth populations. For example, Dalgleish et al. (2008) reports an enormous disparity in rates of PTSD diagnosis when different symptom algorithms are compared to traditional DSM-IV criteria. The disparity underscores the importance of using diverse informants, e.g., both parents and children, to achieve appropriate mental health evaluations. Such a multi-faceted reaction is necessary in confronting the complexities that accompany diagnosing trauma disorders among different age ranges in order to provide on-time and appropriate intervention for young individuals. Lastly, understanding the intricate relationship between trauma exposure and mental health outcome lies at the forefront of devising successful prevention and treatment strategies. Early intervention can have a huge impact on the trajectory of a child's mental health process, especially for someone who has had traumatic exposure. The literature supports the notion that symptoms are in flux, and the need to continue to assess and support. As research in this field develops, the integration of knowledge on neurobiological responses, emotional growth, and successful assessments is important in the development of an integrated framework to treat the trauma and stressor-related disorders. Therefore, in summary, by giving an integrative view into these issues, stakeholders can give greater support to the mental health issues of children and adolescents that have been exposed to the effects of trauma.

Definition of Trauma and Stressor-Related Disorders

Trauma and stressor-related disorders are a set of psychological responses to extremely distressing events or experiences. Trauma and stressor-related disorders include disorders such as post-traumatic stress disorder (PTSD), acute stress disorder, and adjustment disorders, all characterized by the psychological impact created through exposure to traumatic or stressful conditions. In children and adolescents, witnessing or being a victim of such an event as abuse, loss, or accident can drastically alter emotional and behavioral functioning. Presentation of these disorders is variable, and symptoms can range from hyperarousal and intrusive thinking to dissociation and emotional numbing. Phase of the child's development is crucial in the emergence of symptoms, with the requirement for a sophisticated understanding of trauma within the context of their particular psychosocial development. Studies indicate that kids in custody protection are significantly more at risk of mental health issues, an impact that would be traced back to the abuse they have experienced. Recent research indicates that approximately 41.6% of kids in such an environment are diagnosed with mental disorders, with the top being depression and behavioral disorders.

Figure 6.1. The developmental stage of the child plays a crucial role in how these symptoms present, necessitating a nuanced understanding of trauma in the context of their unique psychosocial development.

Source: https://ssir.org/images/blog/SSIR_Interenerational_Trauma-592x333.jpg.

The implications of these results underscore the need for targeted interventions, especially in systems like child welfare that serve as critical stabilization points for vulnerable populations. Furthermore, the chronic stress of such environments can also exacerbate pre-existing illness and establish a pattern of poor health throughout adulthood. These facts highlight the importance of implementing holistic treatment interventions to break across this cycle at an early point since detained adolescents are primarily within grasp of helpful health and social services which can help to lower risk. It is crucial to understand stress as a multifaceted process when working with trauma and stressor-related disorders in adolescents. Stress does not occur independently but instead results from dynamic interactions between characteristic traits of the individual and environmental settings, augmented by factors of history and reactivity of the individual. As noted in the literature, the process of developing an integrated model that can incorporate various stressors could assist in more effective assessment and treatment strategies for these disorders. A more developed typology that considers the multifaceted nature of stress will enable practitioners to tailor interventions to suit the individual experiences of the youths and therefore more effectively manage their symptoms. By recognizing the multifaceted nature of stress and its influence on health and development, mental health practitioners are able to assist in creating more positive outcomes for youth affected by the aftermath of trauma (Beal et al., 2019; Crosswell et al., 2018) (Figure 6.1).

Importance of Addressing Mental Health in Children and Adolescents

The importance of treating adolescent and children's mental illness cannot be overstated, particularly in traumatic stressor-related disorders. The adolescent and childhood years are formative years in emotional and psychological development, and if they experience trauma, it will have long-lasting negative effects on mental health. Prompt management and diagnosis are essential, as attested by the recent literature citing the high prevalence of psychiatric disorders among young children exposed to traumatic exposures, such as motor vehicle crashes. Longitudinal assessment found that some diagnostic algorithms, the alternative symptom algorithm for PTSD being one, outperform traditional assessments, demonstrating a need for age-specific diagnostic criteria and procedures in this high-risk population (Dalgleish et al., 2008). By prioritizing providing mental health interventions early in life, we can avoid the progression of long-term mental health issues. Recognition of resilience to mental health outcomes after stress exposure is also essential. While most children exposed to traumatic events will not develop psychiatric disease, recognition of which factors are associated with resilience is critical in the context of promoting comprehensive mental health programs. The latest research has begun exploring the biological underpinnings of resilience, such as heart rate variability (HRV) and how it relates to brain structure, which can enhance our understanding of differences between people in responding to stressors (Carnevali et al., 2018). By focusing on resilience, clinicians are able to better identify and build strengths in youth and promote effective coping. This multi-component approach can lead to stronger prevention and intervention efforts that not only cure illness but also encourage long-term mental health stability. Incorporating mental health education into the school curriculum is essential to empowering children and adolescents to understand, communicate, and get assistance for their mental health needs. Schools are a primary site where children spend much time, and thus they are most appropriate for mental health promotion. Educational interventions are able to de-stigmatize mental health issues and render them less taboo, opening up to discussions even between teachers and peers. Early interventions such as counseling programs and mental health screening in schools can also respond to timely interventions for those who are experiencing the effects of trauma (Dalgleish et al., 2008). In developing a culture of awareness and support within schools, we establish a setting where healing and resilience become possible. This forward-looking strategy not only resolves existing problems related to trauma and stressor-related disorders but also lays the ground for future generations that are healthier.

6.1. TYPES OF TRAUMA AND STRESSOR-RELATED DISORDERS

The trauma and stressor-related disorders class comprises a range of psychoses that arise secondary to traumatic exposure or extreme stressors. The Diagnostic and Statistical Manual of Mental Disorders, 5th ed. (DSM-5) classifies a number of these, such as Acute Stress Disorder (ASD) and Post-Traumatic Stress Disorder (PTSD). ASD develops right after a traumatic event and can produce significant impairment and distress, whereas PTSD symptoms may arise weeks, months, or years later. The characteristics of the trauma, the history of the person, and their capacity for dealing with them all significantly influence the prevalence and severity of these disorders. Even more precisely, the phase of the person's development during which they undergo the trauma can complicate their psychological responses, which are compounded by the significance of seeing the multifaceted nature of traumas emphasized in recent literature regarding the mental health of children (Fortunato et al., 2018). Besides ASD and PTSD, other disorders with a trauma component are adjustment disorders and reactive attachment disorder (RAD), and both have unique features and clinical concerns. Adjustment Disorders typically appear as an immediate response to a recognizable stressor, with the ensuing overwhelming emotional or behavioral symptomatology. For children and adolescents, such symptoms can manifest as anxiety, depression, or disruptive behavior, impairing social and academic functioning. RAD, by contrast, is typified by unstable capacity to form coherent emotional relationships with caregivers, typically on the basis of severe neglect or unstable caregiving environment. Prevalence of such disorders shows the widespread impact of trauma during childhood on developmental trajectories, placing this population at increased risk for long-term mental illness (Brooks et al., 2015). Understanding the nature of trauma and stressor-related disorders is critical in designing effective prevention and intervention strategies. Early identification of these disorders can avoid long-term consequences of trauma, developing resilience in children and adolescents. This underscores the need for trauma-informed interventions within educational and clinical environments so that professionals are well-equipped to identify and respond to the indices of distress in young people. Additionally, specially designed therapeutic interventions based on a child's particular experience can lead to healing and enhance emotional management, subsequently leading to an improvement in overall functioning. Future practice and research must continue to develop in response to fresh evidence about the complex nature of trauma, reaffirming the need for a multi-dimensional response with attention to developmental perspectives and variation in traumatic response and recovery (Fortunato et al., 2018) (Figure 6.2).

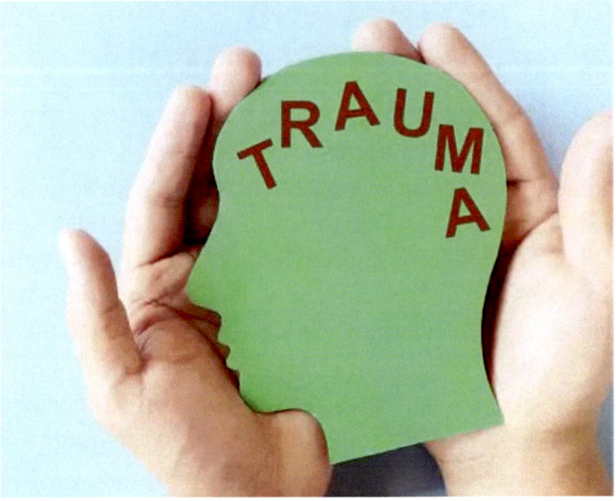

Figure 6.2. Factors such as the nature of the trauma, the individual's previous experiences, and their coping mechanisms significantly influence the onset and severity of these disorders.

Source: https://www.megawecare.com/_next/image?url=https%3A%2F%2Fcdn.megawecare.com%2FFeatured-Images%2Fqt4jGmmJ51N00tYaptAoOY8dLNFpF5R3V50X2PFT.webp&w=1920&q=75.

6.1.1. Post-Traumatic Stress Disorder (PTSD)

The impact of post-traumatic stress disorder (PTSD) among children and adolescents is a complex interaction among individual risk factors and environmental exposures. The condition is a disabling response to traumatic events, often manifested through intrusive thoughts, emotional numbing, and hyperarousal symptomatology. Literature has indicated that children who are exposed to high stressors, including violence, natural disasters, or catastrophic accidents, are at risk for developing PTSD. Early identification is critical as early intervention can prevent long-term impact on emotional and psychological well-being. The subtle presentation of PTSD in children necessitates differential interventions that are mindful of developmental stages and coping mechanisms. Without intervention, the symptoms of PTSD can infiltrate multiple levels of life, resulting in school functioning deficits, interpersonal relationships deficits, and overall quality of life. The significance of the parent-child relationship in PTSD in children cannot be overestimated. Research has shown that children's self-report of symptoms of PTSD is highly variable as compared to parental perceptions, and therefore diagnosis and treatment planning are challenging.

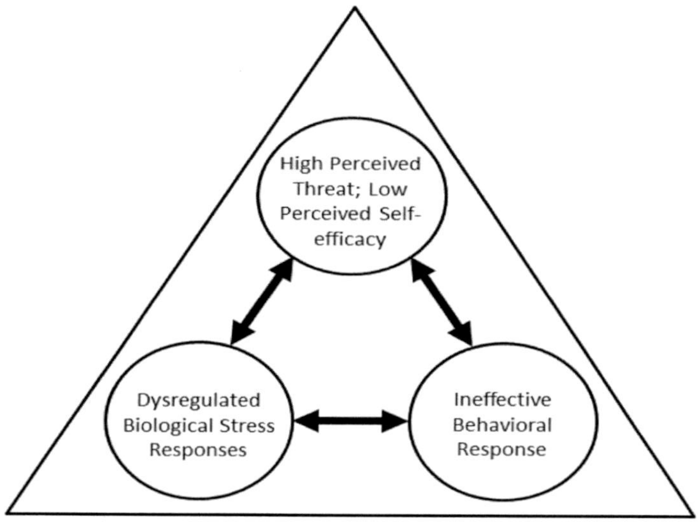

Figure 6.3. Without appropriate support, the sequelae of PTSD can permeate various aspects of life, leading to challenges in academic performance, social relationships, and overall quality of life.

Source: https://media.springernature.com/lw685/springer-static/image/art%3A10.1007%2Fs11126-022-10003-w/MediaObjects/11126_2022_10003_Fig2_HTML.png.

For instance, one prospective study that measured parent-child agreement on PTSD reported that children were more likely to meet criteria on self-report than by parent report. Notably, the Acute Stress Disorder (ASD) consensus was low, whereas it was moderate in the scenario of PTSD and reflected an imbalance in the estimation of emotional distress across generations. The findings uphold the need for children to be involved in the assessment process and suggest that parents may lack an appreciation for the impact of the trauma on their child's mental health, hence the necessity for direct and comprehensive assessments (Thabet et al., 2007). Furthermore, there is a need to consider the broader social contexts in which trauma occurs, namely violence and its psychological impact within communities. Exposure to community violence, e.g., witnessing firearm violence or participating in drug markets, has significant repercussions for youth mental health. Ongoing repeated exposure to such stressors not only increases the risk for developing PTSD but can further lead to a range of negative health outcomes, such as depression and anxiety. Given that trauma accumulates its consequences, one is therefore obliged to explore the long-term outcomes of violence exposure. The interaction between collective trauma and the psychological response of individuals accounts for the necessity of systemic prevention and support interventions (Lynn-Whaley et al., 2017). Addressing these issues in focus, stakeholders are better able to combat the need for adolescent and child mental health in response to the challenges of PTSD (Figure 6.3).

6.1.2. Acute Stress Disorder (ASD)

The emergence of acute stress disorder (ASD) in children is a significant problem within the broader context of trauma and stressor-related disorders. ASD typically follows shortly after the traumatic event, as it is characterized by symptoms of intrusiveness, avoidance, and hyperarousal. These symptoms can impair daily functioning and hinder development progress. Interestingly, certain factors, such as exposure to trauma or individual loss, have a unique risk on the development of ASD in children. In war-affected areas, for instance, children are exposed to violence or experience direct trauma, which leads to increased prevalence of ASD and related disorders. A Palestinian population survey detected over 23% of the subjects with post-traumatic stress disorder (PTSD) exhibiting also symptoms typical of ASD, evidencing the interrelatedness of these conditions in the minds of children (Baubet et al., 2009). Practitioners should be aware of the diagnosis and treatment of ASD in order to value its clinical nuances, particularly the difference in presentation between children and adults. Children may have a more severe manifestation of symptoms but are usually incapable of expressing these in quantifiable terms, making them hard to diagnose. Parent-child symptom concordance is typically poor, as shown in a study in which children were more likely to meet ASD diagnostic criteria based on their own reports than those from their parents (Thabet et al., 2007). This variation exists to ensure direct assessment of children in treatment to effectively identify and subsequently intervene. Identification of these variations is essential to clinicians to enable them to develop effective treatment plans for younger patients, resulting in improved outcomes. Psychotherapeutic intervention is crucial in treating ASD in children and adolescents. There has been evidence that brief psychotherapy may be highly effective in alleviating symptoms among this group. In the study mentioned above regarding war-torn children, 79% of the treated population reported symptom decrease, with even more efficacy in the 15 and under group (Baubet et al., 2009). Psychological treatment varied in intensity and length, which emphasized the need for treatment strategies that can be adjusted on the basis of individual need. The treatment focus is often on developing coping mechanisms and resilience, thereby preparing youth to more effectively navigate their emotional climates. With early intervention and evidence-informed practice strategies, mental health professionals can minimize the long-term implications of acute stress, ultimately leading to healthier development trajectories for traumatized youth (Figure 6.4).

Figure 6.4. The onset of acute stress disorder (ASD) in children and adolescents is a significant concern within the broader context of trauma and stressor-related disorders.

Source: https://cdn-prod.medicalnewstoday.com/content/images/articles/324/324354/acute-stress-disorder.jpg.

6.1.3. Adjustment Disorders

Adjustment disorders are the most important part of the trauma and stressor-related disorders among children and adolescents. Defined by the emotional or behavioral symptoms within three months after a stressor, adjustment disorders may manifest as anxiety, depressive mood, or conduct problems resulting from life events or challenges. Adjustment disorders substantially impact the developing psychological landscape of adolescents with the potential to interfere with school functioning and peer relationships. The necessity of addressing the symptoms of adjustment disorders is precipitated by their likelihood of developing more severe mental disorders in the event that they go untreated. Early identification and intervention strategies are necessary to avert the detrimental effects on a child's psychological well-being and functioning, emphasizing the importance of specialized mental health treatments for compromised adolescents. The link between life stressors and adjustment disorders is particularly firm in contexts such as schools or when there is familial change. Situations involving parental divorce, bullying, or mass moves may create considerable psychological distress, leading to reactive behavior and emotion dysregulation. These stressors for children and young people can exacerbate feelings of isolation and inferiority, further consolidating their undesirable reactions. New research highlights the direct relationship between extrinsic stressors, such as bullying, and psychological outcomes, and reports that victimization increases vulnerability to adjustment disorders (Broome et al., 2017).

Figure 6.5. Adjustment disorders represent a significant aspect of trauma and stressor-related disorders affecting children and adolescents.
Source: https://childmind.org/wp-content/uploads/2022/04/What-Are-Adjustment-Disorders.jpg.

It is important to consider the role of these external determinants for the development of effective prevention and intervention strategies designed to increase resilience and coping skills in these youth populations. In addition, treatment of adjustment disorders involves a multifaceted process addressing therapeutic interventions as well as community awareness. Evidence-based treatments like cognitive-behavioral therapy seek to arm young people with the skills needed to manage their feelings and response to stressors optimally. Apart from individual therapy, having a supportive environment can also do a lot; communities can employ programs to raise awareness and sympathy towards mental health among peers, teachers, and families (Berk et al., 2020). This form of group effort can encourage the elimination of barriers and the establishment of supportive communities, thereby promote open discussion on mental health issues among adolescents. By setting collaborative methods at the center of our actions, we are able to create pathways of recovery and resilience, enabling young people not just to survive their challenges but to thrive in spite of them (Figure 6.5).

6.2. CAUSES AND RISK FACTORS

The etiology of trauma and stressor-related disorders (TSRDs) in children and adolescents is often multifactorial and can have a profound effect on mental health outcomes. Being exposed to adverse childhood events, including physical and emotional abuse, neglect, and family conflict, significantly raises the risk for developing these disorders. For instance, children who have been exposed to domestic violence or neighborhood crime are at a higher risk of developing PTSD and symptoms of anxiety. Additionally, children experiencing chronic illness, or children who have been caring for ill relatives, can also develop trauma. This link emphasizes the significance of proper family and social context assessment in the explanation of how it accumulates over time ultimately leading to a child's mental health trajectory. Moreover, psychological and biological tendencies may also aggravate the trauma situation among juvenile populations. For example, the presence of prior history of mental health disorder, temperament, and personality may all play a critical role in determining the resilience or stress vulnerability of an individual. Recent research suggests that some of these personality traits that are present during childhood may even predict increased emotional reactivity to trauma and stress and complicate processes of recovery. This points to the significance of prevention and early intervention when addressing personality development as a risk factor, agreeing with studies that see the value in considering personality patterns in working with and understanding trauma. New studies indicated that personality traits may be established early in life, which made it essential to examine how early childhood accounts influence adult outcomes on mental health (Fortunato et al., 2018). Lastly, the ecological environment of a child may decrease or exacerbate the incidence of trauma-related disorders. Some of the socio-economic status, family structure, and community cohesion are some of the factors that contribute to playing utmost influence in shaping experiences. For instance, it has been found from research that poor families or socially isolated communities endure cumulative stress that leads to increased vulnerability among children. Concurrently, supportive attachments and caring environments can build resilience and act to buffer against the effects of stressful experience. These different contexts indicate that an integrated perspective on a child's environment is critical in the identification of risk factors linked to trauma. It is crucial to consider how family and community experiences may intensify or diminish the effect of traumatic events on mental health outcomes, allowing for the potential of targeted interventions considering both internal and external factors in TSRDs expression (Paleczna et al., 2017).

6.2.1. Exposure to Traumatic Events

Traumatic exposure significantly influences the mental well-being of children and youth, with potential for developing trauma and stressor-related disorders. Exposure to trauma can be due to many causes, including natural disasters, abuse, and violence. Trauma can have long-term psychological implications, interfering with the emotional and social development of a child. Studies unveil the disparities in access to mental health services among minority youth, highlighting the fact that race and ethnicity become vessels of intensification for the impact of trauma. Through such disparities, mental health practitioners are in a better position to identify and respond to the particular challenges of the affected populations, paving the way for improved care and support systems as outlined by Margarita Alegría and colleagues in their examination of mental health disparities (Green et al., 2015). The uniqueness of exposure to traumatic experiences is central to its impact on youth mental health. For instance, kids who have grown up with exposure to cyclical disasters, such as hurricanes, might possess distinct psychological profiles due to repeated prolonged exposure to threats to life. The Hurricane Exposure, Adversity, and Recovery Tool (HEART) highlight the use of child-centered assessments that will help determine the extent of hurricane-related risks, such as direct and secondary trauma. This assessment demonstrates how the strength of equipment can enable more accurate determination of vulnerable youth and harmonize resources with them to create timely intervention. The linkage between disaster exposure and posttraumatic stress symptoms underscores the importance of early identification and appropriate management of trauma reactions to prevent long-term mental health problems (Dodd et al., 2019). Moreover, the intersection of pre-existing vulnerabilities with exposure to trauma is a significant predictor in the course of an adolescent's recovery. Factors like pre-existing trauma exposure, family dynamics, and community resources are often intertwined, influencing the extent to which a person acts in a healthy way throughout recovery. Protective resources, including social support and resilience, can potentially buffer against the adverse effects of trauma and encourage more beneficial psychosocial development. In attempting to treat such complicated dynamics, clinicians must approach treatment from an integrative perspective that is guided by the influences of both past and present adversity. By prioritizing the integration of strengths into interventions, clinicians can facilitate more resilient recovery pathways for youth who are facing the aftereffects of traumatic experiences, enhancing their overall wellness and quality of life (Figure 6.6).

Figure 6.6. Exposure to traumatic events significantly influences mental health outcomes in children and adolescents, potentially leading to the development of trauma and stressor-related disorders.

Source: https://www.verywellmind.com/thmb/9r9rTNxtizUUSU-O-mIOcTOThcc=/2121x0/filters:no_upscale():max_bytes(150000):strip_icc()/Getty-Images-80487462-59833fb6d088c000112fcc2c.jpg.

6.2.2. Biological and Genetic Predispositions

Understanding trauma and stressor-related disorders involves more specific examination of biological and genetic risk factors that might influence mental health outcomes among children. Genetic factors are significant in the determination of individuals susceptibility to disorders stemming from traumatic events. For instance, variations in genes that control serotonin and dopamine have been linked to enhanced vulnerability to anxiety and mood disorders. In addition, neurobiological mechanisms involving those that utilize the hypothalamic-pituitary-adrenal (HPA) axis are also important in children's responses to stress. Hypothalamic-pituitary-adrenal axis dis-regulation has the possibility of leading to an overactive stress response that can create long-standing mental illness. It is important to know these biological mechanisms in order to understand why certain children are resilient and others develop more severe trauma-based disorders. The interplay between genetic vulnerabilities and environmental factors, specifically childhood maltreatment, further complicates the terrain of disorders related to trauma. Studies have shown that violent or neglectful childhood experiences can serve as potent stressors that not only derail normal developmental pathways but also enhance pre-existing genetic vulnerabilities. The concept of latent vulnerability enters here since neurocognitive alterations in the processes of emotional regulation and threat response can be evident even in children who lack obvious psychiatric pathology (Gerin et al., 2017).

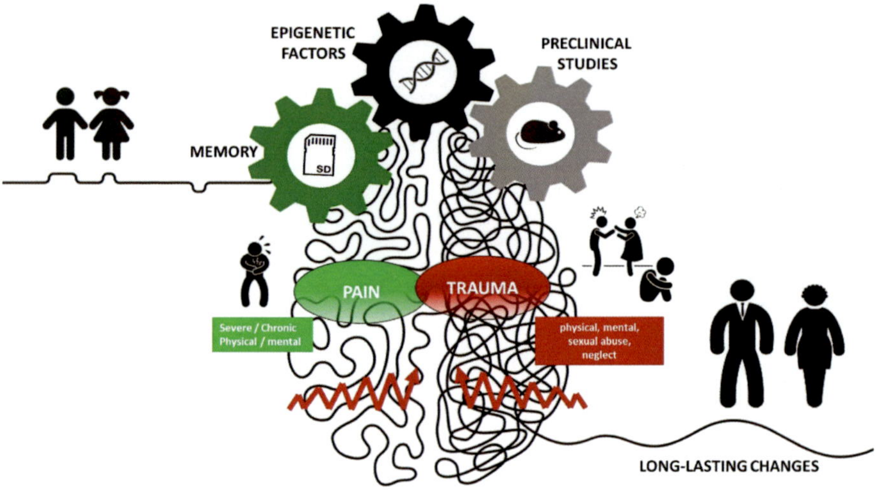

Figure 6.7. Genetic factors play a crucial role in shaping an individual's susceptibility to disorders arising from traumatic experiences.

Source: https://pub.mdpi-res.com/children/children-10-01217/article_deploy/html/images/children-10-01217-ag.png?1689930374.

These neurobiological alterations, although initially protective, if exposed to chronic stressors, can cause an enhanced risk of psychiatric illness in children. This intricate interaction addresses the need for preventative treatments that consider both environmental and biological threats. Moreover, personality pattern development in early life is a key area of investigation for understanding the developmental aspect of trauma-related disorders. According to current studies, there are certain personality characteristics that cause risk for adverse mental health outcomes in children when paired with traumatic exposure (Fortunato et al., 2018). For instance, children who have high neuroticism scores will develop anxiety disorders after they have experienced stress. Early intervention becomes clear as identification of these emergent traits will enable the administration of particular therapeutic interventions that will mitigate the impacts of trauma. By providing utmost priority to personality and genetic risk assessment, mental health professionals can build anticipation interventions that not only address present psychological needs but also assist in building resilience in at-risk children and youth (Figure 6.7).

6.2.3. Environmental Influences and Family Dynamics

Family dynamics and environmental factors interact importantly in shaping the mental health of children and adolescents. Families are usually the initial social setting for a child, and the quality of interaction within such settings has either the capacity to buffer or exacerbate stressors. If in the case of warmth, support, and adequate communication within the family setting, children are likely to develop resilience against adverse experiences. Conversely, however, those families with difficulty in realms such as economic hardship, parent conflict, or psychiatric disease may inadvertently create a home environment with tremendous tension, thereby predisposing a child to trauma and stressor-related disorders. In fact, empirical research indicates that these experiences not only affect immediate psychological response but also long-term health trajectories, indicating that family environments are paramount to understand in the study of child and adolescent mental health. Outside stresses, including socioeconomic status, home, and neighborhood safety, complicate family relationships further and their impact on mental health even more so. Children with a history of having instability or violence in their environment are at higher risk of developing many disorders due to the fact that these external influences interact with family life to create increased levels of stress. Stress, as an emergent process, is not the product of individual vulnerabilities but rather a function of the coming together of external environment and family responses. Effective interventions, taking into consideration both external environment and internal family systems, require an understanding of the multifaceted nature of relationships. The complexity of these interactions emphasizes the need for a multi-dimensional strategy for the treatment of mental illness issues in children, potentially reducing the prevalence of trauma-based disorders among vulnerable populations. Moreover, the collective effect of chronic stress—structured by environmental conditions as well as family dynamics—affects children throughout their life course. Stress can come in various forms, including acute, event-based, and chronic stress, all with their respective psychological and physiological impacts (Crosswell et al., 2018). Moreover, the ability of the family to enhance adaptive coping strategies and health behavior has the power to influence the response of young people to stress to a great degree. A synthesized knowledge of how ecological stressors interact with family processes can offer new paths for prevention and treatment interventions to trauma and stressor-related disorders. Ultimately, these are the complexities that one needs to face in order to effect change in the field of child and adolescent mental health, demanding that multifaceted interventions involve families and their environment in active mental health interventions (Dudgeon et al., 2009).

6.3. SYMPTOMS AND DIAGNOSIS

Recognition of the signs and corresponding diagnosis of trauma and stressor-related disorders in children and adolescents is crucial for effective mental health treatment. The symptoms of the disorders are also very dissimilar from those seen in adults, necessitating age-appropriate diagnostic criteria. In young children, the symptoms may include increased irritability, detachment, or regression behavior, which can be mixed up with normal developmental challenges. The nuances of such symptoms are critical, as proper, and early diagnosis plays a critical role in avoiding long-term psychological harm. More recent studies bear witness to the employment of alternative diagnostic procedures specifically for preschool children, and evidence indicates that such a process can yield increased identification rates of posttraumatic stress disorder (PTSD) compared to conventional DSM-IV criteria (Dalgleish et al., 2008). Given the growing rates of mental health diagnoses in young children, it is essential to make our diagnostic methods more accurate. Trauma and stressor-related disorders diagnosis can also be made more complex by parent-child agreement on variables for symptom reporting. Research finds that children are more likely to report symptoms of ASD or PTSD than parents identify (Thabet et al., 2007). This difference may lead to underdiagnosis of relevant conditions and persistence of unresolved psychiatric disorders. In diagnosing children aged 7 to 10, an integrated diagnostic approach involving parental as well as child reports has been reported to enhance accuracy for the detection of psychiatric disorders. Findings have shown that observations by the caregivers might not capture the child's internal experience comprehensively, highlighting the necessity of applying direct child assessments for informing diagnostic conclusions. Integration of both methods is, therefore, necessary for the building of an educated understanding of the child's state of mental health and ensuring the enhanced effectiveness of treatment. The impact of trauma on children's mental health makes it particularly important to carry out careful symptom assessment and individualized diagnosis. Traumatized children exhibit varying patterns of symptoms in their development and changing with the passage of time, necessitating consistent evaluation. The stable long-term character of PTSD diagnoses following the application of alternative algorithms also highlights the need for specialty management modalities to therapy and intervention (Dalgleish et al., 2008). In particular, traumatized persons, for instance, following a motor vehicle accident, can evolve with variable symptom presentation that requires continuing observation in order to adjust therapeutic modalities accordingly. Early interventions tied to good diagnoses can significantly alter the recovery trajectory of children and adolescents. Thus, continued research into symptom-measuring approaches is required in order to ensure that clinicians can provide care for such groups suitably (Figure 6.8).

Figure 6.8. The diagnosis of trauma and stressor-related disorders can be further complicated by the variable agreement between parent and child reports of symptoms.

Source: https://www.childrensresourcegroup.com/wp-content/uploads/2019/02/Trauma-and-Stressor-Related-Disorders-CRG.jpg.

6.3.1. Emotional and Behavioral Symptoms

The emotional and behavioral symptoms of trauma and stressor-related disorders among children and adolescents are often intense and multifaceted. Following trauma, e.g., maltreatment or violence exposure, adolescents may develop multiple internalizing symptoms like depression, anxiety, and post-traumatic stress disorder (PTSD). Such disturbances are characterized by chronic unhappiness, excessive worrying, and difficulty managing emotions. In addition, trauma can have the ability to create behavioral expressions such as aggression, withdrawal, or defiance that can hinder social relationships and classroom performance. An understanding of how these emotional and behavioral symptoms interact with each other is necessary since they not only impact the individual but also reverberate through family and social systems, subjecting caregivers, and community services to additional stress. Thus, an integrated assessment and intervention strategy is called for the fostering of recovery and resilience in such teenage populations. The physiological reactivity of maltreated survivors during adolescence presents a lens through which one may view their behavioral and emotional symptoms. Studies have confirmed that maltreated teenagers exhibit an unusual stress reactivity pattern characterized by enhanced sympathetic nervous system activity and suppressed cardiac output to social stressors.

Figure 6.9. The physiological reactivity of adolescent maltreatment survivors provides a lens through which to examine their emotional and behavioral symptoms.

Source: https://cdn2.psychologytoday.com/assets/styles/manual_crop_1_1_1200x1200/public/teaser_image/blog_entry/2023-01/shutterstock_2120760704.jpg?itok=A94vvcXx.

This physiological reaction is also mirrored to a large degree by increased externalizing symptomatology, such as aggression and opposition, which can arise as survival mechanisms in response to feeling threatened in their surroundings. This dysregulation model of maladaptive stress response is significant in highlighting the focus on emotional and behavioral symptomology not only as a manifestation of trauma but as a component of the dysregulated state. As these adolescents work their way through the daily issues, their stress sensitivity will exacerbate accompanying symptoms, hence perpetuating a cycle of emotional disturbance and maladjustment behavior (Alves et al., 2014). Parent-child relationship is also held responsible for making the presentation of the emotional and behavioral symptoms following trauma complex. Poor concordance between parents and children regarding whether symptoms happen and to what extent they happen for acute stress disorder (ASD) and posttraumatic stress disorder (PTSD) has been demonstrated by research. Perception mismatch of traumatic symptoms can cause miscommunication and interfere with successful treatment plans. Children are more likely to support more severe symptoms than parents, possibly indicating a disparity between the child's internal and emotional life and those of the parents. Such disparities suggest that child direct interviews are necessary for accurate diagnosis and timely intervention. Furthermore, this challenges the application of parent observations to ascertain emotional disorders and necessitates child-centered approaches to assessment to ensure their emotional and behavioral problems are properly addressed (Thabet et al., 2007) (Figure 6.9).

6.3.2. Diagnostic Criteria According to DSM-5

The Diagnostic and Statistical Manual of Mental Disorders, Fifth Edition (DSM-5) is important in the classification of trauma and stressor-related disorders among children and adolescents. The model provides mental health professionals with the ability to identify and assess the unique symptoms that separate acute stress disorder (ASD) and posttraumatic stress disorder (PTSD). The DSM-5 offers specific diagnostic criteria, for example, the person must have experienced a traumatic event, intrusion of the thoughts, avoidance behaviors, negative thoughts and mood changes, and changes in arousal and reactivity. The criteria assist clinicians during the assessment, making the diagnosis not just precise but even enabling the clinician to plan the appropriate treatment for affected children. Adherence to these standardized criteria is crucial in the application of a standardized approach to diagnosis across various clinical environments. Developmental complications and variations in presentation of symptoms across age ranges complicate the process of making accurate diagnoses of trauma disorders in children. Evidence indicates that the DSM-5 algorithms applied to diagnose PTSD may not fully incorporate the complexity of the disorder, particularly in preschool children. In the research of two- to ten-year-old children who experienced traumatic events, it was discovered that using an alternative symptom algorithm resulted in a higher incidence of PTSD diagnosis than the current DSM-IV criteria (Dalgleish et al., 2008). It emphasizes the necessity of changes within the diagnostic systems for capturing the unique manifestation of trauma in children. Hence, ongoing research on the diagnostic criteria will be the key to refine instruments of assessment that reflect the daily lives of children and adolescents who are exposed to trauma. Moreover, the necessity for obtaining complete symptom reports from the parents and children cannot be overstated in making the diagnosis. Studies have found children to describe symptoms of ASD and PTSD more than their parents, something that indicates the usual parent-child discord in the report of affective disorders (Thabet et al., 2007). Lack of concordance indicates the need for clinicians to employ a multi-informant approach to the diagnosis of stressor- and trauma-related disorders. By combining parent and child perspectives, mental health clinicians can better comprehend a child's psychosocial functioning. Combination of the DSM-5 criteria with developmental considerations and multiple informant data can enhance the likelihood of successful diagnosis and subsequent intervention for adolescents and children who have been traumatized.

6.3.3. Challenges in Diagnosing Disorders in Children and Adolescents

The diagnostic nature of child and adolescent disorders is compound, often complicated by developmental problems and the wide range of variability in symptomatic behaviors by age. Children and teenagers are in the midst of extensive cognitive development and emotional, so it is hard to make a diagnosis on mental health disorders. Symptoms tend to be overlooked as a run-of-the-mill development quirk rather than an indicator of something beneath the surface. Subsequently, therefore, therapists are presented with the daunting task of discerning normative from clinical symptoms, a challenge exacerbated by the variable presentation of disorders like borderline personality disorder (BPD). More importantly, this is in light of the fact that BPD typically escapes diagnosis until adulthood while studies show there may be salient features in adolescence, highlighting the importance of early identification and intervention strategies (Bohus et al., 2015). In addition to developmental variations, external factors such as trauma and environmental stressors also play a significant role in mental health diagnoses among young people. Trauma exposure in the context of direct exposure or vicarious trauma introduces further complexity in assessing mental health. The psychological aftermath of such experience can lead to a variety of behavioral and emotional issues, which make diagnosis complex. Studies show that youth who have experienced high levels of trauma, such as those who have been displaced due to war, display increased internalizing behaviors. For example, one study on Chechen youth found that youth experiencing displacement had higher levels of depression and anxiety than their non-displaced counterparts, highlighting the interaction between the environment and mental health (Betancourt et al., 2004). This refers to the means through which trauma can warp the diagnostic profile, with the outcome of potential misdiagnosis or delayed treatment. Moreover, the quality and availability of assessing devices is another main concern in the identification of mental health disorders in children and youth.

Figure 6.10. Children and adolescents are still undergoing significant cognitive and emotional maturation, which can complicate the identification of mental health disorders.

*Source:*https://img.lb.wbmdstatic.com/vim/live/webmd/consumer_assets/site_images/articles/health_tools/afib_and_anxiety_slideshow/1800ss_getty_rf_young_woman_listening_to_therapist.jpg.

The majority of existing measures of evaluation have not been adequately validated to detect the specialized developmental and contextual factors of the younger populations, with the outcome of diagnostic deficits or imprecision. For instance, while measures are developed to detect indicators of more developed conditions, they may not be optimum for assessing incipient conditions like adolescent BPD. Accumulating evidence underlines the importance of refining measures to align with evidenced neurobiological and psychological development in younger people. The necessity of effective assessments is underscored by the long-term consequences of undiagnosed or misdiagnosed conditions, underscoring the urgency of individualized modalities in screening and intervention methods (Bohus et al., 2015) (Figure 6.10).

6.4. IMPACT ON DEVELOPMENT

The influence of trauma and stressor-related disorders on child and adolescent development is both deep-seated and extensive, impacting both immediate psychological well-being as well as long-term health outcomes. Traumatized children, particularly those who are in protective custody, have increased prevalence of mental health disorders, medical conditions, and health risk behaviors. Around 41.6% of youth in detention have been diagnosed with mental illnesses, the most common being depression and behavioral disorders, and 41.3% have chronic diseases, including obesity and sensory impairments. This overlap of issues hinders developmental trajectories, creating a cycle of instability that can carry over into adulthood. Above all, continuity in such disturbances is an indication of the necessity for targeted interventions and prevention strategies during persistent adolescent attachment to healthcare services, preventing thus the unfavorable health outcome associated with chronic adversity (Beal et al., 2019). Moreover, physiological stress response adaptation has profound effects on maltreated adolescents' developmental trajectories. Dysregulation of the stress response system has also been linked with the onset of psychopathology because maltreated adolescents will typically manifest certain reactivity patterns when they are subjected to social stressors. Based on evidence, these adolescents are prone to manifest a threat response characterized by heightened sympathetic nervous system activity in association with elevated vascular resistance. Even though they may have blunted heart rate responsivity on tasks of difficulty, this dysregulated physiological pattern is irrevocably bound with externalizing symptoms like aggression and defiance. These findings suggest that the emotional and psychological effects of trauma not only influence behavior but also manifest in unique physiological responses, and thus it is all the more arduous for compromised individuals to overcome developmental deficits (Alves et al., 2014). Ultimately, the long-term impact of trauma on youth and children's development necessitates an integrated approach to mental health treatment that addresses both the psychological and the physiologic aspects. Both aspects are particularly important for youth in the foster system or similar protective environments, in which, as noted, they are most likely to face a range of health and behavioral challenges. Understanding the interconnectedness of trauma, stress responses, and health outcomes will be essential for defining effective intervention practices. Providing adequate support to vulnerable populations while still in systems of care could foster healthier developmental paths. By integrating these approaches, mental health professionals will more effectively address the very interactive set of causes which contribute to the adverse effects of trauma and ultimately promote resilience and enhance positive outcomes among traumatized youth (Alves et al., 2014; Beal et al., 2019).

6.4.1. Effects on Emotional Regulation

The impact of trauma and stressor-related disorders on emotional regulation cannot be underestimated, particularly in children and adolescents. They also have difficulty acknowledging and regulating their emotions, and this becomes the cause of maladaptive coping. For example, studies have shown that adolescents who have experienced extreme trauma, such as abuse and neglect, might be unable to integrate the emotional experience in a positive way, resulting in either emotional dysregulation or extreme emotional responses. Emotional regulation is critical for healthy social relationships and academic performance; thus, dysfunction in this area will exacerbate behavioral issues and lead to vulnerability for mental illness. Given that emotional regulation is such a critical piece of the puzzle during these formative years, it is crucial that one examines interventions that specifically address such challenges, potentially undoing long-term negative consequences (Heck et al., 2015). Furthermore, understanding the effects of stress on emotional regulation needs a closer examination of environmental and personal causes contributing to this complex relationship. Findings indicate that stress can manifest in different forms across different contexts and developmental stages. For example, daily stressors may create acute emotional reactions, but chronic exposure may breed higher baseline levels of emotional reactivity and dysregulation. This is particularly dangerous for adolescents under personal and social duress. The cumulative burden of stress can interfere with the use of healthy coping strategies and problem-solving, in the end, reaching their emotional health. According to stress typologies, the relationship between stress exposure and person reactions significantly predicts emotional regulation capacity across life (Crosswell et al., 2018). Further, emotional regulation interventions for traumatized adolescents have also been found to be promising. Skills-based interventions involving the identification of stressors and coping strategies can enable adolescents to manage emotional problems more adaptively. Empirical support shows that cognitive coping and affect regulation can attenuate significantly the relationship between minority stressors and psychiatric distress, particularly in supportive contexts like gay-straight alliances. These peer-to-peer approaches, as well as providing relevant techniques, also build peer support and belonging. Thus, improving emotional regulation skills via targeted interventions may be a significant protective factor against the effects of trauma and stress, promoting healthier emotional development within an important developmental period (Heck et al., 2015) (Figure 6.11).

Figure 6.11. The impact of trauma and stressor-related disorders on emotional regulation is profound, particularly in children and adolescents.

Source: https://www.humanium.org/en/wp-content/uploads/2024/02/shutterstock_232819528-scaled.jpg.

6.4.2. Influence on Social Relationships

The impact of trauma and stressor-related disorders on interpersonal relationships among youth cannot be overstated. The experience of such events is likely to lead to disruptions in developing and sustaining interpersonal relationships, which greatly hinder a young person's social adaptation. With the experience of trauma by an individual, the resulting psychological pain might be manifested as anxiety, depression, or conduct problems that could impair their social interactions with their peers. These emotional and behavioral impairments can initiate withdrawal or acting-out behavior, which again leads to social isolation or conflict with others. Thus, the persistent struggle of navigating social settings has the tendency to develop a loneliness cycle as well as enhance feelings of inadequacy, further fostering negative self-concept and making further social interaction more difficult (Crosswell et al., 2018). Moreover, the formation of secure relationships is crucial in developmental stages since they provide crucial support that builds resilience against mental issues. Children and youth with adverse childhood experiences can cause them to trust others less, thereby finding it challenging to establish healthy relations after experiencing trauma. Research indicates that early exposure to such stressors might be a precursor to stable emotion dysregulation patterns and interpersonal difficulties, primarily driven by fear of abandonment or rejection. These fears might limit vulnerability expression and deny communication openness, which are essential components of good relationships. Here, it is necessary to foster a positive environment both in homes and in schools so that children develop trust and emotional intelligence to maintain healthy relationships (Fortunato et al., 2018).

Figure 6.12. When a young person encounters trauma, the subsequent psychological stress may manifest as anxiety, depression, or behavioral issues, which can hinder their ability to engage positively with peers.

Source: https://alisbh.com/wp-content/uploads/2025/01/674816eb23ef230aef327cef_steptodown.com779911.jpg.

Moreover, trauma not only affects interpersonal interactions but also has great implications for inter-peer relations within groups. Stigma of mental health issues can lead to misconceptions and prejudice among their peers, where victims of trauma are excluded. Due to social hierarchies and peer acceptance being very important at this level, victims of trauma will be excluded and bullied and further exacerbate their social problems. This relationship between ostracism and trauma calls for intervention strategies that work on inducing empathy and appreciation among peers. By interacting with these social processes and fostering healthy relationship building, mental health professionals can assist in the recovery and social integration of affected youth and foster a more inclusive and supportive community (Crosswell et al., 2018) (Figure 6.12).

6.4.3. Academic Performance and Cognitive Development

The interaction between cognitive development and academic performance is synergistically shaped by a range of external conditions, such as trauma and stressor-related disorders occurring in childhood and adolescence. Academic performance is usually a measure of cognitive ability, but the influence of psychological distress can critically distort this path. Children who are traumatized may struggle with attention, memory, and regulation, all necessary for learning and brain health. This makes it harder in a cycle where it is even harder due to poor school performance, which fuels the mental illness, making this in what seems like an endless fight against both school and mental health. Addressing these issues holistic within schools is crucial to sustaining healthy cognitive and academic growth, in recognition of the fact that the effects of trauma extend beyond emotion and are deeply entwined with cognitive capacity. In addition, the physiological consequences of trauma and stress on cognitive growth require equally devoted attention, particularly in those age years occupied by adolescence. Research has identified that adolescents with anxiety disorders present various neural fear processing and emotional regulation, allied to sleep disorder and cognitive impairment. For instance, evidence has proven that clinical anxiety changes the relationship between sleep and the neural reactivity of areas such as dorsal anterior cingulate cortex and hippocampus and influences academic achievement. Because cognitive functioning is optimal in adolescence, trauma-induced damage to cognitive processes can result in lower academic performance, generating a feedback cycle that maximizes stress and compromises school performance. Providing a setting with good mental well-being and health can forestall these detrimental effects by maximizing cognitive resistance to stress. The interplay between trauma, stress, and other cognitive development factors further underscores the need for intervention strategies that are developed with the goal of promoting wellness in school settings. Understanding the effects of trauma on cognition enables teachers and mental health providers to implement supportive systems that offer emotional as well as educational support. Interventions centered on mindfulness, affect awareness, and cognitive-behavioral skills can equip students with techniques for coping with the pervasive nature of stress and anxiety. By providing targeted support, institutions will be in a position to mitigate the adverse impact of trauma on academic performance and lay the groundwork for advanced cognitive development. Finally, understanding the profound interdependence of learning and mental health is the solution for developing learning environments conducive to academic achievement and overall psychological resilience, redressing an area of specific concern in child and adolescent mental health (Figure 6.13).

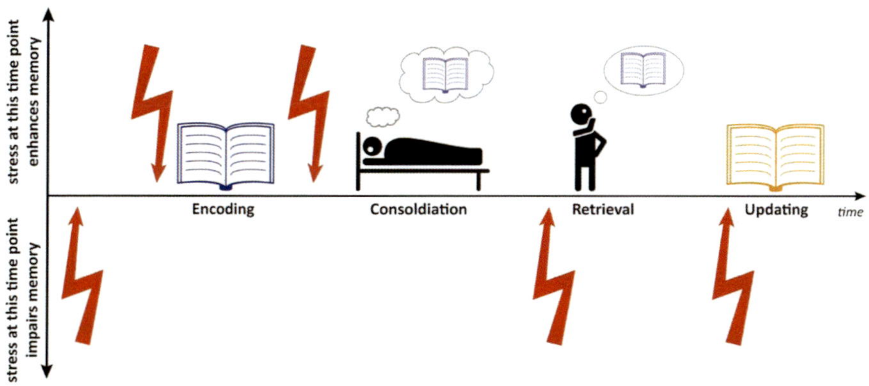

Figure 6.13. As cognitive development peaks during adolescence, disruptions in cognitive processes due to trauma can lead to diminished academic performance, creating a feedback loop that amplifies stress and hinders educational outcomes.

Source: https://media.springernature.com/lw1200/springer-static/image/art%3A10.1038%2Fnpjscilearn.2016.11/MediaObjects/41539_2016_Article_BFnpjscilearn201611_Fig2_HTML.jpg.

6.5. TREATMENT APPROACHES

Trauma and stressor-related disorders in children and adolescents require multi-modal treatment, considering the psychologic and social foundations of such disorders. Cognitive Behavioral Therapy (CBT) is an evidence-based treatment that is renowned to reduce depression and anxiety symptoms in youths exposed to trauma. CBT empowers young individuals with strategies to shift bad thinking and cope with distressful emotions. But what is noteworthy is the fact that trauma-informed care cannot be individualized alone; it must also involve family involvement and social support systems. By blending therapy sessions with family life and community-based services, practitioners are able to create a more integral approach that fosters healing and strength. This integrated system can significantly enhance treatment effectiveness, especially for those at-risk groups like adolescents in foster care or juvenile justice systems that most likely come with more mental health challenges (Beal et al., 2019). Further, familiarity with the individual contexts on which stressor-related disorders emerge is necessary for modifying effective treatment interventions. The majority of adolescents, particularly marginalized adolescents, face amplified stressors such as system discrimination and socio-economic instability. These variables could compound the effect of trauma, both on the development of mental health issues and on treatment efficacy. Current data trend towards youth in protective custody experiencing severe health disparities that are persistent and multidimensional, and therefore the development of targeted interventions becomes paramount. Interventions for long-term health conditions, diagnoses of mental illness, and risk behaviors stemming from trauma must target sustainable support systems that continue even after treatment. Systemic barriers must be reduced to allow continuity of care, especially among detained youth of long duration, as connections to regular health services may avoid negative circumstances (González et al., 2017). Finally, to ensure the greatest possible benefit from treatment, there is a need to incorporate cultural sensitivity and individuality when treating adolescents who are experiencing trauma. Therapists must be instructed to recognize and respect different backgrounds, something that may have a significant role to play in a youth's healing process. Being engaged with interventions which are culturally sensitive, combined with a strengths-based approach, can enhance the therapeutic relationship. For instance, incorporating parts of a child's cultural heritage or belief systems into their treatment plan helps to build trust and ownership. Also, ongoing assessment and treatment plan adjustment based on the changing needs and circumstances of a youth can led to improved resilience and coping skills. Finally, personalized and culturally appropriate care should be paramount in addressing the mounting, interrelated needs of children and adolescents who are suffering from trauma and stressor-related disorders (Beal et al., 2019).

6.5.1. Psychotherapy and Counseling Methods

Psychotherapeutic and counseling strategies play a crucial role in the management of trauma and stressor-related disorders in children and adolescents. Such treatment processes are designed to allow children and adolescents to work through trauma, acquire coping mechanisms, and build resilience. Cognitive-behavioral therapy (CBT) is one of the useful models that focuses on modifying maladaptive patterns of thought likely to be activated by trauma. By teaching kids and adolescents to recognize and challenge these thoughts, CBT encourages healthier emotional responses and reduces symptoms of anxiety and depression. By adapting approaches to the level of development of the child, therapists make approaches accessible to their cognitive functioning and emotional maturity, thus creating an atmosphere to recover. Moreover, group therapy has even been an effective treatment method for trauma, particularly in marginalized adolescents with special stressors. As an example, a new pilot study recently reported on a mental health promotion program for LGBTQ youth carried out in a high school gay-straight alliance (GSA) setting (Heck et al., 2015). The program even addressed minority stressors but, most importantly, promoted coping skills through education and peer support. Patients found the program to be enjoyable and rated it as relevant, thereby showing effective community support in fostering resilience to trauma.

Figure 6.14. Psychotherapy and counseling methods play a critical role in addressing trauma and stressor-related disorders among children and adolescents.

Source: https://cdn.cpdonline.co.uk/wp-content/uploads/2024/04/22161420/The-Role-of-CBT-in-Child-and-Adolescent-Mental-Health-scaled.jpg.

The integration of psychoeducation and structured group sessions empowers participants because they are capable of sharing experience and coping skills, hence building a sense of belongingness essential to emotional restoration. In addition to traditional therapy, newer forms such as psychodynamic therapy are also on the rise in trauma therapy. This approach emphasizes the exploration of unconscious processes and affective states of trauma and attempts to make sense out of relational processes underlying symptoms. One recent study explored how brief psychodynamic psychotherapy affects a patient who had been diagnosed with relational trauma and illustrates how therapeutic dyads are synchronized during sessions when traumatic material is being explored

(Benelli et al., 2015). These findings indicate that a knowledge of interpersonal relationships and how they impact therapeutic outcome is crucial. Integrating clinical observations with neurophysiological measures enables researchers and clinicians to gain information about the relational processes engaged, enhancing the effectiveness of psychotherapy in alleviating symptoms of trauma in child patients (Figure 6.14).

6.5.2. Pharmacological Interventions

Pharmacologic interventions play a critical function in the treatment of trauma and stressor-related disorders within youths. Trauma and stressor-related disorders tend to lead to incapacitating symptoms that can go a long way toward preventing a youngster's social and educational functioning. It is essential to understand that while pharmacologic approaches can be of relief against acute symptoms, these tend to be most effective when utilized in conjunction with psychotherapy. Drugs such as selective serotonin reuptake inhibitors (SSRIs) have succeeded in the treatment of anxiety and depressive symptoms seen in these disorders. Nonetheless, extreme care has to be taken regarding the age and development stage of the child, as pharmacokinetics and drug side effects may vary significantly in children. Pharmacological treatments can be especially useful in the case of anxiety disorders if they complement psychological therapy, like Cognitive Behavioral Therapy (CBT), in cases where CBT by itself proves to be inadequate. Both psychological therapies and pharmacotherapy have, from what is currently documented, proven to be effective. CBT, however, remains the recommended first line of treatment because it has an established safety record and is generally accepted by parents and caregivers. Where anxiety disorders remain undiagnosed, the majority of adolescents suffer more dysfunction within peer relationships, academic achievement, and family functioning and end up developing more psychosocial issues eventually in life. It is with a robust treatment system with the use of pharmacologic options that can provide rapid relief and stabilize the disorder and wait for therapeutic interventions to take effect (Bennett et al., 2016). Furthermore, the selection of pharmacological agents should also consider individual patient variables, including comorbid conditions. For instance, adolescents presenting with trauma disorders may present with signs of post-traumatic stress disorder (PTSD), anxiety, or depression, necessitating detailed assessment and individualized treatment regimens. Through research, it has been confirmed that some pharmacological interventions are effective in treating specific symptoms of these disorders but must be utilized judiciously due to potential side effects. In accordance with the Cochrane Review guidelines, assessing the efficacy of the combined treatments, such as couple and family therapy and pharmacology, is crucial in managing trauma-related disorders (Cowlishaw et al., 2014). Ultimately, an integrated care strategy that encompasses pharmacology along with psychological intervention is critical in optimizing the outcomes of adolescents suffering from such conditions.

6.5.3. Family Involvement and Support Systems

In child and youth mental health, family and support systems play a vital role in cushioning the effects of stressor-related disorders and trauma. Families are the first to offer emotional and social support, which has an influence on the resilience and coping mechanisms of adolescents with psychological issues. Having an intact, stable family supports children's coping ability to endure stressful situations, resulting in good mental health. Family bonds that are disrupted or lacking, such as in instances of child welfare protective custody, leave children vulnerable to mental health issues. Research has established that youth in protective custody also have higher rates of mental illness diagnoses, chronic medical illnesses, and health risk behaviors, highlighting the relevance of intact family presence in their support networks (Beal et al., 2019). Understanding stress dynamics in families is essential in resolving trauma-related disorders among children and adolescents. Stress can have numerous different causes, including family conflict, socioeconomic struggles, and changes in the relationships of a family. These stresses compound with a child's emotional development and are capable of amplifying mental illness, leading to a cycle of distress and instability. An integrative definition of stress takes into account not only the immediate family environment but also the more general social and community environments. By recognizing how these stressors contribute to psychological reactivity and health behavior, stakeholders are able to more effectively develop interventions to construct the family support systems in order to foster resilience (Crosswell et al., 2018). Moreover, the construction of increased family involvement requires that there be deliberate strategies to construct more interrelated connections among children, parents, and caregivers. Family cohesion activities, mental health knowledge, and availability of community resources are principal support networks. Such interventions can assist families in acquiring the skills that enable them to communicate well and build emotional understanding among their members. Through focused interventions, children can be provided with stable support that buffers the negative effects of trauma and stressor-related disorders. Engaging families through therapeutic interventions and providing access to mental health services may result in major improvements in the total well-being of children and adolescents, showing the interdependent work families must do in advocacy for and recovery from mental illness (Beal et al., 2019) (Figure 6.15).

Figure 6.15. Families serve as the first line of emotional and social support, impacting the resilience and coping strategies of young individuals facing psychological challenges.

Source: https://www.unicef.org/sites/default/files/styles/media_large_image/public/UNI205414.jpg.webp?itok=kF4w2Dgr.

6.6. Prevention and Early Intervention

The foundation of effective treatment for trauma and stressor-related disorders among youth lies, to a great extent, in prevention and early intervention strategies. It is important to identify the warning signs of mental illness early since these disorders will progress if left unaddressed. Early interventions have the ability to reverse the impact of trauma by acting on it immediately and by instructing youth on coping skills so that they can overcome their problems. For instance, youth in protective custody, frequently exposed to a variety of stressors, have been identified as a group at higher risk for mental disorders. By targeting prevention efforts at this at-risk group, including frequent screenings and availability of supportive services, we can better guarantee that they are accorded adequate mental health care before complications become more entrenched conditions, as attested by comprehensive studies conducted on young people in these systems (Beal et al., 2019). Furthermore, embedding prevention programs within existing educational systems, like those held in Gay-Straight Alliances (GSAs), shows how early intervention can be implemented effectively in community systems. Programs specifically designed to mitigate minority stressors as well as build coping skills among LGBTQ youth have been feasible and acceptable and have recognized that these interventions are both educational and enjoyable for youth. These early interventions not only equip such teenagers with essential skills but also make them feel accepted and belong to their communities, which is essential to their emotional well-being. The entire approach towards fostering mental health aligns with the greater goal of preventing trauma disorders through enhancing resilience and coping skills among teenagers of various backgrounds (Heck et al., 2015). Summarily, the integration of early intervention and targeted prevention strategies is essential in addressing trauma and stressor-related disorders in child and adolescent mental health. As illustrated by research with youth in protective custody, early diagnosis and treatment has the ability to significantly reduce the long-term consequences of mental illness. Engaging youth in supportive environments and creating community-based interventions can also enhance mental health services access. This proactive work is not just beneficial but necessary in human services if we are to promote long-term health and improve the wellness outcomes in those at greatest risk. Prioritizing these strategies, in turn, positions us to create healthier futures for youth coping with the long-term effects of trauma and stressors in their lives.

6.6.1. Importance of Early Identification of Symptoms

Early recognition of trauma and stressor-related disorder symptoms among children and adolescents is key to effective treatment and intervention. Research has found that children who have experienced traumatic events have a range of psychological responses that may incorporate irritability, fearfulness, and withdrawal. The symptoms, if not diagnosed or treated, escalate to more complex disorders. They can be identified early so that interventions are done at the right time, which can decelerate the deterioration of symptoms and improve long-term outcomes. For instance, studies on preschool and elementary school children who were traumatized confirmed that applying an alternative symptom algorithm to diagnose PTSD was superior to traditional criteria, with a higher rate of identifying individuals at risk for long-lasting psychiatric difficulties (Dalgleish et al., 2008). Identification of such symptoms in a timely fashion is important to facilitate appropriate support and services for affected children and families. In addition, the use of multiple informants, including parents and teachers, is essential in the process of identification. Children cannot symbolize their internal worlds as frequently as adults do, particularly after traumatic experiences. By comparing caregiver and teacher reports, clinicians can gain a greater insight into a child's behavioral and emotional complaints. It was shown to enhance diagnostic validity, especially in children aged 7 to 10 years old because corroborative information procured from caregivers and children report greater case rates of PTSD than from caregiver report alone (Dalgleish et al., 2008). Thus, engaging multiple stakeholders in the identification process guarantees a thorough grasp of the child's symptoms and experiences, leading to more personalized interventions in the end. Finally, the significance of understanding developing patterns in personality in childhood cannot be overemphasized. Literature suggests that personality styles and disorders can arise as early as in childhood, which necessitates the urgency of immediate recognition and intervention. Early identification not only increases the possibilities for mental health interventions but also allows for further refinement of coping mechanisms and resilience. Active intervention of these issues can reduce the susceptibility to chronic mental health problems in later life, thereby supporting healthier developmental trajectories. Since evidence points to the requirement of a development perspective in the evaluation of psychological symptoms, it is necessary that practitioners focus on early symptom detection, creating an environment conducive to the flourishing of children in the presence of trauma and stress.

6.6.2. Community and School-Based Programs

School- and community-based interventions are crucial for the treatment of trauma and stressor-related disorders in children. These programs ensure a setting where kids can be treated with therapy to enhance emotional resilience. Inculcating mental health education within school curricula enables early identification of vulnerable children so that interventions can be delivered on schedule. Also, community programs have a tendency to provide access to resources such as counseling and peer support groups, which are vital in helping young people overcome the challenges caused by trauma. In doing so, these programs not only promote personal well-being but also propel the collective thinking towards mental wellness in communities, hence destroying stigma and establishing supportive communities. One of the most significant advantages of school and community-based interventions is in their ability to assemble different stakeholders towards a shared vision of obtaining better mental health outcomes. Families, schools, and neighborhood organizations have the capability to collaborate and form structured support networks that account for the multifaceted nature of trauma. For instance, community-based interventions can offer parent workshops that educate them further on the impact of adverse childhood experiences on the emotional health of their children. Through their inclusion of families in the treatment process, these programs create a system of support that extends beyond the school. Further, such interventions can lead to increased funding and resources to continue mental health programs, ultimately culminating in more effective interventions for troubled youth (González et al., 2017). In addition, incorporating trauma-informed practices in schools and community life has been transformative in reducing the effects of trauma on adolescents and children. These practices are implemented in programs that provide youth with safe and supportive spaces where they feel comfortable opening up their fears without judgment. This is particularly important for disadvantaged youths who live in contexts where compounded traumas can be inflicted upon them through structural injustices and community violence. By acknowledging the pervasive effects of trauma, such as that experienced by young men of color, community- and school-based initiatives can evolve their initiatives to meet specific needs while promoting healing and recovery (Sered, 2014). By doing so, these settings not only foster personal development but also empower participants to become change agents within their communities, instilling a culture of resilience and support (Figure 6.16).

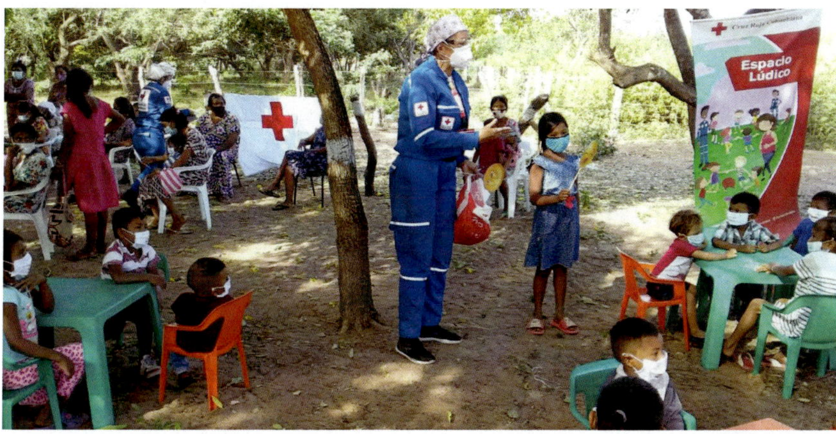

Figure 6.16. Community and school-based programs play a crucial role in addressing trauma and stressor-related disorders among children and adolescents.

Source: https://preparecenter.org/wp-content/uploads/bb-plugin/cache/IMG-20210118-WA0033-002_jpg-panorama-3aca0d45db88a12f8248df7dbdc85fff-61dc9c895040f.jpg.

6.6.3. Role of Parents and Caregivers in Prevention

The role of parents and caregivers in the preventability of trauma and stressor-related disorder in children and adolescents is critical and multifaceted. The earliest interpersonal relations set a pattern for emotional and cognitive development. Literature shows that synchronization of parent-infant development has a significant impact on the child's ability to cope with stress. This synchrony of criticism allows for the development of healthy stress buffer systems, which are essential to psychological adjustment. Responsive caregiving to a child's needs ensures a secure attachment and therefore resilience to adversity. Disruptions in this synchrony, however, can lead to pathological responses, including attachment disorganization, and threaten children for later mental health challenges. Thus, recognizing the importance of involvement of caregivers during these critical times highlights prevention efforts targeting healthy parent-child interactions (Guedeney et al., 2025). Recognition and treatment of early developing personality traits and disorders in childhood are likewise top priorities for parents and caregivers. Recent studies emphasize the continuity of personality styles from early childhood to adulthood and thus the need to detect mental health threats in early childhood. Early intervention is feasible through caregivers identifying signs of stress or maladaptive behavior, allowing for a drastic shift in a child's developmental trajectory. By maintaining open communication and a supportive environment, parents can walk children through emotional challenges and reduce the likelihood of more complex disorders in adulthood. Furthermore, preventative interventions such as parenting programs have been shown to develop caregivers' ability to care for their offspring effectively, reducing susceptibility to trauma-related challenges. Therefore, a proactive intervention by caregivers not only addresses acute concerns but also lays a basis for long-term mental well-being (Fortunato et al., 2018). In addition to cultivating emotional health, caregivers enable children to acquire coping and resilience. By demonstration of effective coping skills, parents enable children to acquire essential tools for coping with stress and adversity. For instance, when parents openly talk about their own stress experiences and demonstrate healthy coping skills, children develop lessons in controlling their emotions. Moreover, caregivers who create a nurturing context for expressing emotions develop emotional intelligence, enabling children to identify and name their emotions. This becomes a habit that can actually reduce the risk of developing stressor-related disorders significantly, as children who feel understood and supported are more likely to cope with adversity successfully. Consequently, the effort of parents and caregivers extends beyond protection alone; it entails the proactive building of resilience and mental health, thus serving as a crucial pillar of trauma-related mental illness avertability (Fortunato et al., 2018; Guedeney et al., 2025).

6.7. CONCLUSION

The impact of trauma and stressor-related disorders on child and adolescent mental health cannot be overstated. As viewed from emerging evidence, the psychopathological response to trauma is very heterogeneous in children, which creates a compelling need for a subtle conceptualization as well as intervention. The recognition that young children, starting from preschool age, can exhibit signs of post-traumatic stress disorder (PTSD) highlights the necessity for the diagnostic criteria to be age-specific among this group. Research shows that symptom algorithms employed in the diagnosis of PTSD can yield more accurate measures than conventional procedures, thus enabling earlier identification and intervention among children exposed to trauma (Dalgleish et al., 2008). This conclusion identifies the importance of regularly revising diagnostic models that consider the unique developmental settings of children. Resilience also is a determining factor in how children and adolescents respond to traumatic events. While the majority will have maladaptive symptoms of PTSD following exposure to significant stressors, others exhibit remarkable resilience, overcoming negative experiences with minimal psychological distress. This difference means that an additional investigation into the biological, psychological, and social factors determining resilience is necessary in the interpretation and management of susceptible groups. For instance, heart rate variability (HRV) measurement has been suggested as a possible biological marker of resilience and is a natural physiological response to stress (Carnevali et al., 2018). Future research endeavors must move even ahead and integrate these biological findings with psychological assessments to foster a more comprehensive understanding of resilience and its applicability in mental health care. To conclude, trauma and stressor-related disorders in children and adolescents can be tackled only with a multi-pronged approach that includes state-of-the-art diagnostic techniques, an understanding of resilience, and targeted interventions. Because of the extensive range in the stress response among individuals, mental health professionals will have to apply an individualized approach that addresses symptomatology and the child's socio-environmental background. Early identification methods, such as incorporating parent- and child-reports of symptoms, will be key in effectively treating these disorders and preventing long-term consequences. Furthermore, interdisciplinary studies on resilience processes provide a promising field that can potentially inform prevention interventions and improve psychological resilience among adolescents exposed to adversity. The potential of such findings underlies the rationale for ongoing inquiry and applied science in mental health clinics dedicated to serving our youth.

6.7.1. Summary of Key Points Discussed

The complexity of the nature of trauma and stressor-related disorders among children and adolescents demands recognition of intricate diagnostic criteria. The research revealed that young children, particularly 2 through 10 years, can demonstrate long-term psychological effects following traumatic experiences, such as motor vehicle accidents. A longitudinal study established that using a different algorithm to diagnose posttraumatic stress disorder (PTSD) can offer better valid results than common DSM-IV criteria. Specifically, 11.5% of the children met the diagnosis by this new procedure within a few weeks after exposure, highlighting the importance of individually tailored diagnostic processes for young populations (Dalgleish et al., 2008). Further, the participation of children and parents in the reporting facilitates a complete picture of child psychopathology, which indicates that reliance solely on parent report can miss children's report of significant symptoms, and hence lead to underdiagnosis or misdiagnosis. The findings of stress as an important player in mental well-being are also strengthened when considering interaction between different types of stressors throughout an individual's lifespan. It is required to mention that stress impacts health across a lifespan, varying in degree of effect from acute stressors, for instance, traumatic events, to chronic stressors that may accumulate over time. An integrative conceptual model is introduced to synthesize knowledge from epidemiological, psychological, and physiological perspectives, enabling in-depth understanding of how stressors interact with people's responses and health behaviors (Crosswell et al., 2018). By defining stress into precise types and timeframes, researchers can better assess the effects of such stressors on the mental health of children and adolescents, ultimately culminating in better intervention strategies and more effective treatment. Additionally, the emphasis on an integrated strategy for diagnosing and addressing trauma-based disorders is a step towards the recognition of the significant role played by environmental and idiosyncratic factors in shaping psychological well-being. The recognition of the fact that traumatic exposures are multidimensional necessitates an integrated response to address child and adolescent mental health problems substantially. When children pass through stressors, be they chronic or acute, the psychological consequence that ensues demands multi-informant strategies and longitudinal follow-up to fully capture existing changes in their mental status. This evolving perspective underlines the necessity to adapt existing diagnostic tools and models so as to be able to better identify and treat trauma and stressor-related disorders to promote healthier psychological development among young people (Crosswell et al., 2018; Dalgleish et al., 2008).

6.7.2. The Necessity for Ongoing Research and Awareness

The child and adolescent mental health landscape continues to shift, especially as it relates to trauma and stressor-related disorders. The more these disorders are being identified, the more crucial the need for continued research and vigilance cannot be emphasized. Study is central in unraveling the delicate dance between stress and mental health, especially as it relates to children and adolescents who are still in the process of developing their emotional and psychological capabilities. The dilemma is how to delimit what constitutes stress and its impact on health outcomes because stress is not a single, unidimensional entity but an emergent process that is operated on by a range of factors. From a holistic conceptual framework, researchers are able to more clearly delineate the settings of stress and differential effects across the life course with emphasis on the demand for resilience and coping by younger generations (Crosswell et al., 2018). Additionally, the importance of the World Health Organizations most recent updates to the guidelines for diagnosis, particularly within the International Classification of Diseases (ICD-11), highlights the applicability of research to the formation of useful therapeutic paradigms for illness associated with trauma. This classification development represents a valuable tool for mental health clinicians, which heightens clinical usefulness as well as broad characterization of mental disorders. The ICD-11 is a key reference point that facilitates research and operational use of evidence-based interventions. Increased understanding of the latest classifications not only enhances more accurately targeted treatment but also embraces interdisciplinary collaboration for addressing the multifaceted nature of trauma and stress disorders in children (Berk et al., 2020). Finally, the application of research evidence to education and community curricula and programs is critical in creating awareness of trauma and stressor-related disorders among families, educators, and medical providers. Enhanced knowledge in the field of the prevalence and impact of the disorders can enable communities to create supportive environments that promote healing. Increased demands on trauma-informed practice in education and health care are called for in order to ensure early detection and intervention and emphasize the community role in evading long-term effect on child and adolescent mental health. Ongoing research gives power to this debate so that newly emerging knowledge is disseminated widely and effectively, hence taking a holistic approach to mental health incorporating awareness, education, and treatment (Crosswell et al., 2018).

6.7.3. Call to Action for Improved Mental Health Resources and Support

Addressing the pressing demand for more mental health services and children's and adolescents' services is a critical step in preventing long-term consequences of trauma and stressor-related disorders. The association between adversity in childhood and later mental illness has been demonstrated repeatedly, calling for prevention instead of intervention. In youth in protective custody, for instance, the prevalence of mental health diagnoses is staggering, and 41.6% have depression and behavioral disorders (Beal et al., 2019). Building robust support networks that address these needs can significantly alter the trajectory for these young adults. Preventive measures such as mental health screening at entry into protective custody and integration of therapeutic assets would identify risk early on to allow for specific intervention to foster resilience and recovery during a moment of vulnerability. Additionally, the impact on the mental health of adolescents of long-term detention cannot be overestimated. Research emphasizes how extended periods of stay in remand regimes under the juvenile justice system have been found to exacerbate pre-existing trauma and contribute to subsequent health issues upon adulthood (González et al., 2017). The custodians of reform need to focus beyond recidivism and economic cost of detention, while emphasizing the negative implications of inadequate mental health treatment among these vulnerable populations. By raising awareness about these concerns, stakeholders like policymakers, mental health professionals, and community groups can make calls for system changes to emphasize mental well-being, rehabilitation, and reintegration. An integrated approach with evidence-based mental health interventions is central to encouraging healthy development and de-institutionalization of trauma. In moving forward, a concerted effort needs to be made to embrace innovative methods of increasing access to mental health care for at-risk youth. Schools, community facilities, and health care providers must work together to put in place a network of care encompassing a broad spectrum of services including counseling, peer support groups, and mental health education. In particular, marginalized youth are most likely to experience compounded layers of trauma and hence culturally responsive and available services are essential (González et al., 2017). Implementing such programs can facilitate individuals to reach care and enhance their well-being. Public and private sectors need to invest in these services, with mental health as a prominent element of child and adolescent development. Developing a culture that acknowledges mental health support is not only beneficial to people's recovery but also leads to healthier societies for future generations.

REFERENCES

1. Alves, S., McLaughlin, K. A., Mendes, W. B., Sheridan, M., et al. (2014). Child maltreatment and autonomic nervous system reactivity: Identifying dysregulated stress reactivity patterns by using the biopsychosocial model of challenge and threat. https://core.ac.uk/download/305124128.pdf (accessed on 14th October 2025).
2. Baubet, T., Casas, G., Espié, E., Gaboulaud, V., et al. (2009). Trauma-related psychological disorders among Palestinian children and adults in Gaza and West Bank, 2005–2008. https://core.ac.uk/download/pdf/9417710.pdf (accessed on 14th October 2025).
3. Beal, S. J., Crosby, I., Greiner, M. V., Nause, K., et al. (2019). Understanding health risks for adolescents in protective custody. https://core.ac.uk/download/212897226.pdf (accessed on 14th October 2025).
4. Benelli, E., Bianco, S., Broggio, A., Kleinbub, J. R., et al. (2015). The words of the body: Psychophysiological patterns in dissociative narratives. https://core.ac.uk/download/80154470.pdf (accessed on 14th October 2025).
5. Bennett, C., Creswell, C., Hill, C., Eapen, V., Ipser, J., James, A., et al. (2016). Anxiety disorders in children and adolescents. https://core.ac.uk/download/46563521.pdf (accessed on 14th October 2025).
6. Berk, M., Brewin, C., Briken, P., Cohen-Kettenis, P., et al. (2020). Mental, behavioral and neurodevelopmental disorders in the ICD-11: An international perspective on key changes and controversies. https://core.ac.uk/download/287582535.pdf (accessed on 14th October 2025).
7. Betancourt, T. S. (2004). Connectedness, social support and mental health in adolescents displaced by the war in Chechnya. https://core.ac.uk/download/78062824.pdf (accessed on 14th October 2025).
8. Bohus, M., Fonagy, P., Hessels, C., Kaess, M., et al. (2015). ESCAP expert article: Borderline personality disorder in adolescence: An expert research review with implications for clinical practice. https://core.ac.uk/download/79495883.pdf (accessed on 14th October 2025).
9. Brooks, M., Bryce, J., Graham-Kevan, N., Irving, K., et al. (2015). Repeat victimization, retraumatisation and victim vulnerability. https://core.ac.uk/download/42138066.pdf (accessed on 14th October 2025).
10. Broome, M. R., Catone, G., Lennox, B., Marwaha, S., et al. (2017). Bullying victimization and psychosis: The inter-dependence and independence of risk trajectories. https://core.ac.uk/download/132201613.pdf (accessed on 14th October 2025).

11. Carlisi, C. O., Ernst, M., Guyer, A. E., Hilbert, K., et al. (2017). Sleep-amount differentially affects fear-processing neural circuitry in pediatric anxiety: A preliminary fMRI investigation. https://core.ac.uk/download/323069555.pdf (accessed on 14th October 2025).
12. Carnevali, L., Koenig, J., Ottaviani, C., Sgoifo, A., et al. (2018). Autonomic and brain morphological predictors of stress resilience. https://core.ac.uk/download/157570373.pdf (accessed on 14th October 2025).
13. Cowlishaw, S., Evans, L., Rodgers, B., Suomi, A., et al. (2014). Couple and family therapies for post-traumatic stress disorder (PTSD). https://core.ac.uk/download/29027137.pdf (accessed on 14th October 2025).
14. Crosswell, A. D., Epel, E. S., Mayer, S. E., Mendes, W. B., et al. (2018). More than a feeling: A unified view of stress measurement for population science. https://core.ac.uk/download/305124133.pdf (accessed on 14th October 2025).
15. Dalgleish, T., Glucksman, E., Meiser-Stedman, R., Smith, P., et al. (2008). The posttraumatic stress disorder diagnosis in preschool- and elementary school-age children exposed to motor vehicle accidents. https://core.ac.uk/download/29109430.pdf (accessed on 14th October 2025).
16. Dodd, C. G., Hill, R. M., Kaplow, J. B., et al. (2019). The Hurricane Exposure, Adversity, and Recovery Tool (HEART): Developing and validating a risk screening instrument for youth exposed to Hurricane Harvey. https://core.ac.uk/download/228022776.pdf (accessed on 14th October 2025).
17. Dudgeon, P., Gee, G., Glaskin, B., Kelly, K., et al. (2009). Social determinants of Aboriginal and Torres Strait Islander social and emotional wellbeing. http://hdl.handle.net/10536/DRO/DU:30058501 (accessed on 14th October 2025).
18. Fortunato, A., & Speranza, A. M. (2018). Personality traits and disorders in childhood. Clinical evaluation and diagnosis. https://core.ac.uk/download/160053023.pdf (accessed on 14th October 2025).
19. Gerin, M. I., McCrory, E. J., & Viding, E. (2017). Annual research review: Childhood maltreatment, latent vulnerability and the shift to preventative psychiatry–the contribution of functional brain imaging. https://core.ac.uk/download/81678173.pdf (accessed on 14th October 2025).
20. González, T. (2017). Youth incarceration, health, and length of stay. https://core.ac.uk/download/216957516.pdf (accessed on 14th October 2025).
21. Green, J. G., McLaughlin, K. A., Alegría, M., & Loder, S. (2015). Disparities in child and adolescent mental health and mental health

services in the U.S. https://core.ac.uk/download/75780891.pdf (accessed on 14th October 2025).

22. Guedeney, A., Welniarz, B., Guedeney, N., Dugravier, R., Tereno, S., Saias, T., et al. (2025). The time of the infant, parent-infant desynchronization and attachment disorganization, or how long does it take for a preventive action to be effective? https://core.ac.uk/download/pdf/6580494.pdf (accessed on 14th October 2025).
23. Heck, N. C. (2015). The potential to promote resilience: Piloting a minority stress-informed, GSA-based, mental health promotion program for LGBTQ youth. https://core.ac.uk/download/213078941.pdf (accessed on 14th October 2025).
24. Kays, D. (2018). Intimate partner violence, anxiety diagnosis, and binge drinking behavior among college students. https://digitalcommons.georgefox.edu/cgi/viewcontent.cgi?article=1242&context=psyd (accessed on 14th October 2025).
25. Lynn-Whaley, J., & Sugarmann, J. (2017). The relationship between community violence and trauma: How violence affects learning, health, and behavior. https://core.ac.uk/download/87085562.pdf (accessed on 14th October 2025).
26. Paleczna, M. (2017). Cancer related PTSD symptoms in patients of all ages and their relatives, and general risk factors. https://core.ac.uk/download/161229435.pdf (accessed on 14th October 2025).
27. Sered, D. (2014). *Young Men of Color and the Other Side of Harm: Addressing Disparities in Our Responses to Violence*. https://core.ac.uk/download/75779904.pdf (accessed on 14th October 2025).
28. Thabet, A., Grills, A. E., Grills, A. E., Goenjian, A. K., La Greca, A., American Psychiatric Association, Bryant, B., et al. (2007). Parent and child agreement for acute stress disorder, post-traumatic stress disorder and other psychopathology in a prospective study of children and adolescents exposed to single-event trauma. https://core.ac.uk/download/29109416.pdf (accessed on 14th October 2025).

Chapter 7

Behavioral and Conduct Disorders

Contents

INTRODUCTION

Conduct and behavioral disorders are a key problem in child and adolescent mental health as exemplified by their prevalence and adverse effects on youth and society as a whole. They represent a group of disconcerting behavior characterized by aggression, oppositionality, and antisocial conduct, which is capable of disrupting school performance and social relationships. The future status of children with conduct disorder is particularly problematic and is likely to lead to severe adult outcomes such as criminality, drug addiction, and other psychiatric disorders (Barlow et al., 2009). Increasing acknowledgment of such difficulties requires a complete comprehension of the etiology of such disorders, possible interventions, and the need for effective treatment approaches based on empirical research. The recent past has witnessed an increase in the development of parenting training schemes aimed at child conduct problem treatment. These systematic interventions provide parents with a systematic means of obtaining effective techniques for managing problem behavior exhibited by their children. Systematic review of randomized controlled trials has revealed large positive effects with such parent programs based both on independent and parent ratings of child behavior (Barlow et al., 2009). However, whilst promising, consideration needs to be given to methodological limitations that may underpin existing research, such as small sample sizes and limited diversity of groups of participants, which affect the ability of findings to be generalized. Thus, further detailed research is necessary for exploring the efficiency of various parenting programs, taking into account that each child has special needs. Mental health at schools is a pertinent field for the treatment of children's and adolescents' conduct and behavioral disorders. Since mental health issues among young students continue to grow, schools are the best locations for preventive interventions and early treatment. A conceptual model including social and emotional learning, resilience promotion, and prevention of behavior disorders can guide the development of effective school-based interventions. A method that embodies an appreciation of the need for a definitions and constructs consensus on the school mental health issues to support researcher-practitioner-policymaker collaboration is preferable. By prioritizing mental health in educational systems, stakeholders can assist in ensuring the comprehensive development of children and youth and eventually lead to healthier practices and improved results.

Definition of Behavioral and Conduct Disorders

Conduct and behavioral disorders are core principles in child and adolescent mental health, described as long-standing patterns of behavior that constitute a violation of others' rights and norms of society. Conduct and behavioral disorders are generally classified under externalizing disorders in which disruptive behavior manifests itself in the forms of irritability, aggression, or defiance. One of the most crucial points of understanding these disorders is their influence in the realm of development because they can impair social behavior, school studies, and family dynamics. They can manifest themselves in a variety of ways, ranging from oppositional defiant disorder (ODD), which is argumentative and defiant, to conduct disorder (CD), where the behavior is more serious, such as aggression towards people or animals, vandalism, and violation of important rules. Early intervention and detection are of primary importance, particularly because undiagnosed behavior issues have been shown to result in numerous negative outcomes later in life or in adolescence. Pathogenesis of conduct and behavioral disorders is multifactorial and based on a combination of genetic, environmental, and sociocultural influences. Biological susceptibilities, such as neurodevelopmental defects, might be implicated, while environmental influences, including family turmoil, peer pressure, and socio-economic disadvantage, are implicated in the development of these disorders. Emerging evidence indicates a stark rise in mental illness in children, emphasizing the relevance of integrative theoretical models that guide intervention strategies (Cavioni et al., 2020). Especially significant is the intersection of behavior and technology, since excessive use of the internet has been linked with increased behavioral and emotional disturbances in adolescents. This would mean that it is crucial to determine the context of the child's environment to be able to effectively diagnose and treat, since curing the resultant behavioral symptoms and their causation will have improved prospects of success.

Figure 7.1. Behavioral and conduct disorders are essential constructs in the field of child and adolescent mental health, characterized by persistent patterns of behavior that reflect a violation of societal norms and the rights of others.

Source: https://cdn-prod.medicalnewstoday.com/content/images/articles/320/320386/boy-shouting-and-mum-in-background-covering-her-ears.jpg.

Prevention and intervention of behavioral and conduct disorders require an individualized response from the perspective of individual, family, and system factors. School mental health programs are particularly critical, as they enhance social-emotional learning and resilience that will hinder the emergence of behavior problems (Cavioni et al., 2020). Also, there is evidence that excessive use of the internet can increase emotional and behavioral concerns, and as such, there is a need for preventive interventions against this emerging problem. Interventions usually involve cognitive-behavioral therapy (CBT), family therapy, and school interventions in an effort to create a therapeutic environment for children and youth. Clear consequences and behavioral expectations in both home and school settings also regulate disruptive behavior. Lastly, understanding definitions, etiology, and potential interventions for conduct and behavioral disorders can contribute significantly to knowing child and adolescent mental health, allowing for the development of effective strategies for fostering resilience and well-being (Figure 7.1).

Importance of Addressing Mental Health in Children and Adolescents

The significance of addressing mental health in children and young people is underscored by crisis levels at which mental illness is rising among the young. The past decades have witnessed increasing cases of conduct and behavior disorder in young people, with long-lasting impacts on their development and well-being in general. Early intervention is necessary as, if not treated early, mental health issues can lead to school failure, relationship problems, and higher chances of unhealthy behaviors. Moreover, the mental health scenario is also further complicated by an enormous spectrum of social determinants that can impact children differently depending on their backgrounds. Successful school-based mental health programs then emerge as a critical tool in identifying not only at-risk youth but also in the creation of learning environments that are emotionally and socially conducive, ultimately leading to the development of students' resilience as implied by contemporary studies (Cavioni et al., 2020). The necessity for a clear understanding of mental health disparities among youths of different racial and ethnic groups cannot be overemphasized. Mental illness has been shown to be the strongest predictors of individuals' overall health and social functioning. Nonetheless, there is evidence of significant differences in mental health conditions and access to services among U.S. minority youth. Of interest are the barriers to mental health care that potentially exacerbate these issues, isolating at-risk youth and impairing their developmental processes. Protective influences in favor of mental health, including community and family engagement, become the response to these inequalities, according to recent studies (Green et al., 2015). Thus, a multi-dimensional model that embraces both universal preventive measures and targeted interventions across communities is needed in upholding equity in mental health care for all children and adolescents. In order to be in a position to address the rising trends in behavioral disorders and conduct, policies must give equal weight to mental health as among general child and adolescent care. This is achieved by building alliances between schools, healthcare professionals, and community agencies in creating an accessible system of mental health resources. Ensuring that mental health instruction is taught in schools could give students and teachers alike the tools they need to identify and address issues early on. These programs must also work to de-stigmatize mental illness so that kids and adolescents would feel okay to seek help without fearing judgment. By constructing a robust foundation that focuses on mental health, society can better prepare its younger generations for the trials of life and thus prepare healthier adulthood in the future (Cavioni et al., 2020) (Figure 7.2).

Figure 7.2. Effective school-based mental health programs, therefore, become essential tools in not only identifying at-risk youth but also in fostering environments conducive to emotional and social learning, thus promoting resilience among students.

Source: https://www.unicef.org/sites/default/files/styles/hero_extended/public/Mental%20health%20UN0418008.jpg.webp?itok=wLCtPyFS.

7.1. TYPES OF BEHAVIORAL AND CONDUCT DISORDERS (CD)

Children and adolescent behavior and conduct disorders are expressed in various ways, typically influencing to a large extent their family, peer, and school relationships. Among all the disorders, the Attention-Deficit/Hyperactivity Disorder (ADHD) stands out due to its distinctive presentation of impulsivity, hyperactivity, and inattention. ADHD children typically present with difficulty maintaining concentration, getting ready on time, and regulating impulses, resulting in disruptive behavior at school and home. Furthermore, if left undiagnosed, the effects of ADHD can be quite marked, in that children will be placed at higher risks of school failure and social relationship problems. Notably, such behaviors continue into adulthood and adolescence, with ongoing issues of mental health and social adjustment, thus pointing towards the significance of early diagnosis and treatment in favor of favorable long-term outcomes. Conduct Disorder (CD) is a significant disorder in which there exist recurring patterns of behavior that violate social norms and others' rights.

Figure 7.3. Conduct disorder (CD) is another prominent condition characterized by persistent patterns of behavior that violate societal norms and the rights of others.

Source: https://opabh.com/wp-content/uploads/2024/08/ODD-or-Conduct-Disorder-A-Side-by-Side-Look-1024x576.jpg.

Children with CD are aggressive, dishonest, reckless in causing damage to property, and genuinely irresponsible and hence significantly impair their ability to relate to other peers and authority figures in a positive way. The subtlety of CD is not only its expression on the behavioral level but also with respect to greater risks for the emergence of other psychiatric diseases, such as anxiety, depression, and drug abuse in adulthood. The CD high-risk course emphasizes the importance of early intervention; effective treatment and intervention, like family therapy and parent training, can lower the risk of adverse adult outcomes, such as crime and drug abuse (Barlow et al., 2009). There is also increasing evidence that early life factors may be yielding the occurrence of conduct and behavioral disorders. For instance, studies indicate that preterm children are at higher risk for developmental complications that have the potential to predispose them to behavioral issues like anxiety, inattention, and social communication impairment (Johnson et al., 2013). The identification of such an association emphasizes the need for prolonged monitoring and intervention programs that are tailored to the specific problems of the preterm child during adolescence. There needs to be an interagency approach from parents, teachers, and mental health professionals to treat behavioral and conduct disorders and offer overall support, which can improve resilience and healthier development pathways of these high-risk groups. Therefore, it is important to comprehend the multifactorial etiology of these disorders in order to treat them and improve outcomes (Figure 7.3).

7.1.1. Oppositional Defiant Disorder (ODD)

Recognition of oppositional defiant disorder (ODD) is especially necessary within the grand scheme of behavior and conduct disorders affecting child and adolescent mental health. ODD is characterized by a persistent pattern of angry, irritable mood, argumentative behavior, and vindictiveness, generally presenting as defiance of authority figures. The disorder significantly affects the child's social, school, and family functioning with a high risk for other mental health issues if untreated. Early intervention and detection are necessary because it has been discovered that early manifestations of ODD can predict the development of severe conduct disorders in adulthood. The impact of these behaviors carries over to later life, making adolescent and adult substance use disorders a problem in need of vigilant surveillance and effective intervention to prevent long-term negative outcomes. The comorbidity of ODD and other conduct disorders, i.e., attention deficit hyperactivity disorder (ADHD), has been examined extensively, exhibiting high comorbidity. Children with Attention Deficit Hyperactivity Disorder are often diagnosed with ODD because there is an overlap of symptoms. ODD occurrence can then complicate the clinical profile of ADHD and thus warrants proper evaluation and certain intervention. For instance, a diagnosis of ADHD has been associated with heightened risk for the later onset of psychoactive substance use disorder, particularly if it co-occurs with conduct disorder (Buitelaar et al., 2013). It is important to have a grasp of these links when developing effective treatment strategies. By appreciating the comorbid nature of the condition, mental health professionals can approach treatment in a more integrated way with consideration for the unique needs of the child, with therapeutic strategies ultimately being more efficacious. Tailored care to treat ODD can significantly enhance caregivers' capacity to manage their children's behavior. One recent intervention aimed at the primary caregivers of adolescents with ODD was designed to enhance self-efficacy and improve family interactions in schools and mental health care systems (Aalsma et al., 2017). By equipping the caregivers with practical tools and strategies, these interventions can establish more supportive home environments, which are vital for the child's growth. Not only do such interventions empower the caregivers, but they also mitigate the influence of ODD on family functioning. Also, successful involvement of parents through structured interventions has the potential to end the dysfunctional cycle and reduce the children's chances of further developing more severe conduct disorders or resorting to unhealthy coping mechanisms like drug dependency. Thus, ODD treatment through structured caregiver intervention is key to enabling sustained beneficial change within child and family (Figure 7.4).

Figure 7.4. Understanding oppositional defiant disorder (ODD) is crucial in the broader context of behavioral and conduct disorders that affect child and adolescent mental health.

Source: https://www.educare.net.au/wp-content/uploads/2020/08/Tips-for-Managing-Oppositional-Defiant-Disorder-ODD.jpg.

7.1.2. Conduct Disorder (CD)

Conduct disorder (CD) diagnosis is among the more severe forms of behavior disorders in adolescents and children with a long history of behavior that violates the rights of others and society's norms. Rule-breaking and aggression towards people and animals, as well as damaging property, and being deceitful are some of the usual presentations of CD, as well as a significant amount of rule-breaking. These behavior patterns not only disrupt the child's performance at home, school, and in interpersonal relationships but also potentially have long-term serious implications, such as educational failure and increased risk for criminality. It is crucial that one identifies and intervenes early because the direction of CD can take a dramatic turn without proper support and intervention, necessitating full understanding of its etiology and context-dependent determinants of behavior. Conduct Disorder treatments need a multiapproach approach, with therapeutic models that engage the child and the family. Parent behavior training has been proposed in literature as being able to lead to statistically significant and clinically meaningful changes in parent behavior, thereby benefiting children with conduct problems. For instance, parents who undergo structured behavioral training report enhanced ability to manage their child's acting-out behaviors and lower parenting stress levels. Parent-based treatments like these can potentially foster healthier family interactions, which is essential because familial and environmental factors are known to cause and sustain CD. Focusing interventions on the specific needs of families, particularly those from underprivileged communities, will likely enhance their effectiveness and accessibility in the treatment of these major behavioral problems (Gerdes et al., 2011). Moreover, the development of community-based interventions depicts the importance of community participation in the prevention of Conduct Disorder. One such example is applying a six-week caregiver group intervention to enhance self-efficacy in primary caregivers of teens with CD. The program emphasizes the collaboration of academic researchers, clinical practitioners, and community stakeholders to assure that the intervention is culturally informed and addresses the unique needs of families. Such interdisciplinarity does not only enable carers to cope with the day-to-day challenges but also establishes a network that can address broader systemic issues related to mental health treatment (Aalsma et al., 2017). Through encouraging resilience within families and equipping them with effective treatments, community programs possess great potential to counter the effects of Conduct Disorder and provide healthier developmental trajectories for affected youth.

7.1.3. Attention-Deficit/Hyperactivity Disorder (ADHD)

Attention-deficit/hyperactivity disorder (ADHD) is typically a behavioral and conduct disorder of child and adolescent mental health. It is characterized by inattention, hyperactivity, and impulsivity and manifests in varied forms, not just negatively affecting school performance but also relationships with others. Insurgent research places the special role of ADHD in influencing relationships with peers, asserting that those with such disorder have difficulty making and maintaining friendships. In fact, they also have fewer and poorer quality friends than their neurotypical peers, and that can actually make them feel even more isolated and even more socially challenged (Gardner et al., 2015). The complex nature of the symptoms of ADHD necessitates a multilevel treatment that focuses not just on the individual behavior but also on the social contexts in which the behavior is occurring. ADHD interventions require treatment beyond mere control of behavior and involve training in social skills. Studies suggest that interpersonal relationship-based programs have been shown to significantly enhance functioning among peers of teenagers with ADHD.

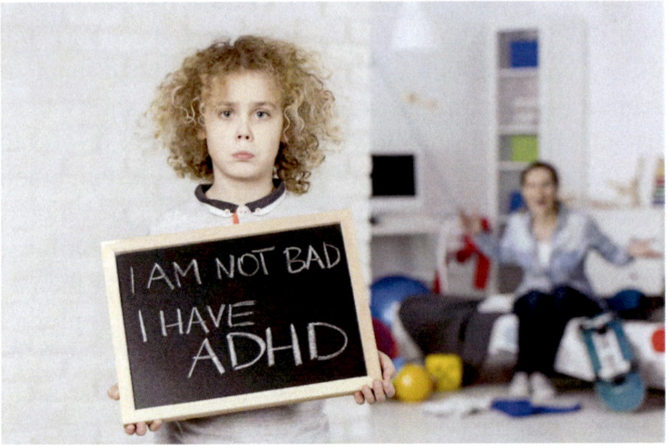

Figure 7.5. Attention-deficit/hyperactivity disorder (ADHD) is frequently categorized as a behavioral and conduct disorder in child and adolescent mental health.

Source: https://northlandchildpsychiatry.com/wp-content/uploads/2023/05/understanding-attention-deficit-hyperactivity-disorder.jpg.

A study of the Program for the Evaluation and Enrichment of Relational Skills (PEERS) is an intervention aimed at enhancing friendship building through parent-supported participation. Findings showed the adolescents who participated in this intervention reported notable gains, from the development of new friendships to increased social information (Gardner et al., 2015). Through the development of these skills, interventions like PEERS not only cure the symptoms of ADHD but also its accompanying social impact, therefore improving the quality of life of the adolescents involved. In addition, the consequences of successful peer relationships reach far beyond childhood and adolescence into long-term emotional and social health. With children developing improved social skills, they are more likely to have less victimization in the peer group and greater social self-efficacy, enhancing their self-esteem and resiliency. The aforementioned pilot study registered large effect sizes for increases in teens' social knowledge and get-togethers as hosts, which is indicative of the promise of formal interventions to engender significant social interactions (Gardner et al., 2015). Thus, it becomes imperative to rank such intervention programs high on the hierarchy of the overall mental health treatment planning since they not only serve to reduce ADHD symptoms but also contribute to the establishment of healthier social environments that foster positive developmental outcomes in young people (Figure 7.5).

7.2. CAUSES AND RISK FACTORS

Several causes lie behind the etiology of conduct and behavioral disorders in children and adolescents, and it is imperative to know these causes to implement effective intervention. Genetic factors contribute to a large extent to decide a child's mental health, as evident from research that indicates that children with genetic disorders such as congenital adrenal hyperplasia (CAH) are predisposed to psychiatric disorders. In research on CAH, it was discovered that there was a significant percentage of children with the condition who developed anxiety disorders and attention-deficit hyperactivity disorder (ADHD), indicating that these genetic factors were capable of materially affecting mental health outcomes. Additionally, family history of psychiatric illness can even raise the risk of behavioral problems emerging in children, validating the argument that genetic and hereditary causes are core elements of etiology of such conditions (Ernst et al., 2010). Environmental causes also become a major element in risk development of behavioral and conduct disorders in children. Suboptimal childhood experience, such as trauma, abuse, and neglect, have been well-documented as the precipitants of various psychological disorders in adulthood. These experiences can lead to disturbance of normal development and pose problems of emotional regulation and behavior. Socioeconomic disadvantage, such as poverty and exposure to violence, also lends itself to environments where maladaptive behavior is likely to be embedded within the environment. The co-action of these environmental stressors could potentially lead to increased incidence of disorders like ADHD and anxiety, particularly in children who lack adequate support systems. It is thus important to understand the multiplicity of environmental factors as causatives of the emergence of behavioral and conduct disorders among adolescents (Johnson et al., 2013). Furthermore, the etiology of mental illness is influenced by environmental and biological factors that determine the neurodevelopmental processes, thus offering a comprehensive explanation of the risk factors and etiology of these disorders. For instance, preterm birth has been found to be a critical risk factor for neurodevelopmental impairment as well as subsequent psychiatric disorders. Studies have established that preterm children experience a higher prevalence of disorders such as ADHD, autism, and emotional disorders relative to children born at term. The relationship reinforces the crucial importance of early diagnosis and intervention among high-risk groups, particularly during the teenage years when mental illness will first manifest. Because behavioral disorders are likely to be associated with overall neurodevelopmental problems, more than one area of risk factor identification—biological, environmental, as well as psychosocial factors—is required to guide effective prevention and treatment (Johnson et al., 2013).

7.2.1. Genetic Predispositions

The contribution of genetic predispositions to adolescents' and children's conduct and behavior disorders is an essential area of study in mental health. Future research suggests that the genetic predispositions have the potential to significantly influence individuals' susceptibility to various psychological disorders, including depression, anxiety, and ADHD. It is also essential to mention here that genetic predispositions do contribute, but they have the tendency to cooperate with environmental stressors, such as socioeconomic status and family environments. Identification of individual genetic markers used in such disorders allows researchers to discover the underlying biological processes. Such hereditary risks have markers that play an important role in making targeted interventions because early detection of risk adolescents has the potential to offer timely and relevant intervention to prevent the development of behavioral issues. Interaction between genetics and the environment is a key aspect in understanding the complexity of mental health among adolescents. Research has confirmed that genetic vulnerabilities are central to the problems of at-risk children, particularly to their school achievement and social behavior. The synergy between genetic markers and the environment provides an understanding of the complex dynamics that impact mental well-being outcomes. For instance, research has demonstrated that the presence of certain genetic vulnerabilities has a multiplicative effect on behavioral disorders when they co-occur with experiences of adversity in childhood. This finding emphasizes the importance of exploring genetic predilections within integrated assessments of children's mental well-being. Gene marker-based experiments as research tools for probing the influence of states of health on learning also illustrate this. Such exploration is demonstrated to be how behavioral disorders can be a product of an interplay between genetics and the environment, necessitating multi-perspective research and practice (Rosenquist et al., 2025). Moreover, the identification of genetic predispositions also assists in directing treatment approaches in addressing conduct disorders and associated behavioral problems. Preventive interventions could also benefit significantly from information regarding these hereditary tendencies, particularly when designing psychoeducational treatments for at-risk groups. For example, research suggests that psychological treatment, as compared to medication treatment, could be more helpful in certain groups, specifically those with genetic susceptibilities. Through an evidence-based psychological approach, practitioners can develop programs that address personal combinations of genetic and environmental factors. This tailored connection makes possible effective prevention and treatment approaches that work to reduce behavior difficulties in youth, ending ultimately in resilience and enhanced mental well-being. The significance of transferring genetic knowledge into pragmatic application highlights a forward movement toward a more individualized model of practice within the field of child and adolescent mental health (Smith et al., 2008) (Figure 7.6).

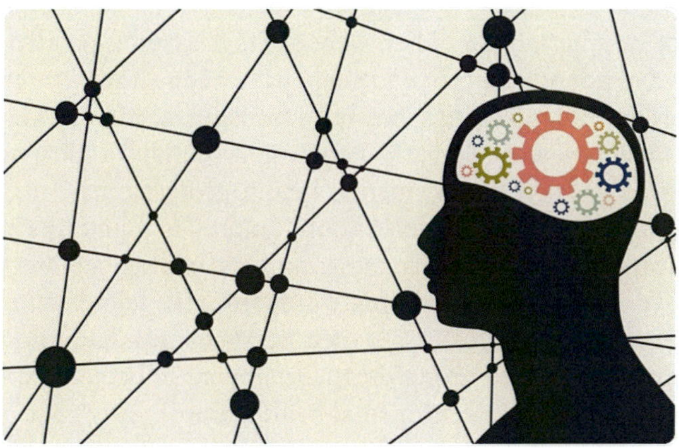

Figure 7.6. The intersection of genetics and environmental factors is a focal point for understanding the complex nature of mental health in adolescents.

Source: https://www.news-medical.net/image-handler/picture/2021/3/shutter-stock_608819573.jpg.

7.2.2. Environmental Influences

Environmental conditions primarily influence children's and adolescents' mental health, particularly behavioral and conduct disorders. Various factors, including family dynamics, financial status, schools, and community, influence the emergence of the said disorders. Research has shown that traumatic family experiences, i.e., neglect or abuse, will increase the probability of developing unhealthy behaviors in adolescents. Those households that provide healthy, supportive environments are likely to encourage resilience among youngsters, while those that include conflict and chaos may initiate the onset of mental illness. Socioeconomic disadvantage can also limit the access to essential resources such as educational assistance and mental health care, further aggravating behavioral deficits. Different studies attribute the interplay between environmental stressors and genetic factors in etiology in psychological disorders. Severe stress has the potential to impact neurobiological processes, particularly during periods of brain development sensitivity in adolescence and childhood. For instance, exposure to traumatic events or chronic stress has the potential to disrupt normal cognitive and emotional development, leading to issues such as depression, anxiety, and conduct disorders. Furthermore, environmental factors including peer relationships and community safety play a significant role in shaping the behavior of an adolescent. Communities with elevated levels of crime or social disorganization are likely to have adverse impacts on the mental health of a young person and contribute to greater risky behavior. The supportive school setting cannot be overlooked either. Schools that assume positive behavioral interventions and adopt supportive settings have been shown to reduce student conduct disorders. Such settings not only transmit academic knowledge but also train social competence and affect control, essential for ideal development. Collaboration between teachers, mental health professionals, and families is crucial in designing preventive interventions tailored to high-risk children. Such as psychoeducational interventions, integrating psychological intervention with education, have an impact on children's outcome. By taking into account the intricacy of environmental factors, it then becomes possible to develop more effective approaches to the prevention and treatment of behavioral and conduct disorders in child and adolescent mental health (Carol, 2013; McClellan et al., 2013).

7.2.3. Psychological Factors

It is important to grasp the psychological determinants that result in behavior and conduct disorders in children and adolescents in order to intervene successfully. Temperament, such as qualities like mood, level of activity, and emotional reactivity, plays a long way in deciding vulnerability to such disorders. Notably, the interdependence among temperament and socio-economic environment makes this relationship more complex. While temperament will predispose an individual to particular behavior, socio-economic disadvantage (SED) will exacerbate them. There is a need for a lack of information concerning how SED modulates relationships between temperament and parenting and between temperament and child psychopathology. Future work must take an interest in learning how SED timing, specificity, accumulation, and duration occur in concert with these dimensions so that it can produce comprehensive theories that inform treatment (Flouri et al., 2008). This subtle understanding can lead to targeted interventions that address both environmental issues as well as psychological inclinations. In addition, the role of school and college settings in addressing mental health cannot be overstated. Schools and colleges are pivotal sites where early interventions can be administered to reduce the impacts of conduct and behavioral disorders. Research indicates that the use of indicated psychological interventions in such settings can be effective in facilitating access to mental health services for adolescents. However, the impact of such interventions is likely dependent on various factors, including intervention characteristics, organizational capacity, and community factors. A systematic review of interventions in schools identified themes that highlight the significance of logistical concerns and staff training.

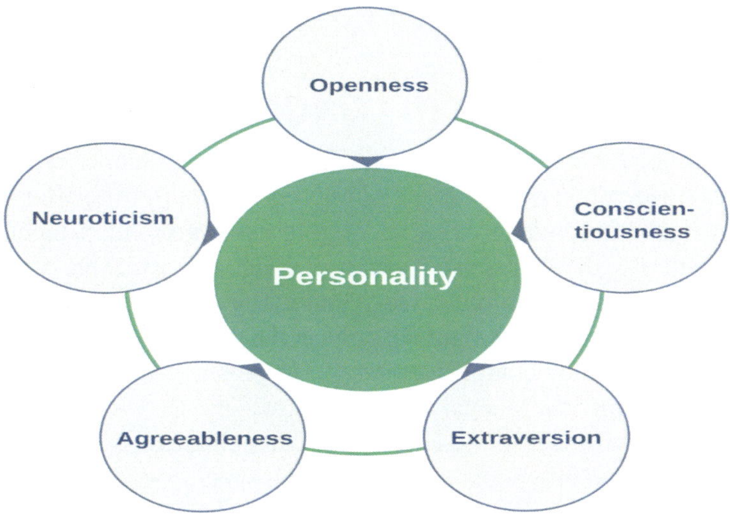

Figure 7.7. Temperament, which encompasses traits such as mood, activity level, and emotional reactivity, can significantly influence the susceptibility to these disorders.

Source: https://upload.wikimedia.org/wikipedia/commons/thumb/c/c0/Wiki-grafik_peats-de_big_five_ENG.svg/1200px-Wiki-grafik_peats-de_big_five_ENG.svg.png.

All these elements must be integrated into mental health interventions in educational frameworks to maximize intervention fidelity and effectiveness. Such an inclusive strategy may yield significant improvements in the psychological adjustment of youngsters (Carroll et al., 2020). Beyond the structured context of schools, the involvement of family and community support emerges as an all-consuming psychological factor in intervention against behavioral and conduct disorders. Parental engagement and relationship quality within the family system have significant effects on a child's emotional and psychological growth. Children growing up in family environments that are nurturing, supportive, and communicative are likely to have improved emotional management and resistance to behavioral problems. On the other hand, parental stress, neglect, or conflict can create increased vulnerability to conduct disorders. Support systems in the community, such as peers and social networks, also contribute to a young person's behavior and coping strategies. Hence, what is needed is an integrated approach taking into account both family functioning and interaction with the community in order to tackle the psychological factors involved in behavioral and conduct disorders effectively and ensure healthier developmental pathways for children and adolescents (Figure 7.7).

7.3. SYMPTOMS AND DIAGNOSIS

Diagnosis of behavior and conduct disorders in youth and children is made on the basis of observation of a cluster of symptoms that will differ in expression from individual to individual. The underlying symptoms often include long-standing patterns of antisocial behavior, hyperactivity, and impulsivity, characteristics of such conditions as Attention-Deficit/Hyperactivity Disorder (ADHD) and Oppositional Defiant Disorder (ODD). These disorders can affect a child's academic and social functioning. Diagnostic criteria outlined in the Diagnostic and Statistical Manual of Mental Disorders (DSM-5) provide mental health professionals with a model to systematically assess these disorders. Clinicians should not only look at frequency and severity of symptoms but also the environment where they appear because behavior can significantly differ according to environmental factors and developmental stages. Diagnosis of the behavioral and conduct disorders can further be complicated by co-occurring conditions that are related to the primary disorders. For example, children with conduct disorder may also present with anxiety or mood disorders, with the result that there is overlap in the symptoms that will conceal the nature of their behavioral disturbance. This complexity highlights the importance of an assessment that is multidimensional in nature and that includes both behavioral observations as well as standardized assessment. There is recent evidence to suggest that early intervention is the key to enhancing outcomes, particularly among children with symptoms associated with anxiety or social communication issues. Research has established that children who present with persistent behavioral difficulties tend to continue carrying these issues into adolescent years, highlighting the need for proper screening and intervention techniques to prevent long-term risks (Johnson et al., 2013). Also, symptom treatment of these disorders entails learning effective treatment methods suited to the specific needs of the individual child. Recent research is directed toward the fact that integrative psychosocial treatments, particularly those that include family participation, are positive prognostic factors for effective outcomes in treating childhood depression and associated behavioral disturbances. Family-based therapy has been found more effective in alleviating depressive symptoms, with significant improvement demonstrated across all measures of functioning and social adjustment. This suggests that the integration of empirically supported therapeutic techniques and family dynamics can improve diagnostic accuracy and effectiveness of treatment. With clinical techniques evolving, there is a great need for continuous development of integrated treatments that meet the complexity of conduct and behavioral disorders to provide wholistic mental health care in children and adolescents (Asarnow et al., 2017).

7.3.1. Common Behavioral Symptoms

The manifestation of common behavioral symptoms in children and adolescents is most crucial to understanding the landscape of conduct and behavioral disorders. Symptoms are usually to include customary oppositional patterns of behavior, such as hostile, defiant, and disobedience, often in combination with Oppositional Defiant Disorder (ODD). The behaviors are likely to disrupt educational and social settings, hindering a child's positive interaction with peers and authority figures. Furthermore, children who exhibit such symptoms tend to be ostracized as well, adding to their emotional issues. The detection and assessment of these behaviors play a pivotal role because they are the basis for interventions that have the potential to alter the developmental trajectories of affected youths. Early identification helps in avoiding the risk of progression into more elaborate conduct disorders, ultimately leading to better emotional and behavior developments later in life. Other than oppositional behavior, Conduct Disorder (CD) encompasses a broader array of manifestations consisting of aggression, deceitfulness, and severe violation of rules. CD children may be violent towards others and show no remorse following their actions. The symptomatology may manifest in varied ways, ranging from bullying and fights to property destruction. These behaviors not only impact the immediate environment but also potentially can lead to problems socially and legally later on, possibly presaging adult antisocial behavior. As such, these symptoms represent a significant warning sign of potential future challenges. As shown by research that identifies significant predictors of ODD and CD symptoms, such as the satisfaction of the parents in marriage, parents and caregivers should establish smooth environments that can reduce such unfavorable behaviors and enhance emotional control and knowledge (Adib et al., 2025). External sources, such as the socio-environmental context, are significant in contributing to the occurrence and expression of behavioral symptoms. Studies carried out during the pandemic have noted a rise in emotional challenges and psychosomatic complaints in children and youths, with a significant jump in irritability and depression symptoms. These were emphasized as important influences by several factors, such as altered routine, social distancing, and stress, to show that extrinsic stressors may worsen pre-existing behavioral disturbances or initiate new onset symptoms (Konopka et al., 2024). Therefore, it is necessary for mental health practitioners to consider such contextual factors while diagnosing and treating behavioral disorders. The inclusion of a family, environmental, and psychological factor can enhance intervention strategies, ultimately facilitating better outcomes for children afflicted with behavioral and conduct disorders. Increased understanding in this area can promote healthy resilient coping strategies, and as such, can promote overall mental health and well-being in the youth population (Figure 7.8).

Figure 7.8. Early recognition helps mitigate the risk of progression into more severe conduct disorders, ultimately supporting healthier emotional and behavioral developments in later stages of life.

*Source:*https://smb.ibsrv.net/imageresizer/image/article_manager/1200x1200/168632/1252678/heroimage0.989734001733802484.jpg.

7.3.2. Emotional Symptoms associated with Disorders

The affective symptoms of certain of the behavioral and conduct disorders experienced by children and adolescents are of paramount importance in understanding the complexity of their mental state. Such symptoms, for the majority of cases, manifest themselves as depression, anxiety, and difficulties with emotional control, which can significantly hinder an individual's capacity to manage social interactions and school pressures. For instance, individuals with conduct disorders tend to exhibit heightened irritability and frustration that leads to explosive violence or withdrawal from social life. These emotional disturbances tend to fuel underlying behavioral issues, creating a cycle of further entanglement that exacerbates their issues. As these teens go on into later adolescence, the persistence of these affective symptoms has been linked to more severe mental health challenges, and it implies that early identification and treatment are necessary for effective long-term outcome in mental health care.

Research has indicated that the emotional consequences of early developmental disadvantage, such as preterm status, are particularly potent. Children born prematurely are at a high risk for various emotional disorders, including anxiety and attention-deficit/hyperactivity disorder (ADHD) (Johnson et al., 2013). Emotional disturbances of these children may result in difficulties with social communication and extreme sensitivity to stress, making it difficult for them to engage in systematic learning environments. In adolescents, these issues often persist, resulting in longer-term concerns rather than merely short-term behavioral difficulties. Preterm adolescents are found to have increased psychotic symptoms, and therefore constant monitoring and therapeutic care. Evidence supports the requirement of specialized mental health interventions which do not only address the behavior but also the emotional symptoms inherent in this population, leading the way to healthier paths of development. In order to enhance emotional wellness, school mental health programs have emerged as necessary components for the same for children and youth. Programs that integrate social and emotional learning in the education process can reap great benefits by a major decline in emotional symptoms and prevention of behavioral disorders (Cavioni et al., 2020).

By enabling students to know and control their feelings, such programs aim at fostering resilience, thus reducing the incidence of conduct disorders among children and youth. Whether such programs work, however, relies on consensus regarding their design and implementation. Having an exhaustive framework that emphasizes the control of emotional symptoms as well as interventions for behavior is essential. This approach can heighten the wider mental health context for children and adolescents, making contexts where emotional health is known to be an integral component of learning and development, ultimately translating into better consequences in life and school environments.

7.3.3. Diagnostic Criteria and Assessment Tools

Diagnostic guidelines and measurement tools employed in the diagnosis of behavior and conduct disorders in children and adolescents are defined elements of effective mental health interventions. Various diagnostic guides, such as the DSM-5, set standard criteria for the classification of disorders such as Attention-Deficit/Hyperactivity Disorder (ADHD) and Conduct Disorder. The criteria help clinicians differentiate between normal behavioral variation and clinically significant issues that warrant treatment. Sound diagnostic assessment not only takes into account measuring for the presence of symptoms, but also their duration and degree to which the behaviors interrupt normal functioning and social interactions. Therefore, standardized testing is necessary to provide a formatted view in establishing the severity and impact of these disorders on the lives of children across contexts and settings. Given the intricacy associated with behavioral and conduct disorders, several psychological assessments have been developed to optimize diagnostic accuracy and general comprehension. Structured interviews, behavior checklists, and rating scales allow clinicians to obtain comprehensive, multidimensional data from parents, teachers, and the children themselves. Scales such as the Child Behavior Checklist (CBCL) are widely used to measure emotional and behavioral problems in a systematic fashion. These assessment tools yield quantitative data that facilitates monitoring of the progress of treatment as well as detection of possible comorbid conditions. Furthermore, they enable ongoing communication about the mental health of the child such that parents, teachers, and mental health workers can collaborate to develop effective interventions sensitive to the individual needs of the child. The nuances of diagnosing disorders such as Reactive Attachment Disorder (RAD) confirm the need for continuous assessment and adaptation of diagnostic criteria. The recent criticisms have directed attention toward the absence of in-depth guidelines of DSM-5 towards RAD, failing to address the whole spectrum of behaviors and symptoms witnessed in the affected children. The limitations inherently constructed in existing diagnostic criteria threaten underdiagnosis or misdiagnosis of such disorders, potentially leading to suboptimal treatment plans. Additionally, the understanding that RAD may be a result of severe early childhood trauma affects not only diagnostic procedures but therapeutic treatments as well. Placing on center stage a trauma-informed approach, mental health professionals are encouraged to rethink more traditional models of assessment and thereby align them with contemporary understanding of the psychosocial determinants of behavioral disorders (Owen et al., 2016). Overall, both the combination of robust diagnostic criteria with multitalented methods of assessment is crucial to the delivery of effective mental health treatment for children and young people (Figure 7.9).

Figure 7.9. Instruments such as the child behavior checklist (CBCL) are widely used to evaluate emotional and behavioral problems systematically.

Source: https://reachoutandread.org/wp-content/uploads/2019/07/home_image_1.jpg.

7.4. IMPACT ON DEVELOPMENT

The course and impact of conduct and behavior disorders in childhood and adolescence can significantly disrupt typical developmental trajectories. These disorders often onset at times of life-critical growth and development, when social, emotional, and cognitive functioning is in the process of being established. Research has indicated that children with conduct disorder exhibit difficulties in developing healthy peer and adult relationships, which hinder them in being able to transition successfully through social environments. Consequently, maladaptive behaviors such as aggression or defiance can lead to an assortment of negative outcomes like poor performance at school and increased cases of social isolation (Maartje et al., 2022). Additionally, once these children reach adolescence, the probability of worsening behaviors may evolve to develop into delinquency or other mental health issues, thereby snuffing out emotional and social development during this pivotal transition period. The relationship between behavior disorders and chronic stress also has a direct contribution to developmental regression. The disorders occur among children and teenagers, who have heightened stress levels due to difficulties such as family conflicts or social rejection, impacting their quality of life negatively (Li et al., 2021). This stress can function as a barrier to engagement with positive experiences such as secure family relationships or education, degrading both psychological resilience and sense of belonging. Chronic exposure to stress can also contribute to additional mental health problems such as depression and anxiety that set up a cycle that detracts from further growth and adaptation in youth. Resolution of stressors in conjunction with behavioral interventions is thus critical in promoting healthier developmental results in those affected. As teenagers with conduct and behavioral disorders make their way through their formative years, the consequences of their disorders do not stop at the individual but instead infiltrate family systems and broader social structures. Dysfunctional amounts of parental distress that stem from managing a child's behavioral difficulties may lead to familial disintegration, further infuriating the child. The impact of these disorders has a tendency to strain not only family relationships, but also the school setting, where teachers and peers alike struggle to provide the individualized support demanded of affected children (Maartje et al., 2022). Therefore, it is imperative that both educators and mental health clinicians assume a multi-dimensional, integrative role with family support and community services. By developing environments that foster positive behavioral change, adolescents and children are able to achieve their developmental milestones regardless of the shadow cast by their disorders, eventually promoting healthier growth trajectories and interpersonal relationships (Figure 7.10).

Figure 7.10. Children and adolescents with these disorders often face heightened levels of stress, stemming from issues like familial conflicts or social rejection, which adversely impacts their overall quality of life.

Source: https://www.newportacademy.com/wp-content/uploads/NA-Website-Resources-Image-EffectsSocialMedia-1386x640-Hero.jpg.

7.4.1. Academic Performance and Learning Difficulties

Academic attainment is an intricate construct that is shaped by a variety of influences including cognitive abilities, emotional states, and environmental factors. Among children and adolescents with behavioral and conduct disorders, there is exaggeration of learning difficulties, having the tendency to result in academic underachievement. These are not only supported by diminished academic performance but also by increased truancy and disaffection from school. New evidence highlights the importance of understanding how these disorders impact learning as well as social integration, both of which are very important to academic success. Addressing the special needs of these students requires tailored interventions that include psychological support and cognitive growth strategies to achieve resilience and academic potential toward their overall performance enhancement (Cavioni et al., 2020).

In acknowledging the consistent setback of the learning environment, the "change without change" phenomenon is a significant source of deterrence to furthering academic success among students with conduct and behavioral disorders. With all the reforms and adjustments undertaken to make learning processes better, systemic obstacles tend to thwart radical improvements. The stagnation affects students' learning capabilities and allows their social problems to continue, fueling an inferior performance cycle. Research on positive youth development and resilience indicates an urgent need for schools to adopt frameworks that are built around social-emotional learning and the care environment (Nicoll et al., 2014). Not only is this beneficial for children with evident learning difficulties, but it may also aid in the creation of a more inclusive school environment, establishing feelings of belonging and agency among all learners. Transformatory education necessitates the blending of mental health within the model of education, particularly for at-risk students to avoid behavioral and conduct disorders. The literature indicates that effective strategies for enhancing resilience call for integrative approaches to tackling skills and emotional functioning through focused interventions. Social-emotional skills can be blended into programs that can significantly enhance students' ability to resist the adversity they face in and outside the classroom. As schools implement such evidence-based interventions, it is essential to create supportive social environments that transcend traditional learning environments. Through the development of resilience and mutual positive peer relationships, teachers can effectively enhance the academic performance of students with learning disabilities, ultimately driving their long-term academic and social achievement (Cavioni et al., 2020; Nicoll et al., 2014).

7.4.2. Social Relationships and Peer Interactions

The multifaceted nature of peer interactions and social relationships is significant to the psychological and behavioral well-being of children and adolescents. Children and youth are faced with a variety of social relationships that include social hierarchies, peer pressure, and friendships, which can all impact their mental health outcomes. Positive peer interactions can enhance resilience and emotional support, and this is significant to the prevention of feelings of isolation and distress. In contrast, aversive social experiences, like social rejection or bullying, can worsen any underlying behavioral and conduct disorders. By having full psychosocial evaluations, as the biopsychosocial model recommends, it is possible to gain a better understanding of these social environments and how they have an effect on mental health. Early identification and intervention of social conflict are essential to prevention of long-term psychological trauma for adolescents, demonstrating the significance of caring environments and supportive networks for their early life (Maartje et al., 2022). Peer relationships play a dual role in the development of children and adolescents; not only do they provide company, but they also play a strong role in influencing self-esteem and the development of identity.

The development of healthy friendships during this early period of life can enhance adaptive coping skills and social competence. Conversely, aggressive, or conflictual interactions can have maladaptive consequences such as increased anxiety, depression, and behavioral disturbance. It has been determined that adolescents with good social relationships have better mental health status and are more resilient under stress. Moreover, the advent of technology, particularly in gaming cultures, brings new social dynamics that can enhance friendships or lead to social isolation. For this reason, it is vital that mental health professionals consider the quality and nature of peer interaction, encouraging healthy relationship-building behaviors capable of reducing behavioral and conduct disorders in children (Granic et al., 2013). In addition, the changing nature of social interactions requires a holistic view of the extent to which different factors impact child and adolescent mental health. Importantly, the role of parental engagement and family dynamics cannot be ignored, as these factors have a considerable impact on children's capacity to establish and retain good peer relationships. A harmonious home environment enhances the likelihood of effective social interaction, while household conflict is likely to cause behavioral issues and hinder social development. As the families navigate through challenges of the therapeutic interventions, it is critical to enforce harmonized mechanisms that extend to both the youth as well as their social relationships. The integration of family-based approaches in clinical treatment has the potential to empower adolescents to overcome and reverse the adverse effect of poor peer relationships as well as to facilitate their overall psychosocial adjustment. Indeed, an interaction between peer relationships and family support plays a central role in evoking an effective model for the management of behavioral and conduct disorders in children and adolescents (Maartje et al., 2022) (Figure 7.11).

Figure 7.11. Young individuals are often confronted with various social dynamics that include friendships, peer pressure, and social hierarchies, all of which can significantly influence their mental health outcomes.

Source: https://www.scripps.org/sparkle-assets/images/peerpressure_web-c44c752859283593e27682ad68de0066.jpeg.

7.4.3. Long-Term Mental Health Outcomes

Long-term mental health effects for children with conduct and behavior disorders are complex and multidimensional. Research has demonstrated that these disorders have enduring issues that can extend far into adulthood, including higher instances of depression, anxiety, and antisocial behavior. Intervention as soon as possible is important because it addresses simultaneous behavioral issues while laying the groundwork for improved mental health outcomes. A focus on the development of coping, emotional regulation, and social skills early in life can reduce some of the ill effects of these disorders. Research highlights the necessity for identification at an early stage and individually tailored intervention plans, which can alter the psychological landscape significantly for the affected individuals in their journey from adolescence to adulthood. In preterm infants, there lies the risk of long-term mental health issues significantly augmented. There is evidence that preterm birth has been linked to a greater occurrence of neurodevelopmental disabilities and psychiatric illnesses, such as anxiety, attention deficits, and impairments in social communication. Such children also develop more serious emotional disturbances with age, and therefore it is important that medical care professionals offer continuous monitoring and intervention to them. The adolescent period is particularly informative inasmuch as issues noted in childhood come to solidify and worsen progressively, raising the chances of developing severe psychiatric illness (Johnson et al., 2013).

Figure 7.12. A focus on enhancing coping mechanisms, emotional regulation, and social skills during formative years can mitigate some adverse effects of these disorders.

Source: https://raisingchildren.net.au/__data/assets/image/0038/97877/Understanding-and-managing-emotions.jpg.

Overall, prevalence among affected adolescents is high and requires specialist treatment and support programs for this vulnerable group (Johnson et al., 2013). In school environments, the promotion and prevention of mental health evolved to address greater numbers of students who report mental health issues. Previous models looked only at academics, but today's trends recognize the importance given to social and emotional learning (SEL) as part of an expansive understanding of wellbeing. Inclusion of evidence-based school programs that promote resilience and prevent behavioral problems by schools shows a shift in the priority of the education system. This comprehensive approach not only assists the short-term correction of behavior, but also it promotes the environment for long-term mental health equilibrium. By striving to treat the co-occurrence of conduct disorders with more general mental health through strict programs and cooperation among educators, practitioners, and policymakers, schools possess a potential to significantly enhance their students' mental health status (Cavioni et al., 2020) (Figure 7.12).

7.5. TREATMENT APPROACHES

Effective treatment programs for conduct and behavioral disorders among children and teenagers call for a firm grasp of the complexities involved in such disorders. The establishment of systematic parent-training programs is one of the more unique approaches, and it has gained greater popularity over the past decade. The programs are designed to equip parents with certain skills and techniques to manage the behavior of their children and thus establish a favorable home atmosphere. Systematic review of randomized controlled trials has demonstrated that these parenting interventions have a significant impact on improving the behavior of children as reported by both parents and also independent reports. Interestingly, meta-analysis identified a significant effect size (SMD –0.67; 95% CI: –0.91, –0.42), indicating that individually tailored parenting interventions have the potential to induce significant improvements in the behavior of these children. While the encouraging results show, there remains a need for more sensitive studies to explore the relative effectiveness of different parenting styles in these programs (Barlow et al., 2009). Aside from parenting programs, family therapy has also emerged as another mandatory treatment system for adolescents with conduct disorder. This approach identifies the family as a critical setting where behaviors develop and can be treated. Systemic family therapy encompasses several methodologies, including structural and strategic family therapy, with the goal of improving family function and communication styles.

These therapies were found to not only reduce teenagers' behavior problems but enhance overall family functioning in a study that was recently conducted. For instance, enhanced family cohesion and parental satisfaction were noted by participants after treatment. Moreover, studies have found that family therapy could be equally impactful but differently so for both genders, emphasizing that it is of prime importance to address individual dynamics of the family unit (Medina et al., 2019). Substantiating further the necessity of customized treatment plans based on the unique characteristics and requirements of adolescent populations and their families. Lastly, the integration of behavioral interventions with therapeutic techniques aligned with the respective stages of adolescents' individual development is essential for the efficient treatment of conduct and behavioral disorders. The combined approach brings together some of the selected cognitive-behavioral strategies in the context of family therapies to facilitate enhanced outcomes. By using interventions that provide positive reinforcement, emotional management, and problem-solving abilities, therapists can efficiently facilitate adolescents' ability to manage their behaviors. In addition, implementing positive school climates under which the youth are able to access mental health care also supports such treatment interventions. Ongoing research continues to affirm that multi-modal interventions, which address developmental and family issues, bring the most success for youth and adolescents with behavior problems. Therefore, a cooperative model that unites formal parent-training and systemic family therapy is a promising avenue for effectively treating behavior disorders (Barlow et al., 2009; Medina et al., 2019).

7.5.1. Behavioral Therapy and Interventions

Behavioral therapy is a cornerstone in the treatment of behavioral and conduct disorders in child and adolescent mental health models. Through systematic approaches, it aims to modify maladaptive behavioral patterns through the reinforcement of positive habits and the cancellation of negative ones. Techniques such as cognitive-behavioral therapy (CBT) have been shown to be extremely effective in treating a variety of disorders, including anxiety and conduct disorders. Furthermore, interventions often include parent training components, which maximize efficacy by reflecting therapeutic techniques in the home. Evidence indicates that such partnerships have the ability to optimize therapeutic gains, emphasizing the significance of combined strategies for behavior therapy. By treating not only the child but also interpersonal interactions within the family, behavioral therapy is a holistic approach that addresses the root of behavior issues, resulting in long-term alteration and emotional resilience among children (Maartje et al., 2022). In the last 10 years, programs like the Children and Young Peoples Improving Access to Psychological Therapies (CYP IAPT) have been a bid to revolutionize the child mental health service sector by learning through the workforce and training up psychological practitioners. The program is centered around evidence-based treatments, where clinicians are taught to deliver low-intensity treatments to address a variety of psychological issues common in children and youth. These interventions are especially aimed at anxiety, depression, and conduct problems, which corresponds with the theoretical foundations of behavior therapy. A meta-analysis presented quite recently highlighted the effectiveness of such low-intensity psychosocial interventions, confirming their capacity to improve symptoms and promote enhanced social functioning among youth. However, the dynamic nature of child development necessitates that such the effectiveness of these interventions not only be established within clinical environments but also in naturalistic ones to establish their feasibility and sustainability in the real world (Ludlow et al., 2020). The integration of behavior therapy with collaborative care models underscores the necessity of an integrated approach to managing conduct disorders in children and adolescents. These models include interdisciplinary teams made up of psychologists, psychiatrists, educators, and primary care providers so that treatment can attend to emotional, social, and cognitive dimensions of health. Through the use of the biopsychosocial model, these teams can tailor interventions that account for the complexity of childhood environment and development. Interventions like increasing parental involvement and positive peer relationships are core components of these interventions, making them more effective overall. Focusing on the building of resilience through behavioral therapy not only addresses immediate concerns but also provides long-term mental stability, as a scaffolding aid for adolescents in coping with the complexities of the adolescent phase (Maartje et al., 2022) (Figure 7.13).

Figure 7.13. Behavioral therapy serves as a cornerstone in addressing behavioral and conduct disorders within child and adolescent mental health frameworks.

Source: https://www.verywellmind.com/thmb/m-GEm-iFyGSJrIdenoo_lboJgqk=/5760x0/filters:no_upscale():max_bytes(150000):strip_icc()/a-professional-child-education-therapist-having-a-meeting-with-a-kid-in-a-family-support-center--1011888356-3db3abdc5d9a4a7c871574ae2d1665b9.jpg.

7.5.2. Medication Management

Medication management is a valuable aspect of the treatment of conduct and behavioral disorders among children and adolescents, providing a regulated means for symptom control that can have the potential to significantly impede a youth's functioning and quality of life. The complexity of the handling of these drugs calls for an integrative strategy that is attuned to the biopsychosocial model, which recognizes the interplay of biological, psychological, and social determinants of a child's development and well-being. Effective medication management is attained through careful balancing of the child's specific signs, careful monitoring of drug efficacy and side effects, and ongoing communication between healthcare providers, children, and families. This continuous coordination ensures that all aspects of the child's health, physical as well as mental, are catered to, for greater treatment outcomes and better family relationships, especially when there is transition in the life of the child, such as developmental milestones and treatment plan transitions (Maartje et al., 2022). Furthermore, constant monitoring cannot be overstressed because children and adolescents may respond differently to medication as they grow up and their conditions alter. Continued monitoring is required to assess the effectiveness of medication prescribed, especially because of side effects that occasionally cause nonadherence or exacerbation of the underlying conditions. Monitoring can include utilizing standard screening tools and clinical ratings that facilitate determining medication changes, dosage increases or even tapering off when necessary. For instance, kids with comorbid disorders, such as ADHD and anxiety, may be treated with specific medication schedules that address both disorders simultaneously, highlighting the necessity for interprofessional practice among healthcare providers (Yoshikawa et al., 2020).

This not only decreases the single symptoms but also enhances the child's psychosocial interactions, leading to a more comprehensive method of mental healthcare. Finally, the psychosocial issues related to medication management need to be addressed to promote compliance and improve the treatment outcome. The caregivers and the mental health professionals should work together to provide a facilitating environment wherein the child understands their treatment, such as open discussion regarding the advantages and disadvantages of medication. Educating young patients as well as their families on the role of medicines in controlling behavioral disorders can dramatically reduce the stigma associated with mental health treatment, thus allowing for a positive discussion of mental health. Moreover, the inclusion of psychotherapeutic interventions along with medication can improve the effectiveness of the treatment regimen. The incorporation of behavioral interventions, such as cognitive-behavioral therapy (CBT), is able to complement the pharmacologic treatment and provide children with essential coping mechanisms to effectively manage their illnesses (Maartje et al., 2022). Not only does this comprehensive treatment help sustain medication compliance, but it also compels children and adolescents to take charge of their mental health process.

7.5.3. Family Involvement and Support

Family involvement and support are a significant determining factor in the resolution of behavior and conduct disorders in children and adolescents. Family relationships can play a significant role in the psychological and emotional development of children, particularly those with conduct difficulties. Active parent involvement, or regular communication, monitoring, and establishing clear expectations, creates an environment that can minimize the severity of conduct problems. Furthermore, research has found that involving families in therapeutic interventions, such as behavior parent training programs, increases the efficacy of the interventions for reducing problem behavior. Through this awareness of the factors leading to behavioral disorders, parents become critical members of the treatment team, bringing about the potential for children to learn prosocial coping strategies and social skills outside the treatment setting. A meta-review of the effectiveness of parenting programs for conduct problems in children has highlighted the effectiveness of these programs when parents are actively involved.

Figure 7.14. Understanding the impact of family support extends beyond childhood and into young adulthood, particularly for those transitioning from residential mental health treatment.

Source: https://dz9yg0snnohlc.cloudfront.net/6-Different-Family-Types-1.jpg.

Formal programs have been shown to have a significant impact on the behavior of children, with meta-analyses identifying a large effect size favoring intervention groups (SMD –0.67; 95% CI: –0.91, –0.42). By equipping parents with the resources, they require to employ consistently discipline methods and positive reinforcement, these programs demonstrate potential to redirect children's behavioral development towards a more positive trajectory. Additionally, unified family participation in treatment protocols not only empowers parents but also optimizes the likelihood for positive outcomes, including reduced disruptive behaviors and overall enhanced family functioning (Barlow et al., 2009). Understanding the role of support from family does not peak in childhood and adolescence but continues into young adulthood, particularly for those transitioning from residential mental health treatment. Research with young adults who previously received this type of treatment depicts the importance of ongoing family support to long-term adjustment and functioning of these individuals. Young adults experience definitions describe that young adults with tight family relationships were more likely to report greater success in significant areas of their life, such as education and social relationships. This indicates the significant contribution that well-developed family systems make to the build-up of resilience and successful adjustment to adulthood. Aligning services and support to the individualized special needs of these young adults entails recognizing the pivotal role of family involvement, guiding them through issues surrounding their previous conduct difficulties (Cameron et al., 2015) (Figure 7.14).

7.6. ROLE OF SCHOOLS AND COMMUNITIES

School and community intervention in the treatment of behavioral and conduct disorders is increasingly recognized as the key to the promotion of mental health in children and adolescents. Schools are first-order environments for socialization and learning, where effective programs can build social competencies and emotional resilience in children. Through the implementation of school-based mental health services, educators can directly address the needs of children with behavioral problems, providing a safe place for every student. Contemporary research highlights the importance of tailored interventions that, beyond taking care of the individual's needs, also create the general schooling climate, thereby averting the development of more severe conduct disorders (Cavioni et al., 2020). This framework underscores the importance of collaboration between teachers and mental health experts in creating integrated programs that serve to address the multiple needs of children, affirming the role of the school as a proactive contributor towards guaranteeing mental health. The success of such intervention further transcends the school into the wider community since children learn from the environment and therefore influence it at the same time. Community engagement is important in solidifying the efforts made within schools because good family and neighborhood relations can neutralize factors that lead to behavioral issues. For instance, neighborhood groups can join hands with schools to develop materials and workshops that educate parents on how to control behavioral issues at home. Such community programs raise the effectiveness of school programs through delivering a consistent message about mental health across settings. This collective support may act as a buffer to protect students against stressors that induce maladaptive behavior among adolescents, thus improving chances of positive outcomes for students who are embedded in such supportive networks (Stanley et al., 2008). Second, the concept of a single model of behavioral health necessitates communication between schools, families, and community stakeholders from time to time. This collaboration can inform policy-making decision-making regarding mental health resources and programming within school and community settings. Additionally, highlighting interdependence of various social systems in addressing conduct disorders can help integrate understanding of each child's individual circumstances. Schools can be those prime centers that bring together promotion of mental health and behavioral interventions through community resources to create a supportive system that addresses the multifaceted nature of adolescent mental health. This holistic approach, where the emphasis is, not only helps to create a help-friendly environment for children with behavioral issues but also attempts to bridge resilience and foster healthier generations.

7.6.1. School-Based Mental Health Programs

School-based mental health programs must be integrated to address conduct and behavioral disorders in children and adolescents. School-based mental health programs are preventive because mental health services are embedded in school settings. Mental health programs can reach students with ease who might be reluctant to seek help due to stigma or be unreachable when they are embedded in schools. The ability to provide services while the students are in school will ensure more participation and engagement. Further, school-based programs can easily enable early intervention, which is a major element in countering the long-term impact of behavioral disorders and thereby ultimately establishing an environment healthy for psychological and emotional growth. Research has discovered that family-based mind-body therapy programs (FMBTs) can make significant interventions for children with attention-deficit/hyperactivity disorder (ADHD) and related behavioral disorders within schools. Through the practice of mindfulness and meditation, FMBTs intervene not only at the level of the individual symptom, but also at the family level, something worthwhile because family life often influences a child's behavior and academic performance. Engaging parents in therapeutic intervention strengthens the support system at the disposal of students and leads to positive changes on school as well as behavioral levels. Creating an overall intervention model that involves families, like FMBTs operate in tandem with the overall goals of school-based mental health initiatives to foster resilience and maintain mental well-being in students (Fang et al., 2024). Besides, school-based mental health services can act on new problems created by technology, such as Internet Gaming Disorder (IGD), which is a significant challenge for adolescents. Since the majority of students play many games in their leisure time, the risk of IGD leading to behavior problems, social anxiety, and depression increases. Mental health programs in schools can be integrated with evidence-based approaches through the application of models such as cognitive-behavioral therapy (CBT) to allow students to manage and understand their gaming behavior. Informing students about the healthy balance between gaming and other aspects can help schools proactively prevent risk factors associated with IGD. Not only do these steps address temporary behavioral issues but also encourage good habits that ensure long-term mental health (Pakpour et al., 2022). Using these holistic perspectives, school-based mental health programs can play a critical role in meeting the multiple needs of youths with behavioral disorders (Figure 7.15).

Figure 7.15. School-based programs often facilitate early intervention, which is crucial for mitigating the long-term impact of behavioral disorders, thereby fostering an environment conducive to healthy psychological and emotional development.

Source: https://upseducation.com/wp-content/uploads/2025/06/Early-Intervention-in-Schools.jpg.

7.6.2. Community Resources and Support Systems

Successful implementation of community resources and support systems is a priority in the treatment of adolescents and children with conduct and behavioral disorders. Schools are also a potential site for mental health services, and their involvement can enhance early intervention and access to appropriate treatment. The selection of appropriate methods and organizational support and training are some of the variables influencing successful implementation of psychological treatments in schools. A systematic review of school-based programs highlights certain of these barriers as logistical concerns and the need for ongoing monitoring and suggests that successful implementation hinges on an integrated process with collaboration between educational and mental health professionals (Carroll et al., 2020). Schools therefore require adequate resources and structured support systems to be in a position to deliver an environment conducive to the mental health and well-being of the students. Community resources are not restricted to schools and encompass a variety of support systems that are critical in conduct disorder management. Family and neighborhood community programs can be employed to enhance the level to which children with behavior difficulties are comprehended. Community-based intervention can also play a crucial role in dealing with causative aspects of such disorders through the generation of awareness and empowerment of parents with coping strategies.

The Inter-agency Plan for Conduct Disorder/Severe Antisocial Behavior recognizes the need to incorporate social systems, such as communities and community values, into the treatment model. Through recognizing the interdependence of such systems, stakeholders can create an enabling environment that reverses conduct problems and fosters children's resilience (Stanley et al., 2008). Last but not least, a partnership approach is essential in ensuring the effectiveness of interventions aimed at meeting the needs of persons with these disorders. The active participation of various stakeholders within the community is essential to the sustainability of conduct and behavioral disorder interventions. School involvement, mental health professionals, families, and community agencies coordination ensures that there exists a strong support system that can adjust accordingly to the changing needs of adolescents and children. Enhanced coordination and communication reduce the possibility of contradictory strategies and enhance the uniformity of treatment methods. Furthermore, ensuring that community services are available and inclusive is fundamental, particularly for marginalized groups who may have additional barriers to accessing assistance. Ensuring that interventions are done based on the specific socio-economic and cultural contexts of families can help to maximize their impact. Hence, the development of support systems and community resources is a change needed in meeting the complexity of behavior and conduct disorders, bringing to the forefront the emphasis on a communal solution to mental disorders facing the younger generation.

7.6.3. Importance of Early Intervention

The importance of early intervention in resolving behavioral and conduct disorders in children cannot be overemphasized. Early intervention in the key early years of a child's life can result in better outcomes as well as prevent some of the long-term effects that usually follow untreated conduct difficulties. Research indicates that early onset of conduct problems commonly precedes a progression to serious antisocial behavior if not treated, such as criminality and other psychiatric disorders during adulthood. It is therefore critical to develop positive environments that promote the mental well-being of children during their early years to discourage the potential progression of these disorders. Early intervention not only enhances the prospects of the child for a healthier course of development but also saves social services and the healthcare system the economic expense of untreated problems of behavior, which, in turn, can lead to detrimental situations in adult life that are difficult to reverse. Parenting programs become an integral part of early intervention programs in order to decrease conduct problems. New group-based parent-training developments have been promising in maximizing children's outcomes with such behaviors. From a review of randomized controlled trials, it has been evident that organized parenting interventions have been proven to achieve significant decreases in conduct problems measured through effect sizes in the intervention group compared to the control group (Stanley et al., 2008). These programs aim to equip parents with effective methods of managing the behavior of their children, eventually reforming family life, and reducing the risk of exacerbating behavioral disorders. Early application of these programs not only addresses existing conduct problems but also prevents more disabling behavioral disorders from evolving in adulthood. This pre-emptive strike is critical in maintaining not only the health of the child but also that of the entire family and that of the general community. Despite the apparent benefits that are typically associated with early intervention, challenges continue to arise with general adoption of effective measures. Global and coordinated action is needed to ensure intervention is timely, especially among at-risk groups such as children aged between 0 and 2 years, who could be at higher risk due to environmental factors. The limitations of the available intervention models, as highlighted by the Inter-agency Plan for Conduct Disorder/Severe Antisocial Behavior, highlight the need for more systematic interventions that address the specific needs of different groups, for instance, adolescent girls who may have various emotional issues (Stanley et al., 2008). Furthermore, facilitating coordination across schools, communities, and health practitioners can enhance the effectiveness of early intervention actions. To establish a supportive system to prevent the occurrence of behavioral disorders, it is necessary to include diverse perspectives and foster evidence-based practices that are in alignment with the needs of the affected children and families (Figure 7.16).

Figure 7.16. Parenting programs emerge as a critical component of early intervention strategies aimed at addressing conduct problems.

Source: https://raisingchildren.net.au/__data/assets/image/0034/98566/quality-childhood-intervention-narrow.jpg.

7.7. CONCLUSION

The prevalence of behavioral and conduct disorders in children and adolescents necessitates prompt intervention by mental health professionals, caregivers, and lawmakers. The evidence suggests that the treatment prognosis for children with conduct difficulties is typically poor and leads to serious outcomes later in life, including criminality and a variety of psychiatric conditions (Barlow et al., 2009). It is so dire a trajectory that it underscores the importance of early treatment and effective interventions. Treatment of such issues is not only required through effective therapeutic interventions but also through system assistance striving to decrease socioeconomic factors that lead to the accumulation of problem behavior. Ultimately, a multimodal intervention uniting behavior therapies with support programs at the community level is required for altering the trajectory of problem youth. Parent-training treatment has, over the last decade, been a potentially useful intervention for youth with conduct problems. Research indicates that structured, replicable parent programs significantly enhance children, as shown by significant improvements in children's behavior compared to control groups (Barlow et al., 2009). Parent-training programs provide caregivers with important tools that not only improve children's behavior but also enable healthier family relationships. The challenge is to research comparative effectiveness of varied parenting methods because current literature indicates a need for thoroughly designed studies to identify what methods result in the best long-term outcomes. These outcomes are critical in order to inform effective and sustainable interventions that suit various family settings. Moreover, it is important to acknowledge that treatment strategies should be adapted in order to tackle the specific problems faced by vulnerable populations, such as the poor. Contemporary studies have shown that evidence-based programs may be effectively implemented in domestic settings, with quantifiable enhancements in the behavior of toddlers. Such adaptability is imperative, considering that some families may encounter challenges in accessing traditional mental health care. By making interventions flexible enough to accommodate the unique needs of these families, mental health professionals can succeed in transforming the lives of young children with behavioral issues dramatically. Continued study and investment in such flexible programs are essential for furthering mental health and improving outcomes for children and adolescents with conduct disorder on a variety of socio-economic stages.

7.7.1. Summary of Key Points

Conduct and behavior disorders of child and adolescent mental illness are significant challenges not only to the individuals themselves but to families and society at large. Research has documented the absence of good prognosis for conduct problems, whereby in the absence of early intervention, conduct problems can lead to devastating adult outcomes, including criminality and psychiatric disorder. Of utmost significance to the treatment of such disorders is the provision of effective treatment methods, chief among which are systematic parenting programs. Systematic review of randomized controlled trials has shown that such programs are able to bring about statistically significant improvement in child behavior, and accordingly, that evidence-based therapy has a most vital part to play in youth mental health treatment as evidenced by Barlow et al. (2009). In addition to parent programs, self-care support interventions have also emerged as a critical component of children and young people (CYP) mental health interventions. New research shows that accessible and flexible self-care approaches can be helpful for mental health symptomology. The findings of wide-ranging service mapping exercises emphasize the importance of partnership working between service providers and CYP and suggest that effective self-care systems are characterized by their ability to respond to the particular needs of young people and their families. The mixed methods approach also emphasizes that self-care is not only corrective but also the pathway to empowerment, as in research investigating personal experience and understanding, emphasizing the applicability of these findings to practice today. Lastly, the trend toward improved mental health outcomes in adolescents and children hinges on the integration of diverse therapeutic modalities, from systematic parental programs to self-care interventions. This multi-dimensional approach acknowledges the richness of conduct and behavioral disorders and provides scope for individualized care that resonates with young people and their families. Ongoing research and innovation are imperative to the refinement of frameworks currently available and to the exploration of under-represented conditions, and to the assurance that mental health provision is not just effective, but also adaptive to the evolving needs of CYP. It is imperative that future work encourages flexibility and sensitivity within treatment settings, in line with the expressed desires of the children and their parents, substantiating the premise that mental health treatment needs to be both effective and humane.

7.7.2. The Need for Increased Awareness and Support

Prevalence of children and adolescents' conduct and behavioral disorders have necessitated an increased awareness and care system in family and educational environments. Recent studies indicate a sharp rise in the problem of mental illness among this group, calling for immediate intervention through awareness-based programs. Schools increasingly find themselves known as the central sites for the advancement of mental health, yet consensus on definitions and models of successful mental health intervention is difficult for both policy makers and educators. By better understanding the complexity of these disorders, stakeholders are better positioned to incorporate integrated mental health programs that respond to classroom achievement as well as emotional and social learning. Since the evidence of demand for such programs confirms, awareness-raising is the top priority to create settings that allow the integrated development of children and adolescents, particularly those at risk of developing behavioral problems (Cavioni et al., 2020). Support systems play a vital role in managing effectively behavioral and conduct disorders, yet numerous families and communities are not aware of the resources available. This has also been shown through research to predict self-injurious behavior among adolescents and, therefore, early identification and intervention are highly critical (Andover et al., 2014). Parent awareness and caregiver campaigns are required in sensitizing them to the signs of distress and parenting. By establishing an educated population, the stigma around mental illness can be diminished, enabling families to receive assistance without fear of punishment. Multidisciplinary treatment systems involving psychological, social, and educational interventions can work towards enhancing the prognosis for youths with mental illness, reinforcing the need for a community-based effort to awareness and support. Also, the building of robust support systems is a collaboration among various fields including healthcare, education, and community organizations. Increased awareness not only works to remove the stigma related to behavioral disorders but also consolidates these sectors' efforts to establish comprehensive support networks for teenagers. Research highlights the role of parental engagement in reversing psychological distress, and it is suggested that there can exist a stark difference in outcomes for youth at risk when effective parenting strategies are in place (Andover et al., 2014). If communities unify to raise the awareness and offer resources, they can effectively establish an environment where young people are willing to be truthful about their struggles. This combined approach of awareness and support is significant in establishing resilience in children and adolescents to promote healthy social-emotional development and mitigate the pervasiveness of conduct disorders in the long run.

7.7.3. Future Directions in Research and Treatment

With the progress of child and adolescent mental health, future research and treatment of behavioral and conduct disorders will also have to adopt the complexity of these disorders. Longitudinal follow-up studies of the destiny of children with these disorders will uncover how early intervention can ward off long-term trouble. Research focusing on individual risk factors, such as preterm birth, has shown a greater incidence of emotional and behavioral disorders in preterm teens that calls for treatment specially tailored to these subgroups (Johnson et al., 2013). In addition, research into genetic, environmental, and sociocultural determinants of behavioral disorders can offer insights into developing individualized treatment protocols. Furthermore, enhancing the intervention method is critical, particularly in the context of ADHD. Present evidence emphasizes the importance of using comprehensive, family-centered programs that not only intervene in the person symptoms but also in social impairment deficit areas that are commonly experienced by adolescents with ADHD. Present studies emphasize the need for implementing long-term interventions, such as the PEERS program, aimed at friend-making skills and social skills (Gardner et al., 2015). This action draws attention to a paradigm that recognizes social skills training as more than a secondary component, but rather as the key to overall therapy success, as it supports both peer relationships and adolescents' own personal satisfaction. Lastly, incorporating technology into treatment modalities is a promising area of investigation for future studies in child and adolescent mental health. Mobile health interventions and web-supported systems might provide extended interaction and supports to both youths and families, facilitating communication about behavior management and emotional support. Future longitudinal studies would examine if these new interventions were successful, particularly in increasing access and adherence among multi-socioeconomic populations. Using technology's power for leverage, mental health practitioners are able to facilitate the scalability of interventions and increased integration in responding to adolescent behavioral and conduct disorders across different populations.

REFERENCES

1. Aalsma, M. C., Brown-Podgorski, B. L., Burke Draucker, C., Oruche, U. M., et al. (2017). Developing a multiple caregiver group for caregivers of adolescents with disruptive behaviors. https://core.ac.uk/download/129148923.pdf (accessed on 14th October 2025).
2. Andover, M. S., Anestis, M. D., Baetens, I., Baetens, I., Baetens, I., Baetens, I., Bandura, A., et al. (2014). Non-suicidal self-injury in adolescence: A longitudinal study of the relationship between NSSI, psychological distress and perceived parenting. https://core.ac.uk/download/55763314.pdf (accessed on 14th October 2025).
3. Asarnow, J. R., Langer, D. A., Sugar, C. A., Tompson, M. C., et al. (2017). A randomized clinical trial comparing family-focused treatment and individual supportive therapy for depression in childhood and early adolescence. https://open.bu.edu/bitstream/2144/24311/1/Public%20Access%20Version%20041717.pdf (accessed on 14th October 2025).
4. Baena Medina, M. S., Hidalgo García, M. V., Jiménez García, L., León, C. M., et al. (2019). Effectiveness of structural-strategic family therapy in the treatment of adolescents with mental health problems and their families. https://core.ac.uk/download/225123947.pdf (accessed on 14th October 2025).
5. Bagner, D. M., Baker, B. L., Baker, C. N., Behan, K. M., Brenner, C. J., Campbell, L. F., et al. (2009). Treatment outcomes for toddlers with behaviour problems from families in poverty. https://core.ac.uk/download/213076118.pdf (accessed on 14th October 2025).
6. Barlow, J., Bayliss, S., Davenport, C., Dretzke, J., et al. (2009). The clinical effectiveness of different parenting programmers for children with conduct problems: A systematic review of randomized controlled trials. https://core.ac.uk/download/48864.pdf (accessed on 14th October 2025).
7. Buitelaar, J. K., Faraone, S. V., Franke, B., Groenman, A. P., et al. (2013). Substance use disorders in adolescents with attention deficit hyperactivity disorder: A 4-year follow-up study. https://core.ac.uk/download/55844599.pdf (accessed on 14th October 2025).
8. Cameron, G., & Frensch, K. (2015). The lives of young adults who have graduated from residential children's mental health programs (FULL REPORT). https://core.ac.uk/download/157835013.pdf (accessed on 14th October 2025).
9. Carroll, B., Clarke, T., Farthing, S., Fonagy, P., et al. (2020). Review: Delivering mental health support within schools and colleges–A thematic synthesis of barriers and facilitators to implementation of

indicated psychological interventions for adolescents. https://core.ac.uk/download/305118502.pdf (accessed on 14th October 2025).

10. Cavioni, V., Grazzani, I., & Ornaghi, V. (2020). Mental health promotion in schools: A comprehensive theoretical framework. https://core.ac.uk/download/322748597.pdf (accessed on 14th October 2025).
11. Cerutti, R., Fontana, A., Guidetti, V., Presaghi, F., et al. (2017). An exploratory study on internet addiction, somatic symptoms and emotional and behavioral functioning in school-aged adolescents. https://core.ac.uk/download/153367682.pdf (accessed on 14th October 2025).
12. de Wit, M., Gajewska, K. A., Goethals, E. R., McDarby, V., Zhao, X., Hapunda, G., Delamater, A. M., et al. (2022). *ISPAD Clinical Practice Consensus Guidelines 2022*: Psychological care of children, adolescents and young adults with diabetes. *Pediatric Diabetes, 23*, 1373–1389. https://doi.org/10.1111/pedi.13428 (accessed on 14th October 2025).
13. Ernst, M., Green-Golan, L., Leschek, E., Merke, D. P., et al. (2010). Psychiatric characterization of children with genetic causes of hyperandrogenism. https://core.ac.uk/download/55802070.pdf (accessed on 14th October 2025).
14. Fang, Y., Liu, J., Zhang, B., Lau, M., Ho, Y. F., Yang, Y., Shi, Y., et al. (2024). A systematic review of the benefits and mechanisms of family-based mind-body therapy programs targeting families of children and adolescents with attention-deficit/hyperactivity disorder. *Journal of Social and Personal Relationships, 41*, 2219–2250. https://www.semanticscholar.org/paper/f0a1c3815cead9290857a39998b37663ab801765 (accessed on 14th October 2025).
15. Flouri, E. (2008). Temperament influences on parenting and child psychopathology: Socio-economic disadvantage as moderator. https://core.ac.uk/download/pdf/82610.pdf (accessed on 14th October 2025).
16. Gardner, D. M., Gerdes, A. C., & Weinberger, K. A. (2015). Examination of a parent-assisted, friendship-building program for adolescents with ADHD. https://core.ac.uk/download/213077596.pdf (accessed on 14th October 2025).
17. Gerdes, A. C., Haack, L. M., & Schneider, B. W. (2011). Parental functioning in families for behavioral parent training and importance of clinically meaningful change. https://core.ac.uk/download/213078223.pdf (accessed on 14th October 2025).
18. Granic, I., Lobel, A., & Engels, R. C. M. E. (2013). The benefits of playing video games. *American Psychologist, 69*, 66–78. https://doi.org/10.1037/a0034857 (accessed on 14th October 2025).

19. Green, J. G., McLaughlin, K. A., Alegría, M., & Loder, S. (2015). Disparities in child and adolescent mental health and mental health services in the U.S. https://core.ac.uk/download/75780891.pdf (accessed on 14th October 2025).
20. Johnson, S. J., & Wolke, D. (2013). Behavioral outcomes and psychopathology during adolescence. https://core.ac.uk/download/9847191.pdf (accessed on 14th October 2025).
21. Konopka, A., Führer, A., Binder, M., Diexer, S., Frese, T., Gekle, M., Girndt, M., et al. (2024). Child and adolescent mental health in a period of fewer COVID-19-related restrictions in an urban population in Germany. *Psychiatry International.* https://www.semanticscholar.org/paper/dd5c040070a19144ff990017efa42cfe026421aa (accessed on 14th October 2025).
22. Li, F., Cui, Y., Li, Y., Guo, L., Ke, X., Liu, J., Luo, X., et al. (2021). Prevalence of mental disorders in school children and adolescents in China: Diagnostic data from detailed clinical assessments of 17,524 individuals. *Journal of Child Psychology and Psychiatry, 63*, 34–46. https://doi.org/10.1111/jcpp.13445 (accessed on 14th October 2025).
23. Ludlow, C., Hurn, R., & Lansdell, S. (2020). A current review of the Children and Young People's Improving Access to Psychological Therapies (CYP IAPT) program: Perspectives on developing an accessible workforce. *Adolescent Health, Medicine and Therapeutics, 11*, 21–28. https://doi.org/10.2147/ahmt.s196492 (accessed on 14th October 2025).
24. McClellan, J., & Stock, S. (2013). Practice parameter for the assessment and treatment of children and adolescents with schizophrenia. *Journal of the American Academy of Child & Adolescent Psychiatry, 52*, 976–990. https://doi.org/10.1016/j.jaac.2013.02.008 (accessed on 14th October 2025).
25. Nicoll, W. G. (2014). Developing transformative schools: A resilience-focused paradigm for education. https://core.ac.uk/download/46603629.pdf (accessed on 14th October 2025).
26. Owen, C. (2016). PTSD from childhood trauma as a precursor to attachment issues. https://core.ac.uk/download/129592830.pdf (accessed on 14th October 2025).
27. Pakpour, S., Fazeli, S., Zeidi, I. M., Alimoradi, Z., Georgsson, M., Broström, A., & Potenza, M. N. (2022). Effectiveness of a mobile app-based educational intervention to treat internet gaming disorder among Iranian adolescents: Study protocol for a randomized controlled trial. *Trials, 23.* https://www.semanticscholar.org/paper/

a11692c082ec86746992aa94b6c5c61625e258f0 (accessed on 14th October 2025).

28. Rosenquist, J. N., Audrain-McGovern, J., Lehrer, S. F., & Ding, W. (2025). The impact of poor health on education: New evidence using genetic markers. https://core.ac.uk/download/pdf/6483352.pdf (accessed on 14th October 2025).
29. Ryff, C. D. (2013). Psychological well-being revisited: Advances in the science and practice of eudaimonia. *Psychotherapy and Psychosomatics, 83*, 10–28. https://doi.org/10.1159/000353263 (accessed on 14th October 2025).
30. Smith, M., & Storey, P. (2008). Methods and approaches to improving the emotional health and well-being of children: A briefing paper concerning interventions to prevent internalizing disorders. https://core.ac.uk/download/pdf/82102.pdf (accessed on 14th October 2025).
31. Stanley, P. (2008). The new multi-ministry response to conduct problems: A SWOT analysis. https://core.ac.uk/download/29196170.pdf (accessed on 14th October 2025).
32. Vazini Adib, F., Shahyad, S. H., & Hushmandi, K. (2025). The role of dimensions of parental marital satisfaction in predicting symptoms of conduct and oppositional defiant disorders in primary school students in Qom, Iran. *The Open Public Health Journal*. https://www.semanticscholar.org/paper/26de43f4ba63bfaf1e70e0f56a010c1daaa73b38 (accessed on 14th October 2025).
33. Yoshikawa, H., Wuermli, A. J., Rebello Britto, P., Dreyer, B. P., Leckman, J. F., Lye, S. J., Ponguta, L. A., et al. (2020). Effects of the global coronavirus disease-2019 pandemic on early childhood development: Short- and long-term risks and mitigating program and policy actions. *The Journal of Pediatrics, 223*, 188–193. https://doi.org/10.1016/j.jpeds.2020.05.020 (accessed on 14th October 2025).

Chapter 8

Eating Disorders and Body Image

Contents

INTRODUCTION

Prevalence of eating disorders among adolescents and children has increased exponentially in the last few decades, a trend that holds significant implications for psychologists and public health officials. Eating disorders like anorexia nervosa, bulimia nervosa, and binge-eating disorder most typically emerge during the adolescent years of an individual and have significant impacts on mental health and quality of life. The intricate dynamic of body image perceptions and eating behavior occupies the central stage in understanding these disorders. With increasing pressures becoming more formidable to meet in terms of beauty standards, adolescents are most likely plagued by body dissatisfaction that could bring about radical behaviors, like disordered eating patterns. Hence, it is important to understand the psychological consequences in terms of perceptions of the self and society to develop successful prevention and intervention strategies. A worry of this issue is the way in which media affect the body image of adolescents because there is extensive research that confirms that there exists a strong relationship between media consumption and eating disorders. Adolescents are bombarded with idealized images of thinness and fitness on various sources of the media, such as television and social media, and stringent implications for their psychological health. Character influence that has been actualized on these platforms has been discovered to be significant in body distress and eating-disordered behavior. For instance, Maria et al. (2017) reveals that the desire to emulate TV characters, coupled with the frequency at which one views, significantly contributes to body dissatisfaction among adolescents. The need to appear like idealized forms in media fosters an unhealthy environment, which spreads ill concepts of oneself and eating disorders. Understanding such dynamics is essential to interpreting the broader sociocultural determinants of youth mental illness. Furthermore, coming to understand the impact of these disorders requires an intervening response that addresses the peer and family dynamics' influence on young people's body image beliefs. Studies indicate that peers hold a pivotal impact on teens' desires to conform to media images, thereby exacerbating mental illness concerns like depression and anxiety. The necessity to foster positive environments, peer and family, cannot be overstated in the fight against eating disorders. Also, Sabo et al. (2004) takes into account the advantages of physical activity and sport as methods of prevention of the prevalence of such disorders. Facilitating sports participation not only enhances good physical health but can enhance self-esteem and body satisfaction in young individuals. Ultimately, it will be most important to develop strategies that integrate media literacy, social support, and healthy lifestyle habits in order to address the spreading epidemic of eating disorders in child and adolescent mental health.

Definition of Eating Disorders

Eating disorders are serious psychiatric illnesses characterized by extreme disturbances in eating behavior, body experience, and control of weight. They mostly present in adolescence and young adulthood and result in a wide range of psychological and physical complications. Anorexia nervosa (AN), the most studied of the types, is defined by strict caloric restriction, an inordinate fear of gaining weight, and an abnormal perception of self-worth in which the individual perceives herself or himself to be fat when actually she or he is underweight. All are complex and inextricably interwoven with sociocultural stress on body image, which can further complicate symptoms and prolong recovery. These disorders not only jeopardize physical health, as understood through rampant malnutrition and fertility issues, but also severely affect mental well-being, requiring a multidisciplinary intervention for effective intervention within the context of child and adolescent mental well-being (Ciobanu et al., 2020).

Figure 8.1. Eating disorders are multifaceted psychiatric illnesses characterized by significant disturbances in eating behaviors, body image, and weight regulation.

Source: https://mapmygenome.in/cdn/shop/articles/Understanding_Eating_Disorders_-_A_Deep_Dive_into_Anorexia.webp?v=1724479592.

Progress in the understanding of eating disorders has included significant shifts in perspective, particularly regarding their connection with sex and social factors. Throughout history, anorexia has most commonly been linked to young women, a trend that underscored its identification with femininity and cultural beauty ideals. Influential professionals in the community of psychiatry, such as Hilde Bruch, criticized earlier psychoanalytic explanations that downplayed more expansive social forces on the independence of women. By reconceptualizing AN as an externally pressures-driven illness, Bruch focused on investigating the dialectics between gender, culture, and mental illness. This paradigmatic shift has resulted in feminist scholars advocating social change rather than individual pathology to tackle the causes of eating disorders (Till et al., 2011). In contemporary discourse, definitions of eating disorders extend beyond the clinical symptoms to include the sociocultural contexts influencing people's perceptions of body image. The contribution of media, peer social interaction, and cultural beliefs is central to the development and perpetuation of these disorders. Adolescents, in particular, are particularly vulnerable to such environmental pressures, leading to distorted body image and maladaptive eating habits. As one considers how mental health professionals can create effective treatments, attention to such broader social forces is necessary. Treatment of eating disorders must involve an integrated approach consisting of psychological counseling, nutrition counseling, and sociocultural criticism, with an aim to inculcate healthier notions of body image among young individuals and minimize the prevalence of these incapacitating diseases (Figure 8.1).

Importance of Body Image in Mental Health

The significance of body image in mental illness cannot be overstated, especially among children and adolescents. At these ages, one is very susceptible to sociocultural messages regarding idealized bodies, and it has the ability to have a far-reaching impact on one's self-concept. The impact of a negative body image has the potential to manifest in several mental health outcomes, including anxiety, depression, and eating disorder behavior. Teenagers, particularly girls, living under a media environment of idealized bodies are said to experience heightened body dissatisfaction, leading to maladaptive weight control behavior and poorer mental illness issues. In particular, media effects have a large contribution to body discomfort, involving that the stress of conforming to idealized ideals of beauty loses mental health and increases vulnerability to eating disorders, thus relating body image to mental health outcomes during adolescence (Maria et al., 2017). Worsening the situation is the stigma associated with eating disorders, which young people might not understand very well. Studies indicate that children often see people with eating disorders as personally at fault, unlike those with other types of mental illnesses such as depression. This stigmatization will impede empathy and assistance to people afflicted with such disorders and lowers the likelihood of openness in discussions regarding body image issues. Moreover, the negative perceptions against people afflicted with eating disorders may discourage teenagers from seeking assistance, further aggravating their psychological illness issues. Thus, de-stigmatization of eating disorders is important in improving the overall mental health setting for adolescents so that they can freely discuss their issues with their body and access help (McNamara et al., 2016). Ultimately, the cultivation of healthy body image among children and adolescents is essential to ensure better mental health and prevent eating disorders. Effective interventions will need to be directed at promoting body positivity and resilience against cultural pressure. Educational interventions that address the unrealistic portrayals presented in media and promote diversity of body type can do much to assist. Empowering young people to love their bodies because of their uniqueness rather than conforming to slimming ideals guarantees an insurance factor against mental illness. It is essential that parents, teachers, and health professionals collaborate in creating an environment that supports a positive environment where issues of body image can be openly discussed, ultimately translating to healthier self-esteem and mental well-being for children in contemporary society.

8.1. TYPES OF EATING DISORDERS

The pathogenesis of eating disorders is highly heterogeneous with several conditions manifesting along varied patterns of aberrant eating. Among the best-described ones are anorexia nervosa, bulimia nervosa, and binge-eating disorder. Anorexia nervosa is characterized by extreme food restriction, intense weight loss, and an intense fear of gaining weight and a distorted perception of body shape. On the other hand, bulimia nervosa entails episodes of binge eating followed by compensatory actions like vomiting or excessive exercise. Binge-eating disorder is marked by recurring behavior of eating large amounts of food without using compensatory behaviors, frequently accompanied by loss of control and distress. It should be noted that such eating disorders can go a significant way in shaping the psychological well-being of children and young teens, particularly their self-esteem and body image. Media portrayal and how it plays a role in the development of body image and eating disorders cannot be overstated. With today's age of social media, young teens are exposed minute by minute to what constitutes a perfect body, which can eventually distort their view of themselves. Evidence supports that media-ideal internalization encourages negative affective experience and unhealthy body self-examination related to one's own body. Subsequently, adolescents can be compelled to extreme dieting and purging as a means of complying with these impossible standards (Dakanalis et al., 2014). This cycle not only heightens the issues with overall body image, but becomes entangled with the psychological disturbances, such as depression and anxiety, which typically accompany these eating disorders. Understandings of cultural values driving beauty standards are central to addressing their impact on adolescents' mental health and prevention. Moreover, peer relations and social interactions become central in influencing adolescents' eating and body image. Empirical evidence shows that identification with media figures can have a powerful impact on adolescents' self-concept and eating patterns, leading to increased body dissatisfaction and disordered eating behaviors. For males and females alike, socializing with peers who attempt to imitate idealized media portrayals has been correlated with increased depression, anxiety, and body distress (Maria et al., 2017). Thus, it is critical to look at individual and media influence on eating disorders as well as the broader social climate through which adolescents are constructing identity. Greater knowledge of such factors helps develop supportive environments that foster healthy body image and facilitate counteracting eating disorders in this high-risk population (Figure 8.2).

Figure 8.2. Anorexia nervosa is marked by an intense fear of gaining weight and a distorted body image, leading to severe restriction of food intake and excessive weight loss.

Source: https://cdn.rehabfiles.com/sites/oasisrehab/wp-content/uploads/2024/10/OR-eating-disorder.svg.

8.1.1. Anorexia Nervosa

Anorexia Nervosa represents a complex interaction of biological, psychological, and sociocultural determinants, and its presence in adolescents highlights the need for targeted intervention. It is characterized by the persistent quest for thinness and excessive preoccupation with not becoming fat, with consequent impairment of physical health and mental wellbeing. Studies have shown that teens might have little knowledge of eating disorders, and frequently they blame personal failure rather than identifying them as medical conditions. This ignorance not only enhances stigma but also makes these individuals' access to treatment and help more challenging. Adolescents will be more likely to view individuals suffering from Anorexia Nervosa negatively compared to other patients due to the fact that they are more likely to view them as guilty of their condition and thereby exacerbating the recovery process (McNamara et al., 2016). Thus, the creation of accurate information regarding eating disorders becomes central in inducing empathy and assisting with the creation of healthier attitudes towards victims. Family functioning has been identified to play a major role in the etiology and maintenance of Anorexia Nervosa among adolescents. The relational-systemic model presumes that pathological family interaction may cause eating disorders. Empirical studies suggest that over-protectiveness and weak open communication within the family, among other factors, might lead adolescents to feel pressured to stick to unreal physical standards. These pressure of family life coupled with cultural ideals of beauty and success can further fuel the unhealthy obsession with controlling weight and pleasing appearance. An awareness of how family relationships affect adolescent eating disorders is of significance, as it underlies treatment plans that actively involve the afflicted themselves, in addition to their families. The use of therapeutic intervention focused on working through family dynamics can improve the rate of recovery and create healthier family relationships as part of therapy (Cerniglia et al., 2020). Despite the complications surrounding Anorexia Nervosa, early treatment and integrated treatment efforts are promising in improving outcomes for adolescents. Multidisciplinary models of treatment targeting medical, psychological, and nutrition intervention are critical in effectively treating this disorder. Cognitive-behavioral therapy has been an extremely effective treatment approach, whose goal is the altering of distorted body image and self-esteem thinking. In addition, the integration of educational interventions addressing teenagers' perceptions and misperceptions regarding eating disorders can create a recovery-friendly environment. These interventions have the ability to de-stigmatize Anorexia Nervosa and enhance peer empathy. Furthermore, interventions should also address building resilience and coping mechanisms for the promotion of positive body image, hence enabling adolescents to resist societal pressures that culminate in the establishment of eating disorders.

8.1.2. Bulimia Nervosa

It is critical to understand Bulimia Nervosa within the eating disorders and body image conversation, particularly in adolescent and child mental health. The condition is characterized by episodic episodes of binge eating followed by the compensatory behavior of vomiting, fasting, or excessive exercise. The cycle of such behaviors fosters an unstable relationship with food and body image. Adolescents with Bulimia Nervosa are most likely to express severe discontent with their shape and weight, motivated primarily by social stress and media portrayals of the ideal body. Stigmatization of eating disorders also makes their problems harder to understand; research has established that adolescents are significantly faster at recognizing the symptoms of other mental conditions, depression for example, compared to eating disorders, which suggests a very poor awareness and understanding of such serious illnesses among friends (McNamara et al., 2016). This imbalance is problematic, as it is likely to hinder supportive dialogue and effective interventions. Family dynamics and relationships are also significant etiological factors for Bulimia Nervosa in the adolescent period. Research indicates that disordered eating is the result of intricate interpersonal problems like family functioning and communication pattern. Families with high conflict, low emotional support, or dysfunctional family patterns can unknowingly cause the development of eating disorders. The relational-systemic model contends that the complete understanding of such family factors is needed to fight Bulimia Nervosa effectively (Cerniglia et al., 2020). By looking at the manner in which adolescents perceive and navigate their family relationships, mental health professionals can develop targeted interventions that not only work on the individual symptom but also promote healthier family relationships.

Figure 8.3. Understanding bulimia nervosa is crucial in the discourse surrounding eating disorders and body image, particularly in child and adolescent mental health.

Source: https://resize.indiatvnews.com/en/resize/newbucket/1200_-/2024/02/dkjuhbdwc-1709021872.webp.

The combined approach, thus, is capable of facilitating recovery and fostering resilience in adolescent patients with this challenging disorder. Moreover, the attitudes and beliefs in society regarding eating disorders contribute to the multifaceted picture of Bulimia Nervosa. The environment of an adolescent, peer relationships, and media exposure are inclined to fuel the sense of inappropriateness or guilt concerning food and body shape. The common stigma attached to eating disorders tends to result in the misinterpretation of the conditions as simple failures in self-control, as opposed to genuine psychological issues (McNamara et al., 2016). The stigma may deter teens from engaging in help seeking as a result of fearing judgment or misconceptions. Hence, it is necessary to promote open discussions about Bulimia Nervosa and other eating disorders in schools and clinical settings for awareness and better understanding. Through the deconstruction of the stigmatization of such disorders, we can enable adolescents to pursue healthier relationships with food and body image while supporting their mental wellbeing (Figure 8.3).

8.1.3. Binge Eating Disorder (BED)

Binge eating disorder (BED) is a big but underappreciated component of eating disorders, particularly in the field of child and adolescent mental health. Unlike anorexia or bulimia, BED is characterized by the frequent recurrence of eating large quantities of food in the lack of control over consumption. This disorder is frequently accompanied by guilt, distress, and shame and is a contributor to the emotional burden of those who experience it. BED is increasingly being seen in adolescents, partly as a reaction to body image pressures created by media depictions of idealized bodies. These stresses may be a cycle of negative emotions, ultimately influencing both physical and mental health, validating the necessity for targeted intervention strategies in this vulnerable age group. The influence of imagery of the media must not be overstated in the context of BED. Teenagers presented with media-perfect images have been proven to internalize these ideals, hence achieving self-objectification and heightened body dissatisfaction. For instance, in a longitudinal study, internalization of media ideals and subsequent self-judgment affected the emotional states of adolescents in relation to their bodies and finally predicted more instances of binge eating (Dakanalis et al., 2014). In addition, the connection between concern about body image and media consumption extends past individual feelings and into peer relationships and social processes. Media desireful thinking among peers can reinforce body dissatisfaction and eating disorders, which offer a fertile soil where disordered eating behavior like BED is able to proliferate (Maria et al., 2017). Their understanding is pivotal in the development of appropriate prevention and treatment programs for BED in high-risk adolescents. The treatment of Binge Eating Disorder necessitates a comprehensive, multi-faceted approach that corrects both the eating behavior and the internal psychological problems. Cognitive-behavioral therapy has been a treatment method that has been most prevalent with its focus on interrupting patterns of negative feelings and binge eating episodes. Healthy body image and media resistance interventions are also needed. With such clear links among body image dissatisfaction, media exposure, and binge eating, educational interventions that help adolescents learn to critically evaluate media messages can become effective prevention interventions. Finally, the treatment of BED requires a joint effort from mental health professionals, educators, and families to establish an environment supporting healthy body image and decreasing the risks posed by societal beauty standards (Figure 8.4).

Figure 8.4. Binge eating disorder (BED) represents a significant yet often overlooked facet of eating disorders, particularly within the realm of child and adolescent mental health.

Source: https://foothillsatredoak.com/wp-content/uploads/2024/08/3-Dangers-of-Binge-Eating.jpeg.

8.2. PREVALENCE OF EATING DISORDERS IN CHILDREN AND ADOLESCENTS

The prevalence of eating disorders among children and teens has emerged as a pressing concern in the field of mental health. Available data indicate that eating disorders, for example, anorexia nervosa, bulimia nervosa, and binge-eating disorder, are increasingly being diagnosed among adolescents. The rise can be explained by a variety of factors, like social pressures and the far-reaching influence of social media glorifying thinness and some body types. As teenagers spend much time on the internet, exposure to unrealistic body shapes can heighten dissatisfaction with the body, thus contributing to disordered eating. Studies indicate that around 1–3% of teenagers can develop anorexia, whereas bulimia and binge-eating disorder develop in about 1–3% and 2–4% of this age group, respectively. Such dramatic statistics point to an urgent need for targeted prevention and intervention efforts in the incidence of eating disorders within this risk vulnerability age group and an impetus toward heightened mental health awareness and education. Several distinct variables account for the higher incidence of eating disorders in youth. These include genetic predispositions, psychological issues like low self-esteem, and environmental factors such as those of the peer group and family. Particularly, adolescents find themselves in an age of exploration when they are discovering themselves and are even more sensitive to others' approval, putting them at risk for embracing unhealthy weight-control behaviors. For instance, the desire to be accepted will lead individuals to go on drastic diets or exercise regimens. Besides, school pressures, social pressures, and changes in life may serve to exacerbate such conditions, making individuals susceptible to mental illness. The intersection of these factors reveals the multidimensionality of eating disorder onset, reflecting the requirement of holistic interventions with psychological, social, and educational components (John et al., 2022). Of particular interest is the fact that the effects of inaction in eating disorder prevention among children and adolescents extend far beyond short-term morbidity; they lead to long-term psychological and physical sequelae. Teenagers with eating disorders frequently have co-occurring mental health conditions, such as anxiety and depression, which can impede their general development and health. Prompt intervention is important, as long-standing eating disorders can lead to serious medical consequences, such as cardiovascular complications, gastrointestinal disturbances, or bone density abnormalities—all of which can have permanent implications into adulthood. Further, evidence indicates high association between eating disorders and poor functioning, compromised academic performance, and reduced quality of life. Countering the prevalence of eating disorders among this demographic thus demands an integrated intervention that fosters healthy body image, resilience, and emotional regulation as well as accessible mental health services (John et al., 2019).

8.2.1. Statistics on Eating Disorders

The prevalence of eating disorders in adolescents and children is staggering, as current statistics show that eating disorders are prevalent among a high majority of this population. Research demonstrates that nearly 1 out of every 5 teenagers has an eating disorder, and the rates for anorexia nervosa, bulimia nervosa, and binge-eating disorder have risen at an exponential rate over the past decade. Up to 70% of teen girls indicate that they are not satisfied with their body image, and this is a key risk factor for the development of disordered eating behaviors. Body image dissatisfaction usually arises from societal pressure and widespread exposure to media-based presentations of idealized, unrealistic standards of beauty. With growing normalization of such ideals, it is important to confront the statistics about eating disorders and their negative effect on the mental health and well-being of young people. The statistics of eating disorders go beyond prevalence rates; they also outline the glaring discrepancies in diagnosis and treatment across demographic groups. Teenagers that belong to marginalized groups often face barriers that deter them from receiving appropriate care, and therefore, underreporting and a lack of targeted interventions ensue. For example, even though white women are most likely to develop such conditions, it has been established that individuals from dissimilar racial and ethnic groups are increasingly becoming apt to develop such problems, though in different rates.

Figure 8.5. Young people from marginalized backgrounds often face barriers that hinder their access to appropriate care, leading to underreporting and a lack of targeted interventions.

Source: https://minorityrights.org/app/uploads/2023/11/african-american-young-people-nasa-hq-photo.jpg.

Understanding these demographic nuances is paramount in the development of successful prevention and intervention strategies. As the research landscape continues to shift, developing greater awareness of how cultural factors are influencing the onset of eating disorders ultimately brings about more comprehensive treatment pathways that are inclusive of diverse populations. The role of media and its connection to eating disorders cannot be overestimated since a number of studies have indicated the powerful effect that idealized body images have on adolescents' self-image. Statistics indicate that media-idealized appearance exposure has a significant contribution to body dissatisfaction, which in turn is associated extensively with eating disorder development. A longitudinal investigation emphasized that teenagers who internalize these idealized media are more likely to develop negative emotions about their bodies, which ultimately lead to behaviors such as diet restriction and binge eating. The connection emphasizes the importance of critical media literacy programs for young audiences to avoid these consequences. By meeting the omnipresent influence of media early on, society has the potential to begin turning the poisonous narratives that drive eating disorders, fostering more supportive body images, and guiding improved mental health for teens (Figure 8.5).

8.2.2. Demographic Factors Influencing Prevalence

The prevalence of eating disorders in children and adolescents is highly influenced by a number of demographic factors, including age, gender, socioeconomic status, and ethnicity. These conditions have been reported to most commonly affect adolescent females, with the issue of body image being most prominent at this vulnerable age. Boys, less frequently diagnosed, are also coming to identify their body image and disordered eating issues as well, marking a shifting paradigm in how these disorders are seen and treated in both men and women. Additionally, socioeconomic status is critical; individuals living in lower-income households may experience higher rates of food insecurity, which drives poor eating habits and greater susceptibility to eating disorders. This gender-economic status demographic overlap recognizes the complexity of eating disorders and requires a nuanced understanding of how these intersecting categories intersect to influence prevalence rates. In addition, the place of internet social media communication in influencing body image perception is also a significant role within the parameters of demographic factors. Teenagers today are bombarded with virtual spaces that glorify idealized body forms and lifestyle, thereby predisposing them to the cultivation of poor self-comparison and discontentment with their very bodies. The state is particularly pronounced in teenagers who extensively utilize social media platforms that spread unrealistic beauty standards. Systematic review has shown that social media use is linked to higher levels of psychological distress, including depression and anxiety, which are known eating disorder onset risk factors. These findings underscore the need to develop awareness and regulations that will mitigate the adverse impacts of overexposure to social media, particularly among vulnerable adolescent groups (Keles et al., 2019). Additionally, cultural and ethnic factors also significantly help in the development of eating disorders in teenagers because different cultures have different beauty ideals and standards for body shape. In some cultures, there is the spread of ideal thinness, and this leads to an increased level of eating disorders among those who feel compelled to conform to it. Alternatively, other cultural models that accommodate other body shapes may help in preventing these disorders. It is essential to recognize these cultural forces for the development of effective prevention and intervention programs. Prevention and intervention eating disorder programs must be culturally responsive and demographically matched to subgroups, with consideration of the unique body image pressures they face. By incorporating demographics into research and treatment, mental health clinicians can better support children and adolescents with eating disorders, resulting in healthier body relationships (Figure 8.6).

Figure 8.6. In some cultures, the idealization of thinness is pervasive, leading to a higher incidence of eating disorders among individuals who feel pressured to conform.

Source: https://cdn.prod.website-files.com/631f6634759e37228184eb55/63ff53e6688e17eb0879a320_How%20diet%20culture%20can%20lead%20to%20eating%20disorders%20THUMB.svg.

8.2.3. Trends Over the Past Decade

Over the past decade, the rise in eating disorders among children and adolescents has been alarming, as various studies have evidenced an upward trend in conditions such as anorexia nervosa, bulimia, and binge-eating disorder. This increase correlates with a growing societal fixation on body image, compounded by the pervasive influence of social media. The portrayal of idealized body types can significantly affect young people's self-esteem and body perceptions. Because adolescents tend to affirm themselves on the internet, they can be extremely susceptible to disorder eating behaviors in their attempt to gain acceptance. The practice is crucial to understanding the psychic milieu of adolescents today as the preoccupation with looks continues to heighten the possibility of eating disorders, calling for prevention that complies with the standards to combat these tendencies in an internet era. Also, childhood obesity incidence has emerged as a strong public health concern, creating a complex relationship with mental health and body image. The rates of childhood obesity have continued to increase, with over 42 million children under the age of five globally estimated to be overweight or obese. These statistics provide an alarming picture; if the current trends continue, an estimated 70 million children will be part of these groups by 2025.

Figure 8.7. The rates of childhood obesity have steadily increased, with estimates indicating that over 42 million children under five years globally are overweight or obese. Such.

Source: https://ichef.bbci.co.uk/news/480/cpsprodpb/EF6F/production/_126059216_gettyimages-992640340-594x594-copy.jpg.webp.

This obesity increase has been associated with most of the psychological effects like depression, anxiety, and decreased self-esteem, each of which is compounded by stigmatization due to social factors and weight bullying. The concurrent epidemics of eating disorders and obesity highlight an imperative need for integrated intervention to address not only eating patterns but the underlying psychological consequences for youth during their formative years (Rankin et al., 2016). As a countervailing intervention to these trends, mental health activism has been more stringent in recent decades, highlighting the need for child and adolescent well-being to be tackled through integrated mechanisms. Efforts at education of the young on positive body image, nutrition, and emotional resilience are increasingly imperative. The perception of how physical health and mental health are one and the same has encouraged policymakers and healthcare providers to create programs that not only tackle eating disorders but also instill overall well-being in a bid to address the negative narrative on body image. Investment in prevention measures not only has an impact on individual mental health outcomes but also has positive economic returns, with each dollar invested in prevention reported to yield up to six dollars in economic benefit. Such measures point towards a shift in committing to an integrated health approach towards the prevention of eating disorders and body image issues, particularly among marginalized populations (Figure 8.7).

8.3. PSYCHOLOGICAL FACTORS CONTRIBUTING TO EATING DISORDERS

The psychological climate of eating disorders in children and adolescents is complex and has numerous contributory factors. A major psychological factor is the far-reaching impact of media portrayal of idealized physical images. Adolescents are very susceptible to the influence of television, where their favorite stars embody unattainable images of beauty. Research confirms an irrefutable correlation between media exposure and body dissatisfaction and consequently eating disorders. For instance, adolescents who identify highly with TV characters have a strong desire to appear as such characters, which also heightens inferiority feelings and body concerns ultimately. Identification with media characters does not just affect self-perception but also creates negative emotional states, i.e., depression and anxiety, which are prominent psychological risk indicators of eating disorder development (Maria et al., 2017). Another psychological factor that has been associated with eating disorders is peer influence and comparison. Adolescents may come under extreme pressure to conform to the peer group norm, including potential body image ideals. This process of comparison will lead to an internalized belief that the worth of oneself is contingent on conformity with these societal and peer-endorsed norms. The desire to be accepted or fit in can lead one to extreme weight loss or other unhealthy food patterns as a means of conforming to perceived standards of beauty. In addition, the impact is increased by the fact that there are close friends present who also compare themselves in similar manners and thus create an environment where unhealthy eating patterns become the expected norm. Hence, the conjunction of psychological processes and social interactions greatly adds to the susceptibility of getting eating disorders among adolescents (Maria et al., 2017). The understanding regarding the psychological factors for eating disorders reaches up to emotional regulation and self-esteem. Low-esteem adolescents are greatly prone to developing abnormal eating patterns as a way of coping with internalized emotional issues. The need for control over one's body form and weight are generally strong enough to act as a buffer against these individuals' perceptions of inadequacy or lack of power. Furthermore, adolescents are able to employ disordered eating as a method of coping with larger psychological stressors, such as family stressors or school stress.

These stressors can be significant during adolescence, and the eating disorder behaviors become maladaptive coping styles to these emotional stresses. Thus, the psychological undertones of self-esteem and mental wellness need to be treated in order to manage and prevent eating disorders among children and adolescents.

8.3.1. Low Self-Esteem and Body Dissatisfaction

Low self-esteem and body dissatisfaction are strongly associated conditions with a significant influence on the psychological well-being of children and adolescents. Body dissatisfaction is likely to appear during phases of development when individuals compare themselves against societal expectations and peer norms. Internalized negative attributions regarding one's body will then frequently result in low levels of self-esteem. Research highlights the way low self-esteem amplifies dissatisfaction with the body, which then creates a vicious circle where negative body image perpetuates poor self-esteem. At a period of identity crisis among teenagers, the pressure to fit the imagined social standards can yield greater prevalence of mental illness, including depression and anxiety. This link underscores the urgent necessity for interventions that specifically address not just body image concerns, but also the foundation blocks of self-esteem that allow for more adaptive development in these formative growth phases. The exploration of low self-esteems role in body dissatisfaction has far-reaching implications for prevention interventions as well as mental health intervention practices. Studies on these correlations have shown that individuals with greater levels of body dissatisfaction tend to engage in maladaptive coping mechanisms, such as problematic internet use, as a coping strategy from their pain (Demetrovics et al., 2013). Also, avoidance can lead to social withdrawal and further perpetuation of mental illness, sustaining the low self-esteem cycle. Thus, promoting positive self-esteem and self-image via interventions such as supportive counseling and exercise programs may be significant in counteracting the negative impact of body dissatisfaction. An understanding of these processes is needed to develop effective comprehensive mental health programs to impact both body image development and self-esteem improvement among youth. In addition, the relation between body dissatisfaction, low self-esteem, and mental illness is also complicated by level of physical activity and race. Studies have established that while body dissatisfaction and depression have an immense impact on teen girls, presentations of these issues may differ among different racial groups (Friedman et al., 2013). For instance, African American girls may report lower body dissatisfaction compared to their White counterparts based on protective factors inherent in their physical and social environment. However, in spite of these differences, a disturbing trend of declining levels of physical activity among all adolescent girls serves to increase the risk of low self-esteem and body dissatisfaction. Because physical activity is a critical instrument for promoting healthy mental well-being, breaking down barriers to participation must become key to resolving these integrative issues and fostering a more robust youthful generation (Figure 8.8).

Figure 8.8. Low self-esteem and body dissatisfaction are deeply intertwined phenomena that significantly affect the mental health of children and adolescents.

Source: https://www.hindustantimes.com/ht-img/img/2023/11/03/1600x900/4637333_1698986034645_1698986045114.jpg.

8.3.2. Influence of Peer Pressure and Social Media

The new social media have also had an enormous impact on the peer pressure dynamic among adolescents, particularly body image and diet. Web sites that are full of photographs celebrating thinness and supporting unrealistic beauty standards play a key role in how young people view their own bodies. With adolescents traversing these online spaces, they are regularly subjected to a continuous flow of material idealizing specific body forms and enacting an omnipresent pressure to conform. Such an event can have negative consequences on mental health, fostering body dissatisfaction and the creation of eating disorders. Therefore, the ubiquitous presence of social media intensifies underlying issues of self-esteem and identity, leading adolescents to pursue acceptance by engaging in destructive behaviors in order to conform to the ideals presented by the internet. Friendships complicate the body image component of social media due to people retaining societal expectations forwarded by their friends and social milieu. As demonstrated by research, the desire to emulate peers and media celebrities can potentially have a strong impact on self-perception and psychological health. This body dissatisfaction is also especially high for women, who most frequently experience stronger pressures to fit into beauty ideals. Surprisingly, friends' desires to emulate media celebrities not only increase body dissatisfaction but also are associated with higher levels of depression and anxiety in both genders. These relational processes create peer influence as part of a very intricate web of social media exposure that can precipitate the onset of eating disorders and affect overall mental health, particularly in vulnerable adolescents. The composite process of peer pressure and social media underscores the necessity of multilevel intervention approaches to cultivating healthy body image in youth. Educational interventions that foster media resistance can aid in enabling adolescents to construct critical thought concerning the beauty constructs that they are exposed to. Further, applying conducive settings, such as family engagement and community programs, may aid in curbing the dangers of peer pressure related to body image. By emphasizing youth agency coupled with protection factors—such as positive role modeling—programs can assist adolescents in coping with the intricate issues girls and boys are required to confront in mapping self-esteem onto external demands. In the end, these multi-dimensional approaches are essential in counteracting the adverse effects of peer pressure and social media in the context of eating disorders and adolescent mental health, fostering healthier developmental pathways.

8.3.3. Family Dynamics and their Impact

Family dynamics can have a strong effect on kids and teens, especially on their body image and the development of eating disorders. Family interactions are responsible for shaping a pattern of behavior and attitude towards food, body shape, and self-worth. The families that have healthy eating habits and healthy body image will be more likely to pass on resilience to kids and provide them with the coping skills to resist peer pressure. In contrast, dysfunctional families, unsupportive family relationships, or imbalanced perception of physical appearance could contribute to a culture that fosters disordered eating practices. This is because it is essential to address the issue of family functioning as an integrated phenomenon when reviewing the eating disorder risk factors among youths since relationship structures are key to understanding the complexities of such mental issues. The empirical studies identify the relational nature of family existence as key determinants in the development and maintenance of eating disorders among adolescent groups. Evidence for the assertion that the role of family relationships plays a weighty part in the development of these disorders is present, with the theory that abnormal patterns in family interaction can complicate the vulnerability of an adolescent to body image issues. For example, those families who may hold thinness or beauty as a value in some forms are likely inadvertently to enhance unhealthy body thinking in their children and encourage a risk of abnormal eating behavior. Relational-systemic practice also reveals that family background is a significant issue in adolescents' distress, and romanticizing interventions in the context of family system involvement in therapy is promoted to grow romanticized thinking and relationships toward eating and body image.

This broad contextual understanding informs intervention strategies targeted not just towards the individual, but towards their home environment as well, an understanding of the intricate web of interrelation that characterizes adolescent mental health. Furthermore, researchers argue that increased knowledge of protective and risk factors among family systems enhances the discourse around eating disorders and body image. Embedding Developmental Psychopathology as a framework facilitates that researchers and practitioners can explore the complexities of family influence further. Relevantly, this framework identifies positive family engagement, communication, and emotional support as protective conditions that can ward off disordered eating behavior. On the other hand, a lack of supportive family communication or emotional relationship can amplify isolation and anxiety in adolescents, driving body dissatisfaction and disordered eating. Combining an understanding of these family processes with interventions empowering families to promote healthier emotional environments points toward ways to improve mental health in children and adolescents (Figure 8.9).

Figure 8.9. Family dynamics exert a profound influence on children and adolescents, especially concerning their body image and the development of eating disorders.

Source: https://toledocenter.com/wp-content/uploads/2023/09/SupportiveEnvironment.jpg.

8.4. PHYSICAL HEALTH CONSEQUENCES OF EATING DISORDERS

The effects of eating disorders extend well past psychological distress, manifesting powerfully through physical health-related complications that affect children and adolescents. Eating disorders are often responsible for severe malnutrition, altering fundamental body functions and annihilating homeostasis. Malnutrition, resulting from a lack of required nutrients, can cause complications ranging from cardiovascular dysfunction to weakened immune systems and stunted growth. These adolescents, who are still in such early development stages, can incur irreversible impacts on their general health and welfare. Further, the risk of osteoporosis increases due to chronic caloric restriction and inadequate calcium, providing yet another risk for fracture. The identification of these physical health complications supports the imperative need for interventions that address not only the psychological aspects of eating disorders but also the deleterious physical health consequences that ensue. Another significant impact of eating disorders is the increasing incidence of obesity and linked health complications in this group. Ironically, while some adolescents struggle with restrictive eating patterns, others may opt for compensatory binge eating and thus are more likely to be overweight or obese. The systematic review indicates that childhood obesity, a significant public health issue, is linked to a number of psychological issues such as low self-esteem and emotional distress. While teenagers tend to have body image problems fueled by societal pressures, the cycle of food disorders can lead to obesity and reinforce the solidification of negative physical and mental health outcomes.

This justifies the necessity for integrated interventions focusing on dietary behavior while bearing in mind the underlying causes of body image dissatisfaction among teenagers. This cyclical interaction between eating disorders and obesity thus necessitates targeted interventions to restrict the associated health threats. In addition, physical health effects of eating disorders can manifest in the form of fatal conditions necessitating immediate medical care. Symptoms such as electrolyte disturbances can arise from both anorexic and bulimic behavior and lead to extreme health crises in the form of cardiac arrest. Teenagers suffering from eating disorders are likely to develop bradycardia and hypotension, indicating compromised heart function. Meanwhile, gastrointestinal ailments such as delayed gastric emptying, esophageal perforation, and chronic constipation frequently emerge as a consequence of disrupted eating patterns. The complexity of these medical conditions places important prominence on the necessity of multidisciplinary intervention strategies that involve healthcare professionals, mental health professionals, and nutritionists. Treating eating disorders holistically can help reduce the severe physical health effects undergone by teenagers, eventually fostering healthier lifestyle habits and increasing body image consciousness among youth, as increasingly recognized in efforts designed to promote effective mental health outcomes (Baker et al., 2016; Sabo et al., 2004) (Figure 8.10).

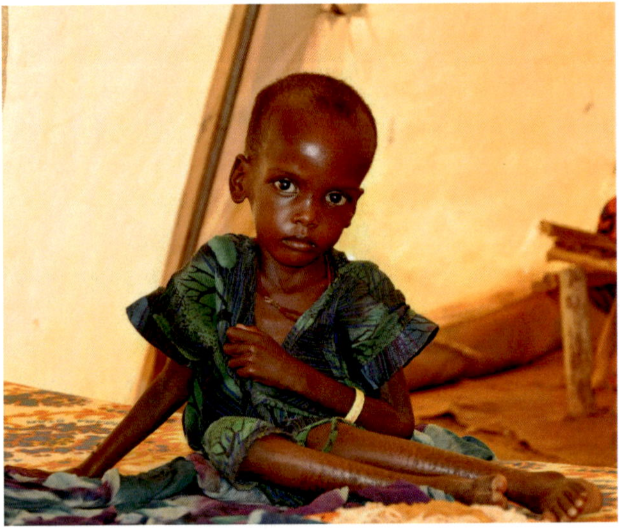

Figure 8.10. Nutritional deficiencies, caused by inadequate intake of vital nutrients, can lead to complications such as cardiovascular problems, weakened immune systems, and slowed growth.

Source: https://upload.wikimedia.org/wikipedia/commons/3/39/A_malnourished_child_in_an_MSF_treatment_tent_in_Dolo_Ado.jpg.

8.4.1. Short-Term Health Effects

Eating disorders immediately and seriously have short-term health effects that crucially impact the body and mind's physiological and psychological health among children and adolescents. For adolescents, the most common disorders, including anorexia nervosa and bulimia nervosa, lead to serious nutritional deprivation based on restriction of food or vomiting. These patterns can have serious immediate medical consequences such as electrolyte disturbances, which in turn are likely to lead to arrhythmias or cardiac arrest, with the implication of urgent intervention. Young patients are particularly vulnerable since their bodies are still in the developing stage; malnourishment, therefore, is likely to distort vital growth mechanisms and may even have long-term consequences if not checked in time. In such cases, medical stabilization is the priority of health professionals, along with treating the root psychological issues of these conditions (Olinder et al., 2022). The psychological impact of eating disorders manifests in several short-term health effects that specifically tend to be high among children and adolescents. As teenagers try to cope with unrealistic images of their bodies, anxiety evokes a nearly crippling high rate of stress and even depression. This emotional distress not only worsens the disorder but also adversely affects social interaction, resulting in isolation from peer groups. The compounding effect of lowered self-esteem can also continue on to reinforce unhealthy dietary habits, perpetuating a vicious circle that is hard to break. Moreover, the chronic preoccupation with weight and shape can create dangerous behaviors such as rigorous exercising or excessive consumption, both of which pose unique health risks that necessitate emergency interventions (Stephen et al., 2021). Education and joint care are necessary in averting the instant health effects of eating disorders in children. Parents and caregivers play an important role by providing an environment where there is open discussion of body image, thus healthy eating habits, and self-esteem. Health practitioners must also practice holistic and culturally responsive education in relation to the signs and symptoms of eating disorders and accept that stigma can hamper treatment. Multimodal interventions involving psychologists, nutritionists, and medical staff are also needed to support nutritional rehabilitation and emotional support. As studies reveal the intricate mechanism of such disorders (Olinder et al., 2022), educational interventions to empower the youth and their families can build strengths against social pressures so that young people navigate their developmental stages healthily and constructively.

8.4.2. Long-Term Health Complications

Serious long-term medical outcomes of child and adolescent eating disorders are extensive and intricate. Eating disorders affect the body's health severely, and they cause serious disorders like cardiovascular illnesses, gastrointestinal issues, and metabolic dysregulation. For instance, individuals with anorexia nervosa tend to develop a decline in heart rate and blood pressure due to malnutrition, which ultimately causes heart failure if not addressed. In addition, bone density effects, especially in those with histories of restrictive eating, may result in osteoporosis later in life, making them more susceptible to fractures. These types of physical health complications are symptoms of a more systemic effect on the body, thus early detection and intervention are important to avoid these severe consequences and maximize the recovery process. Besides the physical health complications, psychological consequences of eating disorders create a cycle that sustains long-term emotional suffering. The relationship between comorbid mental illness and eating disorders is also firmly established, giving rise to a vicious cycle that complicates treatment. Patients with eating disorders often develop lower self-esteem and lower quality of life. In particular, bingeing and the ensuing shame can create a negative feedback loop, extend the disorder and lead to long-term psychological torment. Besides, body image stigma also has the capability to further disconnect individuals from peer support, hence more challenging to reinforce healthy coping and behavior in the long run. The intersection of obesity and eating disorders is also characterized by a unique set of long-term health concerns, particularly in childhood mental health. Childhood obesity has been labeled as an emergent public health issue, and two of the most notable psychological outcomes are: increased risk of eating disorders and the ill effects of weight stigma. Overweight children endure massive pressure in terms of body image that can lead to eating disordered behaviors as a method of coping gone wrong. Long-term health consequences of child obesity include a rising prevalence of metabolic syndrome and type 2 diabetes, potentially laying the groundwork for a pattern of diminishing health which persists into adult life. Comprehension and management of such complex interplay between food consumption, body perception, and mental well-being is imperative, underscoring the need for an overall strategy including physical health and psychological welfare in young people.

8.4.3. Impact on Growth and Development

This bidirectional relationship between eating disorders and body image plays a potent role in the growth and development of adolescents and children and has both short- and long-term consequences. Adolescence is a fast-paced, changing period with accelerated physical and emotional development for which individuals are extremely sensitive to perturbations in body image related to societal norms. Research has shown that viewing idealized media images can lead to internalization of unattainable beauty standards, which may result in increased self-objectification and negative body-related affect (Dakanalis et al., 2014). This is a general process that leads to unhealthy behaviors such as restrained eating and binge eating, not only affecting psychological health but also physical health. As teens struggle with such issues, their development patterns may be hindered and nutritional imbalance and growth stunting due to disordered eating behaviors become pertinent. In addition, some factors, such as medications for co-occurring conditions such as ADHD, make the body image and growth interaction more complicated. For instance, methylphenidate (MPH) has been reported to affect the eating pattern and can contribute to causing disordered eating among children who have ADHD (Akay et al., 2019). It suggests that treatment intervention should be addressed from a holistic perspective while considering that growth can be affected indirectly. In cases where children experience increased concerns about food consumption and body image, their vulnerability to eating disorders is increased, which compromises physical development and emotional strength. Such stringent monitoring of growth parameters along with psychotherapeutic intervention is therefore essential for healthy development in this high-risk group. To treat the impact of eating disorders on growth and development necessitates a multi-disciplinary approach that considers the dynamic interaction of the psychological, social, and physiological processes. Interventions for improving body image need not only to address the person's attitudes and behaviors but also to have educational components that dissect cultural norms surrounding beauty and body ideals. Healthy eating programs and positive body image programs are essential, particularly in environments like school, where teenagers spend a lot of time. In addition, involving families in conversations regarding body image and well-balanced nutrition can help limit the dangers of disordered eating while encouraging growth and development (Dakanalis et al., 2014). Lastly, supporting the culture of self-acceptance and the right lifestyle practices can significantly reduce the prevalence of eating disorders so that adolescents may grow physically and mentally as they experience this period of vital development in their lives (Figure 8.11).

Figure 8.11. Adolescence is a crucial period marked by rapid physical and emotional changes, during which individuals are particularly susceptible to body image disturbances influenced by societal ideals.

Source: https://www.mentalhealth.com/wp-content/uploads/2025/05/adolescent-development.jpeg.

8.5. TREATMENT APPROACHES FOR EATING DISORDERS

Management of eating disorders in children and adolescents needs an overall approach with psychological and physiological management of the disorder. Cognitive Behavioral Therapy (CBT) has been found to be an important therapy in management, emphasizing the need to correct distorted cognition toward the perception of the concept of the body and self-esteem. CBT becomes helpful in the design of coping behaviors in the sense of assisting individuals to cope with their maladaptive procedures. Through a systematic process, the underlying core beliefs that support an eating disorder can be outlined and addressed with patients in conjunction to create healthier thought processes. Further, incorporating family-based treatment becomes critical as family processes are typically implicated in the formation as well as maintenance of such disorders. Family members may be helped by therapists to create supportive environments, thereby enhancing treatment responses in adolescents affected by eating disorders (Till et al., 2011). In addition to cognitive therapies, medical management is essential in addressing the physical health disorders associated with eating disorders. Complete treatment may involve close monitoring in medical facilities, nutrition counseling, and potentially medications for co-occurring psychiatric conditions such as depression and anxiety. The role of nutritionists and dietitians is pivotal; they teach patients the principles of a balanced diet while emphasizing the importance of healthy eating habits as opposed to restrictive behavior. This coordination of healthcare providers ensures an overall response, prioritizing both the physical and mental health of adolescents. As identified in clinical practice, engagement of a multidisciplinary team has a tendency to yield more favorable outcomes, as clinicians can provide treatment-focused interventions that meet the distinct needs and treatment response of each patient (Till et al., 2011). Lastly, ongoing research examining the relational processes used with eating disorders supports intervention practices that consider familial and social contexts. Studies indicate that dysfunctional family relationships exacerbate the emergence and course of such disorders and that interventions must address broader relational factors. Family interventions center on the common role of family members in facilitating recovery through increased intra-familial communication and familiarity. Such an approach, being systemic, resonates with developmental psychopathology models that stress the role played by risk and protective factors for intra-familial relationships. Through the relational understanding of eating disorders, therapists gain the capacity to design treatment that not only heals individuals but also promotes healthier relationships in families with ensuing longer-term advantages (Cerniglia et al., 2020).

8.5.1. Psychological Therapies

Psychological therapies form the core of treating eating disorders (EDs) in adolescents and children, as they are most often intertwined with issues of body image and self-esteem. Cognitive-behavioral therapy (CBT) is known to be an extremely effective type of therapy in modifying distorted thinking and disordered eating behavior. In the majority of cases, the development of a healthy therapeutic alliance—based on trust and collaboration—can strongly influence treatment outcome. Symptomatic improvement in the early stages of treatment has been linked by research to the formation of a robust therapeutic alliance, particularly among younger patients who are more vulnerable to the impact of their illnesses. Establishing a warm setting enhances free communication and interaction, which allows clinicians to tailor interventions more effectively and to increase the potential of positive outcomes in treating EDs (Antoniou et al., 2017). The efficacy of psychotherapies is not only limited to individual therapy but also to family therapies, which promote the inclusion of family members in the recovery process. By addressing family interaction and communication styles, such therapies can help modify behaviors that bring about eating disorders.

Family-oriented treatments mostly lead to the increased participation of parents in the child's recovery process, which results in enhanced communication involving food, body, and emotional well-being. This approach has been promising in reducing conflict and enhancing family functioning, consequently leading to a climate of healing. Moreover, consideration of the psychosocial effects of obesity and eating disordered behavior underscores the importance of multimodal treatment strategies that integrate therapy with nutritional counseling and lifestyle modification. These multistrategy interventions are essential in addressing the complexities of eating disorders (Baker et al., 2016). Despite gains in psychological treatments, challenges remain. The stigmatization of child obesity reinforces psychological suffering and makes it more difficult to treat because children may be teased or bullied, further entrenching their body image issues. Overcoming these social and emotional issues with group therapy or support groups can promote peer relationships and allow for open discussion about shared issues. In addition, it is critical to recognize the comorbidity of obesity and psychiatric conditions like depression and anxiety, which also require simultaneous management with eating disorders. Through the integration of psychological treatments and overall mental health treatments, clinicians are able to develop integrated treatment plans that not only address the symptoms of EDs but also the underlying psychological problems, which perpetuate them (Antoniou et al., 2017) (Figure 8.12).

Figure 8.12. Psychological therapies play a crucial role in addressing eating disorders (EDs) among children and adolescents, as they are often intertwined with issues of body image and self-esteem.

Source: https://familyfirstas.com/wp-content/uploads/2024/09/The-Healing-Link-Between-Body-Image-and-Therapy.jpg.

8.5.2. Nutritional Counseling

Nutritional counseling is also a critical intervention in the treatment of eating disorders and shaping body image beliefs for children and adolescents. Nutritional counseling is a therapeutic process that assists individuals in managing their eating habits and cultivating a healthier relationship with food. The counseling typically begins by conducting a comprehensive assessment of the person's nutritional status, diet, and accompanying psychological issues related to body image. By providing education about balanced nutrition and dispelling myths related to food, practitioners attempt to empower adolescent clients towards smart decision-making. Moreover, creating a relaxed and empathetic environment in nutrition counseling may make an important difference in the treatment process by encouraging teens to ask questions without fear of stigma or judgment. Incorporating nutritional guidance in eating disorder treatment is particularly important, as it combats the physiological as well as psychological components of these disorders. It is well-documented that the interaction between nutrition and mental health is substantial; improper eating habits traditionally exacerbate depression and anxiety feelings in sufferers. Therapists in this field utilize evidence-based methods to help clients overcome negative body image thoughts and acts related to eating disorders. By creating individualized meal plans, which meet both the nutritional needs and individual tastes of adolescents, counselors may bring about constructive changes in their clients' attitudes towards food and body. Responding to these interconnected factors is vital to establishing long-term recovery and preventing relapse. Moreover, it should be ensured that broader social surroundings in which nutritional counseling is being conducted should also be considered. Access to proper mental health care, like food counseling, is hindered by various barriers ranging from economic constraints to cultural stigmatization. As noted, the prevalence of psychological distress is more common than the uptake of clinical help, whereby the majority of teenagers remain unaware of what amenities exist (Benelli et al., 2015). Integrating nutrition counseling with other health care, particularly with primary care, can improve the extent of support offered as it addresses unexpressed psychological requirements. Developing an integrated practice model between mental health professionals and primary care providers will raise the quality of care provided so that nutrition counseling is included in standardized care in the multidisciplinary approach to eating disorders in children and adolescents (Figure 8.13).

Figure 8.13. Nutritional counseling plays a pivotal role in addressing eating disorders and shaping body image perceptions among children and adolescents.

Source: https://susanlandersmd.com/wp-content/uploads/2024/11/image3.jpg.

8.5.3. Medical Interventions

In treating the complexities of eating disorders among children and adolescents, medical treatments have become part of the treatment regimen. Medical treatments would first begin with a complete evaluation by doctors, measuring the patient's physical as well as psychological state. Early medical intervention is crucial because it can forestall the potentially catastrophic health effects of these disorders, including malnourishment, electrolyte imbalance, and heart complications. Further, certain medical procedures may focus on the restoration of physical health at once, typically followed by psychotherapy to address the intrinsic psychological aspects that cause disordered eating patterns. Inclusion of medical recommendations with psychological counseling ensures a multifaceted approach that addresses not only the physical symptoms but also results in better emotional well-being that ultimately leads to long-term recovery. Pharmacologic interventions are also another important part of medical treatment for patients with eating disorders. SSRIs have been found to be useful in managing symptoms of depression and anxiety, which are predominantly associated with eating disorders, particularly in conditions such as bulimia nervosa and binge-eating disorder. While SSRIs do not treat the eating disorder per se, they are able to decrease the accompanying psychopathology so that individuals can function better in psychotherapy. In severe anorexia nervosa, hospital-level medical treatment may be necessary, with medication provided along with nutritional rehabilitation to stabilize the patient medically. The fact that drugs are used signifies the need for multimodal treatment of such disorders to ensure both physiological and psychological aspects are well addressed to achieve optimal recovery outcomes. Moreover, the role of multimodal teams in the medical treatment of eating disorders cannot be properly stressed. Such teams are normally constituted by doctors, psychologists, nutritionists, and other carers who collaborate and formulate individualized treatment plans. Every member in the team contributes their unique expertise to assist in managing the complex interaction of factors driving the eating disorder, e.g., biological, psychological, and sociological. For instance, dietitians might provide personalized nutrition education, while psychologists might focus on cognitive-behavioral approaches to changing distorted body image and self-esteem thinking. This holistic and integrated approach will be required for best handling the multifaceted and diverse nature of eating disorders among children and adolescents, since stigma and mental illnesses complicate recovery and treatment processes further in this population. The imperative need for such cooperative strategies is underlined by the increasing rate of childhood obesity and the accompanying psychological comorbidities, and the imperative of integrated care (Baker et al., 2016).

8.6. ROLE OF PREVENTION AND EDUCATION

In addressing the epidemic of body image disturbance and eating disorders in youths, prevention and education provide a solid foundation. School curricula that promote healthy body image and nutrition education can profoundly influence young people's attitudes toward themselves and their eating behaviors. With school-based programs that create a supportive environment, teachers are in a position to equip students with the necessary skills to challenge cultural ideologies concerning beauty and body shape. Evidence has shown that children exposed to sport and with successful sporting experiences are most likely to have a healthy concept of self and make healthy choices regarding their bodies, thereby reducing the chances of developing eating disorders (Sabo et al., 2004). Such pre-emptive steps not only enable young people but also start a city-wide discussion about the importance of mental well-being, emphasizing prevention in the form of education. Further, inclusion of self-care strategies in the educational curriculum can make prevention even stronger. School programs that teach children and teenagers emotional regulation, stress management, and positive coping skills can directly impact their mental well-being. According to recent studies, self-care support interventions for mental health self-care were found to be moderately effective in improving the mental health outcomes among youth. When youth are educated about self-care practices promoting mental health, they find it easier to deal with the stress that contributes to body dissatisfaction and eating disorders. By encouraging awareness of physical and mental health as part of whole, educational systems can create a healthy approach to well-being, the gateway to healthier living and positive body image for teens. Engaging parents and community in prevention and education also reinforces the healthy body image message. Parents also play a significant role in shaping children's self-esteem and body image through attitudes and behaviors. Educating the families on eating disorder symptoms, encouraging communication, and media representations of body image can establish a robust support group among youth. Furthermore, stakeholder involvement, including health practitioners and community organizations, can ensure that the prevention can be more collaborative and inclusive. As highlighted by recent research, effective self-care support systems in mental health need to be responsive, accessible, and tailored. Through the establishment of a shared platform that integrates prevention and education programs, communities are able to come together and address the eating disorder epidemic as well as promote healthier body image perceptions.

8.6.1. School-Based Programs

School-based interventions are now pivotal strategies aimed at treating eating disorders and body image issues in children and young adolescents. These interventions emphasize the importance of building a healthy setting that promotes positive self-esteem, fosters physical fitness, and fosters general mental health. Schools are the cornerstone of day-to-day existence for adolescents and hence are the ideal site to induce body image and emotional well-being discussions. The implementation of integrative curricula that focus on media literacy, the social norm effects, and fostering resilience can be highly effective in reducing body dissatisfaction among students, particularly during the turbulent period of adolescence.

Figure 8.14. Programs that incorporate physical activity, nutrition education, and mental health support can diminish the prevalence of body dissatisfaction and associated mental health concerns among adolescents.

Source: https://static01.nyt.com/images/2024/04/26/multimedia/00bodybrain-vzjp/00bodybrain-vzjp-videoSixteenByNineJumbo1600.jpg.

With the integration of these issues into the education system, school-based programs can effectively address a diverse range of students with the competencies needed to resist societal pressures on body image as well as eating habits. Research emphasizes the interrelationship between body dissatisfaction and mental health conditions such as depression, and the significant role school interventions play in addressing these issues. Physical activity, nutrition education, and mental health counseling interventions have been shown to decrease the prevalence of body dissatisfaction and accompanying mental health issues among adolescents. For instance, Friedman et al. (2013) highlights the role played by physical activity in attenuating body dissatisfaction and depression across diverse racial groups. Introducing physical activity into schools not only encourages healthier living patterns but also creates a safe and supportive environment that fosters emotional well-being and membership within a community. This multi-dimensional approach is essential in responding to the varied needs of adolescent students and making sure that interventions are tailored to appeal to the particular experience of varied groups of learners. In addition, sensitivity to the effects of media on adolescents' body image awareness is now integral in creating effective school-based programs. Through research, it was discovered that media exposure to idealized body images results in negative self-perception and disordered eating patterns. Courses that educate students on the effects of media and stimulate critical thought regarding beauty standards can be able to counteract such influences. Findings from research, such as those by Dakanalis et al. (2014), shed light on the mechanism through which media ideals enhance self-objectification and the concomitant negative affective states associated with eating disorders. By providing students with the power to critically analyze messages in the media, school-based interventions can encourage a more resilience attitude, allowing young people to avoid negative social pressures and have a healthier body relationship. This organized approach is crucial in supporting adolescents' long-term resilience for mental well-being (Figure 8.14).

8.6.2. Community Awareness Initiatives

Community education initiatives play a vital role in resolving the complex issues of body image and eating disorders in children and teenagers. These programs emphasize public education, developing healthy behavior, and stigmatization reduction of body image-related mental illness. By establishing an atmosphere in which conversation pertaining to nutritional health and self-esteem becomes normal, these programs help immensely reduce eating disorders. For instance, local training workshops led by mental health specialists can guide parents and caregivers in recognizing early signs of body image disturbance among children and thus making appropriate interventions in time. These interventions not only empower the family members but also promote mutual awareness towards the importance of mental health, with subsequent resilience among such concerned youth. The consideration of different perspectives is essential in the conceptualization and deployment of awareness programs for communities. Programs must consider the socioeconomic and cultural aspects of participants for purposes of inclusivity and utility. Research has established that socially disadvantaged racial and ethnic minorities have been exposed to individualized stressors affecting their mental health and body image perception (David, 2018). Programs conceptualized to address these unique experiences can enhance their effectiveness. For example, community campaigns led by influencer and local leader are best positioned to engage more deeply with young people and affirm a sense of belonging and acceptance. Leaning on existing strength in communities, awareness campaigns are successful in facilitating positive discussion regarding body image and eating behaviors, reducing stigma, and provoking help-seeking in young people. Finally, these programs would also need to draw upon partnerships with schools, healthcare providers, and community organizations so as to reach as many people as possible. Schools can incorporate mental health education into their curriculum, providing students with general information on body image and eating disorders. Collaboration with healthcare providers can help to develop materials that inform families about prevention and support systems available in their communities. As has been found by research, the common risk factors and symptomatology across different mental disorders underscore the necessity of comprehensive action in learning and intervention (Caspi et al., 2018). By making effective use of community resources, such programs provide a comprehensive network of support that empowers children and adolescents to learn to develop a positive concept of self and pursue mental well-being.

8.6.3. Parental Involvement and Support

The role of parental influences in the development and maintenance of eating disorders in children and adolescents is critical, given the fact that family contexts are vital factors in self-concept and behavior. Parents can promote a healthy perception of the body and diet through active involvement and interaction with their children. A warm and open communication family climate has been shown to prevent the occurrence of eating disorders. Conversely, studies highlight that dysfunctional family behaviors, such as high conflict or negative body image expectations, tend to increase vulnerabilities in adolescents, leading them to disordered eating habits. The importance of actively engaging teenagers in conversation on their health and self-esteem cannot be overemphasized; it is a protective factor against developing the said disorders and promotes a healthier relationship with food and with the body (Cerniglia et al., 2020). In addition, the inclusion of parental engagement as support in treatment programs makes them more effective. Evidence suggests that working with families in therapeutic treatment enhances the performance of adolescents in treating eating disorders. This is due to the fact that eating disorders are not solely individual concerns but rather manifestations of deeper relational patterns within the family system. Family therapies that embrace working with parents can help treat the underlying emotional and psychological problems associated with these disorders. Through building cooperation dynamics, parents are better positioned to educate children healthier coping mechanisms and attitudes toward body image. Parental participation in the recovery process is thus essential because it facilitates not only healing but also interfamily bonds that provide immunity to subsequent adversity (Sabo et al., 2004). Secondly, parental mentoring subsequently influences youths through role models, eating attitudes, and body image. Parents' attitudes towards physical looks and dieting behavior will usually affect the attitudes and behavior of their children. Caregivers who maintain healthy food relationships and frequent physical exercise will get their children to follow the same. Studies have verified that family attitudes toward exercise and food directly correlate with adolescents' health levels, and this suggests that positive reinforcement can combat the risk of acquiring eating disorders. Therefore, by providing secure support and demonstrating healthy lifestyle practices, parents can significantly alter the trajectory of their children's lives, promoting mental health and well-being. A complete approach like this is critical in the widespread discussion of eating disorders and concern about body image during early development stages (Cerniglia et al., 2020) (Figure 8.15).

Figure 8.15. When parents engage actively with their children, they can foster an environment conducive to healthy body image and nutritional practices.

Source: https://www.unicef.org/ukraine/sites/unicef.org.ukraine/files/styles/hero_extended/public/UN0343212.jpg.webp?itok=f9gj9-qr.

8.7. CONCLUSION

Synthesizing the complex interrelationship among body image, eating disorders, and mental health in youngsters shows that an interdisciplinary approach to prevention and intervention is called for. The far-reaching effect of idealized body representation in the media has enormous implications in internalizing unattainable beauty standards. As exemplified by more recent longitudinal work, the self-reinforcing process of self-objectification and aversive affective states can increase disordered eating behavior in vulnerable teens. The findings underscore the urgency of intervention into cultural ideals glorifying unattainable body ideals as a pressing mandate and demand school-based interventions aimed at dismantling harmful media messages and building resilience against them (Dakanalis et al., 2014). Moreover, peer interactions cannot be disregarded in the influence they exert on perceived body image. Adolescents are likely to find role models among their peers and TV personality figures when it comes to physical appearance. Research indicates that the desire to emulate the characters of reality TV and entertainment television goes together with body dissatisfaction and eating disorder development. Such a relationship suggests that along with focusing on the individual's media exposure, interventions need to involve altering social environments within which teenagers reside. By shaping a positive body image among peer groups and inclusivity, it may be possible to offset the adverse effects of media exposure and enhance mental health among teenagers (Maria et al., 2017). Eventually, the intricacies of eating disorders and body image issues in child and adolescent mental health will need to be addressed by parents, educators, and mental health workers in collaborative efforts. Stakeholders should have the ability to view the interactions among media exposure, peer influence, and psychological processes in shaping young people's perceptions of themselves. Multifaceted approaches through the education of media literacy, counseling focused on body dissatisfaction, and support systems to enhance self-esteem are required. All collaborative efforts toward establishing environments in which diversity and acceptance reign supreme will be a long way toward advancing the well-being of adolescents plagued by such overarching issues. It is through the implementation of such integrative approaches that sustainable change can be achieved in eating disorders and body image (Dakanalis et al., 2014; Maria et al., 2017).

8.7.1. Summary of Key Points

Growing concern over children's and adolescents' eating disorders indicates the need for successful intervention in mental health. Various research has documented the extremely high rates of these disorders, which reflect broader systemic shortcomings in child mental health services. A systematic review of self-care support interventions indicates that even though these programs are fairly effective, there are significant gaps in their availability and responsiveness to youth. Specifically, self-care intervention programs that support flexibility and non-judgmental environments have the capacity to generate healthy mental results. The relationship between the effectiveness of such interventions and their design suggests the necessity of a more child-centered procedure in the ongoing pursuit to provide suitable mental health care to young individuals who are plagued by eating disorders. Apart from therapeutic intervention, intra-family relations play a very crucial role in the study of eating disorders among adolescents. Literature points to the role of family functioning and relationships in the development and sustenance of these disorders. The relational-systemic approach suggests that adolescents would require help not only at the individual level but also in a familial context. Empirical evidence has demonstrated that healthy functioning within the family can serve as protective factors, while dysfunction in the family relationship can be contributory to the facilitation of pathological behaviors. Incorporating these relational factors into treatment protocols allows for the addressing of underlying issues pertaining to eating disorders, ultimately leading to more comprehensive and effective treatment of adolescents (Cerniglia et al., 2020). Moreover, as we explore the complexities of adolescent eating disorders, we must consider the impact of outside forces and body image. Modern culture places an immense burden on adolescents to conform to unrealistic physical expectations, which increasingly plays a role in their self-concept and eating patterns. The interaction of outside expectation with personal wellness—along with inherent mental disorder—poses a negative environment for teens. It is imperative that stakeholders like educators, healthcare providers, and families come together to combat undesirable social norms and promote healthy body image. The collective responsibility is through creating healthy spaces where adolescents are empowered to express their concerns and seek help, thereby facilitating better mental health outcomes and activating resilience to eating disorders.

8.7.2. Importance of Addressing Body Image Issues

The prevalence of body image issues in adolescents is an urgent matter of public health that intersects heavily with mental health outcomes. Body dissatisfaction can be a precursor to numerous psychological disorders, including depression and anxiety, particularly in teenaged girls reporting greater dissatisfaction. Research has established that the body dissatisfaction-depression connection is most pronounced in adolescence, when emotional and social growth is most critical. Given that most adolescent females experience some degree of body dissatisfaction, the need for strong interventions becomes clear. Early prevention of these issues will help reduce the likelihood of serious mental illness, as evidenced by the fact that exercise can be a protective factor. By creating a stronger self-concept and improved physical health, we can create settings that promote healthy growth and allow youth to cope with these concerns more effectively (Friedman et al., 2013). Those interventions to improve body image also need to target the broader sociocultural determinants of discontent. Racial variation in body image views underscores the multidimensional complexities of these issues. Findings suggest that African American girls consistently report lower levels of body discontent compared with White girls, and this suggests that possibly there are resiliency factors in varied cultures. This highlights the necessity for culturally responsive interventions to reach various populations.

Racial and ethnic backgrounds, and how these influence body image perceptions, can be utilized to inform the design of targeted strategies that speak to specific populations. Therefore, comprehensive programs that involve culturally responsive approaches can better address the unique experiences of adolescents and help them become resilient against the pervasive social pressures that create ill effects on body image (Friedman et al., 2013). Moreover, the role of physical exercise as a buffer within the body image-mental health connection cannot be overstressed. Exercise is associated not only with improved physical health but also with improved self-esteem and body satisfaction. As physical activity rates decline during late adolescence, and particularly in the case of adolescent girls, it is essential that participation in sport and recreation is maintained. Increased access to sport and recreational activities can be an early strategy in tackling body image issues. By developing environments that encourage physical activity, we are not only able to enhance mental health outcomes, but we are also able to enhance social relationships and a sense of belonging among youth. For this reason, a holistic approach to body image concerns involving physical, social, and emotional components must be employed within the promotion of overall mental health for this vulnerable population.

8.7.3. Call to Action for Improved Mental Health Support

To reverse the tide of eating disorders and body image issues among children and adolescents, there is a call for action towards increased support for mental health. The existing mental health system only falls below the threshold of properly supporting these vulnerable populations. Evidence reveals a broad disparity in accessibility, response time, and child-centered care in dominant mental health systems (Sabo et al., 2004). Public health experts and educators must combine the prioritization of including holistic services, particularly those aimed at youths in general, on preventing, intervening early, and tailoring the treatment. Not only must there be clinical aid, but there must also be preventive interventions that teach families and communities about the signs and symptoms of eating disorders to provide a stigma-free setting in which the youths would feel comfortable seeking assistance. Moreover, the interagency collaborative effort between schools, healthcare providers, and community agencies can potentially optimize mental health support systems. The significance of universal strategies with the addition of social interaction and physical activity cannot be overstated because the latter two have been linked to improved mental health outcomes in children (Sabo et al., 2004). By creating a supportive environment, families may be empowered to engage actively in children's mental health processes. Offering platforms for discussion of body image and mental health allows for normalizing these problems, leading to earlier detection and intervention. This collaboration must be extended to the youth themselves, their voice leading the development of the services so that care systems are tailored to their actual experiences and demands. Mental healthcare assistance must be reassessed on a regular basis and revised to maintain its effectiveness in our ever-changing social world. The integration of self-care support interventions, as uncovered in current studies, highlights the imperative to equip children and adolescents with coping mechanisms and resilience approaches. This approach not only promotes timely mental health advantages but also supports extended recovery and self-management of mental disease. Stakeholders are called upon to invest in high-quality, evidence-based self-care interventions that are accessible and suitable for youth. By developing these interventions flexible and expandable to accommodate various settings and needs, we can create a solid support system that deals with the underlying issues of eating disorders and body image disturbance, producing healthier results in child and adolescent mental health.

REFERENCES

1. Akay, A. P., & Turan, S. (2019). The effects of stimulants on eating patterns in children and adolescents with attention deficit hyperactivity disorder. https://core.ac.uk/download/232440329.pdf (accessed on 14th October 2025).

2. Antoniou, A., Bachelor, A., Bedics, J. D., Borenstein, J. E., Bourion-Bedes, S., Bravender, T., Brown, T. A., et al. (2017). A meta-analysis of the relation between therapeutic alliance and treatment outcome in eating disorders. https://core.ac.uk/download/323385724.pdf (accessed on 14th October 2025).

3. Baker, J. S., Cobley, S., Han, A., Matthews, D., et al. (2016). Psychological consequences of childhood obesity: Psychiatric comorbidity and prevention. https://core.ac.uk/download/77600894.pdf (accessed on 14th October 2025).

4. Benelli, E., & Bianco, F. (2015). Models of collaboration between psychologist and family doctor: A systematic review of primary care psychology. https://core.ac.uk/download/80154468.pdf (accessed on 14th October 2025).

5. Candler, T., Gregory, J., Murphy, R., Pigott, R., et al. (2017). Fifteen-minute consultation: Diabulimia and disordered eating in childhood diabetes. https://core.ac.uk/download/132207050.pdf (accessed on 14th October 2025).

6. Caspi, A., & Moffitt, T. E. (2018). All for one and one for all: Mental disorders in one dimension. *American Journal of Psychiatry, 175*, 831–844. https://doi.org/10.1176/appi.ajp.2018.17121383 (accessed on 14th October 2025).

7. Cerniglia, L., Erriu, M., & Cimino, S. (2020). The role of family relationships in eating disorders in adolescents: A narrative review. https://core.ac.uk/download/296244843.pdf (accessed on 14th October 2025).

8. Ciobanu, C., Fica, S., Poterasu, M., Rowland, B., et al. (2020). Anorexia nervosa and reproduction: Connecting brain to gonads. https://core.ac.uk/download/304672903.pdf (accessed on 14th October 2025).

9. Cryan, J. F., O'Riordan, K. J., Cowan, C. S. M., Sandhu, K. V., Bastiaanssen, T. F. S., Boehme, M., Codagnone, M. G., et al. (2019). The microbiota-gut-brain axis. *Physiological Reviews, 99*, 1877–2013. https://doi.org/10.1152/physrev.00018.2018 (accessed on 14th October 2025).

10. Dakanalis, A., Dakanalis, A., Dakanalis, A., Dakanalis, A., Dakanalis, A., Dakanalis, A., Field, A. E., et al. (2014). The developmental effects

of media-ideal internalization and self-objectification processes on adolescents' negative body-feelings, dietary restraint, and binge eating. https://core.ac.uk/download/30708901.pdf (accessed on 14th October 2025).

11. Demetrovics, Z., Griffiths, M. D., Koronczai, B., Kun, B., et al. (2013). The mediating effect of self-esteem, depression and anxiety between satisfaction with body appearance and problematic Internet use. https://core.ac.uk/download/30642069.pdf (accessed on 14th October 2025).
12. Faraone, S. V., Banaschewski, T., Coghill, D., Zheng, Y., Biederman, J., Bellgrove, M. A., Newcorn, J. H., et al. (2021). The World Federation of ADHD International Consensus Statement: 208 evidence-based conclusions about the disorder. *Neuroscience & Biobehavioral Reviews, 128*, 789–818. https://doi.org/10.1016/j.neubiorev.2021.01.022 (accessed on 14th October 2025).
13. Friedman, E. (2013). A review of the literature on the effect of physical activity on body dissatisfaction and depressive symptoms in African American and White adolescent girls. https://core.ac.uk/download/12215078.pdf (accessed on 14th October 2025).
14. Gregory, J. W., Cameron, F., Joshi, K., Eiswirth, M. E., Garrett, C., Garvey, K. C., Agarwal, S., et al. (2022). *ISPAD Clinical Practice Consensus Guidelines 2022: Diabetes in adolescence. Pediatric Diabetes, 23*, 857–871. https://doi.org/10.1111/pedi.13408 (accessed on 14th October 2025).
15. Keles, B., McCrae, N., & Grealish, A. (2019). A systematic review: The influence of social media on depression, anxiety and psychological distress in adolescents. *International Journal of Adolescence and Youth, 25*, 79–93. https://doi.org/10.1080/02673843.2019.1590851 (accessed on 14th October 2025).
16. Luna, K. L. (2020). Gendered differences in adolescent body image: Youth agency, protective and risk factors. https://core.ac.uk/download/322958839.pdf (accessed on 14th October 2025).
17. Maria, A., Saliani, A., Baiocco, R., Barcaccia, B., Francesco, F., et al. (2017). Dysfunctional eating behaviors, anxiety and depression in Italian boys and girls: The role of mass media. https://core.ac.uk/download/127586647.pdf (accessed on 14th October 2025).
18. McNamara, N., McNicholas, F., O'Connor, C., O'Hara, L., et al. (2016). Eating disorder literacy and stigmatizing attitudes towards anorexia, bulimia and binge eating disorder among adolescents. https://core.ac.uk/download/30650748.pdf (accessed on 14th October 2025).

19. N/A. (2010). *Wellness Magazine 2010 Issue.* https://core.ac.uk/download/51078251.pdf (accessed on 14th October 2025).
20. Olinder, A. L., DeAbreu, M., Greene, S., Haugstvedt, A., Lange, K., Majaliwa, E., Pais, V., et al. (2022). *ISPAD Clinical Practice Consensus Guidelines 2022: Diabetes education in children and adolescents. Pediatric Diabetes, 23*, 1229–1242. https://doi.org/10.1111/pedi.13418 (accessed on 14th October 2025).
21. Rankin, J., Matthews, L., Cobley, S., Han, A. R., Sanders, R., Wiltshire, H., & Baker, J. S. (2016). Psychological consequences of childhood obesity: Psychiatric comorbidity and prevention. *Adolescent Health, Medicine and Therapeutics, 7*, 125–146. https://doi.org/10.2147/ahmt.s101631 (accessed on 14th October 2025).
22. Sabo, D., Miller, K. E., Heywood, L., & Melnick, M. J. (2004). Her life depends on it: Sport, physical activity and the health and well-being of American girls. https://core.ac.uk/download/71340387.pdf (accessed on 14th October 2025).
23. Till, C. (2011). The quantification of gender: Anorexia nervosa and femininity. https://core.ac.uk/download/29018324.pdf (accessed on 14th October 2025).
24. Williams, D. R. (2018). Stress and the mental health of populations of color: Advancing our understanding of race-related stressors. *Journal of Health and Social Behavior, 59*, 466–485. https://doi.org/10.1177/0022146518814251 (accessed on 14th October 2025).

Chapter 9

Substance Use and Addictive Behaviors

Contents

INTRODUCTION

Over the past several years, there has been a lot of interest in the relationship between substance misuse and addictive behaviors and the mental health of children and adolescents. Children and adolescents are especially susceptible to the psychosocial effects of peers and the risk associated with behavioral experimentation as developmental stages progress. The issue of how drug use might exacerbate already complex vulnerabilities is made more difficult by this group's increasing emotional and social sophistication. Research indicates that these vulnerabilities include factors including temperament, social environments, and family, all of which have a significant impact on the initiation of drug use and addictive behavior. By considering these influences, the researchers are in a position to more effectively assess the multifaceted nature of addiction, particularly in younger populations where interventions may have impacts on long-term mental health outcomes. There exists a substantial volume of literature exploring the relationship between some drugs and the manner in which they impact mental health in youth. For example, the popularity of video gaming among youths has been attributed to social interaction and possible addictive behaviors, especially in multiplayer online spaces. Allahverdipour et al. (2014) points out that problem gaming is associated with depressive moods, loneliness, social anxiety, and academic underperformance, further complicating the mental health profile for those concerned. In addition, there is also an alarming link between substance use—such as nicotine, alcohol, and cannabis—and unhealthy gaming practices among boys. This highlights the importance of dealing with issues of mental health in an integrated way through the incorporation of substance use, gaming practices, and psychosocial effects so that the risks can be handled and curbed effectively. Additionally, the psychosocial effects of substance use extend beyond the risk of addictions to more advanced issues of victimization and trauma. Research has confirmed that marginalized groups like sexual minority women exhibit notably higher rates of lifetime victimization, which is further linked to the harmful pattern of drinking. Drabble et al. (2013) emphasizes that even controlling for demographic variables, sexual minority populations have elevated risk for harmful drinking, indicating a grim interaction between trauma, substance use, and mental health. It is necessary to view these connections in order to develop targeted interventions that account not only for substance use per se, but also victimization histories and underlying mental health issues. As we move forward with this subject, it becomes apparent that grasping these interconnected themes as a comprehensive entity is utterly crucial to informing effective strategies for promoting resilience and healthy adaptation in youth.

Definition of Substance Use and Addictive Behaviors

Substance use is the consumption of psychoactive substances, such as alcohol, nicotine, marijuana, and other illegal drugs. It is not uniform; it varies in terms of frequency, dose, and context of use. In teenagers, substance use can either be in the context of experimentation, which is relatively harmless, or on its way to abuse patterns of loss of control, craving, and impaired functioning. The separation between problematic use and recreational use is most critical, especially among adolescents, because the teenage brain keeps developing, yielding greater vulnerability to addiction. According to new studies, certain forms of substance use have adverse effects on numerous areas of mental health, hence establishing a direct connection between adolescent drug use and issues such as depression and anxiety. Addictive behavior goes beyond traditional substance use, such as behaviors that cause a compulsive action despite negative consequences. Some of these behavior addictions are gambling and unhealthy gaming, both of which have been emphasized in newer studies. For instance, a study on pathological adolescent gaming indicated that teens playing multiplayer games online more often experienced heightened depressive moods, loneliness, and social anxiety compared to those reported by substance use disorders (Allahverdipour et al., 2014).

Figure 9.1. Among adolescents, substance use can manifest in experimentation, which may be relatively benign, or develop into patterns of abuse characterized by a loss of control, craving, and impaired functioning.

Source: https://wellbrookrecovery.com/wp-content/uploads/2025/03/teen-drug-use-1280x724.jpg.

The reward-reinforcement cycle common in substance use as well as addictive disorders demonstrates high similarity of their neurobiological correlates. Identification of these dynamic interplays is important for identifying the most beneficial interventions, since apparently disparate behavior may have concurrent pathways to dysfunctional consequences in adolescent mental health. Difficulty in operationalizing addictive behavior mirrors the conundrum of clinicians and researchers. As the evolution of the field continues, conflict among researchers regarding the definition of Internet addiction (IA) exemplifies these challenges (Griffiths et al., 2015). The broad variation in behavioral addictions complicates attempts to define and identify effective treatment approaches and prevention strategies. Research indicates that IA prevalence can be very discrepant across populations and reflects methodological inconsistencies obscuring our knowledge regarding addiction within a world of digital technology. Since both chemical use and addictive behavior have a tendency to co-occur, mental health responses that are multidisciplinary and integrative are called for. The implications of treatment must address the interplay among these behaviors and reaffirm the need for combined methods aimed at both substance use and behavioral addiction in effort to enhance better adolescent mental health outcomes (Figure 9.1).

Importance of Addressing Mental Health in Children and Adolescents

The increasing incidences of mental disorder among adolescents and young people are in urgent need of focus, particularly considering the fact that these disorders have a direct influence on behavioral outcomes, like the consumption of alcohol and drugs. Anxiety and depression, which are prevalent psychiatric disorders, are likely to arise during these stages of development, thus forming an important connection between psychological well-being and future behavior. Adolescents who have mental disorders tend to use substance as an inappropriate coping mechanism for their conditions. The understanding of this relationship enables provision of timely interventions, a necessity in preventing the onset of inappropriate behaviors. In light of the fact that mental health issues in adolescents are typically underdiagnosed, early intervention will eradicate long-term consequences, foster the establishment of better trajectories and avoid impending substance problems. Additionally, the role of protective environments in guaranteeing mental health for children and adolescents cannot be overestimated. School, family, and community are significant buffers for protection against mental health adversity and can impact coping and resilience. Effective support systems can buffer against risk factors in substance use by providing appropriate emotional support and interventions. Strategies in support of openness regarding mental health in these environments can significantly reduce stigma, which can encourage early seeking of help. Continued engagement of educators and caregivers can provide an oversight mechanism for mental well-being, identifying risk behaviors and influencing positive outcomes. Integration of mental health education and community action can play a major role in deterring youth from drug use, fostering psychologically healthy lifestyles among youth. Cultural influences also significantly define the mental health context of youth and drug-use probability. It is critical to recognize the diverse backgrounds of youth to better address their mental health concerns. Different cultures have unique values, traditions, and beliefs with regard to mental health, which then have implications for help-seeking and treatment adherence. Culturally responsive interventions broaden access and enhance the effectiveness of prevention efforts. For instance, Cook et al. (2017) emphasizes the need for strengths-based practice that incorporates cultural sensitivity to evaluations and interventions as a way to empower youth and families. Furthermore, Sudhinaraset et al. (2016) elucidates how social settings, including peer culture and family dynamics, shape substance uses behaviors. Identifying these subtleties can enable more effective development of integrated mental health interventions that better engage children and youth, ultimately decreasing substance use and improving outcomes (Figure 9.2).

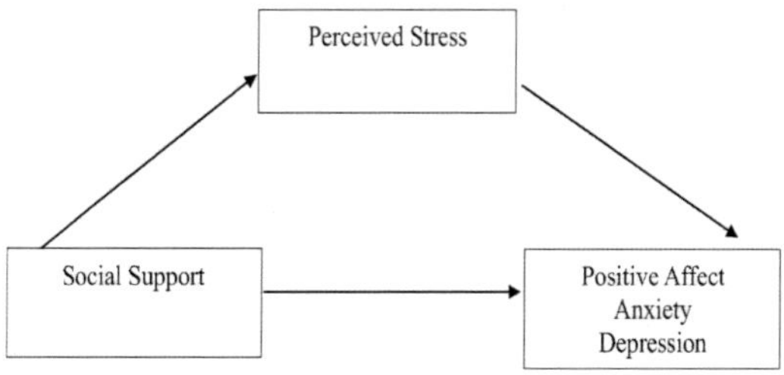

Figure 9.2. Effective support systems can ameliorate risk factors associated with substance use by providing appropriate emotional support and resources.

Source: https://www.frontiersin.org/files/Articles/1330720/fpsyg-15-1330720-HTML/image_m/fpsyg-15-1330720-g001.jpg.

9.1. PREVALENCE OF SUBSTANCE USE IN YOUTH

Substance use among youth has emerged as a significant concern in child and adolescent psychiatry. Data show that adolescents are increasingly becoming exposed to a variety of substances including alcohol, tobacco, and illicit drugs. This is compounded by a variety of factors from peer pressure to accessibility and an evolving social setting fueled by digital communication. As evidenced by a recent scoping review, social media also influence substance use behavior, where social media platforms like Instagram and TikTok have the potential to glamorize and promote the use of substances among youth (Bozzola et al., 2022). This mutually influential dynamic between social media and substance use not only emphasizes the need for targeted preventative interventions but also challenges the long-term implication for adolescents' mental health as they partake in these online spaces. In addition to this, the COVID-19 pandemic has further driven the prevalence of substance use among youth, with use of digital media growing exponentially in periods of physical distancing. The majority of adolescents employed digital sites for their socialization, hence more exposure to risk behaviors like drug use. There was a positive relationship between digital media use and mental health problems among adolescents at the time, as shown by a systematic review that suggested increased screen time could have assisted in propelling an increase in feelings of loneliness and stress (Marciano et al., 2022). This growth in ill-being, as defined in the study, could potentially drive adolescents to consume substances as an unhealthy coping mechanism. Hence, it is crucial to evaluate and recognize the mental health outcomes of increased digital consumption so that comprehensive prevention strategies aimed at substance use can be formulated. The effects of adolescent substance use are broad, with initiation at a young age potentially leading to a range of adverse outcomes, such as substance use disorders and other mental health problems. Public health interventions have begun to focus on the development of evidence-based interventions addressing both substance use and consumption of digital media. It is essential to involve parents, educators, and healthcare workers to build an environment that supports the making of healthy choices. As the findings of the scoping review have so unequivocally shown, there is a pressing need for social media risk education, that is, it is connection to such behavior as use of substances (Bozzola et al., 2022). Through sensitization and exposure to information, stakeholders can better equip young people against such challenges, consequently contributing to better mental health outcomes for this at-risk population.

9.1.1. Statistics on Substance Use Among Children and Adolescents

Substance use among adolescents and children has emerged as a significant public health concern, illustrative of the necessity for intervention strategies in mental health. Studies show that prevalence rates of substance use among this population are overwhelming, typically accounting for multiple psychosocial issues. For instance, evidence suggests that adolescent video gamers with problematic gaming behavior have increased tendencies towards alcohol, nicotine, and cannabis substance use. Particularly, high-risk gamers are almost twice as probable to report drug use compared to their non-gaming peers. These results point towards the relationship between gaming activities and drug use, calling for an integrated strategy to counteract both gaming habits and drug abuse in preventive mental health interventions (Allahverdipour et al., 2014). Besides, social influence also plays an important role in substance use habits among youth. It is discovered by research that peer and family influence play an important role in affecting children's and adolescents' choices regarding the use of substances. In opioid dependence research, teen age, socioeconomic status, family relationship, and coping mechanism are found to be important predictors of substance use in opioid dependence studies. High rates of correlation in such behaviors as smoking and bad education are in accordance with high rates of opioid dependence. Interestingly, the study has shown that educational interventions in problem-solving and coping skills have the potential to decrease the risk for substance abuse among adolescents (Behnampour et al., 2015). Thus, it is important that prevention programs address the complicated social environment in which substance use occurs. In short, statistical data concerning substance use among children and adolescents is useful to explain sophisticated interrelations between various risk factors, including gaming pattern, social environment, and individual coping mechanisms. With mental health professionals seeking to formulate good intervention strategies, in-depth familiarity with the statistics is required. The co-occurring impact of substance uses and addictive behaviors on mental health necessitates specially constructed interventions that not only address the use of substances but also consider psychosocial challenges. An integrated approach can enhance protective factors and ultimately reduce the incidence of substance use issues among youth, paving the way for more favorable developmental trajectories (Allahverdipour et al., 2014; Behnampour et al., 2015).

9.1.2. Trends in Substance Use Over the Past Decade

Over the past decade, substance use trends among teenagers and children have also experienced tremendous shifts by a myriad of social, economic, and environmental determinants. There has been a reported fluctuation in the use rates for most substances, including alcohol, cannabis, and opioids. The shifts can be partly attributed to shifting attitudes towards the use of substances and rising popularity of certain drugs, particularly cannabis, for medical and recreational purposes. These changes in culture will also overlap with mental health, as more use has been linked to more emotional problems in young people. Most significantly, the rise of digital media has also had an influence on how young people use substances, intensifying feelings of loneliness or stress that led to more use. The identification of these trends is at the heart of the development of successful interventions for therapy and public health addressing improvement of mental well-being among youthful populations. Furthermore, research confirms that the intricacies of family life, socioeconomic status, and peer relationships are primary determinants of substance use behaviors among adolescents. Increased family poverty and parental emotional issues have been linked with increased levels of drug use, which suggests that environmental factors highly affect youth behavior. Moreover, the relationship between school-induced stress and drug use cannot be understated, since school pressures tend to compel adolescents towards mechanisms of coping in the form of drinking and drug use. As argued in recent analyses, such trends do not only indicate a troubling trend towards mental health among youth but also illuminate a potential avenue for mental illness to form among young individuals. The compound effects of all these various factors highlight the urgent need for further research into the causality between social dynamics and trends in adolescent substance use, as suggested by evidence from existing epidemiological studies (Armitage et al., 2024; Verhulst, 2015). Finally, following substance use trends over the past 10 years is essential to understanding the evolving state of child and adolescent mental health. While some of the reports show some progress in areas such as less cigarette smoking, increased use of drugs such as marijuana creates new challenges. Various studies speak of the dualism between increasing rates of emotional issues and the complex interplay of drug use behaviors among various groups. Adolescents in the current era have to operate within a complex environment influenced by social media, shifting family dynamics, and economic challenges that can simultaneously encourage resilience and risk-taking behaviors. The need for holistic, evidence-based strategies for understanding such trends is, therefore, essential, as public health efforts have to address the twin challenges of increasing substance use and deteriorating mental health outcomes. Further studies need to concentrate on the collection and analysis of longitudinal data representing those evolving trends, yielding helpful information for practitioners and policymakers (Armitage et al., 2024; Verhulst, 2015) (Figure 9.3).

Figure 9.3. Increased parental emotional problems and family poverty have been correlated with heightened levels of substance use, indicating that contextual factors deeply influence youth behaviors.

*Source:*https://www.unicef.org/eca/sites/unicef.org.eca/files/styles/hero_extended/public/UNI485566.JPG.webp?itok=PZrZ4OHz.

9.1.3. Demographic Factors Influencing Substance Use Rates

Demographic issues are the key determinant of levels of substance use among children. Studies indicate that age, sex, and economic differences can significantly influence prevalence and trend in substance use. That is, for instance, statistically, boys are likely to be engaged in more substance use behavior than girls, particularly under the cover of such activities like gaming, which are likely to precede or accompany substance abuse.

One study found that boys identified as problematic gamers are more likely to use cannabis, alcohol, and nicotine, which is an important site of intersection between gaming activities and substance use. In addition, lower socioeconomic status youth may experience more stressors leading to greater substance use as a maladaptive coping mechanism, so emphasizing the importance of addressing socioeconomic disparities in prevention and intervention programs for substance use (Allahverdipour et al., 2014).

Beyond gender and socioeconomic status, cultural issues also muddy the adolescent substance use picture. Different cultural beliefs and values can shape attitudes towards drug use, potentially leading to varying prevalence rates across populations. For example, drug use could be more accepted or even required in a given context in some cultures while being prohibited in others. The implications are significant, as cultural beliefs have the potential to influence not only the likelihood of drug use but also the effectiveness of prevention initiatives and intervention strategies. Understanding these aspects of culture is valuable in modifying approaches that address specified demographic groups, ultimately resulting in better outcomes in preventing substance abuse among adolescents (Billieux et al., 2018).

Also of interest is the influence of technology and social media on substance use, as such factors are deeply intertwined with demographic realities. Adolescents are particularly influenced by peer norms that filter through online media and can potentially decrease, or augment substance use behavior. Internet gaming, which is now becoming widely popular, is a two-edged sword; though it can foster community and socialization, it also can cause addictive gameplay and secondary drug use. As has been noted in recent studies, pathological gaming is much stronger in boys, who may coexist with higher levels of depressive mood and poor psychosocial functioning in addition to their drug use (Allahverdipour et al., 2014).

Such cross-linked relationships necessitate more integrated strategies that consider the multilateral effects of demographic characteristics on drug use as well as mental health consequences.

9.2. RISK FACTORS FOR SUBSTANCE USE AND ADDICTIVE BEHAVIORS

Determining the risk factors of substance use and addictive habits in children and adolescents is most crucial when prevention interventions need to be applied. Research shows that biological, psychological, and sociological factors contribute to predisposing children to these risky behaviors. For instance, adolescents who have been exposed to parental substance abuse or psychiatric illness are likely to engage in substance use themselves. Moreover, social forces outside of the family such as peer pressure and normalization of drug use in their social environment significantly enhance the risk. Parental involvement and supervision are critical protective factors; children in well-supported home environments are less likely to experiment with drugs or alcohol. Thus, involving the challenging influence of family and social dynamics can provide the foundation for overall prevention and intervention in teen drug and alcohol abuse (Richter, 2020). The COVID-19 pandemic has presented novel risk factors that have further added to the complexity of youth substance use. The crisis has resulted in enhanced isolation, broken family lives, and limited access to supportive community resources, elements known to be significant contributors to mental health issues. In light of schools being closed down and social activity being curtailed, several youths experienced intensified stress and uncertainty. Drug use will be resorted to by vulnerable youth as a way of coping with such emotional challenges in spite of some pandemic features, such as increased parental supervision as a consequence of home confinement, reducing short-term prospects for drug access (Richter, 2020). It is nevertheless necessary to quantify the long-term impacts of the pandemic on youth drug consumption because these experiences will necessarily shape future behavior and vulnerability trends. Co-occurring mental illnesses frequently complicate risk factors for substance use in adolescents. Dual pathology, that is, the presence of both substance disorders and mental illness, presents challenging treatment and intervention issues. Adolescents with dual pathology tend to present more severe psychosocial disturbances and have poorer prognoses than adolescents with substance-induced disorders only. Research has shown that intervention early in life, for example, integrated care that addresses both mental illness and drug use, is crucial to avert the risks of these co-occurring disorders. Recognition of the temporal interaction between the onset of symptoms of mental illness and substance use is essential to make accurate diagnoses and set proper treatment strategies. Through the establishment of awareness and prevention strategies through education systems and healthcare systems, stakeholders can better support high-risk youth and encourage healthier developmental trajectories (Figure 9.4).

Figure 9.4. Adolescents exposed to familial substance misuse or mental health issues are more likely to engage in substance use themselves.

Source: https://bhoperehab.com/wp-content/uploads/2022/07/substance-abuse-families-scaled.jpeg.

9.2.1. Genetic Predisposition and Family History

Genetic predisposition and family history are important in the context of discussing substance use and addictive behaviors among children and adolescents. Genetic factors have been found to significantly contribute to determining individuals' likelihood of developing substance use disorders. A number of studies have found that estimates of heritability for addiction-related traits may explain 40% to 60%, and this highlights a significant correlation between genetic makeup and susceptibility to addiction. This genetic blueprint, when coupled with outside factors such as family dynamics and socioeconomic status, creates a complex portrait of risk. Family history is also significant, in that kids with family members who have issues with drug use are often at higher risk. This intergenerational transmission of risk factors forces mental health professionals to consider family patterns of behavior when assessing an adolescent's potential vulnerabilities and strengths for substance use (Cook et al., 2017). Examining the family environment also explains some of the complexities surrounding youth substance use. Adolescents and children brought up in families with a history of addiction may be at higher levels of exposure to maladaptive coping mechanisms, as well as reduced parental monitoring. These environmental aspects are also capable of amplifying genetic vulnerabilities, shaping one's relationship with drugs. For example, normalization of drug use within the family can cause young people to view such behavior within the norms of acceptable behavior, thus increasing the likelihood of experimentation. Additionally, the absence of protective factors, i.e., supportive parental influence and healthy role models, can also amplify genetic vulnerabilities. Consequently, it is important to identify the interaction of family factors and inherited risk to devise targeted interventions that mitigate the impact of substance use disorders among adolescents (Drabble et al., 2013). Effective intervention methods should not just be aimed at eliminating environmental and genetic effects but also promote resilience among at-risk youth. A strengths-based continuum model would enable clinicians to pinpoint specific risk and protective factors inherent within an individual's family history and allow for individualized treatment plans. This method promotes a full appreciation of the young person's context, allowing mental health professionals to create interventions that build on familial strengths while responding to vulnerabilities associated with addiction. By integrating genetic susceptibility and family dynamics into models of treatment, clinicians are in a better position to treat adolescents with more comprehensive support for substance use disorders. It can also enhance adolescent and family engagement, ultimately promoting a stakeholder-model of intervention focused on reducing stigma and enhancing healthier coping mechanisms (Cook et al., 2017) (Figure 9.5).

Figure 9.5. Family history plays a pivotal role, as children with relatives who struggle with substance use are often at an elevated risk.

Source: https://www.getsmartaboutdrugs.gov/sites/default/files/styles/large_teaser/public/2023-03/Depressed%20Teen.jpeg?h=4ca9cb25&itok=8owRm_uI.

9.2.2. Environmental Influences, Including Peer Pressure

Environmental influences play a crucial part in the etiology of drug use and addictive behavior among youth and adolescents. Peer pressure, among many, is particularly critical in adolescence, a phase characterized by enhanced concern about belonging and social acceptance. Adolescents are typically motivated to model their peers' behavior, including at times drug and alcohol experimentation. Research has shown that peers can have a critical influence on whether an adolescent will or will not use substances, and thus the need for wholesome peer groups that promote wise decisions. If adolescents perceive that drug use is the norm amongst their peers, pressure to conform may result in more experimentation and consequently higher risks of acquiring addictive behaviors, as exemplified by the influence of healthy peer relationships on the outcome of mental health (Shaja et al., 2021). The social environment, particularly the family and school environments, further interacts with peer influences. Parenting and school belongingness have been proven to contribute a lot to the development of a young individual's susceptibility to peer pressure and drug use. Adolescents who are offered warm and responsive parenting and are attached to their schools tend to enjoy good mental health statuses. These protective factors might serve as a buffer to counteract the ill effects of peer pressure. Conversely, authoritarian childrearing methods tend to have the function of rebellion or peer-approval seeking that facilitates drug use, which is likely to augment the risk of negative health consequences. Research indicates adolescents who perceive high school connectedness in themselves are less likely to engage in risk behaviors such as drug use, highlighting the importance of supportive settings (Crano et al., 2020). Moreover, the broader socio-cultural environment has a significant part to play in shaping adolescent attitudes towards drug and alcohol use. Peer pressure can be augmented by cultural norms and values that glorify drug and alcohol use, generating normalized attitudes towards such behaviors among young people. Popular culture representations of drug and alcohol use encourage the belief that drug and alcohol use is essential for social belonging and popularity. Therefore, teens are able to internalize such messages and can feel compelled to indulge in substance-use behaviors for social approval. Such crossroads of cultural pressures, peer pressure, and individual influences necessitate multi-modal interventions. Interventions aimed at building resilience and healthy habits must consider not only individual decision-making but also the environmental contexts that inform such behavior and thus offer a multi-modal path towards enhancing teen mental health (Shaja et al., 2021).

9.2.3. Psychological Factors, Such as Trauma and Mental Health Disorders

Psychological problems such as trauma and mental illness are the leading causes of the development of substance use disorders (SUDs) in children and adolescents. The study highlights that interpersonal trauma during early childhood increases susceptibility to adult drug-related issues. Traumatic events during early childhood are likely to disrupt proper attachments and harm emotional regulation. For instance, mothers with a history of substance use recovery frequently speak about how their own experiences of childhood trauma shape their parenting, suggesting a cycle of trauma that can extend SUDs over generations (Pauw et al., 2019). The narratives illustrate that attachment styles interrupted by childhood adversities can lead to maladaptive coping mechanisms, such as addiction, thus illustrating the intricate dynamic between psychological distress and addiction. Aggressive interventions depend on an emphasis on trauma-informed practices that not only correct present behavior disorders but also explore underlying historical psychological determinants. Gender plays an important role in how psychological components express themselves through adolescent substance use behaviors. Research indicates that both males and females are affected by trauma, although the consequences may be significantly different for each gender and influence their susceptibility to addiction. For example, females present with more psychological distress and more maltreatment and abuse experiences, and these can lead to increased rates of substance use as well as rapid development towards dependence (Simonelli et al., 2017).

Figure 9.6. Psychological factors such as trauma and mental health disorders significantly contribute to the development of substance use disorders (SUDs) in children and adolescents.

Source: https://i0.wp.com/post.healthline.com/wp-content/uploads/2022/05/hugging-siblings-staircase-1296x728-header.jpg?w=1155&h=1528.

9.3. IMPACT OF SUBSTANCE USE ON MENTAL HEALTH

The interaction between substance uses and mental health in children and adolescents is being viewed more and more as a complicated issue, in which one influences the other. The use of substances at early ages complicates any prevailing mental health issue and forms a cycle of addiction and deteriorating psychological health. For instance, adolescents who consume drugs are most likely to develop anxiety and mood disorders because these drugs have the tendency to heighten feelings of loneliness or depression. This correlation can readily be observed in pathological gaming, where adolescents who consume drugs such as alcohol, nicotine, or cannabis are most likely to experience negative mental health outcomes such as social phobia and poor self-esteem. The findings' implications reflect the need for comprehensive strategies to address both mental illness and substance abuse in an integrated response. Certain forms of substance abuse can also serve as maladaptive coping mechanisms for youth who are mentally ill. Research suggests that youth with previously established emotional and behavioral problems are more likely to use substances as a means of coping with psychological distress. Specifically, patients with mental illnesses such as depression or anxiety may seek solace in alcohol or nicotine to self-medicate and find themselves with a dangerous interplay between mental decline and addiction. The occurrence is aided by evidence that reveals more mentally ill teenagers consume tobacco, alcohol, and other drugs than their healthy peers. Such self-treatment practices can impede proper functionality and establish a situation in which mental health keeps deteriorating, necessitating specialized intervention programs targeting both substance use and mental welfare. The crucial intersection of substance abuse and psychological damage among adolescents necessitates widespread interest from medical professionals, educators, and politicians. Not only are adolescents exposed to significant risk factors of drug use, such as peer pressure and access, but those that are also experiencing mental health problems have additional vulnerabilities. For instance, in looking at adolescents that play multiplayer video games, there is evidence of an association between high problematic gaming and lower psychosocial functioning, with increased rates of drug use reported among this group. The co-occurring etiology of these issues highlights the necessity of multi-faceted treatment models that include prevention of substance abuse and mental health education. Active responses like school-based interventions and community support services are hence essential in fighting this multi-faceted issue, ensuring that adolescents receive comprehensive care for them to thrive.

9.3.1. Short-Term Effects on Cognitive and Emotional Functioning

The studies on short-term effects of drug use on cognitive and emotional functioning in children and adolescents give important data regarding their developmental trajectories. These drugs, including alcohol, marijuana, and stimulants, can negatively influence cognitive processes, such as attention, memory, and executive function. For instance, alcohol-using teens may have severe deficits in information processing and concentration, which can influence school performance and learning. Furthermore, the teen brain is particularly vulnerable; because brain functions are in the process of emerging, use of substances has the ability to impair acute performance in a way that does not happen in mature individuals. The impairment can persist even after acute effects have resolved, suggesting the risk of permanent damage, and one that is especially concerning during periods of peak development. Emotional functioning is also disrupted in youth substance abusers.

Figure 9.7. Substances such as alcohol, marijuana, and stimulants can impair cognitive processes, including attention, memory, and executive functioning.

Source: https://www.apa.org/images/2023-06-cannabis-lead-tile_tcm7-317758.jpg.

Research indicates that drugs are known to heighten mood disorders or cause depressive and anxious moods, particularly among vulnerable populations. Adolescents might begin substance use as a coping mechanism or to enhance social experiences, but such use in the short term causes emotional dysregulation in terms of increased irritability or mood swings. The interaction between emotional distress and substance use can build a cycle of violence, where greater substance use exacerbates underling emotional issues, leading to further use of substances as an escape. The danger that such emotional consequences undermine interpersonal relations and schooling cannot be overestimated. This underscores a critical treatment area that requires a complete understanding of the emotional consequence in addition to cognitive deficits. Furthermore, the relationship between addictive behavior and drug use among adolescents should not overlook the new issue of Internet addiction (IA).

As adolescents increasingly rely on digital media, the cognitive and emotional implications of IA come into sharp focus. The acute and short-term effects of IA may mirror those of traditional substance use, where attentional impairments and affective problems become prominent. For instance, IA has been associated with reduced cognitive flexibility and increased anxiety, potentially leading to resistance to face-to-face social contact. The co-occurrence of IA and substance addictions highlights the pressing need for multidisciplinary interventions in prevention and treatment. Mental health professionals and policy makers must note these complicated interdependencies in efforts to form fruitful frameworks that describe cognitive as well as emotional operations within shifting digital realities and drug consumption (Griffiths et al., 2015; Pustilnik et al., 2015) (Figure 9.7).

9.3.2. Long-Term Consequences for Mental Health Development

The long-term effects of adolescent and childhood substance use, and addiction are likely to have a significant impact on mental health development. Adolescence is the peak time for psychological development when core skills of self-regulation and emotional management are developed. It is also noted that studies suggest that adolescents with low self-control are more prone to risky behavior, including alcohol and drug use. These behavior patterns thus exacerbate symptoms of depression and anxiety, creating a vicious cycle of growth and recovery that is difficult to achieve. The value of self-control as a countermeasure to addictive behavior thus highlights the necessity for early intervention that instills emotional resilience in youths. Preventive action in this sense can mitigate the risk of psychiatric illnesses in adulthood, ultimately resulting in healthier adult populations. In addition, the influence of drug use on adolescents' mental health comes into play in terms of legal responsibility and autonomy. Current legal frameworks do not succeed in addressing the particular stage of adolescent development, ascribing adult responsibility while not considering their diminished decision-making capacity. Inconsistency may present inappropriate legal consequences for youths engaging in behavior driven by addiction. With increasing evidence from developmental neuroscience regarding how adolescents process information and think differently from adults, there is a critical need to connect legal norms with empirical understanding of adolescent development. Developing environments that acknowledge these differences has the potential to support healthier decision-making, reducing the prevalence of substance abuse and its associated mental health issues. Finally, substance use has consequences beyond individual mental health, extending to broader social dynamics and community health. Substance-using teenagers isolate their social interactions, rendering them alienated and further enhanced in their states of mental health. These behaviors not only interfere with personal relationships but also do not access support systems that are crucial to recovery and development. Such isolation can actually increase feelings of hopelessness and exacerbate existing mental health problems, leading to a cycle of addiction and emotional distress. These issues are only to be met with long-term community-based initiatives that bring about social bonding, emotional intelligence, and autonomy in a well-organized environment, ultimately paving the way for better generations down the road.

9.3.3. Co-Occurring Disorders and their Implications

The issue of co-occurring disorders, where individuals present with substance use as well as mental health challenges simultaneously, is a challenging problem in the world of child and adolescent mental health. Adolescents are especially vulnerable as a result of the development changes that occur in them, which tend to intensify psychiatric symptoms as well as substance use behavior. The co-morbidity of these disorders also renders treatment more difficult as the teenagers present with co-occurring symptoms that mask or mimic one another. This level of complexity necessitates a comprehensive strategy of assessment and intervention that takes into consideration the particular developmental, social, and environmental variables influencing the youth. Further, co-occurring disorders commonly interfere with adolescents functioning, causing school issues, social isolation, and increased risk of delinquency, calling for effective treatment modalities addressing both sides of their mental health at the same time. Research finds that integrating mental health and substance abuse treatment is able to enhance adolescents' treatment outcomes with these associated issues. Effective treatment is based on an understanding of the dynamics of each disorder and how they can affect each other. Evidence-based practice, such as the research-practice integration (RPI) model, shows the importance of collaboration between clinicians, researchers, and treatment programs to develop interventions tailored to adolescents' needs. It emphasizes the advantages of real clinical application of study findings toward enhancing the quality of care. For instance, in a managed health care plan, findings from research have been used to inform adolescent health services, which then inform effective interventions for individuals suffering from co-occurring disorders (Sterling et al., 2006). An integrative emphasis of this sort is essential to responding to the unprecedented challenge presented by these conditions converging. Moreover, the impact of untreated co-occurring disorders extends far beyond personal health, affecting societal outcomes. Statistical evidence reveals a disconcerting rate of adolescents entering the drug court system with co-occurring mental illness, which ultimately leads to incarceration and school issues (Oliveira et al., 2015). For example, screening tests at court clinic mental health clinics reveal that substance use disorders correlate with an increased likelihood of being immediately incarcerated after mental health assessment. This relates to the contention that co-occurring disorders not only hinder individual flourishing but also contribute to systemic issues in the juvenile justice system. Tracking the interaction between these disorders through focused interventions and policy action helps reduce their impact and enables healthier outcomes among engaged youth, with beneficial dividends for the community at large (Figure 9.8).

Figure 9.8. Adolescents are particularly vulnerable due to the developmental changes they encounter, which can exacerbate both psychiatric symptoms and substance use behaviors.

Source: https://www.news-medical.net/images/news/ImageForNews_779364_17152150118702242.jpg.

9.4. PREVENTION STRATEGIES

Effective prevention programs are an important tool in preventing substance use and addictive behavior among children and adolescents. These programs typically consist of extensive education programs with the aim of developing coping skills and problem-solving skills. For instance, research indicates that education programs aimed at increasing the capacity of young people to handle social pressures can effectively diminish the chances of engaging in substance use. Children with good coping skills are more likely to resist peer pressures or stressors and hence less likely to develop substance use disorders later in life.

This preventive approach also improves mental health and therefore is a crucial element of adolescent health initiatives. Preventive interventions not only reduce drug use directly but also foster a general facilitative environment for healthy development. In addition to educational campaigns, community participation is an important component of prevention. Parent, school, and community-based programs can establish a support system among youth. For example, parents who are educated about the signs of drug use can have open discussions with their children, establishing open lines where issues are addressed before they become serious. Likewise, schools that implement social-emotional learning (SEL) curricula prepare students with the ability to withstand stress and peer pressure and make healthy lifestyle choices. Furthermore, where communities work together to create safe recreational areas and oversee youth activities, protective factors are brought into place that deter the use of illicit substances. Through this, community engagement in combination with educational programs optimizes the effects of prevention measures by utilizing an integrated approach to adolescent mental wellness. Early intervention programs for high-risk groups are another critical component of prevention planning. These interventions are informed by research that shows the impact that socioeconomic factors have on substance use behavior. For instance, research has shown that lower educational attainment and unemployment are powerful predictors of opioid addiction and other substance issues. By identifying and supporting vulnerable youth with specially constructed programs offering mentorship, counseling, and vocational training, communities can buffer against risk factor impact. There is evidence to suggest that enhanced coping skills through targeted support can lead to reduced dependency and accompanying behaviors in high-risk groups. Hence, addressing the root causes of substance use through prevention in early stages is the cornerstone for creating healthier futures for adolescents and youth, underlining the necessity of long-term commitment to evidence-based prevention strategies (Behnampour et al., 2015; Creamer et al., 2018).

9.4.1. School-Based Prevention Programs

School-based prevention programs are a vital means of addressing drug use and addictive behaviors among children and teenagers. They aim to create an environment where there exist healthy decision-making, resilience, and interpersonal skills, ultimately lowering the vulnerability to substance abuse. By incorporating expansive curricula that focus on skill development and awareness, schools are able to engage a diverse group of adolescents and guarantee that warnings regarding the risk of substance use are both accessible and relevant. The effectiveness of these programs depends on their capacity to involve students meaningfully, making connections between knowledge and practical application. An excellent example is the Reclaiming Futures initiative, which emphasizes the importance of youth development and cultural competence in ultimately bolstering responses to substance use in the context of juvenile justice reform. School-based prevention programs are also more effective when aligned with the sociocultural realities of the students. It is necessary to know how social and cultural contexts shape substance use behaviors in order to be more effective at prevention. For instance, alcohol and drug consumption among young people is significantly shaped by peer pressure, family, and community norms. Teachers can create prevention programs based on what they know about these factors and so understand the particular difficulties of their students. Family- and community-stakeholder-engaging programs have the potential to create a more supportive environment that maximizes intervention outcomes. Teen drug use problems demand a multi-dimensional approach incorporating not only educational content but social support systems and cultural competence (Sudhinaraset et al., 2016).

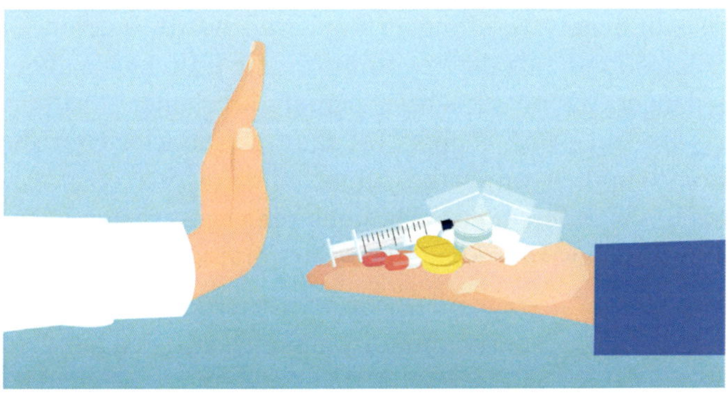

Figure 9.9. By integrating comprehensive curricula that emphasize skill-building and awareness, schools can reach a diverse population of youths, ensuring that messages about the dangers of substance use are both accessible and relatable.

Source: https://isminc-public-assets.s3.amazonaws.com/public/2023-01/article-page-sharing-1200x630-source1-29_1.png.

Lastly, school-based prevention program sustainability is envisioned to be necessary for long-term success in preventing substance use and addiction. Ongoing evaluation and revision of these programs are necessary to meet the shifting needs of the student body. Schools can make informed decisions about program modification by collecting data on drug use trends and program effectiveness. Funding and budgeting are also essential; schools need to put prevention initiatives at the top of their agendas and offer sufficient training for those employees carrying out the initiatives. Interagency school-community and health professional efforts can fortify these programs so that they continue to be relevant and effective. School-based prevention programs ultimately represent a proactive approach to fostering mental health and wellness among youth, paving the way for healthier future generations (Figure 9.9).

9.4.2. Family Involvement and Education

Involvement of the family in treatment and education of adolescents as well as children is crucial to treat substance use and addictive patterns. Familial support can significantly make interventions more effective because it facilitates a feeling of belonging and stability for youth. Family involvement can not only treat the contextual variables influencing a child's behavior but also make the entire treatment plan stronger. When families participate actively in education programs, they are in an excellent position to detect indications of potential use of substances and reinforce prevention at home. Such synergy creates a collaborative environment where youth and caregivers can share concerns and successes, ultimately resulting in improved health outcomes. Education as family participation holds the key to informing individuals about substance use and the dangers involved. These parents are better positioned to offer the necessary guidance and support, as they are educated on the pressures and temptations children might be subjected to (Cook et al., 2017). Such education can be in different formats, including workshops, support groups, and educational sessions addressing the behavioral indicators of addiction and prevention strategies.

By promoting an educated community among teenagers, families encourage acceptance and necessity of discussing the use of substances, reducing stigma, and encouraging openness. The incorporation of schooling activities within the family environment assists in building resistance towards substance use through the enhancement of healthy coping skills and decision-making abilities. The inclusion of cultural competence in family engagement strategies greatly enhances the educational process. Cultural background understanding as having an effect on mental health perception and substance use can be of assistance in adapting education materials and family programming to the specific needs of diverse communities. The culturally aware method not only promotes participation but also recognizes the experiences and issues of families and makes them heard and validated. Also, when families are given culturally responsive training and tools, they are more likely to identify with the information and apply it to their realities. This method empowers families by focusing on creating strengths instead of highlighting risks and thus supporting the broader goal of youth substance abuse reduction and encouraging mental health outcomes (Figure 9.10).

Figure 9.10. Families that educate themselves about the pressures and temptations their children face are better positioned to offer appropriate guidance and support.

Source: https://www.eurokidsindia.com/blog/wp-content/uploads/2024/01/parenting-through-peer-pressure.jpg.

9.4.3. Community Resources and Support Systems

Community support networks and systems play a crucial role in preventing substance use and addiction among adolescents and children. They comprise varied service delivery networks, including preventive education, counseling services, and intervention programs, which play an important role in preventing substance abuse. Community agencies often work with mental health professionals in developing comprehensive plans aimed at fostering resilience among teenagers. These efforts not only provide short-term assistance but also enable long-term recovery options, stressing the significance of strengthening positive community norms. The activation of stakeholders—ranging from schools and families to local businesses—also reflects the shared responsibility in creating an environment conducive to mental health. By using the power of community resources, we are empowered to make a remarkable difference in the course of drug-dependent adolescents and convey the imperative of an intersectoral response to mental health. Under such a system, community-based interventions must be informed by cultural competence in order to respond to the diverse needs of adolescents. The integration of cultural sensitivity into prevention interventions for substance abuse ensures that interventions are not only accessible but also relevant to the young people they are designed to serve. Programs such as the Reclaiming Futures program bring to the forefront the need for youth development practice that incorporates cultural factors, diverging from the intervention approach of one fit all. By prioritizing evidence-based practices for funding innovative practices, communities can adapt their strategies to suit the specific demands of their populations and, in turn, enhance the effectiveness of these programs in curbing the use of substances. The intersection of culturally informed practice and community strengths reinforces efforts to reform juvenile justice systems and presents a multidisciplinary approach to addressing addiction among young people. A model that takes into consideration the complexity of drug use among adolescents is crucial to the provision of successful community support systems. The Adolescent Substance Use Risk Continuum has been suggested as a paradigm for integrating risk and protective factors into strengths-based practices that are applicable within treatment settings. In incorporating aspects such as family systems and cultural influences, this model identifies opportunities for clinicians to engage adolescents in productive and interactive patterns, with a focus on hope and empowerment. As outlined by Cook et al. (2017), this strengths continuum not only facilitates the assessment process but also enhances intervention planning by focusing on solutions rather than problems alone. Consequently, mental health professionals can utilize this model as a vital tool in community settings, allowing for tailored interventions that uplift families and cultivate resilience among adolescents facing substance use challenges.

9.5. TREATMENT APPROACHES

When treating substance abuse and addictive behavior among children and adolescents, one must be particularly careful to respect the developmental subtlety of these issues. Adolescents are most vulnerable to harm from substance use because their brains are still developing, affecting impulse control, decision-making, and risk assessment. Treatment modalities should therefore focus on abstinence but also facilitate healthy coping and resilience for youth. Cognitive-behavioral approaches integrated into programs have proven to alter unhealthy patterns of behavior as well as treat the underlying psychosocial disorders contributing to drug use. This is especially crucial in the context of growing concern over the use of social media and its connection to mental illness disorders, where therapy can help promote logical thinking about teens' online behavior and recognition of the potentially addictive nature of this interaction (Danielle et al., 2018). In addition, a multi-dimensional approach is often necessary since drug use is closely interrelated with other psychosocial problems. Multimodal treatment approaches that incorporate family involvement, community support networks, and instructional interventions will have more success. Family counseling can promote better communication and provide a supportive environment for adolescents with addiction. Furthermore, the incorporation of elements that evaluate physical and mental health factors through both adolescent and parental report may enhance the effectiveness of interventions (Deanna et al., 2017). These comprehensive assessments can allow clinicians to tailor individualized approaches, align interventions to individual risk factors, and foster continued engagement in treatment. Prevention and education are also vital in the fight against substance use and addiction in adolescents. Investment in school-based interventions that educate students about the risks of substance use and addictive technology, including social media, can promote healthy choices. These programs also need to promote peer resistance and wholesome interpersonal relationships. Furthermore, as the prevalence of mental illness grows, screening for substance abuse and emotional health must be done at regular intervals among teenagers at clinical locations. It pays to do it in advance so that it can identify those at risk early and make the appropriate referrals to treatment on time. The combination of early intervention, comprehensive assessment, and community incorporation offers a good foundation that can effectively address the complex dynamics of substance use and addiction-related behaviors for child and adolescent mental health (Danielle et al., 2018; Deanna et al., 2017).

9.5.1. Behavioral Therapies and Counseling

Behavioral treatments and counseling are core in the care of child and adolescent mental health's alcohol and drug consumption and addictive behavior. These treatments emphasize the modification of undesirable behaviors using structured interventions, generally based on the principles of cognitive-behavioral therapy (CBT). As shown in recent studies, procedures such as motivational interviewing and contingency management have been added to treatment models, improving the interactive nature of the therapeutic process. These strategies are particularly relevant in that they address not only the substance use itself but also the psychological factors that commonly accompany it. This two-part strategy is essential, especially in light of the high rate of comorbidity between SUDs and other psychiatric disorders in adolescence, which highlights the need for an integrated model of treatment that targets both realms (Hulvershorn et al., 2015). Moreover, the involvement of family and community in behavior therapies allows for increased intervention efficacy for the teenagers involved in substance abuse issues. Family therapy has proven to increase the support network needed for recuperation and, consequently, the probability of long-term behavioral change. By allowing guardians and parents to participate in counseling, therapists can more effectively tailor interventions based on the distinct needs of each teen, creating a unified environment that is supportive of healing. This integration is significant in that it engages the teen's relational environment, which is critical to effective treatment solutions. Lastly, the modularity of behavioral treatments—allowing modular approaches where components are amendable on the basis of concurrent feedback—is an exciting route to addressing the unique challenges posed by teens with co-occurring internalizing disorders and SUDs (Hulvershorn et al., 2015). Classification of mental health disorders, particularly within new systems like the ICD-11, also informs behavioral therapy methods. As the World Health Organization evolves more specific diagnostic criteria, these advances can help maximize clinical utility and relevance of therapies for substance use disorders. Emphasis on global applicability means that practitioners of mental health are more likely to implement evidence-based treatments in diverse settings. This development highlights the need for ongoing training and adaptation of treatment processes, so counselors are educated in newer protocols and treatments reflecting the sophistication of adolescent mental illness. Ultimately, the marriages of behavioral therapies and evolving clinical paradigms are a solid platform to treat drug abuse and enhance overall mental well-being in adolescents (Figure 9.11).

Figure 9.11. Family-based therapy has been found to strengthen the support network needed for recovery, thereby increasing the likelihood of sustained behavioral change.

Source: https://www.verywellmind.com/thmb/7KqIU6pERziernJ-eLbMrFlmiYI=/2121x0/filters:no_upscale():max_bytes(150000):strip_icc()/family-supporting-daughter-GettyImages-83119807-576c49b03df78cb62c462f4d.jpg.

9.5.2. Medication-Assisted Treatment Options

The landscape of medication-assisted treatment (MAT) for addiction among youth calls for a balanced framework that considers developmental milestones and the complex nature of addiction. MAT entails pharmacological treatment with therapy, which makes a two-pronged approach dedicated to the alleviation of withdrawal signs and symptoms and cravings and the treatment of the psychological dimensions of addiction. Drugs such as methadone or buprenorphine have been found to be effective when administered to adults, but safety and efficacy are the focus of ongoing research when it is used in younger populations. Despite limited research studies targeting adolescents specifically, there remains a pressing need for such research to inform policy and clinical practice because traditional intervention approaches fail to address the singular development-related problems faced by the younger generation with substance use disorders (Reeves et al., 2014).

Treatment approaches must also include psychosocial intervention, such as cognitive behavior therapy, to effect optimal benefits. Multimodal treatment combining medication and psychotherapy has been emphasized as crucial in today's literature. Adolescents have been found to benefit significantly from combined modes of treatment, which can render engagement and maintenance of recovery program more manageable. Whereas stabilization of the individual's status can be attained through the use of pharmacotherapy, psychotherapy addresses the root emotional and behavioral inclinations towards drug consumption. The acknowledgement of such dual viewpoints aligns with research showing that integrative treatment models have greater patient retention in therapy and healthier general mental health outcomes for youths (Karabelnik et al., 2003). The integrated model predicates the importance not just of medication but of establishing a facilitative therapeutic atmosphere. In children and adolescents, integration of MAT into overall mental health care is required due to the high comorbidities of substance use disorders with other mental disorders. The co-occurrence of depression, anxiety, and attention-deficit/hyperactivity disorder among adolescents with substance use disorders demands careful consideration of the interaction between these conditions when formulating treatment plans. As has been illustrated by the research, untreated mental health conditions may worsen substance use trends with unfavorable long-term consequences. Application of evidence-based medication protocols that address such comorbidity can potentially enhance treatment efficacy significantly. For many teens, enrollment in a program that treats both mental illness and substance abuse not only improves their chance for recovery but also instills resilience and coping skills that are crucial to their development (Reeves et al., 2014) (Figure 9.12).

Figure 9.12. While pharmacotherapy can stabilize the individual's condition, psychotherapy addresses the underlying emotional and behavioral patterns contributing to substance use.

Source: https://www.talkspace.com/blog/wp-content/uploads/2024/05/Therapy-vs-Medication.jpg.

9.5.3. Holistic and Alternative Therapies

The emerging epidemic of substance use disorder in children and adolescents necessitates a reevaluation of the treatment approach. Holistic and alternative treatments hold promising interventions to address the multidimensional interaction of physical, emotional, and social issues resulting in addictive behavior. Treating the individual as an integrated unit, these treatments aim at gaining a better understanding of the underlying causes of substance abuse. Research has begun indicating the effectiveness of adding practices such as mindfulness, yoga, and art therapy to traditional treatment regimens. All these interventions not only induce awareness and emotional regulation but also lower stress and anxiety levels, which are typically underlying causes of addiction. Thus, holistic treatments can potentially augment traditional treatment regimens, presenting a more robust treatment paradigm for vulnerable youths with substance issues (Kuss et al., 2016). In addition, other holistic and complementary interventions have also shown effectiveness in the treatment of certain settings of adolescent drug use. For instance, mindfulness-based interventions (MBIs) have been used more and more as effective tools for developing mental health resilience. These practices help adolescents learn present-moment awareness and emotional regulation strategies that are fundamental in the management of craving and substance use cues. In the same vein, community-based interventions that combine aspects of traditional healing rituals can speak to particular social or cultural groups, improving engagement and therapeutic effectiveness. Evidence suggests that when adolescents view their treatment as culturally responsive, attendance and outcomes significantly improve. By taking such steps, holistic therapies can bridge gaps in conventional treatment procedures and thereby become an integral part of curing the multi-aspectual nature of youth substance misuse and addictions (Barker et al., 2025). Further, the increasing inclination to integrate holistic therapies in treatment procedures is transforming the way mental health professionals treat youth substance use disorders. In the determination of the necessity for an integrated care model, therapists increasingly employ multi-disciplinary teams to implement such interventions in combination with standard treatments. Through this integration, professionals are able to deliver more tailored treatment plans considering each adolescent's unique situation and needs. This method allows mental health practitioners to establish an environment without stigma and with easy accessibility for the discussion of mental illness and substance abuse. With the expanding body of research, it is ever more necessary that clinicians and policymakers turn to these other methods as valid components of an integrated treatment regime. The inclusion of holistic and alternative methods not only increases clinical practice but also enables long-term recovery and resilience among adolescents with addictive behaviors (Barker et al., 2025).

9.6. ROLE OF POLICY AND LEGISLATION

The intersection of policy and law has a profound effect on shaping the landscape of child and adolescent mental health services for gaming disorders and addiction. With legislators fighting to grapple with the complexities that affect mental health and gaming disorders, the implementation of regulation comes into focus. The World Health Organization's decision to recognize "gaming disorder" has drawn an international controversy, motivating policymakers to act in haste. Still, the success of these initiatives, particularly in South Korea, where attempts to curb gaming excess have seen limited success, underscores the intricacy of legislative interventions. The concerns voiced by experts regarding the gambling nature of the designation of gaming disorder underscore the necessity of careful consideration and evidence-based justification in policymaking. Lacking solid proof, programs risk making the very issues at hand worse that they aim to curb, requiring a conservative type of legislation of relevant gaming and drug use policies (Ferguson et al., 2020). Dual pathology, or the co-occurrence of addictive disease with other mental illness, raises significant challenges in policy development and enactment. This paradigm places in the limelight the multifaceted nature of adolescent substance uses disorders, which demands comprehensive healthcare policies in favor of early detection and concerted treatment approaches. Since dual pathology patients face greater psychosocial issues, policymakers must pay special consideration to an integrative approach with multiple service domains, such as education, mental health, and substance abuse services. The findings of recent studies clarify the need for a model of care in which substance use, and concomitant mental health conditions are addressed concurrently. This paradigmatic shift is an acknowledgment of the fact that addiction and mental illness are not exclusive of each other; rather, both are impacted by a set of biological, psychological, as well as social factors that must be accounted for by legislation (Torales et al., 2019). Prevention is central in the development of useful policies aimed at preventing the use of substances and addiction among adolescents. Education and awareness projects in schools have the potential to encourage intervention early, which can have the young embracing healthier lifestyles. The findings point out that preventive interventions like behavioral interventions and family therapy will result in a sharp reduction in the development of substance-related problems if they are initiated early. The challenge, however, is in consistent integration of these measures into ongoing systems, where public health policies must be crafted so that they enable flexibility based on new research findings. Even as countries of the world contemplate such policies, an emphasis on early intervention and systems-orientated care identifies the necessity for a nimble legislative system capable of responding to the changing challenges of substance abuse and addictive behavior in the field of child and adolescent mental health (Ferguson et al., 2020; Torales et al., 2019).

9.6.1. Overview of Current Laws Regarding Substance use in Minors

In the examination of current law concerning the use of substances by children, it is significant to determine the contradiction between the liberty given to young people and protective measures initiated by legal frameworks. Law in the majority of jurisdictions typically prohibits the sale and ownership of tobacco, alcohol, and illicit drugs among children, which reflects a universal social consensus concerning the protection of children from the risks involved in the use of substances. However, existing legal approaches reflect inconsistencies in acknowledgment of adolescent autonomy in decision-making. As our recent controversy over legal models has exposed, there is increasing acknowledgment for policy reform that restrains adolescent autonomy in some ways while imposing adult-like responsibilities and sanctions in others (Pustilnik et al., 2015). The legal landscape is therefore evolving to better reflect the developmental neuroscience understanding underlying our comprehension of adolescent conduct and potential for good decision-making. The impact of advertising and marketing strategies on children's use of drugs is also an essential part of the legal discourse. The tobacco industry, for instance, has a history of intense advertisement campaigns that have shaped public perception of smoking as a socially accepted behavior. The research points out the connection between tobacco promotion and smoking initiation among youth, and the argument here is that legal frameworks must aim at curbing the forces that external marketing places on vulnerable young groups (Iyiola et al., 2013). Even though extensive legislation controls the promotion of the drugs to children, its enforcement is generally lacking, thus making it possible for such activities to be sustained that entice them into harmful addictions. Later, the legislation must not only restrict access but also control marketing strategies to cut the risks of the consumption of harmful substances among kids.

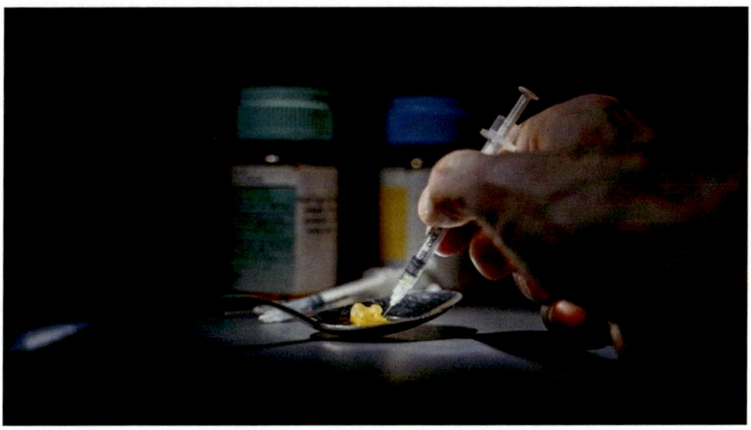

Figure 9.13. Laws across various jurisdictions typically prohibit the sale and possession of tobacco, alcohol, and illicit drugs to minors, reflecting a societal consensus on safeguarding young people from the risks associated with substance use.

Source: https://i0.wp.com/lexforti.com/legal-news/wp-content/uploads/2020/09/blog-image-2-3.jpg?fit=1024%2C576&ssl=1.

Finally, the relationship between legal codes and community resources significantly contributes to the overall picture of substance abuse prevention among teenagers. Most jurisdictions have launched educational programs and interventions that seek to promote a higher level of awareness of the risks associated with substance abuse. These programs typically operate on the premise of existing laws but put additional emphasis on the role of community participation alongside legal enforcement. Decision-makers are encouraged to coordinate educational efforts with regulatory action, ensuring that the legal limitations on drug use are complemented by supportive measures encouraging healthy decision-making. As researchers continue to unravel the biological and psychological susceptibilities of adolescents, legal reforms are also encouraged to embrace an integrated model that is highly conversant in balancing regulation with education, thereby making attempts at curbing drug use and enhancing youth mental health more practical (Figure 9.13).

9.6.2. Impact of Policy on Prevention and Treatment Efforts

In reviewing the policy impact on prevention and treatment practices across the domain of substance use in children and adolescents, consideration should be given to the need for holistic models synthesizing disparate aspects of intervention. Evidence-based interventions and community involvement are priorities within policies that are most effective. For instance, initiatives like Reduce, Reclaiming Futures have yielded evidence that youth development and cultural competence are central in influencing responsive substance abuse treatment in juvenile justice systems. By aligning policy with community needs and evidence-based research, there will be a higher likelihood of inducing positive behavioral change and reducing the rate of substance abuse among vulnerable populations. Secondly, such policies can provide access to recovery services whereby youth are very well cared for while pursuing sobriety. Substantive effectiveness in anti-drug use policies also relies on addressing the macro-level risk factors that lead to addiction behaviors. For instance, alcohol drinking poses severe threats that extend beyond the individual level to involve families and communities. As shown, alcohol abuse contributes to approximately 3.3 million deaths annually, highlighting the importance of immediate policy interventions targeting underlying social and cultural causes (Sudhinaraset et al., 2016). Policies for limiting advertising, community engagement, and educational extension are instrumental in lowering alcohol abuse among youths. By promoting healthy behaviors and reducing risk factors through support of these cultures, policymakers are well-positioned to influence the trajectory of substance use prevalence among children and youth in important ways. In addition, effective policies must take into consideration the interaction between prevention interventions and treatment strategies. Offering a multifaceted response to meet the diverse needs of youth with substance use problems is important. Interventions addressing early intervention, family support, and peer support not only enhance treatment success but also contribute to the overall goal of preventing initiation among youth populations. Inclusion of stakeholders across sectors—healthcare, education, and community groups—can further improve policy implementation of comprehensive policies. Finally, aligning prevention and treatment initiatives with ongoing research and with the inputs of citizens assures that policies are still relevant and responsive, ultimately improving outcomes for children and adolescents who are battling substance abuse and addictive activity.

9.6.3. Advocacy for Improved Mental Health Resources

Increased mental health services are required and ought to be lobbied for in dealing with the complex interaction of addiction and substance use in children and adolescents. Mental disorders have a tendency to comorbid with substance use disorders, and hence, treatment and rehabilitation become more complicated. Increased mental health services will help with early interventions that are crucial in breaking the trajectory of engagement of youth with substances. Projects like Reclaiming Futures underscore the importance of youth development and cultural competency in developing successful interventions within juvenile justice systems. Through the advancement of a holistic practice that integrates mental health services into substance abuse programs, advocates can create supportive environments to enable youth to transcend these obstacles. Investment in coordinated mental health services serves not only to meet the youth's short-term psychological needs but also develops resilience that serves to decrease the underlying causes of substance abuse. Also, the presence of mental health clinics as part of the drug court system is a good example of the demand for coordinated mental health services. The structure allows for comprehensive mental health evaluation at critical junctures in a young person's legal pathway, determination of which interventions to apply based on individualized assessment. For instance, in the Rhode Island Family Court, teens receive personalized recommendations that have a high potential of raising their chances of recovery from drug and alcohol addiction. The integration of mental health evaluation into substance use treatment not only addresses the symptoms of addiction but also contributes to a better understanding of the underlying issues. Therefore, promotion of increased mental health interventions goes beyond provision of treatment; it entails the establishment of tailored approaches from the unique circumstance of each young person, aimed at mitigating eventual recidivism, and enhancing overall welfare in general. Finally, empirical studies shed light on the far-reaching consequences of untreated mental disorders among adolescents with substance use disorders, necessitating urgent advocacy efforts. As noted in current reviews, there have been correlations between substance use disorder diagnoses and increased rates of incarceration shortly after mental health evaluation, showing a clear absence of intervention options. This underlines the strong need for full-range mental health care that treats youth before intensification of their problems. Appropriate resources with an emphasis on prevention, early intervention, and ongoing support can significantly reduce the risk of incarceration while guaranteeing school success. Through the championing of increased mental health resources, stakeholders are able to not just treat the symptoms of drug use but actually redirect vulnerable youth, ultimately leading to healthier adolescent lives and the decades that exist afterward (Figure 9.14).

Figure 9.14. Advocacy for improved mental health resources is critical in addressing the complex interplay between substance use and addictive behaviors among children and adolescents.

Source: https://manochikitsa.com/wp-content/uploads/2024/08/How-to-Convince-Your.GRAPHICS-4TH-1024x704.jpg.

9.7. CONCLUSION

It is crucial to highlight the connection between these two major topics when providing a comprehensive evaluation of drug use and addictive behavior in relation to child and adolescent mental health. Numerous studies have demonstrated that the impacts of drug use go beyond the immediate physical effects, such as those looking at the relationship between problematic video game use and psychological health. Particularly noteworthy is the discovery that teenagers who play excessive amounts of pathological gaming had greater levels of anxiety, depression symptoms, and poorer academic performance, indicating a concerning connection between digital use and psychological deterioration. The finding that addictive behaviors in youth must be respected, as they may exacerbate pre-existing mental health symptoms while creating a feedback system which rewards both habits and psychological anguish, is what these findings demonstrate. Moreover, the general understanding of Internet addiction (IA) reveals striking analogies between traditional substance use disorders and emerging digital dependencies. Research is revealed to indicate that IA, similar to substance abuse, could lead to extreme impairments in psychosocial functioning and daily life. The variable prevalence rates of IA emphasize the necessity for a consistent method of definition and measurement of this phenomenon, given the enormous overlap with the substance use behaviors described in recent reviews. The assessment of IA has to be more than a function of frequency of use, also taking into account the qualitative impact on adolescents' lives, like their relationships, school performance, and self-esteem. This multi-dimensional approach is needed to institute quality preventive strategies and targeted interventions, promoting healthy mental health outcomes in this vulnerable population. Lastly, intervention against children's and adolescents' substance use and addictive behaviors calls for an integrated and holistic perspective that recognizes the nature of such issues as multi-faceted. Interventions must incorporate multi-factorial strategies in addressing individual, family, and social determinants that affect youth behavior. By doing so, one can reduce the destructive effects of both addictive behaviors and the use of substances, thereby increasing enhanced development pathways. The intersection of substance uses, and addictive behavior exacerbates not just the person's mental illness issues but also has far-reaching consequences for society. In the future, ongoing research that crosses boundaries of mental health, addiction, and online behavior will be critical in informing policies intended to protect the well-being of young people and, in turn, healthy generations against emerging challenges.

9.7.1. Summary of Key Points Discussed

The study of substance addiction and addictive behavior in youths reveals seminal trends that intersect with mental health. One is the increasing prevalence of Internet addiction (IA), a high-tech problem that has evolved as an insidious youth culture issue. Research identifies IA's measures as heterogeneous between studies, affecting its reported prevalence at 1% to 18.7% in various national surveys. This heterogeneity in turn can largely be accounted for by methodological variability that permeates the discipline, highlighting the complexities of diagnosing and treating IA as a psychiatric disorder in developmental contexts. Given its commonalities with classical substance dependence, not only does IA warrant concerted research but calls for the institution of targeted psychological and pharmacological interventions based on consideration of differential experiences of affected adolescents. Also, alcohol and smoking during pregnancy are very serious child and adolescent mental health issues. New research reveals stark trends of alcohol and tobacco use among pregnant teens, both at 11.5% and 23.0%, respectively, for past-month use. Surprisingly, pregnant teens are less prone to use alcohol than their non-pregnant peers but consume more tobacco. The use of these drugs concurrently is associated with more advanced mental health states, such as major depressive episodes, in teenage and adult populations. These horrific statistics ought to drive home the necessity of increased public health initiatives aimed at curbing the use of substances among pregnant adolescents as well as addressing the resultant mental health states. Finally, the interconnection between youth alcohol and drug use and mental health requires a multi-faceted approach. The effects of drug use extend further than immediate physical consequences, as typified by the connection between teen tobacco smoking during pregnancy and such psychosocial factors as contact with the criminal justice system. As evidenced by the data, interventions must not only provide cessation of drug use but must also include mental health treatment in order to address the co-occurring disorders so prevalent in such populations. The literature suggests an achingly necessary need for certain interventions and prevention programs that can interrupt the cycle of drug use and the resulting negative impact on mental health among youth and adolescents. Through a focus on gaining such a thorough understanding of these issues, stakeholders can devise more effective prevention and treatment strategies, ultimately resulting in healthier generations to come.

9.7.2. The Importance of Early Intervention and Support

Early intervention and intervention are highly significant in addressing substance abuse and addictive behaviors in children and adolescents, as they serve to redefine the mental health patterns. Adolescence is a stage of vulnerability to numerous external stresses, which results in substance experimentation. According to research, it has been revealed that the earlier individuals are intervened into, the better the outcome will be. Early detection of behavior indicative of potential substance use enables early intervention and provision of support and counseling, which helps to diminish long-term outcomes of such behavior. Early intervention also triggers resilience through promotion of coping skills to alleviate coping with substances as coping strategies. The role of family and social setting is another key consideration in early intervention approaches. Substance use is not a solitary existence for children and adolescents; their worlds, family relationships, and peer groups have a decided influence on decisions about substance use. Involving families in the process of intervention can increase the effectiveness of support networks because family strengths and vulnerabilities can be used to enhance healthier lifestyles. Community-based interventions in which peers are incorporated into educational programs have the potential to make conversations about substance use and its dangers more acceptable. By addressing both individual and environmental elements, interventions are in a position to create a support system that fosters positive behavior change and culture of openness and support, which are the building blocks of those with substance issues. Lastly, evidence-based practices play a critical role in the efficacy of early intervention programs. These practice-informed methods, which are tailored to meet the specific needs of youth, have the capacity to reduce duplication of efforts and enhance impact through programs. Initiatives ranging from the Reclaiming Futures initiative show the potential of combining youth development principles with cultural competence to drive outcomes within interventions. By taking a holistic approach and incorporating emotional, social, and psychological dimensions, these initiatives reflect the complex nature of youth substance use. Enabling awareness of available resources and establishing effective support systems can not only stop the aggravation of substance use disorders but also enhance resilience among youth facing various challenges in life (Sudhinaraset et al., 2016).

9.7.3. Call to Action for Parents, Educators, and Policymakers

Parents have a central role in preventing substance abuse and addictive behavior among children and adolescents because they are typically the initial line of defense. Parents must open channels of communication with their children about the vices of drug use. Open dialogue not only helps to depoliticize such matters but also ensures that children are at ease coming to their parents with questions or concerns. Furthermore, parents must also take proactive measures in learning the signs of drug abuse and intervention assistance. Through parenting classes or coordination with local community health agencies, they are able to equip themselves with the correct information to guide their offspring. The urgency of this call to action is further heightened when considering the early introduction and ignorance that can lead to long-term mental health consequences for teens, ultimately directing us to proactive parenting as the solution to this problem. Teachers also play a gigantic role in making the environment that influences student conduct. Schools may be effective sites of preventive education where well-integrated substance use curricula may equip students with knowledge and management skills. Teachers should be educated to recognize the warning signs of substance abuse and assist in developing school culture that encourages positive decisions. This involves creating environments within which students can discuss their challenges freely without stigmatization. Collaboration between schoolteachers and mental health professionals can lead to integrated support systems within schools. Further, involving parents in education programs can also complement efforts to counter drug abuse. As shown in research assessing healthcare system services for adolescents, teacher involvement in early intervention can lead to innovative interventions that help identify and address such threats at the school level (Harriette et al., 2003). Legislative agendas need to make mental health support and substance abuse prevention priorities for policymakers to develop systemic change. This involves providing proper funding for educational programs raising awareness of the dangers involved with substance use. Policies would also need to close service gaps, providing balanced access for all youth, independent of socioeconomic status. By encouraging materials that are directed to the unique issues of marginalized groups, including young men who are disproportionately vulnerable to problems of substance abuse, policymakers can enable a more inclusive prevention model. Common effort among stakeholders—parents, educators, and policymakers—will be needed in order for there to be a comprehensive support system for youth. Ultimately, a united front is crucial in implementing effective strategies that not only prevent substance use but also promote overall mental well-being in children and adolescents.

REFERENCES

1. Ahmad Shahril, N. S. S., Ahmad, S., & Arshat, Z. (2021). Parenting styles, school connectedness and mental health among adolescents in Selangor, Malaysia. *International Journal of Academic Research in Business and Social Sciences*. https://www.semanticscholar.org/paper/85b67df268171ad9c6924e5a9d0de3be3e0243b6 (accessed on 14th October 2025).
2. Allahverdipour, H., Caplan, S. E., Cohen, J., Cole, S. H., Elliott, L., Engels, R. C. M. E., Evenden, J., et al. (2014). The (co-)occurrence of problematic video gaming, substance use, and psychosocial problems in adolescents. https://core.ac.uk/download/30633243.pdf (accessed on 14th October 2025).
3. Armitage, J. M., Collishaw, S., & Sellers, R. (2024). Explaining long-term trends in adolescent emotional problems: What we know from population-based studies. *Discover Social Science and Health*. https://www.semanticscholar.org/paper/e85592b9c0846117b3736fd86709199bea48fff3 (accessed on 14th October 2025).
4. Barch, D. M., Albaugh, M. D., Avenevoli, S., Chang, L., Clark, D. B., Glantz, M. D., Hudziak, J. J., et al. (2017). Demographic, physical and mental health assessments in the Adolescent Brain and Cognitive Development study: Rationale and description. *Developmental Cognitive Neuroscience, 32*, 55–66. https://doi.org/10.1016/j.dcn.2017.10.010 (accessed on 14th October 2025).
5. Barker, J., Thomson, L., McArthur, M., & Humphries, P. (2025). Effective interventions for working with young people who are homeless or at risk of homelessness. https://core.ac.uk/download/pdf/30677747.pdf (accessed on 14th October 2025).
6. Behnampour, N., Modanloo, M., Mousavi, S., Saghafi, M., et al. (2015). Is opioid dependency related to coping strategies? https://core.ac.uk/download/52205701.pdf (accessed on 14th October 2025).
7. Berk, M., Brewin, C., Briken, P., Cohen-Kettenis, P., et al. (2020). Mental, behavioral and neurodevelopmental disorders in the ICD-11: An international perspective on key changes and controversies. https://core.ac.uk/download/287582535.pdf (accessed on 14th October 2025).
8. Billieux, J., Brand, M., Burkauskas, J., Carmi, L., et al. (2018). Manifesto for a European research network into problematic usage of the Internet. https://core.ac.uk/download/287581533.pdf (accessed on 14th October 2025).
9. Bozzola, E., Spina, G., Agostiniani, R., Barni, S., Russo, R., Scarpato,

E., Di Mauro, A., et al. (2022). The use of social media in children and adolescents: Scoping review on the potential risks. *International Journal of Environmental Research and Public Health, 19*, 9960–9960. https://doi.org/10.3390/ijerph19169960 (accessed on 14th October 2025).

10. Clark, D. L., Raphael, J. L., & McGuire, A. L. (2018). HEADS4: Social media screening in adolescent primary care. *Pediatrics, 141*. https://doi.org/10.1542/peds.2017-3655 (accessed on 14th October 2025).
11. Cook, J., & Miller, A. (2017). The adolescent substance uses risk continuum: A cultural, strengths-based approach to case conceptualization. https://core.ac.uk/download/213072254.pdf (accessed on 14th October 2025).
12. Crano, W., & Ruybal, A. L. (2020). Social psychological contributions to the mitigation of adolescent depression. https://www.semanticscholar.org/paper/ca10d4917742c3c86751e799b5c273be4f56e182 (accessed on 14th October 2025).
13. Creamer, M., Hoelscher, D., Kelder, S., Wilkinson, A. V., et al. (2018). Special issue introduction: Youth at risk. https://core.ac.uk/download/147566855.pdf (accessed on 14th October 2025).
14. De Pauw, S., Meulewaeter, F., & Vanderplasschen, W. (2019). Mothering, substance use disorders and intergenerational trauma transmission: An attachment-based perspective. https://core.ac.uk/download/237011860.pdf (accessed on 14th October 2025).
15. DiNitto, D. M., Oh, S., Reingle Gonzalez, J. M., Salas-Wright, C. P., et al. (2017). Prevalence and correlates of alcohol and tobacco use among pregnant women in the United States: Evidence from the NSDUH 2005–2014. https://open.bu.edu/bitstream/2144/26190/3/%255bClear%20Manuscript%255dAlcohol%20and%20tobacco%20use%20among%20pregnant%20women_revised%20011917.pdf (accessed on 14th October 2025).
16. Drabble, L. A., & Trocki, K. (2013). Alcohol in the life narratives of women: Commonalities and differences by sexual orientation. https://core.ac.uk/download/70410109.pdf (accessed on 14th October 2025).
17. Drabble, L. A., Hughes, T. L., Korcha, R. A., Lown, A., et al. (2013). Sexual orientation differences in the relationship between victimization and hazardous drinking among women in the National Alcohol Survey. https://core.ac.uk/download/70410106.pdf (accessed on 14th October 2025).
18. Ferguson, A. M., Bean, R., Nielsen, M., & Smyth, M. (2020). Policy on unreliable game addiction diagnoses puts the cart before the horse. *Psychology of Popular Media Culture, 9*, 533–540. https://www.

semanticscholar.org/paper/7008e087bd554d569f62b93ed7ab39a5622b988f (accessed on 14th October 2025).

19. Fox, H. B., Shejavali, K. I., & McManus, M. A. (2003). Is the health care system working for adolescents? Perspectives from providers in Boston, Denver, Houston, and San Francisco. https://core.ac.uk/download/71352449.pdf (accessed on 14th October 2025).
20. Griffiths, M. D., Kuss, D. J., & Pontes, H. M. (2015). Clinical psychology of internet addiction: A review of its conceptualization, prevalence, neuronal processes, and implications for treatment. https://core.ac.uk/download/30633161.pdf (accessed on 14th October 2025).
21. Hulvershorn, L. A., Quinn, P. D., & Scott, E. L. (2015). Treatment of adolescent substance use disorders and co-occurring internalizing disorders: A critical review and proposed model. https://core.ac.uk/download/46964468.pdf (accessed on 14th October 2025).
22. Iyiola, O. O. (2013). Social problems of tobacco marketing in southwestern Nigeria: A behavioral study. https://core.ac.uk/download/18294982.pdf (accessed on 14th October 2025).
23. Karabelnik, L., & Thomas, C. R. (2003). Practical child and adolescent psychopharmacology. *Journal of the American Academy of Child and Adolescent Psychiatry, 42*, 616. https://www.semanticscholar.org/paper/cc19da008ab5cf94ee3863c3c6f338d027128b56 (accessed on 14th October 2025).
24. Kuss, D. J., & Lopez-Fernandez, O. (2016). Internet addiction and problematic internet use: A systematic review of clinical research. https://core.ac.uk/download/30650974.pdf (accessed on 14th October 2025).
25. Marciano, L., Ostroumova, M., Schulz, P. J., & Camerini, A. L. (2022). Digital media use and adolescents' mental health during the COVID-19 pandemic: A systematic review and meta-analysis. *Frontiers in Public Health, 9*. https://doi.org/10.3389/fpubh.2021.793868 (accessed on 14th October 2025).
26. Oliveira, C. (2015). Juvenile substance uses and effects of substance use disorder on incarceration and grade retention in a sample referred for court clinic mental health evaluation. https://open.bu.edu/bitstream/2144/13285/10/Oliveira_bu_0017N_11627_web.pdf (accessed on 14th October 2025).
27. Pustilnik, A. C., & Tennison, M. N. (2015). And if your friends jumped off a bridge, would you do it too? How developmental neuroscience can inform legal regimes governing adolescents. https://core.ac.uk/download/56360509.pdf (accessed on 14th October 2025).

28. Reeves, G., & Riddle, M. (2014). A practical and effective primary care intervention for treating adolescent depression. *JAMA, 312*(8), 797–798. https://www.semanticscholar.org/paper/98e831b5977e89d554f8c668a10e368d4112ed45 (accessed on 14th October 2025).
29. Richter, L. (2020). The effects of the COVID-19 pandemic on the risk of youth substance use. *Journal of Adolescent Health, 67*, 467–468. https://doi.org/10.1016/j.jadohealth.2020.07.014 (accessed on 14th October 2025).
30. Simonelli, A., Mapelli, D., Cerniglia, L., Parolin, M., Cristofalo, P., & Cimino, S. (2017). Cognitive functioning, clinical profile and life events in young adults addicted to drugs. Does being a girl make a difference? https://core.ac.uk/download/141698670.pdf (accessed on 14th October 2025).
31. Sterling, S., & Weisner, C. (2006). Translating research findings into practice: Example of treatment services for adolescents in managed care. https://core.ac.uk/download/323072702.pdf (accessed on 14th October 2025).
32. Sudhinaraset, M., Takeuchi, D. T., & Wigglesworth, C. (2016). Social and cultural contexts of alcohol use: Influences in a social-ecological framework. https://core.ac.uk/download/323077110.pdf (accessed on 14th October 2025).
33. Tekin, E., Liang, L., & Mocan, N. (2025). Do adolescents with emotional or behavioral problems respond to cigarette prices? https://core.ac.uk/download/pdf/7210118.pdf (accessed on 14th October 2025).
34. Torales, J., Castaldelli-Maia, J. M., da Silva, A. G., Campos, M. W., González, I., & Barrios, I. (2018). Even more complex… When mental disorder meets addiction in youth: Dual pathology. *Current Drug Research Reviews, 11*, 40–43. https://doi.org/10.2174/258997751166618112816535 8 (accessed on 14th October 2025).
35. Torales, J., Castaldelli-Maia, J., da Silva, A. D., Campos, M. W., González-Urbieta, I., & Barrios, I. (2019). Even more complex… When mental disorder meets addiction in youth: Dual pathology. *Current Drug Research Reviews, 11*(1), 40–43. https://www.semanticscholar.org/paper/a2c9125462c7a8cf3eb54fd350157550ea79370e (accessed on 14th October 2025).
36. Verhulst, F. (2015). Commentary: Physical health outcomes and health care have improved so much, so why is child mental health getting worse? Or is it? A commentary on Collishaw (2015). *Journal of Child Psychology and Psychiatry, and Allied Disciplines, 56*(3), 394–396. https://www.semanticscholar.org/paper/6d44d1efd083367e4f6dd62e8f57c365263b873d (accessed on 14th October 2025).

Chapter 10

Mental Health in Schools and Communities

Contents

INTRODUCTION

Due to its cumulative influence on the health of teenagers, school and community mental health has gained more attention from educators, legislators, and mental health specialists. Since schools are an important setting for learning and socialization, treating mental health issues benefits both the individual student and the community as a whole. Since emotional and psychological well-being is recognized as a crucial component of academic success, the integration of mental health programs into educational institutions highlights the significance of early intervention and support system frameworks. According to the literature, governments are incredibly disparate in the amount of support provided to mental health programs, calling attention to the need for consistent policies promoting a systemic approach to mental wellness within schools (Askell-Williams et al., 2011). Also, the "Healthy Universities" model has been an innovative strategy to enhance mental health provisions in higher education. The model recognizes that university life can be unique sources of distress that have immediate adverse consequences on students' mental health, necessitating a broader approach to support. In this, the development and initiation of a National Healthy Universities Framework aim to leverage the work towards advancing mental health. Following a collective action by multiple universities, the focus is put on implementing sustainable measures that support meeting the needs of students with integrated institution-wide efforts. Not only do these measures serve as an advisory standard for universities, but they also stimulate collaborative practice among education institutions and community healthcare resources (Cawood et al., 2010). Lastly, the intersection of mental health, education, and community only serves to highlight the worth in a unified approach in the face of immediate concerns for mental health. In establishing spaces where students' mental health becomes priority, schooling systems can become agents for change for the communities in which they operate. This more expansive strategy goes beyond treating solely mental health complications, working instead to foster resilience in individuals who need to survive the trials of modern life. Through effective implementation of school and university mental health initiatives, all stakeholders can unite and ensure that support systems are available so that they not only exist but also get used effectively. The commitment to mental health promotion would be essential in building healthier generations and consequently stronger communities.

Importance of Mental Health in Educational Settings

The importance of prioritizing mental health in school settings is brought to light by how psychological well-being impacts students' overall performance in learning and social growth. Mental health concerns like depression and anxiety can significantly hamper a student's concentration, engagement, and achievement potential. When schools integrate mental health awareness in their curriculum, they establish a learning atmosphere that improves learning as well as personal growth and resilience among the students. These programs build an encouraging learning atmosphere that encourages students to seek help, thus reducing stigma for mental health issues. By sequential interventions that are tailored to student needs, educators can build an active strategy that is beneficial to all the students in a school, at the same time highlighting the importance of mental health training and services in schools. Furthermore, teachers' work is more than simply teaching academics; they also have a central role in screening and responding to mental health issues. Schools are effective places for early intervention, but many fail to implement evidence-based mental health approaches effectively. As illustrated in how mental health promotion in, say, Australia is being tackled, in terms of programs such as KidsMatter Primary, combining mental health programs with education systems must be solidly supported and financed.

Figure 10.1. Mental health challenges, including anxiety and depression, can significantly inhibit a student's ability to focus, engage, and achieve their potential.

Source: https://static1.squarespace.com/static/64959c1091617327d9ef78bf/t/654cfa8cdb74ee2df8c03ea9/1699543693032/Squarespace+Homepage+-+2023-11-09T152935.060.png?format=1500w.

While these initiatives indicate the merit of mental health, they are confronted by challenges such as varied institutional will and uneven enforcement of best practices. Ensuring quality assurance in implementation and assessment of such programs is critical to realizing long-term gains for students. This underscores the need for ongoing investment in mental health training for teachers as well as building robust support systems within schools. Furthermore, the benefits of school-based mental health programs extend beyond individual students to the broader school community. A healthy student body is crucial in encouraging a positive school climate, which results in more relationships and collaboration. When the students are understood and cared for, they become more involved in participating in school activities, enhancing their sense of community, and belonging. Despite the realization of the importance of social and emotional well-being, as described by Askell-Williams et al. (2011), there are still inequalities in the government's provision of mental health programs among areas, leading to variations in program quality and delivery. For the optimal effect of mental health promotion in schools, stakeholders ought to advocate for equitable policies and resource allocation. Mental health investments not only demystify academic achievement but also empower students, equipping them to face future challenges in their community (Figure 10.1).

Overview of the Impact of Mental Health on Communities

The relationship between health at a community level and mental health is intricate and crucial to the encouragement of good social environments. Mental illness has the potential to complicate significantly lives of individuals and hence communities' texture. When a community's population is faced with issues of mental health, they may spread within social networks to influence diminished productivity, increased unemployment, and unsuccessful family life. Besides, mental illness often leads to increased levels of substance abuse and crime, which can accelerate community tensions as well as public safety. It is for this reason that community-level treatment of mental health is crucial not only for the well-being of individuals but also for maintaining healthy social frameworks. The COVID-19 pandemic showed us the far-reaching impact of mental health on community resilience. Extended social solitude, fear of infection, and vagueness in economic conditions have elevated fear and despair levels among worldwide populations. Those societies that failed to develop robust mental health support mechanisms felt severe downturns in overall well-being. The ones that prioritized mental health services, however, witnessed more cohesive community reactions and recovery efforts. The importance of mental health has come to the forefront more and more, highlighting the importance of systemic change and the importance ascribed to mental health within public health thinking. As summarized in current studies, for instance, the impact of the pandemic, fostering mental wellbeing can do a lot towards building community resilience in the face of crisis (Charlene et al., 2020; Wang et al., 2020). Effective mental health interventions foster not only individual recovery but social cohesion. Interventions that engage community members in mental health awareness, such as workshops and support groups, provide essential information and access to resources. These interventions have been found to reduce stigma and trigger help-seeking behavior, hence leading to early intervention and prevention of more complex mental health issues. Additionally, encouraging supportive environments among schools and community organizations assists in building resilience in youth and vulnerable populations. The collective responsibility of community stakeholders—citizens, NGOs, and governments—is central to addressing mental health problems through complementary efforts. Through the emphasis on mental health, communities can shape communities where there is an environment supporting the emotional well-being of all residents, thus enhancing overall quality of life as well as stability (Charlene et al., 2020; Wang et al., 2020) (Figure 10.2).

Figure 10.2. Communities that failed to implement robust mental health support systems witnessed significant declines in collective well-being.

Source: https://theamikusqriae.com/wp-content/uploads/2024/07/all-about-bullying-1440x810-1.jpg.

10.1. THE CURRENT STATE OF MENTAL HEALTH IN SCHOOLS

School mental health today is a complex portrait in which increased awareness is coupled with insufficient funding. As schools are stretched to address rising student levels of anxiety, depression, and behavioral concerns, the demand for comprehensive mental health services intensifies. Early intervention has already been shown through emerging research to have a powerful effect on student achievement and well-being. But very few schools possess the requisite infrastructure, trained human resources, and the necessary budget to implement quality mental health programs. The growing awareness of the significance of mental health in a school setting highlights the gap between awareness and actual practice. Lastly, the success of school mental health initiatives relies on a multi-faceted approach that not only emphasizes the need for increased funding but also the coordination of educators, mental health professionals, and policymakers to align resources in a corresponding manner. The racially disparate effect permeates the current mental health environment of schools, and it becomes increasingly difficult to improve the challenge of providing equitable mental health care. Students of color might have unique stressors including systemic racism, socioeconomic problems, and cultural stigmatization of the quest for mental health interventions. These have been shown to exacerbate these underlying mental health problems to lead to higher levels of distress in minority students. Interventions that are not designed with a specific equity focus can, by default, actually create these inequalities, highlighting the need for individualized approaches that address the diverse experiences of students. To achieve this, schools must adopt policies that increase not just accessibility to mental health interventions, but also cultural and socio-economic literacy among students. This renders mental health interventions highly effective and relevant to populations they are intended to help, resulting in an inclusive school setting. Moreover, the integration of mental health education within school curricula is an extremely worthwhile opportunity to de-stigmatize mental illness for students. By proactively teaching students about mental health, schools can foster an environment that renders it okay to talk about emotional health and encourages students to seek out services when necessary. School programs that incorporate SEL can help students acquire essential coping skills and resilience, eventually leading to a healthier school climate. Mental health has increasingly come into focus in response to the contemporary challenges of the COVID-19 pandemic, which further amplified the levels of stress and anxiety among students. Mental health education not only solves problems in the short-term but also lays the groundwork for a lifetime of skills needed to handle personal and academic problems. By doing so, schools can empower students to be in charge of their own mental health and, in turn, build a community that values well-being as an intrinsic part of success in school.

10.1.1. Prevalence of Mental Health Issues Among Students

Treatment of the prevalence of mental illness among students necessitates an integrated examination of the various determinants of teen psychological well-being. Mental illness is especially common among teens, with studies indicating that nearly a third of students present symptoms of mental health distress. A cross-sectional survey among rural Gujarat schools revealed shocking facts regarding the mental health condition of adolescents, which revealed that 37% of the sample had normal SDQ scores (Kharod et al., 2015). While nearly 30% were in the borderline score category and a further 33% had abnormal scores, the findings suggest a dire need to introduce effective interventions at the school level. These interventions would involve life skills education, which targets mental health issues alongside increasing access to primary mental health care within schools and communities. In addition to the statistical prevalence of mental health issues, implications for various student groups must be considered.

Specific demographic characteristics are found to have a significant influence on outcomes in mental health, revealing disparities requiring targeted responses to mental health programming. For instance, the study in Gujarat found that girls and students with backgrounds of problematic families had higher scores of abnormal mental health (Kharod et al., 2015). Furthermore, PTSD, depression, and anxiety were disproportionately observed in marginalized groups, including Asian youth exposed to unique social adversities. A study that surveyed over 300 Asian American teens indicated profound concerns such as depression and victimization, highlighting the intersection of mental health with society and culture pressures.

Figure 10.3. Mental health problems are notably common among adolescents, with research indicating that nearly a third of students display signs of mental health distress.

Source: https://humanoo.com/wp-content/uploads/2023/08/generation-psychische-gesundheit-arbeit_1.jpeg.

This indicates the necessity of culturally responsive mental health paradigms in schools to foster resilience and respond appropriately to the diverse mental health needs of students. Lastly, the call for heightened sensitivity and responsive action in addressing mental health issues in schools calls for partnership and community action. As much as the reported prevalence of mental health issues among students, stakeholders—educators, parents, and mental health workers—must advance holistic efforts with mental health training and support at the top. Interventions should emphasize early detection and prevention mechanisms, particularly for vulnerable groups. For instance, integrating life skills education into school curricula can give students the essential coping strategies to build resilience against academic and social pressures (Kharod et al., 2015). Programs that are advocacy-promoting and community-driven, like the Asian Youth Advocacy Network, can also contribute to the ability of marginalized youth to maintain quality mental health management. Therefore, an effort from all is critical to minimize the influence of mental health problems on students, improving education outcomes and overall community well-being (Figure 10.3).

10.1.2. Barriers to Accessing Mental Health Resources in Schools

A significant hindrance to mental health availability in schools is based in socioeconomic challenges that affect students' overall well-being. Homeless students, for instance, might face coordinate issues that hamper their ability to seek help. More than 1.3 million homeless students accounted for by the 2013–2014 school year illustrate the scope of the issue, presenting a frightening swell in numbers year by year (Reed et al., 2016). Such students, hard-pressed to satisfy their basic survival needs, might find it difficult to focus on academic or mental health counseling efforts. Consequently, the trauma of homelessness can lead to adverse mental health outcomes, perpetuating a cycle of disaffiliation and lower achievement. Absent targeted interventions and services in schools, such vulnerable students are likely to become increasingly behind their peers, underscoring the necessity of comprehensive mental health services in school settings. Other than socioeconomic status, school location is also critical in determining access to mental health care. Rural or distant students are reported to face exceptional barriers including, but not limited to, far distances for making visits to health centers, scarcity of mental health professionals, and inadequate means of transport (Heath et al., 2014). These concerns are responsible for substantial latencies in seeking help, and students find themselves without the timely interventions of their mental health. Moreover, stigma in more rural settings may lead to individuals not seeking the care they require, contributing further to the issue. This geographic imbalance speaks to the necessity that policymakers ensure that how resources and infrastructure are distributed can be made more effective to support students in these under-resourced neighborhoods. Lastly, organizational issues within schools themselves can hinder access to mental health services. School counselors and mental health practitioners both have gigantic caseloads, which means not enough individualized time with students who need it. With increasing awareness about mental health, school service need has increased but has not been supplemented by staff and resources (Reed et al., 2016). Without adequate training of teachers and staff to deal with issues of mental health, the issue is aggravated because teachers may lack the necessary skills to appropriately screen and deal with students' needs. Therefore, students can feel invisible within a school system where their mental health needs go unrecognized and unaddressed. Therefore, rectifying these systemic shortcomings is crucial to building a system that puts student mental health and well-being front and center in educational systems.

10.1.3. Role of School Counselors and Mental Health Professionals

Their efforts are key to building supportive learning environments that address students' psychological needs. Over the last few years, there has been an acknowledgment of the advanced mental health issues that face students, exemplified by increasing levels of anxiety and depression among young people. School counselors are first-line advocates who serve as key sources of support and guidance for students facing personal, social, and academic challenges. Through the creation of mental health awareness programs, school counselors directly impact students' emotional education and hardiness. They also serve as a link of communication between students and mental health services, allowing young people access to the correct interventions at the right times. With the increasing demands being placed on such professionals, continuous training and development become essential in an effort to enhance their capacity to meet the diverse mental health demands of schools (Gallagher et al., 2009). Amidst this evolving setting, mental health professionals also have a significant role to play by complementing school counselors' work. Their campus presence allows for a more comprehensive model of mental health services, which is necessary to address the increasing challenges of student stressors and trauma. Collaborative work between school counselors and mental health professionals can facilitate the development of multi-tiered systems of support, including interventions from universal mental health promotion to targeted therapeutic services. This partnership is particularly important in determining the particular challenges that underserved and marginalized populations are likely to face. Blending mental health professionals' expertise with the school setting not only makes the support system for students more effective but also fosters a culture of inclusiveness and understanding, essential to facilitating student success academically and personally (Gallagher et al., 2009). The interprofessional overlap of school counselor and mental health professional roles brings to the fore the necessity for their professional identity to be re-shaped to address increasing demands to provide support for student mental health. As the profession's role evolves, school counselors must be re-shaped to integrate their educational leadership with being mental health advocates to break down silos typical of mental health services in schools. This blend contributes to their ability to advocate for system changes that prioritize mental health resources, benefiting the greater student body in the end. Barriers such as resource limitation, mental health stigma, and success at all costs in the classroom might, however, impede productive collaboration. To overcome these challenges, ongoing lobbying for school policies that benefit mental health programs in schools is crucial so that mental health professionals and counselors can work together to enable integrated student development (Auger et al., 2013) (Figure 10.4).

Figure 10.4. The role of school counselors and mental health professionals is crucial in fostering a supportive educational environment that addresses students' psychological well-being.

Source: https://cloudmain.vocovision.com/wp-content/uploads/2025/08/The-Role-of-Mental-Health-Professionals-in-Schools-1136x757.jpg.

10.2. THE IMPACT OF MENTAL HEALTH ON ACADEMIC PERFORMANCE

Mental health has a major impact on the academic performance of students, with many studies recordings the negative effects caused by poor mental health such as anxiety, depression, and trauma. Students with poor mental health tend to experience poor concentration, memory loss, and lack of motivation, which contributes to lower academic performance. For example, students who have high levels of anxiety are likely to have high absenteeism based on stress-related illness or direct avoidance of schools. This can create a vicious cycle where low academic performance contributes to mental illness, which then contributes to increasing disengagement from schooling. Because of this, teachers and policymakers must realize how academic achievement intersects with mental health, since interventions aimed to foster good mental health will need to account for the educational environment that they belong to. The prevalence of homelessness among students creates a significant area of focus on how mental health impacts educational success. Many students living in homelessness will generally have difficulty with the instability of housing, a main barrier to their educational success. Over 1.3 million homeless students were reported in a given school year, as per recent statistics, indicating the magnitude of this issue. These students are particularly prone to mental health issues, which can lead to absenteeism and poor performance. The psychological tension of homelessness can discourage their ability to form important relationships with fellow classmates and educational administrators, thereby discouraging academic advancement. Addressing the particular needs of homeless students, therefore, is at the forefront of establishing lines of advancement towards enhanced educational attainment and general well-being (Reed et al., 2016). Investments in a comprehensive mental health support system across an entire school can mitigate the negative impacts of mental health on educational performance. Such systems would need to involve access to counseling, stress management workshop attendance, and peer networks supporting resilience. Further, mental health education for teachers can assist in building an environment in which students feel both safe and supported. It is important that school policy is integrated with mental health initiatives because effective intervention contributes to a decline in dropout rates and students' overall academic performance. With comprehensive assistance, students can cope with their challenges more effectively, which later translates into better educational experiences and life (Gallagher et al., 2007). As mental health emerges as a more public aspect of education policy and practice, paying attention to well-being at school will enhance not only individual student success but the educational community's climate as well.

10.2.1. Correlation between Mental Health and Academic Success

The intersection of mental health and academic achievement is increasingly being valued as a determining factor of educational attainment. Children with mental health problems often experience severe challenges that hinder their ability to do well academically, leading to reduced involvement and achievements. For instance, depression and anxiety are common among school children, and they directly negatively impact their concentration, motivation, and overall learning ability. Consequently, mental disorders affect not only learning, but also interfere with social interaction, further isolating students from others and complicating the learning process. Understanding this connection is relevant to teachers and policymakers alike because enhancing the environment can directly contribute to student success and happiness. Moreover, extrinsic conditions such as socio-economic status have a serious influence on mental health and learning. Homeless students, for example, have unique challenges which further compound mental health issues, impacting their continuity and academic performance. From the latest statistics, more than 1.3 million homeless students were recorded in the 2013–2014 school year, showing the need to address this problem.

Figure 10.5. Students grappling with mental health issues often face significant barriers that hinder their ability to perform academically, leading to decreased engagement and achievement.

Source: https://ibcces.org/wp-content/uploads/2019/04/Impact-of-Anxiety-and-Depression-on-Student-Academic-Progress.jpg.

The students typically experience discontinuity in their learning, which reduces their performance and increases the incidence of school dropout. Furthermore, the majority of education systems lack the facilities and support structures to effectively address the mental health demands of these excluded groups. Interventions and assistance services may be utilized to make schools yield a more leveled playing field in which academic success is guaranteed to all students irrespective of whether or not they live in housing situations (Reed et al., 2016). Addressing the mental health problems faced by students must occur at the system level in education and community systems. Recently developed strategies for trauma-informed care and mental health intervention offer evidence of the potential to increase the success of high-risk populations. Strategies that target early intervention, particularly among boys and men of color, have been identified as central to sustaining school success. Strategies attempt to turn unproductive discipline, minimize dropouts, and provide vital mental health services targeted toward the unique needs of a variety of populations of students (Bird et al., 2013). Efforts by schools, communities, and mental health professionals are required to ensure that students obtain broad support. Placing mental health first in educational policy and practice can generate not just academic achievement but also students' overall development, ultimately creating healthier and more resilient communities (Figure 10.5).

10.2.2. Effects of Stress and Anxiety on Learning

The prevalence of worry and stress in schools is a significant challenge to student learning as well as overall cognitive performance. Excessive stress can interfere with memory recall, focus, and critical thinking, which are essential components of successful learning. Furthermore, anxiety might be manifested through various forms such as physical ones like headaches and fatigue, which further distracts students from educational activities. Since students experience stress from academic requirements and interactions, the build-ups of stress can lead to diminished capacity for participation and class involvement. Schools must make mental efforts towards health that address these stressors, ultimately developing a learning and development culture. By introducing coping strategies and emotional guidance, schools of learning are able to act upon the adverse impact of anxiety and stress on academic achievement, thus providing the maximum facilitative experience for all students. Mediating effects of community influences on stress and anxiety cannot be overlooked since these elements significantly contribute to the mental well-being of students. Research informs us that the vast majority of boys and young men of color are confronted by challenging contexts, many of which are punctuated by violence and instability that both enhance anxiety and distress. These experiences affect not just their emotional well-being but also interrupt their ability to focus on learning. Effective interventions must be sensitive to the force of context, including communities' support systems and assets that are congruent with students' life experience. With communities and schools collaborating to develop programs of specialized assistance, they can build strength and provide students with the tools necessary to manage their issues. By putting into practice, a unified approach taking into consideration the individual alongside the people surrounding them, students' mental health and scholastic performance could be dramatically improved overall, leading to a healthier learning environment. When discussing mental health in school, there should be comprehensive strategies that incorporate social and emotional learning (SEL) as well as resilience-building interventions. Rising evidence underlines that not only do SEL programs strengthen students' well-being but also have positive effects on student achievement. By equipping students with critical emotional regulation and interpersonal skills, such programs can reverse the detrimental effects of anxiety and stress that disrupt learning. Additionally, the incorporation of preventive strategies to confront behavioral concerns enables students to excel academically while managing their mental health. Educators and policymakers must align their actions with current research evidence in school mental health as brought forward in recent reviews. Developing an integrated framework around mental health promotion within education can ensure equal access to resources and support for all students, ultimately contributing to better learning experiences and academic outcomes (Cavioni et al., 2020) (Figure 10.6).

Figure 10.6. Schools must prioritize mental health initiatives that address these stressors, ultimately fostering an environment conducive to learning and growth.

*Source:*https://static.wixstatic.com/media/84da7d_7c4948bd6f9149798cc09feeeb75194b~mv2.png/v1/fill/w_568,h_378,al_c,q_85,usm_0.66_1.00_0.01,enc_avif,quality_auto/84da7d_7c4948bd6f9149798cc09feeeb75194b~mv2.png.

10.2.3. Strategies for Supporting Students' Mental Health to Enhance Performance

Supporting students' mental health at school needs to be tackled with a multi-faceted approach that embraces the diverse challenges of their lives. Key strategies include implementing mass mental health schemes that promote awareness, resilience, and control of emotions among students. These schemes should be integrated into school curricula and may include schemes such as mindfulness exercises, stress management classes, and peer support groups. By building a culture that puts mental well-being at its core, schools not only help shape coping strategies on the part of students but also reduce the stigma associated with seeking help. All these have become increasingly important in the recent past, especially after the pandemic, when many students reported declining mental health and increased levels of loneliness (Son et al., 2020). A key strategy involves training staff to identify and deal with mental health issues. Educators and school counselors need professional development focused on detecting distress signals and how to have conversations about mental health with pupils.

Figure 10.7. Teachers and school counselors should receive professional development that focuses on identifying signs of distress and navigating conversations about mental health with students.

Source: https://www.lillio.com/static/589c3c56acf73dd4159237639b5dcf8b/1ed4907c-1ee1-4a4e-8bfa-ce59212b73f7.png.

This provides teachers with the ability to foster supportive classroom environments where learning is encouraged. Further, cooperative efforts with mental health professionals can augment the workforce invested in students so that aid is readily accessible. Such partnerships facilitate personalized interventions focused on meeting specific needs and emphasizing holistic education with a balancing of mental health and academic achievement. With schools ongoing to evolve, such training initiatives represent a valuable investment in the health and performance of students (Brenda, 2020). Finally, developing strong community relationships strengthens the support infrastructure for student mental health. Schools can develop partnerships with local mental health agencies, whereby students may be able to access resources beyond the abilities of the school. Community outreach can take many forms, from providing workshops, support groups, or functions that promote mental well-being and resilience. Further, schools can involve the family by offering training to the family in order to identify mental health problems and teach them strategies to assist their children at home. By fostering a sense of community and belonging, students will be well positioned to perform better academically as well as emotionally and even improve well-being. It sees that mental health is not solely the school's but is a shared responsibility among various stakeholders (Son et al., 2020) (Figure 10.7).

10.3. COMMUNITY RESOURCES FOR MENTAL HEALTH SUPPORT

The integration of community resources into school and community mental health support structures is most critical in addressing the increased mental health challenges within school and community settings. School represents the central location where children's emotional and psychological challenges can be addressed prior to their becoming more complex. One of the key components of this system is the collaborative relationship between schools and community mental health organizations, giving students multiple support networks, including counseling and referral to agencies. School mental health programs can create a culture of openness, de-mystifying mental illness and enabling early intervention strategies. This collaborative approach not only enhances the professional competency of teachers who are otherwise on the frontline in the identification of students in need but also assists in creating a support community network that goes beyond schools, thereby establishing an entire safety net for students and their families (Askell-Williams et al., 2014). To that effect, successful mental health assistance programs usually incorporate trauma-informed care that recognizes the pervasive impact of trauma on learning and behavioral responses. Community resources are able to provide specific training to school personnel so that they are able to learn about and react to the needs of students who have had adverse experiences. For example, responding to issues such as exposure to violence or family turmoil demands an awareness of mental health some teachers may not have unless trained. Solutions put forward, for example, trauma-based interventions, are essential to offering a good and safe learning environment. By offering teachers the training required to recognize and act on students' trauma, communities are in good position to prevent student disciplinary issues and school dropout while monitoring resilience and recovery in schools (Bird et al., 2013). Encouraging mental health services at the local level also means reaching caregivers and families and informing them and supporting them better. Parent education classes and support groups can provide parents with knowledge about mental health, developing awareness on symptom identification and how to improve home well-being. This method, being holistic in nature, does not only improve mental health literacy among families but also fosters collaboration between parents and schools in the implementation of interventions to promote students. As conversations about mental health become a normalized part of family and community life, the probability of students reaching out for help rises, leading to greater collective well-being overall. Ultimately, the utilization of community resources in mental health assistance works to establish a more educated, resilient, and interconnected environment that operates for the betterment of students, families, and educators, which enriches the educational environment (Askell-Williams et al., 2014).

10.3.1. Overview of Local Mental Health Services and Programs

Information regarding local mental health programs and services is essential in fostering an atmosphere of support among schools and communities. Local mental health services tend to include a diversity of programs designed to address the distinctive needs of diverse populations, including children, teenagers, and adults. These programs tend to offer psychological assessment, counseling, crisis intervention, and prevention services. Mental health programs in schools have increasingly been used as an evidence-based approach for early recognition and intervention of students with mental health issues. By integrating mental health services into the school curriculum, these programs provide students with direct support at the point of need, enhancing resilience and promoting sound mental well-being. Coordination between the schools and local mental health organizations is essential in developing a holistic support system for addressing the various levels of mental health challenges among the youth within the community. The focus on combined strategies is one of the essential considerations to the success of local mental health care, as it facilitates coordination of the resources and capabilities of various stakeholders. Schools typically work with community mental health agencies in an effort to develop special programs that cater to the unique needs of their student populations. Such cooperation is critical in consideration of the complexities of adolescence and variability of factors that impact mental health disparities. Recent reports reveal the challenges of providing effective coordination of such programs and accessibility, particularly to vulnerable children. Funding, staff, and availability of services are primary determinants of the extent and effectiveness of such programs. Mitigation of such issues can enhance the provision of mental health services and enable youth to manage more effectively their transitions, thus lowering rates of school and community disengagement (Fernandes-Alcantara et al., 2014). Federal youth policy development underscores the sustained activity aimed at improving the mental health care of young people in local areas. Previous policy shifts have established federal programs that intervene with vulnerable youth so that there will be an integrated system of protection. Both preventive interventions and the development of protective factors are guided by these efforts, which can buffer adverse mental health outcomes. An effective mental health program should not only provide for short-term psychological needs but also build resilience in the long term through education resources and vocational training in skills for youth (Fernandes-Alcantara et al., 2018). With mental health concerns becoming increasingly complex, mental healthcare at the local level must keep up and grow in accordance with these new needs. An ongoing focus on enhancing program coordination at the federal, state, and community levels will ultimately translate into improved mental health outcomes for children in schools and communities (Figure 10.8).

Figure 10.8. Local mental health services often encompass a range of initiatives designed to address the specific needs of diverse populations, including children, adolescents, and adults.

Source: https://data.unicef.org/wp-content/uploads/2020/05/UN0787144.jpg.

10.3.2. Importance of Community Awareness and Education

Community educational awareness is an essential tool in constructing school and community mental health. When families and individuals are aware of mental illness, they can recognize symptoms and gain the appropriate treatment. Educational awareness eliminates myths regarding mental illness, which disintegrates stigma and allows the afflicted to feel more accepted. By incorporating mental health education into school curriculum, programs can enable students with the knowledge to learn about their own mental health and why seeking help is so important. Taking this proactive approach ensures that mental health is addressed early on, so schools are healthier environments in which to learn and develop. All these can also involve community forums and workshops that open up discussions concerning mental health so as to share experiences that bring about resilience and peer empathy, leading to overall community well-being. In addition, engaging the stakeholders in the community in the education of mental health is crucial in the development of a support system that caters to diversity. The agencies in the community can collaborate with schools to design tailored programs that address local needs. For instance, partnerships with public health initiatives can provide resources and knowledge regarding effective mental health treatments that address the specific social determinants affecting the population. Not only do such collaborations enhance the quality of mental health training but also provide varied learning opportunities, such as internships in community environments. These experiences allow students to experience mental health from a practice perspective, hence bridging the gap between theory and practice. As illustrated by initiatives that strengthen the training capabilities in healthcare, interagency working significantly enhances the capacity to address mental health requirements successfully, both at the student and societal levels (Gallagher et al., 2007). Also, engaging members of marginalized communities in mental illness awareness programs fosters diversity and inclusiveness, and amplifies discussion about mental illness. Underrepresented group interventions can tailor messages that speak to communities, thus amplifying outreach and participation. For example, partnerships with correctional facilities have been beneficial, as it exposes students to various social determinants of health and offers varied learning experiences for nursing and public health students (Bouchaud et al., 2017). Such exposure promotes awareness and sensitivity in cultures, which are essential while working on mental health issues. By understanding that a community has differing experiences and needs, the stakeholders are best placed to develop effective outreach that will resonate with different groups, leading ultimately to a more empowered and informed community. Such a comprehensive knowledge base is central in dismantling barriers to mental health treatment and creating a culture of care for everyone, most importantly youth in schools.

10.3.3. Collaboration Between Schools and Community Organizations

Collaboration with the community and school has also been increasingly necessary in order to respond to mental health issues within schools. By collaborating with local agencies, schools can leverage the knowledge and skills of such agencies to establish a more comprehensive support system for students. Community partners possess unique competencies and services not available or unaffordable to schools, which enable targeted interventions that specifically address students' mental health issues. Also, such collaborations enable the sharing of resources and therefore enhance program effectiveness. For instance, mental health education and counseling programs can be assisted significantly by the services of local mental health agencies. Not only do such collaborations enrich the educational experience but also offer a safety net for students to enable them to receive the help they require both within and outside the classroom. Collaborative work requires a dedication to the building of trusting, solid relationships between schools and community partners.

Figure 10.9. Community partners often possess specialized knowledge and services that schools lack, allowing for the implementation of targeted interventions that directly address the mental health needs of students.

Source: https://www.wgu.edu/blog/2018/10/importance-mental-health-awareness-schools/_jcr_content/root/container/imageandtext.coreimg.85.800.jpeg/1705598842574/worriedteentakingatest-j-525364.jpeg.

Establishing dialogue and shared objectives is critical to the success of collaborative work. Schools must understand the benefits that community organizations can provide, such as access to other sources of funding and specialized programs addressing the special needs of students. As observed in the policy guide introducing solutions to increase the possibility for children outside of the school environment, effective collaboration with community partners can produce innovative solutions that bridge the gap between academic success and mental health (Wright, 2005). Additionally, such partnerships offer an open environment where numerous various voices can contribute to mental health initiatives, consequently contributing to better overall well-being in the community. To ensure optimal gain from partnership, ongoing monitoring and feedback by all stakeholders are essential. Schools and community agencies must continue to assess the effectiveness of their partnerships and the interventions they provide. This not only allows one to identify areas for improvement but also strengthens the school-community partnership relationship. These practices can help to build a responsive and adaptive support system that evolves with the shifting needs of students. The experience of the greater Omaha region, which stepped up and made gains in building service delivery to meet the needs of high-risk populations, is an example of how collaborative models can strengthen service delivery in schools (Skrypek et al., 2010). In the end, long-term collaborations could be central to advancing mental health awareness and access, confirming the idea that community health is everybody's business (Figure 10.9).

10.4. STIGMA SURROUNDING MENTAL HEALTH

Elimination of stigma towards mental health is vital in creating inclusive environments within schools and society. The stigma would otherwise lead to stigmatizing individuals with mental illness, which prevents them from accessing help. In schools, students who are mentally ill will be confronted with stereotypes and misconceptions that alienate them and aggravate their condition. Thus, ignorance can result in poor academic performance and a decline in social interaction. Combating stigma must therefore include comprehensive education programs that not only inform students but also teachers and staff on mental health. Through the establishment of an inclusive climate, schools can mitigate the adverse effects of stigma and promote students to seek help if they need it. In addition, mental health stigma is not only manifested at the level of individual attitudes; it also has an impact on systemic barriers within mental health care provision. As per recent evidence, the mental healthcare treatment gap has also been recognized as a major issue, and barriers have been described in terms of insufficient funding, the lack of human resources, and inaccessible services (Axelsson et al., 2020). This gap in treatment thus not only reflects societal attitudes towards mental wellbeing but also serves to highlight the imperative of improved mental health care. Hence, communities and schools must advocate for policy changes that enhance the provision of services in number while defining public mental health awareness. Progressing these systemic challenges through this channel enables the provision of pathways for enhanced access to mental care by communities, slowly closing the gap as far as stigma and mental well-being are concerned among residents. Finally, the scope of mental health stigma is extended to the general membership of individuals with disabilities. Importantly, the progress achieved following the enactment of the Americans with Disabilities Act (ADA) establishes the importance of community integration and treatment of individuals with mental illness (Priaulx, 2015). Alarming trends, however, such as the emergence of disability-only spaces, imperil inclusivity. Though such challenges confront communities, advocacy interventions are key to equip individuals with mental health conditions with the services and support they need in order to thrive in integrated settings. Both stigma hurdles in social lives and lobbying for policies that accommodate the ADAs vision of integration need to be addressed through initiatives that ultimately build healthier and more open-minded communities in schools and communities (Figure 10.10).

Figure 10.10. Schools and communities must thus advocate for policy changes that enhance the availability of services while promoting an understanding of mental health issues.

Source: https://upload.wikimedia.org/wikipedia/commons/thumb/9/9a/Primary_school_children_in_classroom.jpg/640px-Primary_school_children_in_classroom.jpg.

10.4.1. Understanding Stigma and its Effects on Individuals

Stigma of mental health is a common issue that significantly affects individuals' experiences, particularly in schools and community settings. The social stigma exists as negative prejudices and discrimination, marginalizing people with mental health problems and exposing them to misconception. Far too frequently, these negative social attitudes are adopted by individuals facing mental health problems, which has the effect of amplifying the emotions of guilt and shame, thus preventing them from searching for help. Such internalized stigmas not only contribute to their mental illness but can also derail their learning and social development within school environments, where empathy and peer acceptance are crucial to positive outcomes. Thus, stigma must be addressed to create an environment of comfort for support and acceptance that will enable sufferers to pursue much-needed treatment and manage their afflictions effectively. Moreover, stigma's impact does not end at personal level but seeps through to community relations and even schools. For example, stigma has the unintended consequence of deterring schools from being open about mental health issues, thereby denying students and parents exposure to available resources and support systems.

Through this shunning, ignorance and misconception give birth to a cycle of ignorance and misconception where myths and misconceptions surrounding mental health remain unchallenged. As contended in existing literature, raising public awareness by effective campaigning has the ability to develop local capacity to resist adversity in the form of male suicide and increase shared knowledge about mental illness experience (Braybrook et al., 2013). By creating a setting that is inclusive and encourages the discussion of mental health, schools can destroy the barriers placed by stigma and encourage a more compassionate community setting that ultimately ensures the resilience and mental health of all parties involved.

Examining some cases, such as the varying perceptions people have of autism in varying cultural settings, further illustrates the impact of stigma on community responses to mental health. One Jamaican comparative study highlighted that few beliefs and resources significantly influence the perception and treatment of autism and general mental health perception (Curran et al., 2014). Under such low-perception mental health communities, stigma may prevent the family from seeking services and altering the child's life trajectories of mental disorders.

This is compounded by socioeconomic factors, which create additional barriers to the receipt of care. Through comprehension of the insidious way stigma works within differing cultural and socioeconomic backgrounds, stakeholders are positioned to tailor interventions to address particular community needs. It is obvious that through the encouragement of a greater than stigma understanding of mental health, communities and schools are positioned to create a more equitable and empathetic environment for individuals who are living with mental health needs.

10.4.2. Strategies to Reduce Stigma in Schools and Communities

Decreasing stigma in schools and communities is most important in the development of a mental health and well-being-positive environment. Incorporating education programs into mental health awareness can be a powerful move towards shifting attitudes. Mental health education can be incorporated into school curricula so that students, teachers, and families learn mental health issues, how prevalent they are, and the importance of empathy. Studies have found that education interventions could neutralize stigma by increasing understanding and sympathy towards the suffering individuals. For instance, interventions providing training to teachers and peer leaders in recognizing and acting on mental health problems can empower them to create a more inclusive environment. By limiting stigma in school settings, schools can ensure healthier social relationships and support systems (Nancy et al., 2020). Involving members of the community in lessening stigma is equally important in developing acceptance and awareness.

Figure 10.11. Addressing stigma in schools and communities is critical to fostering an environment conducive to mental health and well-being.

Source: https://www.behavioralhealthnews.org/wp-content/uploads/2022/07/AdobeStock_386371173web.jpg.

Community outreach programs have the potential to mobilize local leaders, organizations, and health workers to advocate for mental health as well as win acceptance of people who are suffering from mental health disorders. These programs can include mental health fairs, workshops, and forums that allow mutual sharing as well as open discussion among members of the community. Providing arenas to share narratives can potentially create connection points that reduce fear and stigma of mental health issues. For instance, some campaigns on HIV stigma are evidenced to show that community-level dialogue might provide social support that is vital while, concurrently, undermining more pervasive societal misconceptions about health conditions (Nabunya et al., 2020). The greater the variety of voices engaged in such conversation, the more powerful the initiative will be in dismantling assumptions. Peer support programs have also been effective in combatting stigma within students. By developing safe spaces where people share personal stories of mental health, schools create meaningful relationships.

The programs allow students to connect with others and develop a sense of belonging and terminate loneliness. Training the peer supporters to listen and support their peers without bias is at the core of the strategy. In addition, utilizing resources from mental health professionals to assist with continued guidance and education can enhance such programs' effectiveness. Peer-led programs not only facilitate students' participation in destigmatization but also empower them to become contributing members of the community. Collectively, these approaches create a support network that must be the top of the list for promoting mental health and reducing stigma at school and community levels (Nancy et al., 2020) (Figure 10.11).

10.4.3. Role of Media in Shaping Perceptions of Mental Health

The media is pivotal in the construction of social attitudes towards mental health, particularly within educational environments and communities. Mental health narratives are built and shared by media, including television, online media, and newspapers. This matters because it shapes public opinion, making mental illness less stigmatizing or even more stigmatizing. For instance, when the media presents mental health through sensationalism or lies, it tends to generate misconceptions among those who seek to portray mental illness. Thus, it becomes crucial to address the media portrayal of mental health as a method of producing healthier messages.

This is particularly applicable in schools since students tend to be vulnerable to these media messages, thus changing their understanding of mental health and their receptiveness to assistance. The media representations have influences beyond individual beliefs but extend to community support systems and mental health resources as well. Specifically, access to mental health services and the accessibility of information make significant impacts on attitudes toward treatment and awareness. As highlighted in research, there has traditionally been a wide disparity in research pertaining to specific populations, including people with mental health disorders. The effectiveness of pro-mental health campaigns relies on the media's penetration in multicultural populations, such that the message reaches multicultural backgrounds as well as socioeconomic levels. The media can give voice to these communities, thereby leading to increased awareness and comprehension. Baezconde-Garbanati et al. (2019) emphasizes that culture-sensitive public health campaigns must be created and suggests that an evolved strategy to media messages will help foster acceptance and trigger mental health literacy in diverse audiences. In addition, medias influence on the attitudes towards mental health is firmly rooted in cultural context, which determines reception and interpretation of stories about mental health.

As observed in foreign settings, as carried out in Jamaica, the social setting may have a significant influence on individuals' understanding of mental illness such as autism within a community. Curran et al. (2014) suggests that variability in the perception and availability of mental health care may lead to varying levels of acceptance between groups. These cultural determinants make the grand narrative supported by the media and often not considering local practice and belief in relation to mental health more complex. Therefore, an integral media plan respecting and integrating multicultural views must be used for enabling a fuller awareness of mental health that ultimately aids in developing healthy environments in schools and communities (Figure 10.12).

Figure 10.12. The media plays a pivotal role in shaping societal perceptions of mental health, particularly within educational environments and community contexts.

Source: https://www.apa.org/images/health-advisory-adolescent-social-media-use-hero_tcm7-316469.jpg.

10.5. PREVENTION AND EARLY INTERVENTION STRATEGIES

Effective prevention and early intervention activities are essential to addressing mental health issues in schools and communities. These range from a wide variety of programs aimed at enhancing better mental well-being and mitigating risk factors before they become complicated problems. Some school-based programs, for instance, usually involve mental health literacy programs, which educate students, staff, and parents on recognizing signs of distress and available resources to them. Building a robust infrastructure for mental health fosters an environment of ease in which the student can express their concerns and access support. By enabling awareness and education, such initiatives can potentially reduce the stigma related to mental health disorders, convincing people who are in need to seek aid and intervention services early enough. Community-targeted prevention efforts can significantly improve the mental health outcomes for populations who are at risk, including underserved youth. Research indicates that boys and young men of color are disproportionately burdened by environmental stressors because of poverty and segregation (Sandstrom et al., 2015). Interventions need to therefore address not only individual students but also the systemic reasons for their challenges. Providing access to mental health services, establishing supportive environments, and developing community partnerships can create an interwoven network of protection for vulnerable youth. These strategies are key to developing resilience and allowing individuals to navigate the complexities of their environments successfully without succumbing to the adversities that they too frequently undergo. Furthermore, attempts to address some of the difficulties of society, such as domestic violence, are part of the mental health profiles of schools and communities. New strategies aimed at adolescents and young parents must be introduced in order to make breaks in cycles of trauma and build healthier family and social environments (Rosewater, 2003). By emphasizing prevention, such programs can engage actively with youth in conversations about healthy relationships, conflict resolution, and coping skills. Such programs not only protect vulnerable populations but also create a culture of engagement and awareness with mental health. By so doing, communities can contribute concretely to a preventive model of health that emphasizes early intervention and better mental health outcomes across all groups.

10.5.1. Importance of Early Identification of Mental Health Issues

The significance of the early identification of mental health issues among schoolchildren cannot be overestimated. Early identification of such issues allows early interventions that can alter the direction of a student's academic and personal life. Research has established that mentally ill students, such as those with depression and anxiety, are more likely to develop academic decline and behavioral problems. Therefore, the implementation of early detection strategies can be employed as a measure to prevent such upper-level complications like school violence. With the establishment of an environment that prioritizes awareness on mental health, teachers are able to create supportive learning environments that promote open communication and compassion towards issues of mental health. Interventions such as peer support programs and mental health literacy can be a source of empowerment for students and staff and can lead to a healthier school community and improved overall learning outcomes (Lugo, 2024). Additionally, the effects of early identification extend past the immediate school environment and impact societal systems as well. By schools adopting trauma-informed practices and proactive mental health measures, they establish a culture that is conducive to enhanced academic attainment and emotional well-being. Specifically, benefits of such programs include increased attendance rates and lower dropout rates, which are vital to long-term academic success and future life opportunities. Moreover, research highlights the critical role that mental health services play in addressing the more universal problems of the marginalized groups, such as boys and men of color, who may face specialist challenges in school settings. Such interventions do not only contribute to academic success but also prepare children for future work by equipping them with coping strategies and resilience (Bird et al., 2013). Ultimately, early identification of mental illness enables longitudinal positive results on the individual and social level. Development of mental health literacy in students, teachers, and parents builds collective awareness of mental health among community members, closing the gap of stigma and encouraging people to access help where needed. Additionally, as school systems implement systematic monitoring and screening of students' mental health, they create a system of early intervention that can prevent crises before they become unmanageable. In doing this, schools position themselves not only as learning entities but as key stakeholders in the well-rounded development of youths. By the integration of structured mental health interventions, schools may foster the adaptation of resilient individuals who are more likely to flourish within and outside the school setting (Bird et al., 2013).

10.5.2. Programs and Initiatives for Mental Health Education

One of the most important elements in moving forward with mental health education within schools and communities is establishing and enforcing specific programs and initiatives. These programs aim to improve the capabilities and consciousness of students to allow them to better traverse the emotional nuances of well-being. Federal policies have changed in recent years to allow for youth-centered mental health programs that focus on protective factors that drive the resilience of adolescents during their move into adulthood. Specifically, the report highlights the idea of disconnection among youth and raises the importance of programs to address these problems, ultimately leading to the accumulation of emotional and social skills necessary for healthy adult life (Fernandes-Alcantara et al., 2014). By creating a healthy setting through mental health instruction, schools can eliminate dangers of mental health diseases and enhance students' well-being. A very good case of successful mental health programming is Australia's KidsMatter Primary, which emphasizes the importance of social and emotional health from early childhood to secondary schooling. The program illustrates how schools are significant settings for promoting mental health through using preventive and intervention strategies aimed at addressing their students' own specific needs. Even as mental health programs are gaining more recognition for their significance, there are challenges to their implementation and sustainability. Challenges such as inconsistency with the provision of funding from the government and the need for quality assurance when applying evidence-based interventions can be counterproductive to the success of such programs (Askell-Williams et al., 2011). Resolution of all these concerns is necessary to make mental health education highly prioritized in the education system. Integrating mental health education into educational curricula is necessary to create positive learning environments. Mental health awareness and coping skills-based programs can significantly reduce stigma and enable students to avail themselves of help when needed. A comprehensive strategy must be implemented, not just academic education but also auxiliary support by means of counseling services and peer-led programs. In addition, coordination among schools, mental health practitioners, and community organizations can broaden the scope and magnitude of mental health programs. Through forming partnerships, schools can call on resources and expertise to better serve vulnerable populations so that all children have fair access to the mental health education and services to foster healthy growth. The need for innovation and adaptability in program planning remains essential to maintaining mental health education initiatives in schools and communities.

10.5.3. Role of Parents and Guardians in Supporting Mental Health

Parent and guardian engagement is paramount in developing a sound mental atmosphere for children, particularly in schools and communities. Parents are the primary and substantive carers and sources of emotional support, and they have great influence in the shaping of their children's behavioral responses to adversity and stress. Parents have a central role in teaching children coping mechanisms that make them resilient to mental illness. Recent studies highlight that parental support is capable of functioning as a buffer to stress effects, enabling children to cope with the emotional dynamics of challenges that they confront in daily life, including the pandemic generated by COVID-19. The support is especially relevant to children living with chronic illness since the psychological status of parents has a direct influence on the well-being of their children, not only emotionally but also on educational outcomes and social interactions. In addition, the stress experienced by parents during times of distress, including those caused by the COVID-19 pandemic, can have a significant impact on their capacity to provide this critical support.

Figure 10.13. Parents serve as the primary caregivers and initial sources of emotional support, significantly influencing their children's behavioral responses to stress and adversity.

Source: https://4687378.fs1.hubspotusercontent-na1.net/hubfs/4687378/childrens%20emotional%20awareness.png.

As parents face uncertainties, job loss, and alterations in responsibilities, the psychological health of parents begins to deteriorate, hence affecting their children. Stress has been proven to increase parental stress, leading to higher vulnerability among children, and thus it is crucial that parents seek assistance and maintain their well-being to provide a nurturing environment. The link between parents' mental health and child outcomes shows the need for intervention in mental health programs in a holistic manner such that support systems need to encompass the parents as well. School programs offering family mental health services can encourage such an excellent balance so that kids are always supported at home and at school. In addition to direct emotional support, parents and caregivers also have important roles to play in advocating for necessary mental health services for their kids. Through awareness of mental health services and educational programs, carers are better equipped to access and utilize optimally community services for their children. The advocacy can include requesting professional support, when necessary, participation in school boards or in community health programs, and establishing open discussions about mental health in the domestic environment. With schools progressing towards full mental health models, parents need to participate actively in such discussions. Their engagement can lead to de-stigmatizing mental issues, facilitating an acceptance that mental and physical health are as important as one another. Combining parental engagement and community support mechanisms provides a levelled framework significantly enhancing children's mental well-being outcomes, thus fostering resilience, and thriving in today's challenges (Nancy et al., 2020; Williamson et al., 2020) (Figure 10.13).

10.6. POLICY AND ADVOCACY FOR MENTAL HEALTH IN EDUCATION

Policies and advocacy for education mental health are paramount in fostering healthy environments for student well-being. This focus emanates from the realization that mental health plays a significant role in learning and development. Education policies must be based on an integrated view of mental health, advocating for programs that encompass mental health education in curricula and creating awareness. Along with this, teaching teachers to recognize and intervene when mental illness is a concern is important. These programs can facilitate developing school climate that reduces children's stigma toward mental illness and open discussion of mental illness so children will feel seen and heard. In doing so, structural competency-guided strategies, as described in the proper literature, can enhance the education system with the capacity to address systematic health disparities among their students (Jonathan et al., 2014). Interagency collaboration among schools, families, and mental health professionals must also be advocated for in order to create an integrated system of support for students. This multi-faceted approach ensures that mental health services are readily accessible and are phrased in forms that address the diverse needs of the student body. Through coalitions with community mental health agencies, schools are able to bridge the gap between school and mental health service environments, leading to better student outcomes. This coalition is crucial in creating a continuum of care which will extend beyond the classroom. Policies are to encourage funding and support to carry out these alliances in an efficient way. Additionally, development of protocols, as proposed by guides such as the SPIRIT 2013 Statement, could be effective in structuring such alliances and encouraging the quality and consistency of school-based mental health programs (Chan et al., 2013). Besides, ongoing monitoring and evaluation of mental health policies within schools are necessary to ensure their efficacy and relevance in addressing the shifting needs of students. As social perceptions of mental health change, education policies must also change to provide an encompassing approach. Ongoing monitoring of the establishment and impact of mental health programs can inform developments and innovations, ensuring an evidence-based policy-making strategy. It also matters to involve students and families in feedback procedures because their experience provides valuable information about the program's effectiveness. By holding to a dynamic policy context that emphasizes mental health, schools can significantly influence the well-being of students, thus resulting in healthier school communities and a better mental health outcome for all youth learners.

10.6.1. Overview of Current Policies Affecting Mental Health in Schools

The landscape of school mental health policy is increasingly shaped by the recognition of the important role that mental health plays in academic success and overall student development. More recent policy efforts concentrate on comprehensive ways of addressing students' mental health problems in order to build healthy learning environments. These policies favor co-located mental health services for education systems to facilitate early assessment and intervention of students at risk. They also favor teacher training, having the capacity to recognize mental health issues and to foster student resilience. A compelling argument for inclusivity within these policies highlights the imperative of serving diverse student groups, addressing the unique needs of disenfranchised populations in hopes of delivering equal access to mental health care and support systems. This multi-pronged approach aims to reinforce the understanding that mental health is germane to education achievement and personal development. In addition to overall policy initiatives, local governments and education administrators increasingly emphasize mental health as a core component of school curriculums. These programs typically consist of intensive mental health instruction focused on awareness and demystification of mental illness among students. Schools are instituting programs in social-emotional learning (SEL) designed to develop self-awareness, self-management, and interpersonal skills. As illustrated in the example of teachers' struggles, for instance, during the pandemic (Jefferson, 2025), mental health support as a reinforcement is essential not just for pupils but also for staff members, who must have proper supports to deal with their multifaceted roles. Policies aimed at improving teacher health and reconciling professional obligations further empower teachers to offer a consistent presence to their pupils. Finally, an enlightened approach that integrates mental health education with general courses can contribute to improving student achievement and school culture to a great extent. Finally, it is essential to acknowledge the role of community engagement towards the implementation and long-term survival of mental health policies in schools. Effective strategies encourage inter-institutional cooperation among schools, families, and neighborhood health centers for a cohesive support system that is able to respond to diverse learners' needs. Recent studies have reaffirmed the impact of socio-educational violence on mental well-being, and thus integral interventions outside of the school setting have been called for. Facilitating effective collaboration among community stakeholders facilitates sharing of resources and provides the support network that not only supports students but also families with mental health needs. By providing open communication and complete involvement by everyone involved, policies can be modified to respond to the constantly changing issues within schools to ultimately result in healthier schools where all students are better equipped to succeed.

10.6.2. Advocacy Efforts for Improved Mental Health Resources

Advocacy for improved mental health services in schools and communities is required to address the growing mental health crisis among children. While anxiety, depression, and other mental illnesses are on the rise, it is crucial that advocacy bodies insist on raising awareness and adequate resource allocation. Such initiatives have the tendency to involve cooperation among several different stakeholders, including teachers, mental health practitioners, parents, and local organizations, in framing an inclusive approach towards mental health learning and assistance. Awareness-raising not merely reduces stigma but also focuses on early intervention techniques, which can actually lower the long-term effects of mental illnesses upon youths remarkably. School initiatives that include mental health services as part of existing school frameworks can demonstrate the positive impacts mental well-being has on academic achievement and social relationships, hence highlighting the importance of interlinked policies in schools and communities (Costa, 2024). Enforcing policies that enhance mental health education in schools is another key aspect of advocacy. By advocating for the integration of mental health education into standard curricula, stakeholders can promote empathy and understanding among students, which are necessary to the development of positive school climates. This is part of the broader educational equity efforts in which not only are mental health services made accessible, but they are systematically woven into students' lives. For equipping teachers to identify and respond to mental health concerns, it is a crucial step; they become first-line responders who can render spaces safe for students to express their needs. Also, engaging parents through workshops and content is important to enable them to perform supportive roles towards the mental health of children. Integrated, these advocacy measures promote the resilience and support system of the community for youth to thrive (Abdul et al., 2024). Finally, effective advocacy for improved mental health services must be a sustained effort to address the institutional barriers that restrict access to these necessary resources. Advocacy groups must push policy changes at the local, state, and national levels, such as appropriations for mental health initiatives targeting schools and low-income communities. These include efforts to position mental health as a higher priority on school budgets and increased coordination with health professionals. With the establishment of partnerships and community involvement, campaigners can fight existing inequalities in resource allocation and promote practices inclusive of groups from different backgrounds. All in all, a concerted effort to implement and refine this advocacy measures can greatly improve school and community mental health outcomes, with a favorable setting where every student receives the support needed (Costa, 2024) (Figure 10.14).

Figure 10.14. With increasing rates of anxiety, depression, and other mental health disorders, it is imperative that advocacy groups work to raise awareness and ensure that resources are allocated effectively.

Source: https://yourcommonwealth.org/wp-content/uploads/2025/02/prioritizing-mental-health-copy.jpg.

10.6.3. Importance of Legislative Support for Mental Health Initiatives

The cornerstone of mental health programs is legislative backing, which has a significant impact on the scope and efficacy of youth-limited programs in educational and community contexts. Federal policy must be directed to offer appropriate solutions as the prevalence of mental health difficulties among teenagers rises, as seen by an increase in behavioral problems, anxiety, and depression. Recent reports on the evolution of federal youth policy highlight the need of interagency coordination and protective variables that might shield vulnerable populations from negative outcomes. The acquisition of finances and resources required to implement mental well-being programs is made possible by legislative initiatives, demonstrating the clear link between policy advocacy and the effective delivery of mental health services in communities and schools (Fernandes-Alcantara et al., 2014). The intricateness of mental health demands legislative models that are flexible and integrated. Programs must go beyond addressing immediate mental health treatment and consider the broader context of youth development with a focus on the environmental and social determinants of mental health outcomes. For instance, federal programs targeting at-risk youth generally emphasize an integrated strategy that addresses mental health education, community engagement, and skill development. The necessity for such deep programming is evident in the discussion of disconnectedness as a construct, where legislative support leads to cooperative efforts that not only target treatment but also assist in building resiliency in youth (Fernandes-Alcantara et al., 2018).

This is essentially adopting the position that legislation needs to support infrastructure that integrates mental health as a central component of education and community development. Furthermore, legislative activism is important for demystifying mental illness in youth. By situating mental health as a public health issue through legislation, policymakers can promote cultural transformation in schools and communities toward greater openness and acceptance. This is particularly important in schools, where stigma can keep students from discussing their challenges or seeking help. Legislative measures can establish school-mental health partnership, which ensures partnership between schools and mental health professionals to ensure that resources are in place to address student needs. The effective interaction of legislation and mental health initiatives is the importance of ongoing advocacy and appropriations for funding to fund spaces in which young people can thrive—harnessing supportive frameworks rooted in policy (Fernandes-Alcantara et al., 2014) (Figure 10.15).

Figure 10.15. With the rising prevalence of mental health challenges among adolescents, evidenced by increasing rates of anxiety, depression, and behavioral issues, comprehensive federal policy is imperative for structuring adequate responses.

Source: https://s3.amazonaws.com/utep-uploads/wp-content/uploads/online-regis-college/2023/04/20020602/RC-MSN-2022-Q4-Skyscraper_-Understanding-the-Youth-Mental-Health-Crisis-01.jpg.

10.7. CONCLUSION

Understanding the complexity of teenage mental illness is essential to formulating a rational conclusion regarding the problem of mental illness in schools and communities. Evidence indicates that diet and mental health are closely related, hence nutritional therapies may be the key to improving mental health. Unhealthy eating habits, especially increasing consumption of sugar-sweetened beverages, are linked to higher levels of anxiety and depression symptoms in teenagers, according to findings from one of the large longitudinal studies. The consumption of fruits and vegetables, on the other hand, is favorably connected with psychological well-being, supporting the inclusion of healthy food options and nutritional education in school curricula (Dabravolskaj et al., 2024). Therefore, addressing mental health from a biopsychosocial perspective that incorporates nutrition could result in significant gains in mental health outcomes in communities and schools. Furthermore, cyberbullying is a serious problem that complicates adolescents' mental health. Studies' empirical results demonstrate the significant incidence of cyberbullying victimization and its connection to major mental health conditions like stress, anxiety, and depression. A coordinated and well-organized approach to prevention and intervention is necessary since socioeconomic factors, such as household income, have a significant impact on mental health outcomes, making these issues more challenging (Amin et al., 2024). Policymakers, mental health practitioners, and educators must come together to develop educational interventions aimed at generating awareness about the impact of cyberbullying considering the diversity of adolescents' socioeconomic contexts. These programs could assist in building a healthier, more supportive community where students can thrive emotionally, in addition to academically. Ultimately, the overlap between nutrition decisions, cyberbullying, and financial situations reinforces the importance of comprehensive strategies that include mental health interventions for both schools and communities. Programs need to incorporate not just prevention, but also long-term support systems that facilitate open discussions about mental health concerns. School counselors and mental health professionals must be equipped with training to recognize warning signs of distress and employ effective coping skills to develop resilience in adolescents (Amin et al., 2024). By providing an educational environment that prioritizes mental health and addresses nutrition and cyberbullying, we are not just responding to the immediate needs of our students but making an investment in a healthier, more equitable future for our communities. It demands multi-pronged solutions, tolerating the complexity of mental illness while demanding broader system reforms that prioritize the well-being of future generations.

10.7.1. Summary of Key Points Discussed

Mental health has become an issue of concern in both education and community settings because both organizations are important in the welfare of children and teenagers. There are reports that schools, being part of a child's normal life, greatly affect the path of mental health. These colleges should not just provide academic support but also inclusive models that integrate mental health care in their systems. This model provides access without compromising the stigma that normally accompanies seeking help, allowing for a system where mental well-being is esteemed as much as academic achievement (Torrey et al., 2007). The collaborative efforts of families, mental health professionals, and teachers can create a solid support network that is effective in dealing with multiple mental health issues. Further, school discussion of mental health needs to include an expanded perspective encompassing the interconnectivity of social variables impacting adolescent well-being. Research indicates that environmental factors such as family, safety of the community, and economic status have significant impacts on mental health outcomes. In particular, policies to enhance the support networks of communities and families work in reducing threats to adverse mental health indicators. Through bringing preventative interventions and positive exemplars into prominence, communities can enhance their youth development capacity (Shore et al., 2009). This multi-level intervention recognizes the importance of collective action in influencing mental health and psychological resilience-friendly environments. In addition, the issues facing teenagers today, including violence, drug addiction, and mental health crises, are urgent issues calling for rapid response in schools and communities. Alignment of school policy with mental health initiatives can achieve a more coordinated approach to addressing these issues. Schools may include social-emotional learning curricula that equip students to deal with life's pressures. Community-based partnerships can provide added assistance, such as counseling and after-school programs, aimed at dismantling barriers blocking access to care. Through creating a coordinated response to such emergent issues, stakeholders can foster resilience in youth, eventually enhancing mental health outcomes among generations to come (Shore et al., 2009; Torrey et al., 2007).

10.7.2. Call to Action for Schools and Communities

With the increasing number of mental health problems among young people, there has never been a more critical time for a comprehensive call for action from schools and communities. Schools play a key role in assisting in the nurturing of mental well-being, but most of them are not prepared to cope with the challenges that accompany mental illness. This lack requires intervention by educators, mental health professionals, and families in creating supportive systems. Engaging stakeholders in a dialogue concerning mental health programs can create awareness and reduce stigma. Schools can also implement targeted programs which not only inform students on mental health but also equip them with coping strategies. Schools can collectively empower students to access care, providing them with a climate where mental health is equated with academic achievement. Community involvement is also essential in this project, as it requires an integrated effort to appropriately implement mental health programs. It can be highly productive to have school and community organization collaboration, as it ensures resources are utilized effectively in helping vulnerable children. Outreach programs can bridge gaps between schools and community services, thus ensuring mental health care for families in need. Given that Gilgoff et al. (2015) highlight the pivotal role of community-led programs in mobilizing support for vulnerable adolescents, such programs help ensure they attain equitable educational, economic, and health benefits. Combining school resources with care systems within the community has the capacity to create an integrated safety net and thus render mental health care conspicuous and accessible to students and their families. Lastly, it is essential for policy decision makers to recognize the necessity for long-term funding and support for school mental health programs. Fluctuating degrees of government support can have a direct impact on the efficacy and long-term sustainability of mental health programs as determined by Askell-Williams et al. (2011). Long-term commitment to evidence-based practices, staff training at the school level, and ongoing evaluation of programs is required to sustain successful implementation of mental health promotion programs. By insisting on comprehensive policies that channel resources into mental health promotion in schools, communities are able to cause fundamental transformations in the lives of adolescents. Lastly, a collective effort on the part of schools and communities can lead to an atmosphere that favors the mental well-being and overall welfare of students so that they are able to achieve well academically and as individuals.

10.7.3. Vision for a Future with Improved Mental Health Support Systems

The future vision for improved mental health care systems in schools and communities must be all-encompassing in terms of prevention, intervention, and ongoing support. Most important in this vision is integrating mental health services in schools, which makes the environment more accessible and supportive for students. Trauma-informed care should be given priority by schools and staff should be trained so that they are attuned to the mental health needs of all the students, particularly those from marginalized backgrounds. By supporting evidence-based practices such as early interventions and mental health screenings, schools can be positioned to address mental well-being before it becomes a crisis. Building strong collaborations among schools and community mental health agencies can continue to enhance these efforts, creating a robust safety net for students that addresses the subtlety of mental health challenges. Moreover, addressing the unique needs of boys and men of color within these systems is essential to advancing equitable mental health outcomes. The data presented by Bird et al. (2013) indicates the primary concerns of these populations, particularly schools where systemic barriers have a tendency to exacerbate mental health issues. In restructuring punitive disciplinary measures and implementing trauma-informed practices, schools can provide a less exclusionary climate promoting emotional well-being. Mentorship opportunities and programs of support that address the culture can empower these individuals, making it easier to process issues experienced in schools. Having career training programs included can also further enhance self-efficacy, providing avenues for success that can even alleviate some of the mental health issues. Building a support network addressing these specific experiences ultimately fosters a more equal society. Finally, the "building up" of mental health care systems also includes the deliberate allocation of resources toward training healthcare professionals who have the ability to treat a growingly diverse patient base. As evident from efforts outlined by Gallagher et al. (2007), building up training systems for healthcare can significantly impact the provision of mental health services. By providing appropriate training in cultural competency and trauma-informed care to mental health professionals, communities are positioned best to meet the needs of their residents. Furthermore, by supporting interdisciplinary collaboration among educators, mental health professionals, and community organizations, a more integrated mental health system may be fostered. This collaborative strategy not only enhances the quality of care but also fosters community resilience and ultimately helps build an environment where the mental well-being is cherished and enriched in every sphere of life.

REFERENCES

1. Abdul, S., Adeghe, E., Adegoke, B. O., Adegoke, A. A., & Udedeh, E. H. (2024). Promoting health and educational equity: Cross-disciplinary strategies for enhancing public health and educational outcomes. *World Journal of Biology Pharmacy and Health Sciences*. https://www.semanticscholar.org/paper/8849cdda2ab62105a29905baabb120bb0db30f80 (accessed on 14th October 2025).
2. Amin, S. M., Mohamed, M. A. E. S., El-Sayed, M. M., & El-Ashry, A. (2024). Nursing in the digital age: The role of nursing in addressing cyberbullying and adolescents' mental health. *Journal of Psychiatric and Mental Health Nursing*. https://www.semanticscholar.org/paper/054a9c48bff49a64bffe30929af67bbf43134f45 (accessed on 14th October 2025).
3. Askell-Williams, H., & Cefai, C. (2014). Australian and Maltese teachers' perspectives about their capabilities for mental health promotion in school settings. https://core.ac.uk/download/43327038.pdf (accessed on 14th October 2025).
4. Askell-Williams, H., Dix, K., & Slee, P. T. (2011). Whole-school mental health promotion in Australia. https://core.ac.uk/download/46603607.pdf (accessed on 14th October 2025).
5. Auger, R. W., DeKruyf, L., & Trice-Black, S. (2013). The role of school counselors in meeting students' mental health needs: Examining issues of professional identity. https://digitalcommons.georgefox.edu/cgi/viewcontent.cgi?article=1008&context=gsc (accessed on 14th October 2025).
6. Axelsson, M., Bockting, C., Buysse, A., Desmet, M., et al. (2020). Healthcare professionals' perspectives on mental health service provision: A pilot focus group study in six European countries. https://core.ac.uk/download/288817269.pdf (accessed on 14th October 2025).
7. Baezconde-Garbanati, L., Byron, M. J., Carroll, D. M., Cruz, T. B., et al. (2019). Pro-tobacco marketing and anti-tobacco campaigns aimed at vulnerable populations: A review of the literature. https://core.ac.uk/download/323062757.pdf (accessed on 14th October 2025).
8. Bird, K., Harris, L., & Bryant, R. (2013). Investing in boys and young men of color: The promise of opportunity. https://core.ac.uk/download/71361431.pdf (accessed on 14th October 2025).
9. Bouchaud, M., & Brooks, M. (2017). Prisons as learning environments for nursing and public health practice. https://core.ac.uk/download/129192343.pdf (accessed on 14th October 2025).

10. Bowser, R. (2013). The Affordable Care Act and beyond: Opportunities for advancing health equity and social justice. https://core.ac.uk/download/pdf/18491830.pdf (accessed on 14th October 2025).

11. Braybrook, D., Robertson, S., & Robinson, M. (2013). "Talk" about male suicide? Learning from community programmers. https://core.ac.uk/download/29018317.pdf (accessed on 14th October 2025).

12. Browne, N. T., Snethen, J., Greenberg, C. S., Frenn, M., Kilanowski, J. F., Gance-Cleveland, B., Burke, P. J., et al. (2020). When pandemics collide: The impact of COVID-19 on childhood obesity. *Journal of Pediatric Nursing, 56*, 90–98. https://doi.org/10.1016/j.pedn.2020.11.004 (accessed on 14th October 2025).

13. Bryant, R., & Phillips, R. (2013). Improving supports for youth of color traumatized by violence. https://core.ac.uk/download/71364662.pdf (accessed on 14th October 2025).

14. Cavioni, V., Grazzani, I., & Ornaghi, V. (2020). Mental health promotion in schools: A comprehensive theoretical framework. https://core.ac.uk/download/322748597.pdf (accessed on 14th October 2025).

15. Cawood, J., Doherty, S., Dooris, M. T., Powell, S., et al. (2010). Healthy universities: Concept, model and framework for applying the healthy settings approach within higher education in England. https://core.ac.uk/download/6113134.pdf (accessed on 14th October 2025).

16. Chan, A. W., Tetzlaff, J., Gøtzsche, P. C., Altman, D. G., Mann, H., Berlin, J. A., Dickersin, K., et al. (2013). SPIRIT 2013 explanation and elaboration: Guidance for protocols of clinical trials. *BMJ, 346*, e7586–e7586. https://doi.org/10.1136/bmj.e7586 (accessed on 14th October 2025).

17. Costa, N. R. (2024). Mental health education in secondary schools in Uganda: Strategies to use and way forward. *International Journal of Research and Innovation in Social Science*. https://www.semanticscholar.org/paper/4d29f62aa6315ef1b89c80fc7537e1adb44b0234 (accessed on 14th October 2025).

18. Cuadra, J. M. (2025). The dynamics of the mental and physical health of Filipino special education educators during the COVID-19 pandemic: A hermeneutics approach. *Qualitative Research Journal*. https://www.semanticscholar.org/paper/de7aab0cb095aa347f9182218df88ef98c5abd10 (accessed on 14th October 2025).

19. Curran, S., & Naqvi, L. (2014). Mental health in Jamaica: An approach to awareness and treatment in children. https://core.ac.uk/download/56326249.pdf (accessed on 14th October 2025).

20. Dabravolskaj, J., Patte, K., Yamamoto, S., Leatherdale, S., Veugelers, P.

J., & Maximova, K. (2024). Association between diet and mental health outcomes in a sample of 13,887 adolescents in Canada. *Preventing Chronic Disease, 21.* https://www.semanticscholar.org/paper/2e3cfaec86a843aaefd1e21bdd033b234987c4ae (accessed on 14th October 2025).

21. Dewey, C. M., Hingle, S., Goelz, E., & Linzer, M. (2020). Supporting clinicians during the COVID-19 pandemic. *Annals of Internal Medicine, 172*, 752–753. https://doi.org/10.7326/m20-1033 (accessed on 14th October 2025).
22. Fernandes-Alcantara, A. L. (2014). Vulnerable youth: Background and policies. https://core.ac.uk/download/19523873.pdf (accessed on 14th October 2025).
23. Gallagher, K., & Beer, T. (2007). Solving Colorado's health professionals' shortage: Initial lessons learned from the Health Professions Initiative evaluation. https://core.ac.uk/download/71346999.pdf (accessed on 14th October 2025).
24. Gallagher, K., & Beer, T. (2009). Solving Colorado's shortage of health professionals: Final evaluation findings and recommendations. https://core.ac.uk/download/71341041.pdf (accessed on 14th October 2025).
25. Gilgoff, J., & Ginwright, S. (2015). Toward more equitable outcomes: A research synthesis on out-of-school time work with boys and young men of color. https://core.ac.uk/download/75786240.pdf (accessed on 14th October 2025).
26. Heath, S., Hippe, J., Jesso, B., Maddalena, V., et al. (2014). Access to health services in Western Newfoundland, Canada: Issues, barriers and recommendations emerging from a community-engaged research project. https://core.ac.uk/download/213625635.pdf (accessed on 14th October 2025).
27. Henning, K. N. (2012). Criminalizing normal adolescent behavior in communities of color: The role of prosecutors in juvenile justice reform. https://core.ac.uk/download/70374966.pdf (accessed on 14th October 2025).
28. Kharod, N., & Kumar, D. (2015). Mental health status of school going adolescents in rural areas of Gujarat. https://core.ac.uk/download/386381278.pdf (accessed on 14th October 2025).
29. Lugo, J. (2024). The impact of school shootings on children's mental health. https://core.ac.uk/download/648636090.pdf (accessed on 14th October 2025).
30. Metzl, J. M., & Hansen, H. (2014). Structural competency: Theorizing a new medical engagement with stigma and inequality. *Social Science &*

Medicine, 103, 126–133. https://doi.org/10.1016/j.socscimed.2013.06.032 (accessed on 14th October 2025).

31. Nabunya, P., Byansi, W., Sensoy Bahar, O., McKay, M. M., Ssewamala, F. M., & Damulira, C. (2020). Factors associated with HIV disclosure and HIV-related stigma among adolescents living with HIV in southwestern Uganda. *Frontiers in Psychiatry, 11*. https://doi.org/10.3389/fpsyt.2020.00772 (accessed on 14th October 2025).
32. Reed, B., Ingram, E. S., Bridgeland, J. M., & Atwell, M. (2016). *Hidden in Plain Sight: Homeless Students in America's Public Schools*. https://core.ac.uk/download/75761432.pdf (accessed on 14th October 2025).
33. Rosewater, A. (2003). Promoting prevention, targeting teens: An emerging agenda to reduce domestic violence. https://core.ac.uk/download/71354063.pdf (accessed on 14th October 2025).
34. Sandstrom, H., Dubay, L., Astone, N. M., & Popkin, S. J. (2015). Promoting healthy families and communities for boys and young men of color. https://core.ac.uk/download/75780436.pdf (accessed on 14th October 2025).
35. Shore, B., & Shore, R. (2009). *KIDS COUNT Indicator Brief: Reducing the Teen Death Rate*. https://core.ac.uk/download/71346741.pdf (accessed on 14th October 2025).
36. Skrypek, M., & Idzelis, M. (2010). Intimate partner violence in Omaha. https://core.ac.uk/download/75784806.pdf (accessed on 14th October 2025).
37. Son, C., Hegde, S., Smith, A., Wang, X., & Sasangohar, F. (2020). Effects of COVID-19 on college students' mental health in the United States: Interview survey study. *Journal of Medical Internet Research, 22*, e21279–e21279. https://doi.org/10.2196/21279 (accessed on 14th October 2025).
38. Torrey, N., & Rosenberg, S. (2007). Role of school-based health centers under universal coverage for children and youth in California: Issues and options. https://core.ac.uk/download/71354638.pdf (accessed on 14th October 2025).
39. Wang, G., Zhang, Y., Zhao, J., Zhang, J., & Jiang, F. (2020). Mitigate the effects of home confinement on children during the COVID-19 outbreak. *The Lancet, 395*, 945–947. https://doi.org/10.1016/s0140-6736(20)30547-x (accessed on 14th October 2025).
40. Wiederhold, B. K. (2020). Connecting through technology during the coronavirus disease 2019 pandemic: Avoiding "Zoom fatigue." *Cyberpsychology, Behavior, and Social Networking, 23*, 437–438. https://doi.org/10.1089/cyber.2020.29188.bkw (accessed on 14th October 2025).

41. Williamson, B., Eynon, R., & Potter, J. (2020). Pandemic politics, pedagogies and practices: Digital technologies and distance education during the coronavirus emergency. *Learning, Media and Technology, 45*, 107–114. https://doi.org/10.1080/17439884.2020.1761641 (accessed on 14th October 2025).

42. Wright, E. (2005). Supporting student success: A governor's guide to extra learning opportunities. https://core.ac.uk/download/71355316.pdf (accessed on 14th October 2025).

Index

J

K

L

M

N

O

P

T

V

W

FSC
www.fsc.org
MIX
Papier | Fördert gute Waldnutzung
FSC® C083411

Kolibri 360 GmbH
Ferdinand-Jühlke-Straße 7
99095 Erfurt, Deutschland
produktsicherheit@kolibri360.de